Publishing *The Prince*

PUBLISHING
The Prince

HISTORY, READING, &
THE BIRTH OF POLITICAL CRITICISM

Jacob Soll

THE UNIVERSITY OF MICHIGAN PRESS
Ann Arbor

First paperback edition 2008
Copyright © by the University of Michigan 2005
All rights reserved
Published in the United States of America by
The University of Michigan Press
Manufactured in the United States of America
⊗ Printed on acid-free paper

2011   2010   2009   2008   5   4   3   2

A CIP catalog record for this book is available from the British Library.

Library of Congress Cataloging-in-Publication Data

Soll, Jacob, 1968–
    Publishing the Prince : history, reading, and the birth of
political criticism / Jacob Soll.
        p.   cm.
    Includes bibliographical references and index.
    ISBN 0-472-11473-5 (cloth : alk. paper)   1. Political science—
History.   2. Political science—Philosophy.   3. Europe—Intellectual
life—18th century.   4. Europe—Intellectual life—17th century.
5. Europe—History—18th century.   6. Europe—History—17th century.
I. Title.
JA83.S594   2005
320.1—dc22   2004021664

ISBN-13: 978-0-472-03343-0 (pbk : alk. paper)
ISBN-10: 0-472-03343-3 (pbk : alk. paper)

To J. H. M. Salmon

NICOLAS MACHIAVEL
Citoien & Secretaire de
FLORENCE

F. Ertinger sculp.

Fig. 1. Abraham-Nicolas Amelot de La Houssaye's translation of Machiavelli's *The Prince* (Amsterdam: Henry Wetstein, 1684), frontispiece (*a*) and title page (*b*). This edition of *The Prince* was

LE
PRINCE

DE NICOLAS
MACHIAVEL,

CITOIEN ET SECRETAIRE

DE FLORENCE.

Traduit & Commenté par

A. N. AMELOT,

Sieur de la Houssaie.

A AMSTERDAM,

Chez HENRY WETSTEIN. 1684.

the most widely read in France for the one hundred years after its publication. (Courtesy of Annenberg Rare Book and Manuscript Library, University of Pennsylvania.)

Acknowledgments

Behind every book is a history. This book began in Paris in 1991, in Roger Chartier's old office at the Maison des Sciences de l'Homme on the boulevard Raspail. Roger first suggested that I look at Amelot de La Houssaye's translation of *L'Homme de cour*. I looked into its pages, followed its references, and began a long voyage of scholarship. Roger has worked on this project with me ever since, and my debt to him is grand. Indeed, this book is in many ways his. He and Christian Jouhaud sent me to work at the Bibliothèque Nationale, where Christian suggested that I do a "material bibliography" of the works of Amelot, thus providing the project an analytical framework. Christian has given much inspiration, tough criticism, and useful advice, as has his seminar at the Groupe de Recherches Interdisciplinaire sur l'Histoire du Littéraire at the Centre de Recherches Historiques, *haut lieu d'érudition*. Daniel Roche has been a constant friend and teacher. His seminar at the rue d'Ulm was the basis of my graduate education. Many thanks are due to Robert Descimon, who first took me to the Archives Nationales on the hunt for Amelot and has ever since been a source of guidance. Annie Parent-Charron took the time to read my work, give me valuable advice, and publish my first article in the venerable *Bulletin du Bibliophile*. For this, I will always be grateful. Many thanks also go to François Moureau, great erudite and patron; Pierre-François Burger, my first real reader; André Gunthert, my original friend and teacher in Paris; Diogo Ramado Curto, my teacher, friend, guide, and patron in the early days between Paris and Lisbon; and Marc Fumaroli and his seminar at the Collège de France.

The second phase of this research took place at Cambridge University. Under the guidance of Peter Burke, my work became a study of political criticism. He turned me toward the critical traditions of the sixteenth and seventeenth centuries and made me understand how early modern culture worked on a pan-European scale. Peter's erudition, humanity, and intellectual agility were mirrored in the rich collections of the Cambridge University Library. To have access to them both at once was a great privilege. Quentin Skinner took the time to read and guide this work throughout my time at Cambridge.

I am grateful for his support and honored that he trusted me enough to lend me his books. Thanks also go to James Raven, who brought me to Magdalene College; to Elizabeth Leedham-Green and Cecil Courtney for generous friendship; to Filippo de Vivo, a valued reader and friend; and to Stuart Gillespie in Edinburgh and to his journal, *Translation and Literature.*

I first met Anthony Grafton in the Bibliothèque Nationale. Due to his friendship and mentoring I moved to Princeton where I continued working on this project while teaching as a lecturer. Much of the form and content of this book come from long conversations with him—part Talmudic master, part Erasmus, part Lipsius—and reflects his influence as a reader and teacher. His seminar on humanist rhetoric and those who took part in it inspired and gave shape to this book. I would neither have written this book, nor had the possibility to pursue my academic career without his support. I hope my footnotes are an ample reflection of my admiration and gratitude. Between precepts at a lunch at Palmer House, Ted Rabb explained how to turn my dissertation into a book. This book thus bears his strong mark. He has worked tirelessly ever since, reading versions of the manuscript and giving valuable, frank advice and much support. I am grateful for long talks with Peter Gordon that did much to help formulate the framework of the first chapter. I thank Robert Darnton for his advice, comradeship, and confidence; thanks also go to the Princeton History Department and especially to Judy Hansen.

Many thanks go to Donald Kelley and the *Journal of the History of Ideas;* to François Rigolot and the Princeton Renaissance Seminar; to Michael Warner's Center for the Critical Analysis of Contemporary Culture seminar at Rutgers; to Lloyd and Dorothy Moote's Princeton/Rutgers seminar on early modern history; to Peter Stallybrass for his support and many wonderful dinners and to his seminar on material texts at the University of Pennsylvania; to the Washington Area Group for Print Culture Studies; to Orest Ranum; to Rudy Bell; and to the Department of History at Rutgers University, Camden, a model of collegiality and nurturing. I am particularly grateful to my chair, Andrew Lees, who provided active support for publication.

Those who read final drafts of this book will see their influence in its pages. Thanks to my anonymous readers at the University of Michigan Press for their generous and erudite comments. John Salmon was the first to look at a complete manuscript. Peter Miller did much to guide the revision and reconsideration of the book. I am grateful for his advice and patience in responding to my many questions. Geoff Baldwin made many useful commentaries. Tamara Griggs took the time to read and critique the manuscript, showing the value of friendship mixed with deep learning. Of particular value were Robert Darnton's corrections and critiques. His work has been an inspiration since my undergraduate days and, therefore, his comments had both scholarly and personal relevance. J. G. A. Pocock also took the time to read a final draft, and with clear reference to Amelot de La Houssaye, filled the margins of his copy with dozens of manuscript notes: corrections, additions, and most of all, a Tacitean erudite commentary. Needless to say, I would have liked to have published my book with his annotations in the margins, but publishing practices have changed since the seventeenth century, and thus the Pocock hand-annotated edition will remain a private tool of historical analysis and personal development.

None of this project could have been done without the libraries and librarians who provided their support and learning. At the old Bibliothèque Nationale in Paris, the reference librarians were my first research instructors, and librarians in the Réserve des livres rares and the Salle des Manuscrits, such as Isabelle de Conihout, acted daily as teachers, helping me track down and, in many cases, interpret the books and documents I used for this project. For years I researched this book at the old site at the rue de Richelieu—it is fundamentally a product of that place, and I shall always miss working under its beautiful arches and ceilings. I owe debts to the Bibliothèque de l'Arsenal, the Bibliothèque Mazarine, the Archives Nationales, and the Bibliothèque de l'Institut. The University Library at Cambridge is one of the grandest collections in the world, and working there with my cart of sixteenth- and seventeenth-century books from the Acton and Peterborough collections was an utter pleasure. The Firestone Library at Princeton provided not only the wealth of its collections but also the wonderful experience of doing deep research in the stacks late into the night. Floors B and C have become a spiritual second home. Thanks also to the Rutgers University Library; to Susan Halpert at Harvard's Houghton Library; and to John Pollock of the Rare Books Department at the University of Pennsylvania's Van Pelt Library, who helped me research the final chapter of this book and provided most of its images. I am grateful for the financial support of Magdalene College, the Cambridge Overseas Research Fund, the Prince's Trust, the Bibliographical Society, the Royal Historical Society, the Rutgers Research Council, and my department.

I enthusiastically thank Chris Collins, the editor of this book, his staff, and the University of Michigan Press. Editors are, in many ways, the authors of the books they publish. Chris helped this one see the light of day. He and the press have been exceedingly generous and patient, and most of all, they have had unshakable confidence in this project. They are the model of what an academic press should be.

Richard Serjeantson has taught me much as we traveled across Europe and North America, from great university to great university, from ancient libraries to antique book dealers, from the wine cellars of Trinity College to the three-star Michelin restaurants of the Old World, and beyond. He is a true comrade in erudition, oenology, and life. This book owes much to him. My old friend at Magdalene College, Roger O'Keefe, showed me the value of a good Australian Jesuit education, read numerous versions of this project, corrected spelling in four languages, and inspired me to keep going with his own particular eloquence. Colin Hamilton has been reading versions of this book since I started it in Paris. He has gone through it all in what has always been a brotherhood of books. I am grateful for his friendship, learning, and constancy. I will never forget my debts to my undergraduate mentor, Alan Spitzer, as well as to Becky Rogers, David Hamilton, Steve Ungar, Olivier Dehors, and Emmanuel Barrault. I am grateful to my parents—my mother for supporting me, introducing me to reading, European culture, and helping me get a French education; my father for his moral as well as financial backing, going so far as to fly to Paris to bring me a computer when I needed one. My father put up great sums to allow me to follow my pursuits in Paris, Lisbon, Cambridge, Princeton, and Philadelphia. He never wavered in his belief that this book was important, and he always said, "Publish." Finally, Ellen Wayland-Smith has read more versions of this book more times than anyone else and has provided advice, support, and the inspiration of an unwavering love of letters.

As an epilogue to this short history of a book, I must thank Patrick Fray and the Restaurant des Zygomates. They housed me, fed me, gave me much fine Burgundy, and taught me how to cook. While I learned the canon of literature at the Bibliothèque Nationale by day, the Zygomates taught me the canon of French wine and food by night. All graduate education should follow this model. *L'histoire est une certaine cuisine.*

Contents

Illustrations

1. POLITICAL THEORY
AS TEXTUAL CRITICISM

The French revolution was written out in full in the books of Tacitus and Machiavelli, and we could have sought the duties of the people's representatives in the histories of Augustus, Tiberius or Vespasian, or even that of certain French legislators; because, except for a few nuances of perfidy or cruelty, all tyrants are alike. For ourselves, we come to make the world privy to your political secrets, so that all our country's friends can rally to the voice of reason and the public interest.
—Maximillien Robespierre,
Report on the Principles of Political Morality (February 5, 1794)

Joseph de Maistre, the fanatical Catholic philosopher of the early nineteenth century, saw the French Revolution in terms of a culture war. Looking back on 1789 from the vantage point of the shaky Bourbon restoration, he blamed the Revolution on Voltaire. In his eyes, Voltaire's insistence on satire, political criticism, and irreligion weakened the thousand-year-old bonds of blind faith that had kept the order of monarchical civilization since Charlemagne. De Maistre was an extremist and a romantic, but despite his feverish approach to political theory, he understood an essential element of the Enlightenment.[1] Doubt and skepticism, sharpened into tools of political criticism, had cut away at the foundation of Christian, monarchical authority. In de Maistre's Manichean world, there was no liberal middle ground—either Europe returned to the monolithic faith of church and king, or it would descend into the hellish fires of chaos. Absolute monarchy, he insisted, could not coexist with political criticism.

While de Maistre might have understood a cultural cause of the French Revolution, he certainly did not have a solid concept of its origins. The buildup of political criticism had indeed weakened the absolutist order of Old Regime Europe. An esoteric array of secular critics, from the Protestant Pierre Bayle to the champion of noble privilege, Montesquieu, along with Voltaire, Gibbon, Diderot, and others, forged a new vision of politics based on political and legal criticism.[2] What de Maistre did not see was that this critical, skeptical view had its roots in absolutist intellectual life. Pioneered by

Machiavelli and effectively applied by absolutist philosophers such as Jean Bodin, pragmatic political criticism was developed as a tool for princes. Ironically, this earthly science of politics, called "reason of state" by some and commonly referred to as the idea of prudence, was a product of the very world that de Maistre claimed it had destroyed.

If the secular political ideology of the Enlightenment is the foundation of modern politics and society, we still do not understand the process by which it evolved out of the absolutist political tradition of the seventeenth century. How do we explain the fact that the Venetians, the Dutch, and the English developed republican and/or revolutionary political traditions by the mid-seventeenth century, yet the arch-absolutist state of France was the setting for the great statements of political ideas that have shaped the subject since Hobbes and Locke? What was the cultural process by which monarchical authority evolved toward Kantian public enlightenment?

The goal of this book is to answer these questions by tracing the evolution of secular political culture from its Machiavellian origins into the absolutist period of the sixteenth and seventeenth centuries and, finally, to the eighteenth-century Enlightenment. It will expand Paul Hazard's classic thesis that "almost every idea that appeared to be revolutionary in around 1760 or even around 1789, was already in existence in 1680,"[3] by showing the unlikely, though close, relationship between monarchist politics, erudite scholarship, skeptical culture, and the Enlightenment. This book will resituate the shift away from divine monarchical legitimacy and a long crisis of political authority, toward the world of books and editing—in a middle zone between the hungry world of Grub Street popular culture and the meta-sphere of elite philosophers. It will reveal that the dynamic site of political criticism arose in the realm of humanist learned culture, where editors, commentators, and printers used old editorial strategies to publish historical and political information. Central to the understanding of the rise of political criticism between the Renaissance and the Enlightenment is the story of humanist erudite practices and their consequences.

Building on classical tradition and Machiavellian tradition, absolutist scholars of the sixteenth century developed a philosophy of practical politics through the creation of critical-reading methods for the analysis of historical information. This quest to create a truly accurate, critically assessed, source-based history was driven by ambitions to help strengthen the French monarchy. However, by the end of the seventeenth century, a drastic change took place. The critical historical method of "reason of state," or the "capacity to calculate the appropriate means of preserving the state," had been appropriated by critics of the crown.[4] Indeed, eighteenth-century political philosophers forged new methods of political criticism from the old tools of republican humanist and absolutist historiography. By doing so, they publicly circulated an intellectual tool that could be used not only to bolster royal authority but also to criticize and dismantle it. The popularization of skeptical political culture was not Hazard's "crisis of consciousness" but, rather, the triumph of an old skeptical tradition that emerged in Venice in the works of Paolo Sarpi and Trajano Boccalini and found its way to France via the works of Tacitus and the royal obsession with political prudence. Thus, the republican tradition did indeed set the stage for the Enlightenment, but not necessarily by providing a philosophy of virtue. Instead, it produced a set of universal critical tools that could be used by republicans, monarchists, and subversives alike.[5]

WHAT IS CRITICISM?

Modern scholars have called Pierre Bayle the "father of the Enlightenment." Indeed, his *Critical and Historical Dictionary* (1697) was the first great best seller of the eighteenth century. Bayle's work was much more than a simple dictionary. It was a great compendium that showed how to use historical evidence to attack established authority. Bayle locked his readers into a circle of reading and critical questioning. The idea was that if established historical facts could be undermined with other established facts, the reader would have to exercise great critical abilities to ascertain the truth. It was not just a scholarly method. It was the mechanics of a new worldview.

Once Regent Philippe d'Orléans lifted the ban on Bayle's book after the death of Louis XIV in 1715, readers waited in line to consult it at the Bibliothèque Mazarine.[6] Of 500 private library catalogs between 1750 and 1780, 288 contained Bayle's masterwork, far more than any other book.[7] Yet while Bayle was a great innovator, he obviously did not write for an enlightened, eighteenth-century audience. He died in 1706, nine years before Louis XIV. His *Dictionary* was the product of an earlier age, researched and written in exile in Holland, at the height of Louis's quest for absolutist government. It thus reflects the concerns of the seventeenth century. It was neither an attack on absolutism nor a paean to reason. Rather, it was a monument to criticism and doubt beyond political ideology.

Bayle wrote his work in the ambiguous context of seventeenth-century humanism and skepticism. As Reinhart Koselleck has observed, Bayle drew on Richard Simon's attempts at understanding theology by subjecting the Old Testament to philological analysis.[8] Simon himself built on an older humanist tradition of textual criticism that scrutinized texts for historical, linguistic accuracy. In the sixteenth century, the great northern humanist Erasmus had shown that poor translations of the Bible changed its fundamental meaning: a historically mistranslated word or a poorly interpreted allegory could twist the meaning of the Bible or of a classical text.[9] Taking up a central theme of Dutch proto-Protestant humanism, Erasmus insisted that linguistic and hermeneutical accuracy brought the reader closer to the true meaning of revelation. This implied that good readers made good Christians. Simon (1638–1712), a Catholic, sought to reform the reading practices of the Reformation. He attacked the Calvinist tenet of the personal interpretation of the Scriptures by showing that without careful training in textual criticism—a skill he obviously claimed to possess—readers could never truly understand their meaning. He believed that his innovation proved once and for all the necessity of the Catholic Church as a scriptural guide.[10] However, orthodox Catholics, such as Jacques-Bénigne Bossuet, recognized dangers in Simon's approach. In Bossuet's eyes, Simon had illustrated that the rules of criticism operated independently of faith. The very idea of subjecting the Bible to an extensive, rational, historical critique of any sort went against the fundaments of faith and undermined its inherent authority.

Bossuet was not the only one to see the subversive potential of Simon's work. Pierre Bayle and Spinoza were quick to recognize the significance of Simon's achievement.[11] Bayle realized that Simon's methodology of historical erudition could be used not only for religious texts but for secular history as well.[12] Koselleck notes that the difference between Simon and Bayle was that Simon's goal was "revelation" while Bayle's was "reason."[13] Bible criticism was just a step away from political criticism.

Thus, there is a great paradox at the heart of Bayle's *Dictionary*. It reveals that the critical tradition so cherished by Enlightenment thinkers had its roots in the work of "erudite philologists, grammarians and translators of ancient languages," the foot soldiers of royal absolutist and post-Tridentine humanism.[14] It also reveals the intellectual path by which the scholarly techniques of textual criticism would form the basis of the new secular order, an order that ideally would use the rational analysis of history to formulate its political theories and whose only constraints were the laws of nature themselves. In short, absolute monarchs had turned to faith in reason as a weapon, and, in turn, this new cult undermined absolutism.[15] Rather than the traditional view of absolutism in which *auctoritas non veritas facit legem,* the secular culture of "truth" actually competed with raw power and effectively undermined it.[16] Praxis would become enlightenment.

To ground the origins of secular political theory in erudite historical criticism has important implications for intellectual history. It reveals why traditional intellectual history has not successfully explained the origins of the Enlightenment. What Koselleck calls the "reign of criticism" at the end of the seventeenth century was an intellectual movement that sought not to write great books and ideas but, instead, to translate, examine, compile, reedit, and criticize existing works. J. G. A. Pocock has pointed to the importance of this concept for the eighteenth century: "The capacity to read texts critically, vital . . . to the writing of Enlightenment history, was also a great part of what the age meant by 'philosophy.'"[17] No one can assign a political *grande idée* to

Bayle's *Dictionary*. That is why, until quite recently, intellectual historians have come up empty-handed when trying to connect the Enlightenment to the obscure parentage of the seventeenth century.[18]

As the complex page setting of Bayle's *Dictionary* illustrates, criticism involved more than simply writing (figs. 2a and 2b). Authors such as Bayle saw the production of meaning not in terms of words alone but, rather, in terms of a textual bricolage: they cited, translated, commented on, reproduced, pasted, and juxtaposed texts against each other in vast collages and compilations. Philosophy could be found not only in primary texts but also in introductions, annexes, and the margins of books. Medieval and early modern authors arranged and even rearranged. To write meant to produce discourse, but meaning was also strongly attached to the materiality of books and the presentation of texts.

This raises the question of how to study the history of political philosophy during the age of humanist textual practices. What constituted political philosophy during the sixteenth and seventeenth centuries? What did it look like, or what was it meant to look like? The textual collage of Bayle's *Dictionary* illustrates that the study of early modern political philosophy is a more complex problem than has previously been considered.[19] When reading the compendia and erudite encyclopedias of the sixteenth, seventeenth, and eighteenth centuries, it becomes clear that the criteria of what constituted a major work of political thought were very different during this period than they are now. Political philosophy was not clear-cut discourse, and it was a textual practice closely associated with the culture of printed information. If modern historians are to understand the complex intellectual world that produced the Enlightenment, they must think like humanists and study textual practices as political statements.

Indeed, intellectual historians who simply skip from high spot to high spot—like tourists who stay on a tour bus and ignore the gritty reality of the monuments they visit—cannot hope to understand what writers and their readers had in mind. They must explore the backstreets of bibliography and follow the steep paths of the social history of knowledge.[20] This does not only mean "grubbing in the archives," as Robert Darnton insisted in his now classic critique of Peter Gay.[21] In this instance, it means taking into account that high culture was messier and more complicated than has been previously recognized.[22] So-called high culture was not as high and pristine as it appears today in the seemingly stable classic editions published by Cambridge University Press and Penguin Books. High books such as *The Prince* could lead low lives, as socially nonelite scholars and printers helped shape their meaning and as a heterogeneous reading public made multiple interpretations. In short, we have much to discover about the canon itself. Rather than obstinately embracing the canon or righteously rejecting it, the time has come to reassess its very nature and measure its nuances. As Rousseau and, ulti-

de Tachus, & se fit élire Roi par les Egyptiens.   Cela fait il envoia des Ambassadeurs au Roi
Agesilaus pour le prier de se joindre à lui, & ne manqua pas de lui faire de magnifiques pro-
messes.   Tachus de son côté n'oublia rien pour le retenir. Chacun de ces concurrens envoia des
Députez à Lacedemone.   Agesilaus y en envoia aussi ; mais beaucoup plus afin de recommander
les intérêts de Nectanabe, qu'afin de recommander ceux de Tachus. Il reçut un plein pouvoir
de faire tout ce qu'il jugeroit le plus à propos pour le bien de sa patrie, & il jugea qu'il étoit
(b) Tiré de beaucoup plus utile aux Lacedemoniens d'abandonner Tachus, que de le maintenir ; desorte
Plutarque, qu'il passa au service de Nectanabe avec les soldats qu'il commandoit : ce qui, comme l'a remarque
in Vit.Age- son Historien, ne méritoit pas d'être apellé autrement que trahison, quelque couverture qu'on y
silai. donnât de l'utilité publique. Tachus ainsi abandonné s'enfuit où il put (b), & je ne crois point que
(c) Theo- l'Histoire l'ait jamais retrouvé. Quelques-uns (c) ont dit qu'il se retira en Perse. Il faut bien
pompus, que tout bon asyle lui manquât, puis qu'il se refugioit chez un Prince qui ne le pouvoit re-
& Lyceas garder que comme un chef de rebelles. Athenée donne au ressentiment d'Agesilaus une cause
Naucrati- fort diférente de celle qu'on vient de voir ; mais j'aimerois beaucoup mieux en croire Plutarque,
tes, apud
Athenæum, qu'Athenée (A).
Libr. XIV.
pag. 616.

(A) J'aimerois beaucoup mieux en croire Plutarque qu'A-
thenée.] Ce dernier attribue tout à un mot de raillerie ; il
(1) Athen. veut (1) que Tachus se moquant d'Agesilaus, en le voiant
Libr. XIV. de si petite taille, lui ait dit, *Une montagne a été en travail*
pag. 616. *& s'enfant, Jupiter en a eu peur, elle s'est delivrée d'une souris.*
Ωδίνεν ὄρος, Ζεὺς δ' ἐφοϐεῖτο, τὸ δ' ἔτεκεν μῦν. Il ajoû-
te qu'Agesilaus se mit en colere, & qu'il répondit, *Vous*
m'éprouverez un jour que je suis un lion. La menace fut suivie de son effet ; car une sédition aiant été excitée contre
Tachus, il se vit abandonné d'Agesilaus, & contraint de
s'enfuir en Perse. Je ne trouve point de vraisemblance à
cela. Premierement Plutarque, qui raporte assez au long le
mépris que les Egyptiens firent d'Agesilaus en le voiant si
mal équipé, & de si mauvaise mine, & en conoissant son
mauvais goût par le choix qu'il fit sur les presens qu'on
lui avoit envoiez, ne dit point que Tachus se soit mêle
de ces railleries. Il dit bien que la foule du monde qui
accourut au rivage, pour voir ce grand Capitaine dont la
renommée parloit tant, lui apliqua la fable de la montagne qui enfanta une souris ; mais il ne dit point qu'A-
gesilaus ait répondu la moindre chose, & Tachus n'étoit
point là. Le bon mot, qu'Athenée fournit au Roi de Lacedemone, auroit trouvé sans doute place dans le Recueil
que Plutarque nous a laissé des Apophtegmes de ce Prince, s'il fût venu d'une bonne tradition. De plus y a-t-il

aparence qu'un homme, qui avoit tant de besoin d'Age-   *(2)* ...
silaus, ait été assez imprudent pour l'irriter par une si pi-   ...
quante raillerie ? Je ne nie pas que Plutarque n'ait observé   ...
qu'Agesilaus eut à souffrir de la vanité de Tachus (2) ;   xxx xm-
mais encore un coup, cet Historien n'auroit pas oublie en   ...
ce lieu-là le conte de la Montagne, & la vive réponse   ...
d'Agesilaus. Je croirois volontiers qu'il faudroit réduire à   ...
ceci la narration d'Athenée ; on raporta au Roi de Lace-   ...
demone que les Egyptiens après l'avoir vu si petit , lui   ...
dont ils s'étoient fait une grande idée, avoient parlé de la   ...
montagne qui enfante un rat ; il répondit aprement ,   ...
*Ils verront bientôt je suis comme un lion, ou ; & il qu'il   ...
ont eu sur le rivage.* Il ne pretendoit point menacer Ta-   ...
chus, mais le remplir d'esperance. J'ai oui dire que ces   ...
Generaux François se trouvant en Allemagne , & remar-   ...
quant qu'on n'y avoit pas bonne opinion de certains Ré-   ...
gimens qu'ils y commandoient , on l'on ne voioit pas de   ...
grands corps, ni de grosses masses de chair bien nourries &   ...
bien vetues , instruroient les gens par ces paroles, *Vous vo-   ...
rez ces petits soldats , maigres & descharnez , aller au feu   ...
comme des lions , & faire plier les plus gros colosses.* Quoi   ...
qu'il en soit , on peut voir dans ce conte d'Athenée vrai ou   ...
faux une leçon importante, c'est que les Princes ne doivent   ...
jamais offenser personne p.r des railleries (3) : il leur en   ...
coûte bon quelquefois.

(a) D'au-   TACITE (Caïus (a) Corneille) Historien Romain, a fleuri dans le prémier Siecle.
tres lui On ne sait rien de ses ancêtres, & aparemment la gloire de sa Famille commença en sa personne.
donnent ne. Son prémier emploi, dit-on , fut celui de Procureur de Vespasien dans la Gaule Belgique (A).
pour Pré- Etant retourné à Rome , il reçut de l'Empereur Tite un grade plus honorable (b). Il fut Pré-
nom Pu- teur sous l'Empire de Domitien (B), & Consul sous Nerva (C). Mais toutes ces dignitez ne
blius,& en lui donnent qu'une gloire fort petite , si on la compare à celle qu'il s'est procurée par les travaux
sont repris de sa plume. Ses Annales & son Histoire (D) sont quelque chose d'admirable, & l'un des plus
(b) Voiez
la Remar- grans
que (A).

(1) Dans la   *(A) De Procureur de Vespasien dans la Gaule Belgique.*]   au Regne de Trajan ; & c'étoit l'occupation qu'il réter-
Rem. (K). Vous trouverez ces paroles dans la Vie de Tacite compo-   voit pour sa vieillesse : je ne crois pas qu'il ait pû executer
(2) Taci- sée par Juste Lipse, *Initium dignitatis sub Vespasiano*   ce dessein. *Quod si vita suppeditet, principatum Divi Ner-*
tus.Hist. *suit , a quo Plinio auctore, procurator datus Gallia Belgica*   *væ,& Imperium Trajani,uberiorem securioremque materiam*
Libr. I. *rationes Principi administravit.* Se citeroit ci-dessous (1) ce   *senectuti sepoui :* Trova-t-on, orum senectuti, hæc jeuvre que
Cap. I. qu'a dit Pline , & l'on y verra qu'il n'a fait aucune men-   *dst, & que sentin dicere licet* (11). Les paroles montrent
(3) Dans la tion de Vespasien. Pourquoi donc le cite-t-on, comme un   qu'il commença son Histoire après la mort de l'Empereur
Rem. (K). Auteur qui nous aprend que cet Empereur donna à Tacite   Nerva , & pendant la Vie de Trajan. En effet, il donne
(4) Lipse.in cette Charge ? Est-ce parce que l'on a trouvé que Tacite l'a   au premier le Titre de *Divus* qu'il ne donne pas à l'autre.
Vita Taciti, exercée sous l'Empire de Vespasien ? Mais cela donne-t-il   Il ne nous reste que V Livres de son Histoire : ce n'est
l'on exposant le droit d'attribuer aux Auteurs ce qu'ils n'ont point dit ?   que la plus petite partie ; car ils ne comprennent pas un an
(5) C'étoit Qui qu'il en soit , on ne doute guere que Tacite n'ait   & demi : sur tout l'Ouvrage devoit comprendre environ
l'an 841, & possédé cet emploi sous Vespasien, & voici sur quoi l'on se   vingt neuf ans. Ceux qui s'interessent aux cinq Livres com-
le 30eme.selon fonde : *Dignitatem nostram à Vespasiano inchoatam , a*   me la suite des Annales divisées en XVI Livres sont bla-
Dyon,ou *Tito auctam , a Domitiano longius provectam non abnuerim*   mables ; puis qu'il est certain que les Annales doivent être
le Secr. selon (2). C'est Tacite qui parle. Nous verrons ci-dessous (3) si   considerées comme un Ouvrage sepáre. L'Auteur les com-
Calvisius. cette opinion est bien fondée.   posa après qu'il eut achevé l'Histoire (12) : elles commen-
(6)Tacitus,
Annal.   *(B) Il fut Préteur sous l'Empire de Domitien.*] Vertranius   çoient à la mort d'Auguste , & s'étendoient jusques a cel-
Libr. XI. met cette Préture sous le neuvieme Consulat de cet Empe-   le de Neron. Il ne nous en reste qu'une partie, savoir les
Cap. XI. reur (4) : mais il l'eut du mettre sous le quatorzieme ;   IV premiers Livres , quelques pages du V , tout le VI , &
(7) 849.se- car elle concourt avec le tems que Domitien celebra les   depuis l'onzieme jusques au XV , & une partie du XVI :
lon Calvi- jeux séculaires : or il est certain qu'il les celebra cette Con-   les deux dernieres années de Neron & une partie de la
sius. sul pour la quatorzieme fois (5). Citons Tacite: *Is (Domi-*   precedente nous manquent. C'etoient les derniers Livres
(8)Plinius, *tianus) quoque edidit ludos fæculares : iisque interestui assui*   de l'Ouvrage. Au reste , les cinq premiers Livres furent
Epistola I. *Sacerdotio Quindecimvirali præditus : ac tum prætor. Quod*   trouvez en Allemagne par un Receveur de Leon X. Il les
Libri II. *non jactantia vitero , sed quia collegio Quindecimvirorum anti-*   aporta a Rome à un Pape , & en reçut une gratification de cinq cens
(9) Ulrman *quitat ea cura , & magistratus potissimum exequebantur*   ecus. *Coroeta quod ad Vspirginem Monasterium est , à quæstore*
Princi- *officia sertimonicarum* (6).   *Pontifuci fuere inventi, qui cui ad Leonem X. detulit , ac*
pii rationes   *pag. 110.*
prætermitto,   *(C) . . . & Consul sous Nerva.*] Il fut subroge en la   *ar'vidige loco quingentos accepit aureos* (13). Philippe Hero-
soit narra- place de Virginius Rufus , qui étoit mort dans son troisieme   alde eut ordre de les publier (14). Je me souviens d'avoir   *rene sopra*
tes libris Consulat l'an de Rome 850 (7) , & il l'honora d'une fu-   oui dire à feu Mr. l'aure Docteur en Theologie de la Faculté   *Tacite in*
quibus suis nebre funebre. *Laudatus est a Consule Cornelio Tacito,*   de Paris, que Leon dixieme aiant publie un tiret par le-   *pag. 110.*
Imperatori- *nam hic supremus felicitatis ejus cumulus accessit, laudatur*   quel il promettoit tant seulement une indulgences a ceux   *XIII.*
bus Domitiani *eloquentissimus* (8).   qui decouvriroient les Manuscrits de Tacite , sans aucun de   *Herodi. in*
tempofui.   l'argent & de sa gloire (15) , il y eut un Allemand qui fure-   *Xm m bene*
Tacitus,   *(D) Ses Annales & son Histoire.*] Il fut l'Histoire avant   ta toutes les indulgences , & qui trouva enfin quelques Li-   *Blege de Lol*
Annal. les Annales ; car il nous renvoie a l'Histoire dans l'onzie-   vres des Annales dans le Monastere de Corwey. Il les alla   *presente*
Libr. XI. me Livre des Annales (9) ; il nous y renvoie, dis-je , tou-   presenter au Pape , qui les reçut avec un plaisir extreme, &   *pag. 110.*
Cap. XI. chant des choses qui concernent Domitien : or il est sur (10)   qui lui demanda qu'elle recompense il souhaitoit. L'Alle-   *Blege de Lol*
(10) Voiez que son Histoire s'étendoit depuis l'Empire de Galba in-   mand le contenta d'etre rembourse de la depense qu'il avoit   *Stace di*
Tacite, commence- clusivement , jusques a celui de Nerva exclusivement. Il   faite pour aller voir les Bibliotheques , tant que un eu   *courant.*
ment de son destinoit un Ouvrage particulier au Regne de Nerva, &   *volage*
Histoire.

Fig. 2. Pierre Bayle, *Dictionnaire historique et critique* (Basle: Jean-Louis Brandmuller,
1738), vol. 4, pp. 310–11. Bayle's chapter on Tacitus gives a sense of his complex page setting and of the secondary role played by his primary text (*a*). Notice the reference to

grans efforts de l'esprit humain, soit que l'on y considere la singularité du style, soit que l'on s'attache à la beauté des pensées, & à cet heureux pinceau avec lequel il a su peindre les déguisemens & les fourberies des politiques, & le foible des passions. Ce n'est pas qu'il n'y ait bien à reprendre dans l'affectation de son langage, & dans celle de rechercher les motifs secrets des actions (E), & de les tourner vers le criminel ; mais c'est un grand éloge pour son esprit, que de voir l'estime que plusieurs Princes ont eue pour ses Ouvrages (F). Un Auteur moderne en a fait ce jugement : *Tertullien l'accuse de nous debiter beaucoup de mensonges. Non seulement il estoit ennemi de la veritable religion, mais on voit en divers endroits qu'il n'en avoit point du tout. Son style est assurément assez obscur ; il est mesme quelquefois dur, & n'a pas toute la pureté des bons Auteurs de la Langue Latine. Cependant son art à renfermer de grands sens en peu de mots, sa vivacité à depeindre les évenemens, la lumiere avec laquelle il penetre les tenebres du cœur corrompu des hommes, une force & une éminence d'esprit qui paroist par tout, le font regarder aujourd'hui presque généralement comme le premier des Historiens* (c). On en a fait tant de Versions, & on l'a tant commenté (G), que

(c) Tillemont: Hist. des Empereurs Tom. II, l'Art. pag. 511 Edit. de Bruxelles.

[16] Notes. sur Me-sieurs desoit qu'il avoit lû ce narré dans la Pré-face de la l'Edition de ses Livres de Tacite. Voïez l'E-loge de Mr. Faure dans le Journal des Savans du 16 Nov. 1691, pag. 471 Edit. de Hollande.

[17] Les XVI.XVII. XVIII du II Volume Avere l'Edition, 1875.

[18] Libr. I, d'Eloquence, Prélud. II.

[19] Professe. leur à Pise.

voisinage de Rome. Leon jugea que c'étoit trop peu, & lui fit donner davantage ; & afin de lui procurer de la gloire & du profit, il voulut lui laisser le soin de publier ce Tacite. Mais l'Allemand s'en excusa sur ce qu'il manquoit de l'Erudition nécessaire)16).

(E) *Ce n'est pas qu'il n'y ait bien à reprendre dans l'affectation de son langage, & dans celle de rechercher les motifs secrets des actions.*] Muret a fait trois Harangues (17) pour repondre à ceux qui ont critiqué Tacite. Leur Critique étoit trop aigre, elle étoit injuste à certains egards, il n'a donc pas été difficile à l'Apologiste, bon Orateur & subtil Rhetoricien, de l'eluder. Vous aprendrez dans ces Harangues ce qu'on reproche à Tacite. Vous l'aprendrez aussi dans les *Prolusions* de Famien Strada (18). Il déplut par là à Paganinus Gaudentius (19), qui non seulement lui critiqua (20) plusieurs endroits de son Histoire du Pais-Bas, mais tâcha aussi de justifier Tacite. Ce Gaudentius n'étoit pas un rude champion : il savoit un peu de beaucoup de choses ; & n'aprofondissoit rien. *Magis literis tinctus quàm imbutus . . . , nihil in ingenio solidum, cum per artes & disciplinas peregrinaretur nulli penitus insistens* (21). Il me semble que le Cardinal du Perron a trop méprisé Tacite (22).

Le Livre intitulé *Anonymiana ou Melange de Poësies, d'Eloquence, & d'Erudition*, qui fut imprimé à Paris l'an 1700, contient un Discours qui n'est pas trop favorable à nôtre Historien. Voici ce que l'on y juge de son langage (23): „ Tacite paroît bien Latin, mais trop obscurement pour ce qu'il a voulu écrire. Sa diction dure „ & resserrée pourroit estre prisée ailleurs que dans une „ Histoire, où tout doit être clair & bien établi , où l'é-„ loignement des faits, leur diversité, les epoques, & leur „ changemens toûjours contestées la rendent obscure d'elle-„ même, tant que le stile soit de la partie.... (24)." C'est „ un abus de pretendre que la maniere d'écrire de Tacite „ puisse la rendre recommandable ; s'il y a des vins enfu-„ mez par un peu d'amertume, ils le sont par une bonne „ qualité : mais une maniere d'écrire dure & scabreuse „ n'acquit jamais de reputation à une Histoire. Bien loin „ d'elever l'esprit à de plus grandes connoissances, com-„ me le pretend ce Scavant (25), elle l'embarrasse & le „ rebute. Diroit-on, par exemple, que Cesar le fût au-„ tant d'attention s'il avoit été plus obscur & moins „ naturel? N'eleve-t-il pas l'esprit jusques à ses pensées, „ qui doivent toûjours être dans la lecture de ses Histoi-„ re, la juste borne des nôtres; au lieu que dans une ma-„ niere d'écrire obscure, l'esprit du lecteur se promene ou „ il lui plaît, quand il ne le laisse pas, & se forge des „ imaginations qui n'ont souvent aucune justesse, ni au-„ cune proportion avec les choses. Cesar par sa netteté „ le reduit au naturel, & ne laissa jamais à souhaiter plus „ de lumiere dans les actions qu'il a decrites ". Je sous-„ crirois volontiers à ce jugement , & il me semble que ce „ qu'on ajoute touchant l'autre affectation de Tacite n'est „ pas moins bon (26). „ (27) Tacite est un habile politi-„ que , & trouve dans les plus judicieux écrivain; il a entre des „ consequences fort justes sur les evenemens des Regnes „ dont il a fait l'histoire , & il en fait des maximes pour „ bien gouverner un Etat. Mais s'il a donné quelquefois „ aux actions & aux mouvemens de la Republique, leurs „ vrais principes, s'il en a bien démêlé les causes, il faut „ avoüer qu'il a souvent suplée par trop de delicatesse & „ de penetration à celles qui n'en avoient pas; tant il est „ vrai que l'on se caracterise dans tout ce que l'on fait , „ & que l'Histoire se fait imagines entre les mains qu'elle „ doit être , lors que ceux qui s'en mêlent n'en écrire don-„ nent pour la veritable cause de ce qu'ils ne connoissent „ pas ce qu'ils ont imagine de moins sensible & de plus „ caché aux yeux du Peuple : Il leur arrive souvent de „ faire d'un secret particulier au Prince , une affaire con-„ nue à tout le monde , & c'est un defaut si familier à „ Tacite (28); que j'oserois dire , apuié d'ailleurs d'une „ infinité de bonnes raisons, que c'est lui faire trop de „ grace que le regarder comme un Historien fort exact , „ & qui a écrit selon les regles.... (29) Il a choisi „ les actions les plus delicates & les plus susceptibles des „ delicatesses de l'art ; les Regnes ausquels il s'est princi-„ palement attaché dans son Histoire n'en sont pas une „ petite preuve. Dans celui de Tibere, qui est sans con-„ testation son chef-d'œuvre, & où il a le mieux réüssi, „ il y trouvoit une espece de gouvernement plus accom-

modé au caractere de son genie. Il aimoit , comme „ nous l'avons dit , à démeler les intrigues du cabinet, à „ en assigner les causes , à donner des desseins aux pre-„ textes , & de la verité à de trompeuses apparences. Ge-„ nie trop subtil, il voit du mystere dans toutes les actions „ de ce Prince. Une sincere déference de ses desseins au „ jugement du Senat , étoit tantôt un piege tendu à son „ integrite , tantôt une delicate maniere d'en être le mai-„ tre ; mais toûjours l'art de le rendre complice de ses „ desseins , & d'en avoir l'execution sans reproches. Lors „ qu'il punissoit des factieux , c'étoit un effet de la dé-„ fiance naturelle pour les Citoiens, ou de legeres mar-„ ques de colere répandues parmi le peuple, pour dispo-„ fer les esprits à de plus grandes cruautés. Ici la contra-„ rieté d'humeurs de deux Chefs , est un ordre secret de „ traverser la fortune d'un competiteur , & le moyen de „ lui enlever l'affection du peuple. Les dignités deferées „ au merite, étoient d'honnêtes voies d'éloigner un con-„ current, ou de perdre un ennemi, & toûjours de fata-„ les recompenses. En un mot tout est politique, le vice, „ & la vertu , y sont également dangereux, & les faveurs „ aussi funestes que les disgraces. Tibere n'y est jamais „ naturel, il ne fait point sans dessein les actions les plus „ ordinaires aux autres hommes. Son repos n'est jamais „ sans consequence , & ses mouvemens embrassent toû-„ jours plusieurs menées ". Les maximes que j'ai „ leues dans cette Dissertation de l'Auteur de l'Anonyma-„ na sont plus sujettes, ce me semble , à une juste contes-„ tation.

(F) *L'estime que plusieurs Princes ont eue pour les Ouvrages de Tacite.*] Le Pape Paul III avoit usé tout son Exemplaire à force de le reire. Cosme de Medicis premier grand Duc de Florence faisoit ses delices de cette lecture. Muret nous va dire tout cela en plus beaux termes, *Paulo III P. M. quo multum sapientiorem senem nostra vidit atas, Tacitum sape relegenda conterebatur, neque ullum profusum scriptorem aquè libenter legebat. Cosmus Medices, qui primus Magnus Etruria Dux fuit , homo factus ad imperandum, qui eam, qua vulgo fortuita dicuntur, in consiliis & prudentia consistere docuit, Tacitos libros in deliciis habebat , eorumque lectione aviditssimè fruebatur, Neque nos hodie multis aut Principum, aut optimi cujusque virorum à Principibus in consilium adhibeatur, rendendum studiosissimè legunt, & quasi pranmagistro quendam prudentia habent* (30). Faisons suivre ce Latin par un Passage de Balzac. Dans une Lettre qu'il écrivit à d'Ablancourt le 4 de Juin 1643, „ Ta-„ cite étant devenu vostre, ma mauvaise humeur contre „ luy ne sçauroit durer. Je ne puis hair un homme que „ vous aymez : Et , si vous dire le vray , il me semble que „ cettuy-cy c'est fait plus doux & moins espineux, depuis „ qu'il a passé par vos mains. L'importance est que vous „ ne vous eites point sali en mesmé de faux matieres,& „ que parmy les ordures de la Politique vostre Morale s'est „ conservée en sa pureté. Un Philosophe Stoique du der-„ nier siecle , comme vous diriez Juste Lipse , a eu la mes-„ me delicatesse pour Tacite dans le dernier Capitaine, comme vous „ dirièz le Marquis Spinola , à faire sa langue la mesme „ traduction, quoy qu'elle n'ait point esté publiée : & je „ vous apprens ce secret , que je tiens d'un de ses plus par-„ ticuliers Confidens (31) ". Joignen à cela ce Passage de Guy Patin : *Corn. Tacite, qui est son Breviaire d'Etat & le premier ou le grand Maitre des secrets du Cabinet , & même que Monsieur de Balzac à quelque sort apellé l'ancien original des finesses modernes , a est le parfait de l'Ivre* (32). Souvenez-vous ici de l'empressement de Leon X: j'en ai parlé ci-dessus (33).

Joignons la Reine Christine aux exemples que l'on vient de voir. Mr. Chanut dit qu'elle ne faisoit de la Langue Grecque *que son divertissement aux heures perdues, sans que l'etude de cette langue & des autres troublast les resfours souveraines. C'est de ce dernier nom qu'elle qualifioit entre autres l'estime de Tacite, dont il ne se passoit point de jour qu'elle ne luel quelques pages. Cet Auteur qui donne de l'exercice aux plus sçavans lui étoit très familier* (34).

(G) *On en a fait tant de Versions, & on l'a tant commenté.*] Mr. Amelot de la Houssaye, qui a traduit en François les trois premiers Livres des Annales , a mis au devant de sa Traduction un Discours Critique , où vous trouverez le nom de plusieurs personnes qui ont travaillé sur cet Ecrivain. Vous y aprendrez le jugement que l'on fait de leur travail , & du style & de la morale de Tacite. Tout cela est fort curieux. Mais ne croiez pas que ce Traducteur

[20] Voïez son Livre de Candore, Politico, imprimé à Pise l'an 1646.

[21] Octav. Ferrarius, in Prolusio-nibus Titu-lis Litera-torum Tom.

[22] Voïez son-ventana, pag. 7.

[23] Ibid, pag. 9.

[24] C'est à-dire la Mauthe de Vayer.

[25] Anon-nyu, vel ici fer-mentant parlant. Voïez la Citat. (18).

[26] Anon-nymiana, pag. 10.

[27] Ilau a saleu-nuus fac dire qu'il avoit etre ce qu'en nuus plus bele, eux kun quia que mnme. Le ce-lle est mêché dans Es. ser-venit.

[30] Muret, Orat. XVI Vol. II, pag. 342. Edit. Lipsi. 1672.

Voïez Orationes. Helm. iii, pag 5 & la Preface du III Li-vre de la Ariena Anteria; & l'aquilet, Lettres , Tom. II, pag. 442. & juce.

[31] Balzac, Lettre à d'Ablan-court. C.2 le XXI du XII Livre, & le XXI l'an La ore en la I Partie des Lettres Choisies, pag. 128. Edition d'Amsterd.

[32] Patin, Lettre CXXVI. pag. 171 du II Tome.

[33] Dans la Remar-que (D).

[34] Voïez Mr. Bail-let, Vie de Des-Cartes Tom. II, pag. 305.

Amelot de La Houssaye at the bottom of page 311 (*b*). (Courtesy of Annenberg Rare Book and Manuscript Library, University of Pennsylvania.)

mately, Robespierre made starkly clear, the works of Tacitus and Machiavelli could be put to more radical uses than those of Voltaire. In the end, high philosophy helped fuel popular revolution.

Pierre Bayle was not the first to try to reveal the mechanics of critical practice. He knew what modern scholars have overlooked: that the tools of political criticism had circulated for nearly a century in the works of political reason of state. His *Dictionary* represented the next stage in the life of the old critical tradition. Precisely the circulation of reason-of-state literature and of an apparatus of scholarly criticism within a growing public sphere made available the methods of decoding the crown's strategies for retaining power.2[3] Once this happened, points out political philosopher Marcel Gauchet, the state quite literally lost its mystery, and opposition to absolute power became more widespread. The process of publishing critical historical works concerning reason of state and prudence broke the sacred balance between the absolute monarchist state and its subjects, turning the crown into a subject of critical analysis.[24] The diffusion of political criticism during the seventeenth century illustrates the ambiguity of the concept of the "public" at that time.[25] Strategies and critical historical readings circulated through publication, yet they entailed very private reading. They were, after all, about dissimulation—how princes do it, how to read their strategies, and how to do it yourself. What is less clear is the process by which the world of reason and state—first royal and then individual and private—became public.

AMELOT DE LA HOUSSAYE AND THE MATERIAL RHETORIC OF PRUDENCE

A key to understanding the publication and popularization of codes and strategies of reason of state is an erudite scholar from the late seventeenth century, Abraham-Nicolas Amelot de La Houssaye (1634–1706).[26] Amelot was single-handedly responsible for reediting the greatest works of secular political theory at the end of the seventeenth century. He translated and commented on the works of Tacitus, Machiavelli, Gasparo Contarini, Paolo Sarpi, the Cardinal d'Ossat, Baltasar Gracián, and La Rochefoucauld. Before Bayle, Amelot took these works of critical history and political sociology and re-presented them with his prefaces, notes, and commentaries, all of which "helped" the reader use these books to criticize royal despotism. Authors such as Tacitus, who had been a staple of absolutist historical culture, were now presented as tools of subversion.

When eighteenth-century French thinkers read Machiavelli, they most likely saw him through Amelot's much-published critical version.[27] In understanding how Amelot appropriated these essential works of critical political history, introducing them into the wide market for political criticism created by Versailles, we will see for the first time how a monarchist, absolutist program of history evolved into the basis of public political criticism.[28] Amelot's critical project marks the moment when the knowledge of political history and historical criticism became public and widely accessible. To be sure, he was not the first political thinker to understand that by publishing historical information, he could transform it into political criticism. This was, of course, Paolo Sarpi's great project. But beyond Sarpi and before Bayle, Amelot was the first to create a complex program to systematically publish a reading apparatus to help the public understand political criticism.

In his article "Tacitus and the Tacitist Tradition," Arnaldo Momigliano claimed that he did "not know of an adequate study of A.-N. Amelot de La Houssaye, the greatest Tacitist of France and the translator of Baltasar Gracián, who was also the writer of the *Histoire du Gouvernement de Venise* (1676), a classic in the interpretation of the Venetian constitution."[29] Momigliano was stating what Pierre Bayle knew at the end of the seventeenth century: that Amelot de La Houssaye was personally responsible for re-presenting and transmitting the major works of secular, historical political prudence during a period of "crisis" that we now recognize to be pivotal in the evolution of classical Renaissance culture into the Enlightenment.[30] The tradition of the *saeculum* (the historical realm of humankind's earthly affairs) passed through Amelot's hands, and during the thirty years of Louis XIV's reign, Amelot nurtured and protected the ancient methods of pragmatic political analysis, repackaging the political texts he edited to fit their era. A highbrow version of Menocchio, the subversive, freethinking miller from Carlo Ginzburg's *The Cheese and the Worms*, Amelot appropriated the works he read and recast royal prudence as a weapon for political criticism.[31]

Amelot's most notable works include a translation and commentary of Paolo Sarpi's *History of the Council of Trent* (1683) and *Treatise on Beneficial Matters* (1685), as well as a translation of Minucci and Sarpi's *History of the Uscoques* (1682).[32] Amelot's translation of *The Prince* (1683) was the primary French version of Machiavelli's seminal work throughout the eighteenth century and was still being reedited in the 1960s.[33] Containing Amelot's preface and commentary and, in its margins, eighty-three maxims from Tacitus, this edition was published twenty-three times between 1683 and 1789. His best-known translation was that of Baltasar Gracián's *Oráculo manual y arte de prudencia,* better known under the French title that Amelot gave to it, *L'Homme de cour* (1684), which was a best seller in its time, with ten editions between 1684 and 1808. It is still published today, making Amelot one of the most successful translators in French history.[34] Amelot's later works include commentaries on Cardinal d'Ossat's *Lettres* (1698) and La Rochefoucauld's *Mémoires de la minorité de Louis XIV* (1688) and *Réflexions, sentences et maximes morales* (1711),[35] as well as a prefatory commentary on Frédéric Léonard's compilation of royal treaties, *Les préliminaires des traités des princes* (1692). Amelot's posthumous *Mémoires historiques, politiques, critiques et littéraires* (1722), an eighteenth-century best seller, was likely a forgery.[36]

Amelot was, above all, a translator of Tacitus, publishing three different translations of his favorite author: *Tibère: Discours politiques sur Tacite* (1683), *La Morale de Tacite* (1686), and *Tacite: Les six premiers livres des Annales* (1690).[37] Five editions of French translations of the works of Tacitus were published by the Protestant academician and Richelieu's ally Perrot d'Ablancourt.[38] Amelot was the only other French translator of Tacitus with translations published between 1680 and 1700. He was the most important translator of Tacitus of the age of Louis XIV, with fourteen editions of his translations of Tacitus between 1683 and 1731.

In total, between 1676 and 1706, the year of Amelot's death, at least 59 editions of his eighteen different works were published in French. Between 1706 and 1808, 47 editions were published, including 5 previously unpublished, posthumous works. Thus, between 1676 and 1808 (the year Amelot's works stopped being regularly reedited), at least 106 editions of twenty-three different works by Amelot appeared in print. On the basis of these numbers, Amelot would appear to be one of the most prolific and popular writers of his time and one of the most successful translators of all time. Multiple editions of his work were published well into the eighteenth century, and eleven editions of two of his works were published during the twentieth century. His books were carefully studied and much appreciated by Pierre Bayle. Queen Christina of Sweden annotated her edition of Amelot's translation of *The Prince* while in exile in Rome. Montesquieu wrote notes in the margins of his copies of Amelot's books and cited him in *De l'esprit des loix*. Voltaire vilified Amelot but reedited his critical edition of *The Prince*. Gibbon's library contained the *Histoire du gouvernement de Venise*, and even Napoleon copied down passages from this work with Jesuit-like diligence.[39]

Yet Amelot has been forgotten by modern intellectual historiography precisely because of his own authorial strategy, which fits poorly into the conventional definition of what it means to be an author. Writing critical—and possibly republican—political theory during the Sun King's rule was a near impossibility for an author working in the oppressive atmosphere of Paris.[40] Therefore, Amelot used time-tested strategies of editorial dissimulation—translation, commentary, and writing with double meanings—to mask his work. When carefully examined, Amelot's editions of Tacitus and Baltasar Gracián, for example, are facades that cover the carefully constructed edifice of his own political thought. Understanding how Amelot interpreted and represented his immense corpus of major works of critical political historiography will allow us to understand how their meaning evolved between the

Renaissance and the Enlightenment, as well as illustrating the grander picture of the evolution of secular political culture in early modern Europe.[41]

REPRESENTING REASON OF STATE

Little is known about the life of Abraham-Nicolas Amelot de La Houssaye, who was born in Orléans in 1634 and died on December 8, 1706, in Paris, where he was buried in the cemetery of Saint-Gervais. Amelot occupied a gray zone in the literary political world of his time. He was not an author in the conventional sense of the term. Nor was he a member of an academy or a recipient of a royal pension. At the end of his life, he appears to have lived solely from the patronage of a wealthy benefactor, the abbé Henri de Fourcy.[42] Amelot was a print-shop corrector, editor, and professional publicist, and in this tradition of humanist printing and editing, he re-presented a large number of the most influential works of secular history and rhetoric of early modern Europe. In examining how he re-presented such works as Machiavelli's *The Prince,* it is clear not only how translators, editors, and printers manipulated established works to serve their own agendas but also the extent to which texts must be interpreted in the context of how and when they were reproduced, as well as how the editor or author intended them to be read at the time. In the end, does it matter if Machiavelli intended his work to be republican, since we can never definitively establish what his true intentions were? Or is it more fruitful to examine what editors such as Amelot thought of the work, how they presented it, and how their readers read and then interpreted it? Amelot had his own political agenda, and to meet it, he edited the books of existing authors, bending their meaning to fit his intentions.[43] With Amelot de La Houssaye, print-shop editor and Tacitean political theorist, the history of the book intersects with the history of ideas.

In his youth, Amelot was a poor student *aumonier* (ward) of the Jesuits at the Collège de Paris, working as a copyist to earn his board.[44] In 1667, at the age of thirty-three, he received the relatively advantageous appointment of second secretary to the ambassador to Portugal, Louis de Verjus, comte de Crécy.[45] Verjus recommended Amelot to Nicolas Prunier de Saint-André, the ambassador to Venice, where Amelot was once again secretary in 1669. In a strange turn of events, Verjus, on his return to Lisbon, apparently discovered that Amelot had stolen a number of important documents and valuable objects. According to a police report, Amelot sold these secret ambassadorial minutes to "foreign powers."[46] Verjus wrote to warn Saint-André in Venice, where Amelot was removed from any sensitive duties, forbidden to work again for the king, and, as a distraction, sent to the Biblioteca Marciana to "find as many documents as he wanted for his commerce [in illicit documents]."[47]

Amelot was thus removed from the service of Louis XIV. What options were left open for a former Jesuit copyist and ambassadorial secretary with a tarnished reputation and a talent for languages? As a police report states, Amelot began a business of finding documents and publishing them for money.[48] Amelot was not yet an author. At one level, he was a proto-newsman. At another, he worked in the spirit of the monastic tradition of the scribe in the scriptorium—living in the printing shop, where he researched, corrected, and translated various documents, which were then printed by the royal printer for a profit.[49] This odd mix of trafficking in diplomatic documents and editing political works began as a professional opportunity for a poor corrector and translator but turned into something more important. By publishing documents and history pertaining to reason of state, Amelot crossed the line from impoverished gadfly to subversive critic. He was giving new life to what had been secret archival documents. It was treason to sell secret treaties and ambassadorial relations. To publish them was sedition.

With his *History of the Government of Venice* (1677), Amelot discovered both the force and danger of openly publishing texts that revealed the workings of reason of state.[50] What brought Leopold von Ranke fame in the nineteenth century brought legal worries to his predecessor. As in the case of Ranke, Amelot's commerce in Venetian diplomatic relations served as the basis of a revolutionary method of critical political history. However, as the police report states, Amelot's Venetian archival research first landed him directly in the Bastille.[51]

Amelot had been thrown in jail for a book with which he and the royal printer, Frédéric Léonard, had hoped to make significant profits.[52] Despite Amelot's six weeks in the Bastille and despite the Venetian ambassador's threat to bring Amelot's severed head back to Venice, Amelot and Léonard's gamble paid off. One document in the archives of the Bastille states that the *History of the Government of Venice* was reprinted for a second time despite its ban, and in fewer than three years, at least twenty-two editions of the book appeared across Europe in Dutch, English, Italian, and Spanish.[53] With this first success, Amelot not only became an internationally known author but also learned a lesson in writing about politics under Louis XIV: while it could be a source of revenue, it had to be done with calculated prudence. To avoid further prison terms, Amelot turned to methods of writing that reflected his role in Léonard's printing shop as much as long-standing traditions of Tacitean authorship.[54] Rather than "writing" books himself, Amelot slipped into the traditional role of a *correcteur d'imprimerie*—a sort of in-house scholarly editor.[55] Working and often living in Léonard's shop, Amelot earned his bread publishing critical editions of political works.[56]

The nonauthor of his own works, Amelot managed to keep his literary identity ambiguous. In the preface to his first translation of Tacitus, *Tibère:*

Discours politiques sur Tacite, Amelot explains the ambiguity of his authorial practice.

> As for myself, Reader, it is not easy to tell you precisely what my Work is, although I know well what it concerns. And in reality, it is difficult to give it an appropriate name. Because if you consider only the title, or the text of the Chapter headings, it is a pure translation of passages from Tacitus; if you examine the content of the Chapters themselves, it is a Political, and Historical, Commentary, on his Works; if you have observed, that Tiberius is always the principal subject of each Chapter, it is in part the History, in part the Examination of his reign, from the beginning to the end: the reason for which the book is entitled TIBERIUS. But if you have remarked, that the basis of the content concerns all Princes in general, it is no longer the reign of Tiberius, but the Art-of-reigning. Finally, if you examine the instructions, and the Maxims of State, which are spread throughout the body of the Work, you will find that it is an abridgment, and like an elixir of all the Works of Tacitus, rather than a Commentary on the six first Books of his Annals. Such that I can say about my work, as did Justus-Lipsius about his *Civil Doctrine,* that the invention and the form are such, that it is correct to say, that everything in it is by me, and and that nothing of it is.[57]

Placing himself firmly in the Tacitean tradition of Justus Lipsius, in which books of political theory were crafted like commonplace collections of classical citations, Amelot says, with a hint of irony perhaps directed at a royal censor, that his works are an "elixir" of the works of Tacitus. Thus, at the same time, all is by him and nothing is.[58] Amelot was making an important point: he could not be arrested for parroting the words of Tacitus, the semiofficial historian of the Bourbon regime.[59]

At the same time, Amelot was using translation and commentary to formulate his own libertine political philosophy. How exactly did he manage to re-present such authors as Tacitus, Machiavelli, and Baltasar Gracián to the extent that he in effect became the author of their works? Using many of the editorial devices inherited from both manuscript and print traditions, Amelot manipulated the *mise en page* (page setting) and *mise en livre* (organization of compiled texts within a book) of his text and the texts on which he commented.[60] Through prefatory texts, footnotes, concordances, and commentaries, Amelot hijacked the texts presented in his books.[61] He saw the practice of pasting together collages of texts as a kind of writing, which I will refer to as *material rhetoric.*

In *The Bibliography and Sociology of Texts,* Donald McKenzie repeats the proposition made by Fredson Bowers—in his classic book *Textual and Literary Criticism*—that the form of a text affects its meaning.[62] In a now famous study of Congreve's works of theater, McKenzie showed that the author or the editor of a work controls its format, typographical conventions, and page settings. These material aspects have an "expressive function" that influences the reception and interpretation of a work.[63] Thinkers such as Lipsius and Bayle thought about writing and rhetoric in the material terms of how different text presentations and page settings would appear to the reader. Their discursive vision was far more complex than the simple linear narratives studied by historians of political philosophy and literature. In studying humanist compilers and historians, it is thus necessary to understand how they perceived their own authorial practice as well as how their page settings affected the meaning of the texts they represented. The idea of *material rhetoric* goes one step further than only taking into account the material form of texts. Material rhetoric implies that the act of changing the meaning of a text by changing its formal presentation was a conscious method of expression for humanists and should be studied as such.

Amelot's editorial practice not only sought to comment on authors such as Tacitus; by manipulating the texts of the works he edited, he changed their meaning to fit the intellectual market of his time. This is particularly relevant in the case of Amelot's greatest best seller, *L'Homme de cour*.[64] In this work as in others, Amelot's material rhetoric not only modifies the meaning of the primary text by way of the constant intervention of his commentaries; it frames the text between various "paratexts" that both introduce and then reexplain how the text is to be read.[65] Furthermore, Amelot reorganizes the text with numerical maxims (which are not in Gracián's original) and then gives lists and indexes of these maxims. In addition, he provides a collection of courtly maxims by other authors, drawing parallels with the primary text by page references so as to help the reader interpret the "oracle of prudence" in the context of the world of the court.[66]

That Amelot was famous and infamous for prefacing, translating, and commenting on political works was an advantage at one level: under the guise of paraphrasing the sanctioned Tacitus, he could write about sensitive subjects such as tyranny and flattery.[67] However, the very methods that veiled Amelot's authorial responsibility also diminished his reputation in the pantheon of historical philosophy. Bayle would be remembered as the author of the *Dictionnaire,* but Amelot would be remembered only vaguely—as Momigliano characterized him—as "the author of the *Histoire du gouvernement de Venise* and the French translator of Tacitus and Baltasar Gracián."

My goal here is not just to resuscitate Amelot but to reconstruct the long-term scholarly tradition of which he was a part. Amelot's works serve as a lens through which to view a tradition that began in earnest in the sixteenth century and evolved in unforeseen and revolutionary ways during the Age of Enlightenment. They provide us with a unique opportunity to revise the way in which we study the history of philosophy today. They show that we need to relearn the material, textual practices inherent in the production of early modern political philosophy and literature. Seventeenth-century readers recognized the complexity of Amelot's critical project. It becomes very clear that what they saw as authorship and political philosophy differs greatly from the piously removed readings of literary scholars and the pure discourse analysis of modern historians of philosophy. Indeed, many modern traditions of literary criticism seem almost scholastic in their lack of teleological consciousness. For early modern critics, ideas were important, but so was the materiality of texts; therefore, we must focus on both. By juggling page settings and various texts, Amelot was speaking an editorial language that was familiar, yet innovative within the genre of critical editions.

Fortunately, Amelot's works were widely reviewed in the burgeoning erudite press, and it is thus possible to form an idea of how seventeenth-century readers read political philosophy. One of the most voracious readers of the second half of the seventeenth century, Pierre Bayle, reviewed almost all of Amelot's works.[68] In the June 1686 edition of the *Nouvelles de la république des lettres,* Bayle wrote the fourth of six different reviews that he published between 1684 and 1688 on Amelot de La Houssaye's works. The work in question, *La Morale de Tacite: De la flaterie* (1686), was Amelot's second translation and compilation of maxims of Tacitus, accompanied by voluminous commentary (figs. 3a and 3b). *La Morale* was printed in Paris by Martin and Boudot, whose books (the title page tells us) were sold in Amsterdam by Henri Desbordes, the publisher of the *Nouvelles.* Bayle, the exile, was never far from Amelot, the Paris publicist, who published a quarter of his works on the Protestant printing presses of Holland. Over the years, Bayle kept up with the vicissitudes of Amelot's career.[69] More than that, Bayle was intrigued by Amelot's consciously created page layout. In his glowing review of *La Morale,* Bayle pauses from his examination of the question of flattery to describe Amelot's material rhetoric.

> Here is the order the author follows. First he shows the Latin passage by Tacitus that concerns flattery. Underneath, side by side, he puts his own translation and next to it the translation of the late Mr. D'Ablancourt. Underneath this he gives his attacks against this famous translator. After that, he gives his commentary on this passage, which is itself nothing but a fabric woven from passages from Tacitus, Pliny the Younger and Paterculus, which are cited at the bottom of the page.[70]

Step-by-step, Bayle goes over Amelot's page, describing the layout of each material device. The so-called father of the Enlightenment was above all a reader of the seventeenth century, steeped in its rich mix of Renaissance literary and textual practices.[71] Bayle recommended that his readers focus on Amelot's notes and prefaces.[72]

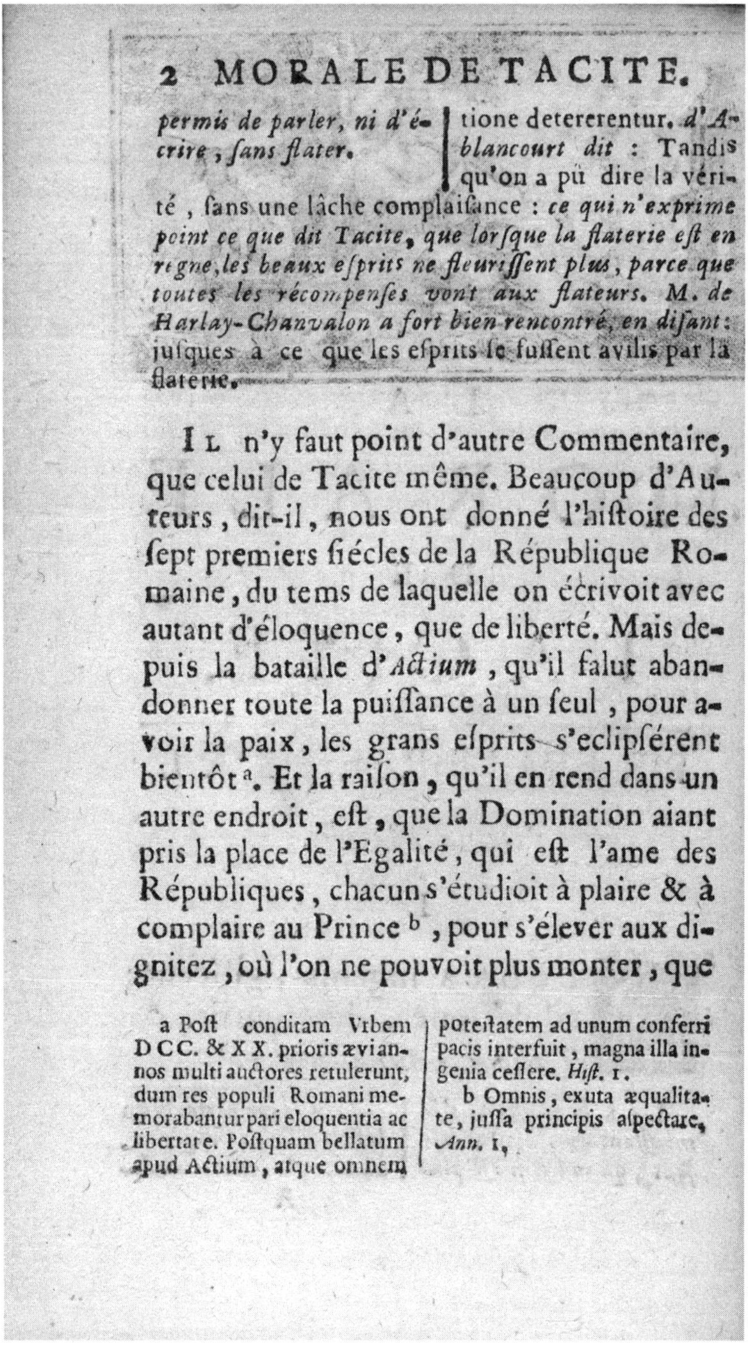

permis de parler, ni d'é-
crire, sans flater.

blancourt dit : Tandis
qu'on a pû dire la véri-
té, sans une lâche complaisance : *ce qui n'exprime*
point ce que dit Tacite, que lorsque la flaterie est en
regne, les beaux esprits ne fleurissent plus, parce que
toutes les récompenses vont aux flateurs. M. de
Harlay-Chanvalon a fort bien rencontré, en disant :
jusques à ce que les esprits se fussent avilis par la
flaterie.

Il n'y faut point d'autre Commentaire,
que celui de Tacite même. Beaucoup d'Auteurs, dit-il, nous ont donné l'histoire des
sept premiers siécles de la République Romaine, du tems de laquelle on écrivoit avec
autant d'éloquence, que de liberté. Mais depuis la bataille d'*Actium*, qu'il falut abandonner toute la puissance à un seul, pour a-
voir la paix, les grans esprits s'eclipsérent
bientôt[a]. Et la raison, qu'il en rend dans un
autre endroit, est, que la Domination aiant
pris la place de l'Egalité, qui est l'ame des
Républiques, chacun s'étudioit à plaire & à
complaire au Prince[b], pour s'élever aux dignitez, où l'on ne pouvoit plus monter, que

a Post conditam Vrbem
DCC. & XX. prioris ævian-
nos multi auctores retulerunt,
dum res populi Romani me-
morabantur pari eloquentia ac
libertate. Postquam bellatum
apud Actium, atque omnem

potestatem ad unum conferri
pacis interfuit, magna illa ingenia cessere. *Hist.* 1.

b Omnis, exuta æqualita-
te, jussa principis aspectare,
Ann. 1.

Fig. 3. Abraham-Nicolas Amelot de La Houssaye, *La Morale de Tacite: De la flaterie* (Paris:
Veuve Martin and Boudot, 1686), pp. 2–3. These opening pages of *La Morale de Tacite*

par les degrez de la fervitude ᶜ. Or eſt-il, que
la fervitude & la flaterie ſont les deux compagnes inféparables ᵈ. Et c'étoit à l'ocaſion
des flateries honteuſes du Sénat, que Tibére
s'écrioit ſi ſouvent, *O les grans efclaves* ᵉ ! Le
Jeune- Pline, que je citerai ſouvent, à cauſe
de la conformité de ſes maximes avec celles
de Tacite, à qui il faiſoit éxaminer ſes écrits,
parlant des livres de ſon Oncle, en excuſe
huit, qui nétoient pas du même ſtile, ni de
la même force que les autres, ſur ce qu'il les
avoit compoſez du tems de Néron, ſous qui
la fervitude ne permétoit pas d'écrire avec
liberté ¹. Et dans une autre létre il dit, qu'il
a vû un regne, ſous lequel le Sénat étoit devenu muet, & même hébété, à force de
garder le ſilence ².

c Quanto quis ſervitio promptior, opibus & honoribus extollerentur. *Ibidem.*

d Quippe adulationi fœdum crimen ſervitutis ineſt, *Hiſt. 1:*

e Cùm fœda & nimia cenferent, quoties Curia egrederetur, eloqui ſolitum : O homines ad ſervitutem paratos ! *Ann. 3,*

1 Dub'i ſermonis octo ſcripſit ſub Nerone noviſſimis annis, cum omne ſtudiorum genus paulò liberius & erectius periculoſum ſervitus fe-

ciſſet. *Epiſt. 5. lib. 3.*

2 Proſpeximus Curiam ; ſed Curiam trepidam & elinguem, eum dicere quod velles periculoſum eſſet. . . . Iam ſenatores, jam participes malorum, multos per annos vidimus tulimuſque, quibus ingenia noſtra in poſterum quoque hebetata, iracta, contuſa ſunt. *Epiſt. 14. lib 8. Il parle de Domitien. Et dans ſon Panégirique de Trajan il apelle céte ſervituae du Sénat,* mutam ac ſedentariam aſſentiendi neceſſitatem.

contain Amelot's commentary on servility as well as an enunciation of his own authorial strategy to comment on Tacitus with passages from "Tacitus himself" (*a, b*). (Author's private collection.)

Bayle was not the only critic who recognized Amelot's authorial practice for what it was. A great, though unrecognized, critic of the end of the seventeenth century, the lieutenant of the Châtelet (police chief) Gabriel Nicolas de La Reynie (1625–1709), wrote his reports not for the republic of letters but, instead, for the crown.[73] Much like the literary critics who were the subjects of his investigations, La Reynie looked not just at ideas but at how they were presented.

> Amelot is working as a print-shop corrector and he has translated Paolo Sarpi's History of the Council of Trent, and far from sweetening a text that is filled with sympathy for heretics, Amelot misses no occasion in his preface and his notes which are found in the margins, to mark and favor the libertine sentiments of Sarpi.[74]

La Reynie recognized that the works Amelot translated, such as *The Prince* and the *History of the Council of Trent,* were in themselves subversive. Re-edited in French with Amelot's notes, they were even more so.

> At the same time, the Sieur Amelot has also translated from Italian The Prince by Machiavelli and he has also published this work in Holland filled with notes, in which he has mixed maxims that are so dangerous that they deserve to be condemned for the good of Morals and Politics. For this he deserves much blame.[75]

However, the lieutenant of the Châtelet did not arrest Amelot. The former Jesuit novice was hiding behind the works of others, and this made it less pressing and perhaps harder to arrest an author who was well-connected with the powerful Louvois Le Tellier family. La Reynie understood his man, and more important, he understood the force of critical political history. He recommended that Amelot be put under surveillance but not harassed. Amelot and his critical eye would be far more dangerous in a foreign country, he aptly noted.[76] La Reynie's instinct would be proven correct only ten years later, when Pierre Bayle's *Dictionary* showed exactly how influential a good French critic could be if able to work in the freer air of the more tolerant Dutch Republic.

It seems a perfect contrast, then, that Pierre Bayle found Amelot's critical version of Sarpi's *History of the Council of Trent* laudable for the same reason that La Reynie condemned it. In his review of Amelot's translation, he speaks not so much of Sarpi's work but, rather, of how Amelot reframed it. It is Amelot's commentary that he recommends to the reader.

> The publication of the first edition of the History of the Council of Trent well-informed the Public as to the importance of this work, the usefulness of its notes, and the beauty of its Preface, in which one sees reigning overall the force of [Amelot's] esprit. . . .[77]

Although working on opposite sides of the critical fence, Bayle and La Reynie offer valuable insights in how to study political philosophy during the age of humanist criticism. Long before Koselleck, they knew that the key to political criticism was textual criticism. They also knew that the publication and circulation of secular history was a potential dagger of Brutus. But they did not know how effectively it would cut to the heart of the monarchical state only half a century later.

In 1690, Amelot published his third and final translation of Tacitus, *Tacite: Les six premiers livres des Annales.* This heavily annotated translation is the only seventeenth-century French edition of Tacitus that contains an illustration of the Roman historian on its frontispiece. Yet Tacitus is only part of the authorial bill. Sitting at a table in a library, dressed in Renaissance clothing, Tacitus is shown writing a book. Around him are crowns and symbols of the Roman Empire. This scene is presented on a stage, on the front of which is written, "Tacite, par le Sieur Amelot de la Houssaie." Amelot is billed like a theater director and Tacitus as his star. Tacitus provides the raw talent, but Amelot must interpret it and present it. In this context, the printing shop is backstage. It has been said that a "book is like the tip of an iceberg," that it is "the visible one-fifth or so that is left of the writing and re-writing, editing and re-editing, research and revision that lie beneath it and have produced it."[78] In the case of Amelot de La Houssaye, we may go so far as to say that his political thought is also like the tip of an iceberg of humanist rhetorical and editorial practices. These editorial practices and their relationship to political philosophy are crucial to understanding the origins of secular culture in France.

Above all, tracing the humanist, monarchist origins of eighteenth-century political criticism allows us to situate the Enlightenment in its own era. At one level, a project that situates the origins of the Enlightenment in the tyrannical politics of absolutism might appear pessimistic. Yet this study neither seeks to cast a negative light on secular political theory nor insists on the existence of a negative "dialectic of Enlightenment."[79] In showing the complex origins of secular political theory, it reveals the complexity of the secular tradition in western Europe. There were certainly *grandes idées* of the Enlightenment, and implicit to their formulation and expression was the evolution of an older culture of criticism. Enlightenment philosophies did not simply evolve from the messianic hope of Christianity into a new secular mythology. Nor was it the clear outcome of a high-minded tradition of republican or merchant virtue; nor did it spring primarily from a spontaneous movement of popular sedition or from a simple trend of de-Christianization. Rather, in its original essence, the critical spirit of the eighteenth century grew from a practice—or as the French would say, a *geste*—embedded in the learned culture of Renaissance humanism, both republican and, later, monarchist. It came from a tradition whose origins were elite but whose uses spanned class and ideology.

The ideas of the Enlightenment would find a home in this culture based on what Peter Burke so aptly called the "Renaissance sense of the past"—the great humanist movement that, for the first time since antiquity, sought to understand the past not as an immobile constant but, rather, in terms of change, difference, and human possibility.[80] It would permit some Europeans to believe that they at least had a chance to wrest the *gubernaculum*, or tiller of human affairs, from the hand of God. [81]

In the end, this book seeks to show that Enlightenment thinkers were products of their own time. Voltaire and Montesquieu were educated during the seventeenth century, and Robespierre himself, as the quotation at the beginning of this introduction so dramatically illustrates, was a lawyer and Latinist trained in the great French humanistic legal tradition. These thinkers attempted to mold abstract ideas such as empathy, humanity, justice, liberty, reason, and revolution out of the ideas and intellectual traditions most available to them. In this light, Robespierre's desperate tyranny seems less criminal than it does hopelessly Oedipal. Much like the Soviet aparachiks who transformed into capitalists but retained their totalitarian tendencies, the apostles of revolutionary terror could not shake off the weight of their humanist origins. They, too, would remain true to the grand, yet potentially treacherous, heritage of critical history.

Historians must recognize that the thinkers who produced one of the grandest moments in human history were nurtured and educated by the ancien régime; it was in a way their muse. But this does not diminish their contribution. Indeed, it renders it more complex and surely richer. Michel Foucault warned against what he called the "blackmail of the Enlightenment"—that if one was not wholeheartedly for the historical concept of Enlightenment reason, one risked casting a vote by default for the authoritarian alternative.[82] In response, Foucault proposed a model of perpetual Kantian critique of the Enlightenment, which he characterized as a "complex historical process" in a "state of tension."[83] To avoid a teleological turn as we analyze and critique the Enlightenment, we can ground our own analysis in an earlier tradition. Before Foucault, Habermas, and even Immanuel Kant, Amelot de La Houssaye and Pierre Bayle developed critical historical methods that are still the foundation of historical epistemology today.[84] Had Bayle lived a century later, his *Dictionary* surely would have had an ironic chapter on the Enlightenment, because for Bayle, the practices of doubt and protest were stronger than ideology.[85] Bayle's complex page setting is surely testimony to the fact that books could be subversive, but, of course, only readers had the power to make revolutions.

True to the spirit of Pierre Bayle, the first clues in the hunt for the origins of secular political culture are found in the world of erudition. The origins of the political criticism so treasured by modern democracy began not humbly by the sweat of an honest dissident but, rather, in the halls of the Florentine chancellery and, later, in the grand antechambers of the French monarchy. Its seeds were the classical works of Greek and Roman nobility, and its harvesters were the humanist scholars, masters of reading, who were the proud and often eccentric gatekeepers to the political wisdom of the ancient world.

2. HOW TO TEACH KINGS TO READ HISTORY
Humanist Culture and the Disenchantment of Absolutist Power

Machiavelli is not often considered a pioneer in the history of Renaissance reading practices, yet he was one of the greatest promoters of reading in early modern Europe.[1] More than just perfecting his own methods of communing with the classics, he started a movement that allied humanist reading with politics, which was the very basis of political science. At one level, he read the classics to escape from his problems and enter into a sphere of high ideas. At another, he read to find practical lessons for politics. Kings needed to learn to read history, he insisted, to apply past wisdom to current politics. For this reason, Ernst Cassirer considered Machiavelli's works a declaration of political modernity.[2] In his *Discourses,* Machiavelli changed the rules of Renaissance politics by bringing humanist techniques of reading into the sphere of practical politics.

> [O]ne finds neither prince nor republic who repairs to antiquity for examples. This is due in my opinion . . . to the lack of a proper appreciation of history, owing to people failing to recognize the significance of what they read. . . . Since I want to get men out of this wrong way of thinking, I have thought fit to write a commentary on all those books of Titus Livy which have not by the malignity of time had their continuity broken. It will comprise what I have arrived at by comparing ancient and modern events, and think necessary for the better understanding of them, so that those who read what I have to say may the more easily draw those practical lessons which one should seek to obtain from the study of history.[3]

No longer in the hands of God, the rudder of state—the *gubernaculum*—was now in the hands of a historically conscious prince. Thus, Quentin Skinner remarks, "history became an ideology: the conduct of political argument came to be founded to an increasing extent on the presentation of rival theses about the alleged dictates of various 'ancient constitutions.'"[4] Slowly, political authority shifted from the "laws of nature" to "appeals to the past."[5] But more than an ideology, history brought with it a cultural practice. Building on Tacitus and Livy, Machiavelli used history to create a "permanent political science," or as Ernst Cassirer termed it, a historical "technē," an "art" of political action.[6] Butterfield also defined this inductive practice as the "insistence upon empirical data, the idea of grounding the sciences upon a firm basis of verifiable observations, the patient and assured promotion of knowledge by the collection, the collation, and the analysis . . . of facts."[7] Machiavelli's works are not only about ethics and politics; they are laboratories for his own method for reading history. The *Discourses* and *The Prince* are both compilations of historical examples from which he draws his famous political maxims.[8]

Machiavelli's political method of historical reading was influenced by the defeat of the Florentine republic in 1511.[9] After eighteen years in exile, the Medici family reentered Florence as triumphant dictators. A leading diplomat and second chancellor of the republic, Machiavelli was jailed.[10] Stunned by the republic's collapse, he now sought a method to maintain the state against the unpredictable whims of *fortuna*.[11] Florentine elites had long used historical, archival documents and examples to guide their political decisions and form their civic identity.[12] Machiavelli would now transform Florentine historical consciousness into a revolutionary political methodology.[13] Working from humanist tradition, he based his historical approach to politics on the philosophy of prudence. Prudence, or *phronesis*, defined Aristotle, was "a truth-attaining rational quality, concerned with action in relation to things that are good and bad for human beings."[14] It was based on "the fruit of the years"— on personal experience or the knowledge of history.[15] The equation was simple. Prudence could be used to stabilize politics, and the basis of prudence was the knowledge of history, which entailed a historical information science.

Machiavelli drew from the Greco-Roman historian Polybius (203? B.C.–ca. 120 B.C.), who emphasized the relationship between politics and history.[16] Polybius maintained that history was the basis of politics, because it could be used as a replacement for personal experience by the provision of *exempla*: "For there are two ways by which all men can reform themselves, the one through their own mischances, and the other through those of others."[17] Polybius was the first to link historical reading practices with political effectiveness, outlining an inductive historical method of "practical wisdom."

The peculiar function of history is to discover, in the first place, the words actually spoken, whatever they were, and next to ascertain the reason why what was done or spoken led to failure or success. For the mere statement of a fact may interest us but is of no benefit to us: but when we add the cause of it, the study of history becomes fruitful. For it is the mental transference of similar circumstances to our own times that gives us the means of forming presentiments of what is about to happen, and enables us at certain times to take precautions and at others by reproducing former conditions to face with more confidence the difficulties that menace us.[18]

Yet Machiavelli did more than just resurrect the classical tradition of prudence. He fine-tuned it for the rough-and-tumble world of sixteenth-century Europe. Aristotle referred to prudence as a political means to doing "good," and Cicero insisted that prudence needed to be based on a firm foundation of ethics and law (*sine iustitia nihil valebit prudentia*).[19] But Machiavelli discarded the inherent "good" of Aristotelian and Ciceronian prudence, replacing it with a logic of practicality.[20] In chapter 15 of *The Prince, prudenza* is purely practical.[21] A prudent ruler, Machiavelli said, cannot keep his word.[22]

This new form of political prudence was a potent mix. It resurrected the Polybian tradition of historical reading and knowledge for political wisdom, but it joined it with a stark, secular vision of politics—one heavy with the ancient cynicism of Livy and Tacitus, devoid of ethics, and based only on tangible political results. Few could openly defend Machiavellian political pragmatism, but they could embrace his political approach to reading history. With the slow spread of Machiavelli's works (*The Prince* was first printed in 1532), history's stock rose as princes, republics, and courtiers turned to historical analysis as a tool to obtain political results. Kings became critics, and historians became political philosophers.

The idea that divine-right French absolutists adopted and developed a highly sophisticated critical historical culture poses difficult questions for the history of modern politics. Were absolutist kings responsible for undermining the very authority of the cosmology of divine-right monarchy? What was the process by which monarchists fostered secular political historicism, and what were the links between divine-right monarchy and the new empirical culture of the Scientific Revolution?[23]

PRUDENCE AND THE DECLINE
OF MYSTICAL GOVERNMENT

Although it appeared decrepit and reactionary by the eighteenth century, at its beginnings in the sixteenth century, French absolutism was an innovative approach to government. From Jean Bodin to Jacques-Bénigne Bossuet, late sixteenth- and seventeenth-century thinkers designed a powerful concept of sovereignty based on the principle of royal independence—independence from papal authority, independence from parliaments in legislating laws, and independence from noble barons in fighting wars.[24] To maintain this innovative independence, the monarchy would draw on new, secular political tools. At the end of the seventeenth century, Louis XIV exposed the great internal conflict in absolutist political theory when he remarked that independent royal power came from the opposing poles of God and reason of state.

> [The] tranquility of subjects is found only in obedience, [and] . . . it is always better for the public to support rather than influence even the bad government of kings, which only God can judge, and . . . those actions that they seem to take against the common law are founded most often on reason of State, which is the first of laws, as everyone agrees, but the least understood and the most obscure to those who do not govern.[25]

Whether or not the French monarchy ever achieved true political independence is debatable, but the very concept of independent royal power based on reason of state constituted a cosmological revolution in traditional political thought.[26] According to feudal tradition, kings were "emperors in their own empires" [*rex est imperator in regno suo*], yet their sovereignty was dependent on the ancient constitutional laws of the kingdom.[27] In theory, the medieval monarchy was not absolute; rather, it was a major link in the corporative chain of society and in the hierarchy between heaven and earth.[28] French feudal tradition required that the king consult with his three estates and, at least in theory, respect the authority of the pope. Absolutism altered this balance by placing the monarch's rights over those of the corporative community and thus above law. In his study of secular politics in France, *The Disenchantment of the World: A Political History of Religion,* Marcel Gauchet claims that the rationalizing tendency in absolutist government during the religious wars in France was the key element in the shift toward secularism. When the French state turned to practical political science as its modus operandi over religion and tradition, the state's very legitimacy became earthly.[29]

The disintegration of French society during the religious wars fueled a process of political desacralization—or "disenchantment," to use Weber's and, later, Gauchet's term—as the crown turned to the ancient political idea of prudence and its modern offspring, reason of state, as a pragmatic response to religious fanaticism.[30] The classical moral virtue of prudence taught reason, or the practical wisdom with which an individual discerns the most profitable course of action. Reason of state was the reformulation of political prudence as a strategy to pursue and protect the state's interests by any means.[31] The very idea that reason or a pragmatic political science was a possible tool of power had important cultural ramifications. It implied that the outcome of politics lay outside the static realm of tradition and, most important, that if kings were to reason about politics, they would need the critical tools and terms with which to reason.

With the rise of prudence and reason of state came the development of a complex political information science.[32] The practice of prudence, or reason of state, was based on the establishment and analysis of accurate historical and political documents.[33] The crown collected past historical examples to understand the general mechanics of politics and distill universal maxims of statecraft. Its eventual goal would be to control access to important archives and the publication of historical works based on authentic documentary sources—the raw material of political legitimacy and the basis of political truth and mythmaking alike.[34] Historical analysis transformed the very essence of mystery of the state—the *corpus republicae mysticum*—from the old religious mystery of the body of Christ and the human dominion of the *saeculum* into the classical, secular concept of *arcana imperii*, or "secrets of empire." The "secret of state" was not the mystery of God but, rather, secret political information and analysis. *Arcana imperii* implied hidden human information, which by its very definition could be discovered and deciphered by humans.[35] Thus, historical political culture was both the key to absolute power and the critical basis for subverting it.

The idea that part of the great Western process of political disenchantment and criticism began during the sixteenth century forces a reassessment of the sphinx-like question, what are the cultural origins of the French Revolution?[36] In other words, what are the earlier origins of this movement of royal desacralization? Clearly, a long process of political desacralization and de-Christianization began two hundred years before the Revolution, when royal mystical authority began evaporating as politics evolved into a battle over political information and critical understanding.[37]

The implications of this struggle over political criticism and the culture of reason of state problematize Jürgen Habermas's concept of the public sphere, which has informed much of the work done on the cultural origins of the French Revolution.[38] Habermas claims that political authority shifted away from the crown with the rise of a bourgeois civil society in the eighteenth century. He maintains that the emergence of private citizen-readers led to the development of a collective public opinion that gradually sapped away the authority of the absolutist state.[39] Yet Habermas's model does not take into account the fact that before the full genesis of "public opinion," the absolutist state created a mechanics of private royal opinion.[40] The idea that politics could be based on opinion at all has its roots in the theory of reason of state and the development of a secret royal sphere of political reasoning and analytical opinion forming.[41] As unsettling as it might seem, political criticism and the terms of future public debate were monarchist creations. At issue is less when the sphere of public opinion emerged than when private individuals appropriated the royal *res publica*'s hold on political criticism.[42]

With the goal of developing a historical science of reason of state, the French crown turned to classical humanist scholars to develop historical tools of practical politics, based on observation and historical analysis. Reason of state was not only an idea about how to practice politics; it was also a scholarly methodology based on the analysis and presentation of historical information. The rise of historical criticism and secular politics at the turn of the sixteenth century was not just the triumph of a secular and legalist approach to government; it was the triumph of a humanist historical movement sponsored by the French crown.

PRUDENCE: *A Historical Information Science of Politics*

While Machiavelli pioneered the use of historical induction for practical politics, it was Jean Bodin (1529–96) who first created a systematic method of historical political analysis. Where Machiavelli suggested that princes read history, Bodin developed a complex methodology to show them how to do so. Bodin was hardly the "anti-Machiavelli" some have suggested.[43] While he condemned unethical politics, he promoted and developed Machiavelli's historical methodology of politics.[44]

Bodin lived at a time when history had become a tool of polemic. During the French religious wars, extremist Catholics and Protestants alike used history as an argumentative weapon for claiming legal rights and justifying civil disobedience and factional retribution.[45] However, among competing groups, only the French crown sought to develop a historical methodology of prudence to further its cause. No longer the unchallenged mediators between heaven and earth, French monarchs were forced to create a new political legitimacy in the context of a now unavoidably multireligious, strife-ridden kingdom.[46] To conceptualize this new practical role, the crown turned to legal scholars and historians to justify the legitimacy of absolute power.[47] Machiavellian critical reading and analysis took on a significant role not previously present in royal political culture.[48] To master the passions of the religious wars, the king studied the history and present condition of his kingdom in order to establish wisdom for effective political control.[49]

Jean Bodin was a leading figure in this burgeoning world of historical political theory and empirical methodology.[50] While he believed in divine right and the mystical aspects of religion, his masterwork of historical method, the *Methodus ad facilem historiarum* (1566), was a model of the new marriage between politics and historical technology.[51] Bodin used the Roman historian Tacitus as a historical model for critical politics, for he considered Tacitus's historical style "full of prudence."[52] He praised Tacitus as a rigorous alternative to the eloquent Cicero, due to Tacitus's experience in politics: "It is true that on account of his unpolished manner of speaking Tacitus usually is repudiated by those who prefer the lighter trifles of grammarians to the more serious accounts of those who have spent the whole of their lives in public affairs."[53] While Bodin rejected Machiavelli on ethical grounds, he admitted that like Tacitus, he made history useful for understanding the workings of politics.[54]

In the quest for a politically applicable history, Bodin looked for a method of establishing criteria of accuracy for the reading of historical documents. In the *Methodus,* he insists that only true history is useful for the demands of politics.[55] After establishing what were relatively primitive criteria of textual reliability, Bodin extracts universal political maxims from historical sources— the raw material of politics.[56] In the dedication to the *Methodus,* Bodin outlines his method for the triage and analysis of historical sources.

> At the beginning I outlined in a table a form of universal law, which I have shown you, so that from the very sources we may trace the main types and divisions of types down to the lowest, yet in such a way that all members fit together. In this exercise, truly, I have appreciated the saying of Plato— nothing is more difficult or more nearly divine than to separate accurately. Next I have established postulates, on which the entire system rests as on the firmest foundation. Then I have added definitions. Afterward I laid down as briefly as possible precepts called "rules" according to the proposed form, as if to a norm. At one side I added, in brief notes, the interpreters of Roman law, so that from the same sources whence I have drawn, each man can take his own satisfaction.[57]

For Bodin, the exposition of the truth was attached to the research, analysis, and presentation of sources. The work Bodin describes in the preceding passage—a work he would later publish as the *Juris universi distributio* (1580)—is a grand compilation of documentary evidence. Although quite short, it contains eighty-three numbered, marginal notes, themselves often containing more than one source reference. Bodin provides historical proofs—referenced on the page as material evidence—from which he formulates the laws of civil science.[58] Not only did Bodin write historical and legal theory, but in creating critical compilations such as the *Juris,* he acted as a scholarly editor.

In his *Six Books of the Republic* (Les six livres la république) (1576), Bodin applied what he discussed in the *Methodus* to French politics, thus smuggling a fine-tuned version of the Machiavellian method into mainstream absolutist political theory.[59] The *Republic* is an absolutist masterwork of historical induction, filled with historical references and political analysis.[60] While repudiating tyranny, Bodin developed Machiavelli's historical practice and promoted it for the monarchist cause.[61]

JEAN DU TILLET: *Political Prudence and the Art of Compilation*

Fourteen years after the publication of the *Methodus,* Jean Du Tillet, another history-writing lawyer, reproduced original documents and used extensive source references in the hopes of creating a royal political science.[62] While not openly a reader of Machiavelli, he did reference Tacitus. Here, finally, was the prudential, Italian tradition of reading history for politics, created for and presented directly to a French monarch, Charles IX.[63] Du Tillet's great historical compilation, the *Recueil des roys de France, leurs couronne et maison* (1580), methodically shows the reader how to use archival documents to gain political prudence. It presents a list of the genealogy, ranks, and laws of the French kings.[64] After each section, he provides the "Inventaires sur chasque Maison des Roys et grands de France," consisting of a compilation of royal sources, collected from official archives, listed after the history of the reign of each king.[65]

As its title, meaning "collection," implies, the *Recueil* is a descriptive bibliography, intertwining text and corresponding sources. The principal text consists of a very simple chronology of royal politics, notable for the fact that the chronological narrative corresponds to sources given in the *inventaire* that directly follows the text.[66] In each bibliographical reference, Du Tillet lists the title or subject of the document, the document's location, and even its carton number (*layette*).

Why did Du Tillet go to such lengths to reproduce his historical sources? Due to his position as chief archivist of the Paris Parliament, Du Tillet was commonly asked to provide documents to form royal Gallican policy.[67] His historical legal tract *Pour la majorité du roi treschrestien contre les escrits des rebelles* (1560) attempts to establish royal authority through the context of feudal laws. Du Tillet represents the ambiguous cultural crossroads— between parliamentarianism, Gallicanism, royal constitutionalism, and nascent absolutism—where royal politics met archival and historical practices. Significantly, Du Tillet was commissioned by François II to reorganize and classify an index of the royal archives.[68] In his dedication to Charles IX, Du Tillet claimed that royal history and politics were inseparable from material historical documents and their mode of referencing and textual representation.

> Having visited at great labor and expense since my taking office, a great number of registers in your Parliament, having researched the libraries and titles of a number of Churches in your Kingdom, and with the permission of the late King your Father (who God absolves), having entered into the treasure rooms of your charters, and having looked at everything by his command, and with the declaration that he would carry the expense and pay me for my help (which was necessary due to the great number of such documents), I undertook to organize in the form of histories and the order of reigns, all the disputes of this third line of Kings with its neighbors, the Domains of the Crown by Provinces, and the laws and ordinances since the Salic Law by volumes, reigns and by a separate compilation that concerned the Royal persons and houses, and the ancient form of government

of the Three Estates and the order of Justice of the aforementioned Kingdom. . . .[69]

At one level, Du Tillet was here little more than an erudite, Gallican editor publishing a document catalog. At another level, however, he was a political theorist. His historical practice had political ramifications, for in showing how secular, historical knowledge could be harnessed for royal politics, it illustrated the Machiavellian *technē* in blunt textual terms. Indeed, it is in the spirit of Polybian prudence that Du Tillet offers to Charles IX the historical documents of his realm.

> The writings of past events, even domestic ones, are (SIRE) not only very useful, but also very necessary as much to Kings and Princes, as to their subjects. Because (as Polybius said [in book 1 of his Roman history]) there is no easier path to learning about life than from the knowledge of precedence, because there are two ways for everyone to correct their faults (from which no one is exempt): one is to accept the calamity that comes from disorder caused by one's self, which must be accepted as the wrath and chastisement of God. . . . The other way that must be sought out actively and early and embraced, is the science of good and bad Governments, and the similar events truly experienced by one's predecessors, which serves everyone as experience of the good and bad of others, from which one can profit with no loss or pain.[70]

In showing how true documents taught science through concrete historical examples, exemplarity was tied to historical accuracy.[71]

By the time of Charles IX, Du Tillet had lived through the reigns of four kings. It was surely this long and loyal service to the crown that allowed him to speak so frankly to the French king. Du Tillet was selling multiple humanist historical skills to the crown. Only the unfettered truth, he told his king, could best serve the monarch. In other words, a good king needed to hire a trusty historian with knowledge of how to find historical documents and extract their political wisdom.

LIPSIAN PRUDENCE

Bodin and Du Tillet transformed Machiavellian historical politics into a historical method applicable to French royal government. However, these two authors do not represent a widespread cultural movement. It would take the work of the Dutchman Justus Lipsius (1547–1606) to market the practices of historical prudence to a pan-European audience of republicans and monarchists alike.

Justus Lipsius was the most popular humanist at the end of the sixteenth century and was particularly influential in France.[72] While Machiavelli lived in the chaos of the French and Spanish Italian invasions, Lipsius, like Bodin, lived and worked in a Europe shattered by the Protestant Reformation and the terrible wars that ensued. While Machiavelli was a civic patriot in the old northern Italian mold and Bodin a proto-nationalist, Lipsius was a cosmopolitan. His temperament suited the times. The Reformation was an international crisis, and humanism had become an international movement. Lipsius changed cities and jobs as often as he changed religions. Like Henri IV, the "politique" king who converted to Catholicism after ascending to the French throne in 1589, Lipsius was an accommodator.

Not only did Lipsius adapt to the events that surrounded him. He also accommodated the work of Machiavelli to fit the intellectual market of absolutism by using the Roman historian Tacitus as a convenient stand-in for the Florentine master of politics.[73] While Machiavelli's approach to the critical understanding of politics was similar to that of Tacitus, the Roman historian was not tainted by a reputation of immorality. Publius Cornelius Tacitus (A.D. 55–ca. 117) was a praetor, senator, and proconsul; servant of emperors; defender of the senatorial class; and leading orator of his day.[74] Despite his own proximity to imperial power, his work defended old Roman republican liberties—a stance that was tolerated under Trajan. Some humanists, such as Guillaume Budé, called him "the most wicked of writers," due to his harsh attitudes toward Christians, but most saw Tacitus as a political moralist.[75] Like Machiavelli, he was a political cynic and a pessimistic observer of human nature, who portrayed the Roman emperors not as glorious figures but, rather, as monsters, unmasking their hypocrisy and cruelty.[76] French kings desperately wanted a practical political science to confront the mayhem of the religious wars, and through Lipsius, they adopted Tacitus as their official historian.[77]

TACITISM: *A Tradition of Reading for Politics*

Lipsius was not only a philologist interested in reestablishing Tacitus's original text but also a commentator who sought to extract moral and political sententiae from Tacitus's works.[78] Having experienced firsthand the upheavals and vicissitudes of the religious wars that culminated in the St. Bartholomew's Day massacre of August 24, 1572, Lipsius promoted Tacitus as a political guide for restoring stability. In dedicating the 1581 edition of his translation of Tacitus, *C. Cornelii Taciti opera omnia quae exstant* (1581), to the states of Holland, he says that the works of Tacitus can be used as a tool to crush civil war and restore liberty and stability. He concludes that Tacitus "should be in the hands of those in whose hands are the rudder and tiller of the state."[79]

Lipsius's goal was to construct a textual apparatus for controlling the tiller of the state, by illustrating how to read Tacitus with a critical eye for politics. Lipsius used the editorial device of commentary to teach his reader how to analyze history for politics. Underneath the primary text of Tacitus, he filled the bottom margin of the page with historical examples that mirror Tacitus, as well as political commentary that leads to the formation of maxims. These maxims are listed in an index at the end of the book, effectively turning Tacitus's works into a handbook applicable to politics.

In 1589, Lipsius published his *Politicorum libri sex,* a collection of princely commonplaces. Characterized by Montaigne as a "learned and laborious tissue," Lipsius's collection of historical and political sentences contained more than a thousand citations; not surprisingly, 547 were from Tacitus.[80] Forming a cento of sententious examples wholly from citations of classical authors such as Tacitus, Lipsius declared of his own work "that all is mine and that nothing is."[81]

> For the invention and the order are entirely ours, while at the same time, we have collected the words of ancient authors, principally historians, that is to say, as I believe, the sources of political prudence.[82]

Publishing this collection was an act characteristic of Renaissance humanism. Like Du Tillet, Lipsius harnessed history to extract political wisdom for the prince. In was in the spirit of Lipsius's commentaries that Tacitists would write their work for the next two hundred years.[83] The Lipsian practice of commentary was similar to biblical exegesis, only the authority had changed. Tacitus, not God, had become the supreme oracle of human affairs.

More than any other figure, Lipsius epitomized the Tacitist movement. Tacitists did not write theoretical narratives, like other political philosophers. The Tacitist movement represents the convergence of a humanist learned culture of reading with politics. "Tacitists" translated, commented on, and emulated the style of the Roman historian. Like modern computer users, they cut and pasted.[84] Outside of espousing practical politics, they did not always express clear political ideologies. Instead, they championed critical practices involving commentary, commonplaces, proof, and source references. They did not write in linear, Ciceronian forms. Instead, their texts were collages of extracts or concordances of historical examples.[85] Increasingly, to be a good political theorist, one needed to be a good textual editor, which implied that to be a good prince, one needed to be a good reader.[86]

As classical humanists, Tacitists were not only Latin experts; they were teachers and experts in reading methods. Early humanists earned their money teaching Latin and philology in schools and to wealthy patrons.[87] Their basic expertise was thus rhetorical, but the practices they taught had wider applications. By the sixteenth century, humanists touted a new skill:

hermeneutical methodology. Medieval Bible scholars had looked to extract wisdom from the Scriptures and patristic works, but humanists such as Desiderius Erasmus were the first to extract moral and behavioral aphorisms in order to apply them to life.[88] Humanists—later Jesuits—developed the practice of what they called "reading with fruit," or reading to extract sentences and maxims, which was to be applied beyond the realm of the Bible.[89] A good student would learn to use humanist reading methods when reading Greek and Roman works, to extract the "marrow," or the essential material, out of a text.

The methodology of reading for both learning and application to practical life was outlined in such manuals as Francesco Sacchini's *De ratione libros cum profectu legendi libellus, deque vitanda moribus noxia lectione, oratio Francisci Sacchini* (1615). Sacchini not only detailed which books were best to read but also outlined practices for extracting knowledge from books. In chapter 11, Sacchini explains that "it is important to write down extracts from reading" so that one can organize personal compilations of useful material.[90] The product of "reading with fruit," as one translator later called Sacchini's method, was the commonplace book.[91] Florilegia, the textual basis of the great culture of collecting in the Renaissance, were the writings of fruit.[92] These collections of examples were designed for students or compiled by students themselves, to help them memorize the wisdom of the ancients as an aid in argument. A florilegium was comprised of a long series of citations organized under topic headings (*loci,* or "places"). Humanist pedagogues routinely published books of florilegia that consisted of collections of thematically organized essential quotations from classical and holy works.[93] The educational methods of the trivium emphasized the use of commonplaces and instilled a common culture of quotes and historical maxims in the young social elite of Renaissance Europe.[94] At the top of the humanist market, where classical learning met royal power, humanists such as Erasmus designed pedagogical manuals specifically for princes.[95]

Much like the church fathers, who, at least until the Reformation, guarded the "true" interpretation of the Scriptures, Tacitists worked as textual guides.[96] The job of the interpreter was also one of pedagogue. Like the Renaissance teacher, who provided the text to the student (whose responsibility it was to extract and memorize commonplaces), the Tacitist extracted exempla or maxims, presenting them to the reader with commentary or, usually, more maxims.[97]

Tacitists championed the commonplace practices of humanism but did so with the single focus of political wisdom. Lipsius's critical edition of Tacitus was the flagship of a widespread Tacitist movement that exploded after 1581. Published the same year as Lipsius's critical edition of Tacitus, Carlus Paschalius's 1581 commentary on the first four books of Tacitus's *Annals* is the other great founding work of Tacitean critical reading.[98] Like Lipsius,

Paschalius was a scholar living in the whirlwind of the religious wars. An Italian resident of Paris and sometime Protestant, he was a political counselor and diplomat in the entourage of Marguerite de Valois.[99] His Tacitean notebook is an inductive guide that shows the reader how to squeeze political wisdom out of Tacitus's main text.[100] It is a textual version of an orange press: at the top of the page is Tacitus's text in large print; underneath, with the heading "Observationes," are maxims and political interpretations that have been squeezed from specific passages referenced in the text with letters (fig. 4). In the margins, in small print, are brief bibliographical references of related ideas or parallel historical sources. Luxurious red borders frame the three distinct texts, leaving ample marginal space for annotations, much like a commonplace notebook.[101]

In the margins of one copy of Paschalius' commentary (found in the Cambridge University Library), an anonymous reader did exactly what Paschalius recommended.[102] The reader's annotations illustrate how he or she learned to analyze Tacitus by using Paschalius's method. On the flyleaf and on the blank back of the title page, the anonymous reader, whose notes date from August 1650, created his or her own list of maxims from each book of the *Annals, Histories,* and *Agricola.* For the works of Tacitus on which Paschalius did not comment, the reader continued what Paschalius began; by writing political maxims in the lower margins, the reader created a personal manuscript version of Paschalius's printed guide. With the right tools—historical text, pen, and paper—any well-trained reader could practice political prudence.

THE LIPSIAN TRADITION AND FRENCH ROYAL TACITISM

While he inspired Tacitists across Europe, Lipsius's Tacitist methodology of prudence was particularly successful in France, where his books circulated in great number and where influential political theorists made ample references to his work. Michel Senellart has identified at least forty Latin reeditions of the *Politica* after 1578, primarily published in France, Holland, and Germany.[103] Charles Le Ber first translated the *Politica* into French in 1590, followed by Simon Goulart in 1594.[104] The catalog of the French Bibliothèque Nationale lists at least sixteen editions of French translations and adaptations of the *Politica* between 1597 and 1609. Perhaps more revealing of Lipsius's wider cultural influence is the presence of at least thirty editions of his critical commentary of the works of Tacitus (*C. Cornelii Taciti opera omnia quae exstant*) in the French national collection, as well as at least ten copies of his collected works published between 1585 and 1675.

A number of French political theorists of the beginning of the seventeenth century drew on Lipsius's method of reading history for prudence and

nienfes tot cladibus extinctos,fed ᵃ conluuiem illam nationum comita-
te nimia coluiſſet. hos enim eſſe Mithridatis aduerſus Sullam, Antonii
aduerſus diuum Auguſtum ſocios,etiam vetera obiectabat, quæ in Ma-
cedones improſperè, ᵇ violenter in ſuos feciſſent, offenſus vrbi propria
quoque ira,quia Theophilum quendam Areo iudicio falſi damnatum
precibus ſuis non concederent. Exin nauigatione celeri per Cycladas,
& compendia maris adſequitur Germanicum apud inſulam Rhodum,
haud neſcium quibus inſectationibus petitus foret:ſed tanta manſuetu-
dine agebat,vt,cùm orta tempeſtas raperet in abrupta, ᵇ poſſetque inte-
ritus inimici ad caſum referri, ᶜ miſerit triremeis, quarum ſubſidio di-
ſcrimini eximeretur. ᵈ Neque tamen mitigatus Piſo, & vix diei moram
perpeſſus,linquit Germanicum,præuenitque: & poſtquam Syriam, ac
legiones attigit,ᵉlargitione,ambitu infimos manipularium iuuado, cùm
veteres centuriones,ſeueros tribunos demoueret, locaque eorum clien-
tibus ſuis,vel deterrimo cuique attribueret,deſidiam in caſtris,licentiam
in vrbibus,vagum, ac laſciuientem per agros militem ſineret, eò vſque
corruptionis prouectus eſt,vt ſermone vulgi, ᶠ parens legionum habe-
retur.Nec Plancina ſe intra decora fœminis tenebat,ſed ᵍ exercitio equi-
tum, decurſibus cohortium intereſſe:in Agrippinam, in Germanicum

OBSERVATIONES.

a *Cù imitatione virtutis verius, quàm nomine & imaginibus fiat fides generis nobiliſsimi, perſæpe
iniuria gloriantur homines ſe iis eſſe prognatos,quos vniuerſus orbis terrarum , ob ſingularem vir-
tutem,admiratur,ſi in ipſis nulla antiquæ virtutis veſtigia apparent. itaque etſi populus Athenien-
ſis,aut alius quiſpiam fama celebris, re ipſa illorum, quos aſſerit eſſe maiores ſuos, perquam diſſi-
milem ſe præſtat,ac degeneres animos arguit ignauia,huic verò illud obiectari verè poteſt , illorum
quidem,à quibus ſe eſſe ortû inſolenter & falſò gloriatur,progeniem longâ ſæculorum ſerie,multiſ-
que caſibus eſſe extinctam;ipſum verò aliunde illò conueniſſe,eſſeque non ſtirpem illam præclariſsi-
morum hominum,ſed colluuiem omnium nationum.*

b *Impune tunc inimicum vlciſci poſſumus , cùm quicquid illi aduerſi accidit , id ad caſum
referri poteſt.*

c *Is verè & generoſus,& manſuetus dici debet , qui cùm ita poſsit de inimico pœnas ſumere , vt id
caſu , non ipſius conſilio factum eſſe dici poſsit , tamen de eius ſalute adeò laborat , vt eum ſua
opera ac diligentia periculo eximat. Quantam laudem meretur hic, tanto certè odio dignus eſt is,qui
cui ſalutari opera adeſſe poteſt,hunc perire patitur. mihi quidem paria videntur eſſe , aliquem ne-
care , & quem potes non ſeruare.*

d *Malus animus , & iniquus nullo beneficio mitigari poteſt.*

e *Quemadmodum ſtrenuus imperator cauet ſedulo,ne otio miles corrumpatur,eumque crebris expe
ditionibus,patientia periculorum , laboribus, & experientia durat,ita ignauus exercitum corrum-
pit largitione,atque ambitu, infimos manipularium , hoc eſt, obſcuriſsimum quemque militem iu-
uando ; veteres centuriones,& ſeueros,antiquam,duramque militiam reuocantes demouendo , &
& eorum loca deterrimo cuique attribuendo ; ſinendo deſidiam in caſtris,licentiam in vrbibus , ac
militem vagum & per agros laſciuientem.*

f *Vulgus plerunque deterrima quæque laudat.*

g *Haud ſatis decet fœminam intereſſe exercitiis militaribus, atque adeò ijs omnibus, quæ virorum
propria ſunt.*

O ij

Marginal notes:
1. Nam 5 oratế tantum philo-
ſophum capitis damnaruni.vi-
de huius apolo
giam apud Pla-
tonem.ac The-
miſtoclem virû
de patria opti-
mè meritum
expulerunt.vi-
de Thucy.lidế
libr.1.de bello
Pelopõeſf. &
Plutarchum in
Themiſtocle.
& ſocio. graui
tate tributorû
preſſerunt.vide
eandem Thu-
cyd. lib.1.hiſt.

refashioned it in the context of early French absolutist political philosophy. Pierre Charron cited Lipsius's definition of prudence in his famous work *De la sagesse* (1601), a complex weave of long passages from Montaigne, Bodin, and Lipsius.[105] A great libertine neo-Stoic rationalist, Charron was a humanist priest, famous for his sermons and for preaching personally to Marguerite de Valois and Henri IV.[106] In *De la sagesse*, Charron cites Lipsius citing Machiavelli to justify royal practical politics.[107] He admits that he has based his long chapter devoted to the idea of prudence on Lipsius's *Politica*, from which he, as a good Lipsian, has extracted the "marrow."[108] Like Lipsius, Charron is concerned with reading and observation as tools for politics. He claims that political power is based on observational knowledge: "Prudence is the knowledge and the choice of things, which one must desire or avoid; it is the just estimation and triage of things; it is the eye that sees everything, that drives and orders everything."[109] He insists that while personal experience is a preferable source of prudence, the "Science of History," which comes from "reading," is a more common source of practical wisdom.[110]

Significantly, this concern leads Charron to clearly enunciate the new, desacralized role of the monarch. His definition of sovereignty is based purely on the laws of knowledge and power: political power is based not on a natural hierarchy but, rather, on the knowledge of history and of the "nature" of one's subjects.[111] Rather than God and tradition, Charron argues, it is the sovereign analytical "eye" that reads society with the goal of ordering it. Thus, he concludes, monarchical power and authority became reliant on earthly effectiveness as the king read history and carefully observed his kingdom.

Six years after *De la sagesse*, a Parisian magistrate, Adam Theveneau, not only quoted Lipsius's passages on prudence but tried to tailor them into a method of princely education. His advice book *Les Morales* (1607) was dedicated to the future Louis XIII and his younger brother, Gaston d'Orléans. Significantly, he, too, saw the king in the role of a reader. Although the civil wars were over, *Les Morales* illustrates that, more than ever, the crown was interested in Lipsius's concept of prudence.

In his *Advis et notions* (1608), another educational manual dedicated to the young Louis, Theveneau reiterates the idea of ethical relativity and promotes the empirical practices of prudent monarchy. Copying a passage directly from the *Politica*, he states that it is ethical for the prince to lie for the cause of "public utility."[112] He calls prudence the "eye" of all royal virtues, which guides action toward justice and shows the path for other virtues to follow.[113] For Theveneau, the eye of prudence has a holy, supernatural quality. He compares it to the "Angel of the Lord," who discovers everything, lifts the veils created by men, and, finally, exposes all truths, seeing through "ruses," "finesses," and "subtitlités."[114] This clairvoyant, royal form of supernatural reading must, above all, be used for justice in ruling the state—and with the "fear of God."[115]

Theveneau's maxims represent a significant step for humanist prudential culture as it became a staple of French royal education. Henri IV believed that his son needed to learn how to think critically, so he recruited his own doctor, Rodolphe Le Maistre, as a royal professor of prudence. In his role as preceptor to Henry IV's children, Rodolphe Le Maistre wrote *L'Institution du Prince: Ensemble La Sagesse des Anciens* (1613), a handbook of maxims from classical authors. Repeating an absolutist mantra of the day, Le Maistre insisted that an effective ruler had to be schooled in the art of prudence.[116] Thus, Le Maistre framed political education in natural terms: "Prudence, which is the perfection of man, is not hereditary: it comes from Experience and by Instruction."[117] Le Maistre said that the young heir to the throne would need to learn the "observation of politics, and the contemplation of Counsels, Enterprises and the great Plans of Great Princes, and Great Republics."[118] He concluded that for this "serious Instruction of both the Body and Soul," the young Louis XIII would need to study "History."[119]

In the dedication to the second edition of his translation of the works of Tacitus, *Le Tibère Français, ou les six premiers livres des Annales de Cornelius Tacitus* (1616), Le Maistre evokes Tacitean prudence, arguing that "History is the Academy of Kings" and that Tacitus is the most useful historian for the "maintenance of a great Empire."[120] Le Maistre claims that Henry himself instructed Le Maistre to translate Tacitus into French, a duty that he found to be "extremely difficult and time consuming."[121] Citing Lipsius, Le Maistre claims that Tacitus will be useful for controlling the "mutinies," "seditions," "conspiracies," and "treasons" of the "People" and the "great Senate."[122] Thus, he argues, the young king will have to read Tacitus critically, in order to extract prudence.

> History, (I say) teaches the good to follow, and the bad against which to guard: it is filled with Maxims of State, that appear as Oracles, for the Instruction of Kings, and those who hold the reigns of government.[123]

Le Maistre's royal edition of Tacitus was more than just a manifestation of the idea that princes should be practical. It was the triumph of a set of learned cultural practices that Bodin had developed half a century earlier. To teach young princes prudence, tutors could not assign *The Prince,* but they could recommend the works of Tacitus, the most popular Roman historian of the age, who had inspired Bruni, Bodin, and countless humanists. Obviously, the Bourbons could never declare themselves Machiavellians. But they could openly seek a new political culture to help stabilize the power of the crown.

The pedagogical commonplace manuals of prudence represent an early, royal moment in Norbert Elias's concept of the "process of civilization," in which rules of self-control and symbolic tools of politics gradually replaced the physical violence and military prowess of medieval monarchs.[124] Kings would have to learn a set of critical practices and political manners. To master prudence and succeed as an effective prince, the king would have to learn to conceal his intentions, while reading the intentions of those around him in studied secrecy. This implied social and even scholarly expertise. Not only would he have to read the intentions of others, but he would also have read about his kingdom, the history of politics, geography, and natural history.[125] Thus, the king would have to learn reason and science to master the bodies of his realm. Rather than a soldier, the absolutist monarch emerged as a "royal eye," establishing political control by silently observing and analyzing his kingdom.

By the early seventeenth century, Tacitus had become the most popular ancient historian in France. The popularity of his works rivaled even Cicero's. At least thirty-three editions of eleven different translations of Tacitus were published in France between 1582 and 1663.[126] These Tacitean editions were particularly prestigious, expensive editions. Beginning in the 1580s, French translations of Tacitus were published in larger formats than those of other classical authors. Of the editions of Tacitus published in France before 1660 and found in the catalog of the Bibliothèque Nationale, four are in folio, fourteen in octavo, nine in quarto, two in duodecimo, and one in vicesimo-quarto. Folio and quarto editions are particularly large. The first major French translation of Tacitus's works, Etienne de La Planche's *Les oeuvres de C. Cornelius Tacitus* (1582), is in folio, measuring 35.4 × 25 cm. In comparison with the six editions of Sallust published between 1616 and 1663 (four are in quarto, one in octavo, and another in duodecimo), the Tacitean works in folio are comparatively monumental. Achilles de Harlay de Champvallon's translation of Tacitus's works, published in Paris in 1644 and 1645, is another example of a particularly luxurious folio edition. The 1644 edition found in the Bibliothèque Nationale measures 37 × 24.5 cm. It contains an exceptional, full-page portrait of Anne of Austria and is bound in Gaston d'Orléans gilded arms. The edition of 1645, also found in the Bibliothèque Nationale, has the same measurements and portrait. Editions of this size and quality would probably have been produced in limited printings, with fewer editions than the typical print run of twelve hundred.

One hundred and fifty years after Gutenberg invented printing by movable type, books remained luxury items. Paper represented the major cost in publishing.[127] The larger the format of the edition was, the more expensive the edition was. Books were often sold in sheet form, to be later bound by the purchaser. To a certain extent, the format of the paper of a book was a measure of its intended public. Thus, a large-formatted book would have been destined for a well-to-do reader. Bookshop owners and printers would have been reluctant to invest in printing a wide-bordered edition in folio without the assurance of a purchaser or a patron. In some cases, private patrons had books published, paying for the initial impression and launching their re-edition. The size and quality of the late sixteenth- and early seventeenth-century editions of Tacitus are a testimony to the prestige he enjoyed and the privileged place his books occupied at the top end of an already exclusive book market.

The demand for editions of Tacitus came directly from the crown itself, which actively institutionalized the new critical, learned culture necessary for inductive political science. In the sixteenth century, it recruited classical scholars such as Le Maistre, as well as historical critics and political theorists in the law courts. With the foundation of the Académie Française in 1634, Cardinal Richelieu assembled a royal stable of humanist scholars to help develop the tools and practices of inductive politics.[128] The Académie was filled with Tacitists who looked to the great Tacitist traditions of Italy and Holland to import practical political culture for their royal masters. Tacitean translators were almost exclusively ministers, magistrates, or important humanists close to the monarch to whom their works were dedicated. Of the ten individuals who translated Tacitus between 1582 and 1660, eight held positions at court.[129] Five were either members of or closely associated with the Académie Française.[130] Five were known as translators.[131] Four wrote poetry or oratory.[132] Two were royal historiographers, and a third was at least nominated by Colbert for the job.[133] Le Maistre was a royal doctor, Ithier Hobier was a bureaucrat, and Marie de Jars de Gournay was the only woman in the group.[134]

Tacitus became the official classical historian of France. François de Cauvigny, Marie de Jars de Gournay, Rodolphe Le Maistre, Achilles de Harlay de Champvallon, and Perrot d'Ablancourt all dedicated their translations to a reigning French monarch. Commissioned by the king for a translation, Le Maistre called Tacitus the "Oracle of Princes" and the "only Author worthy of Kings, for the knowledge to govern states well."[135] Throughout the first half of the seventeenth century, the crown actively encouraged the translation of Tacitus. In his dedication thanking Cardinal Richelieu for his appointment to the Académie Française, Perrot d'Ablancourt maintains that Tacitus is the only author "great" and "admirable" enough to be offered as a gift to a prince.[136] The same idea is expressed in Harlay de Champvallon's dedication to Anne of Austria, which goes one step further. De Champvallon claims that only the queen has the acuity to penetrate the meaning of Tacitus.

I know, MADAME, that the service that I intend to render to your Majesty, will not be advantageous to Tacitus, and that my Translation has much diminished the force of his spirit. Yet your Majesty's spirit, which is even above Royalty, will penetrate easily into the fog with which I have covered this great light, and return it to its original brilliance that I was unable to conserve.[137]

Tacitus alone among authors had the privilege to enter into the cabinet of the prince, and it was claimed that only the royal eye could penetrate the secrets of his politics. The French crown had fostered and developed the Tacitist movement. The old Renaissance sense of the past had evolved into a textual, pedagogical commodity in the realm of royal politics. Machiavelli's tools, far from being seen as republican, had become the basis of royal political culture. The crown created a new field of political knowledge, but it was only a matter of time before other eyes peered into the *arcana imperii* of the *corpus mysticum* of the state.

3. POLITICAL POWER IN THE ARCHIVES
From Reason of State to Critical History

B y harnessing reason of state and printed propaganda as modern informational tools of governance, the French crown created a public sphere without truly understanding its full ramifications. The very fact that the res publica entered into a dialogue with its opponents opened the Pandora's box of public criticism. Every pamphlet or official work of history not only evoked a response but begged to be critiqued and analyzed. The polemics of the Reformation and Counter-Reformation caused an arms race of criticism and attacks, and the crown's sophisticated use of reason of state did the same in the realm of politics. Conscious of the possibilities of the public use of reason, a number of subversive scholars began the project of publishing not only historical information but also—and perhaps more important—the tools with which to analyze and criticize politics.

THE DE THOU AFFAIR, 1605–9

At the turn of the sixteenth century, the French crown actively sponsored the textual and political culture of Tacitist historical studies, but it found very quickly that these traditions also posed a certain danger. The old humanist tradition of accurate history and the crown's relationship to political criticism came to a head in the work of the great legal scholar Jacques-Auguste de Thou (1553–1617).[1] Like other historical thinkers of the late Renaissance, de Thou was marked by the religious strife that gripped France at the end of the sixteenth century.[2] Coming from an ancient line of magistrates and presidents of the Paris Parliament, de Thou rallied to Henry IV's moderate political solution to the religious wars. A Catholic, de Thou nonetheless condemned the fanaticism responsible for the butchery of the St. Bartholomew's Day massacre. He worked as a diplomat for Henry, traveled in the royal entourage, and played a leading role in finding a legal response to the wars that culminated in the Protestant Henry's conversion to Catholicism. With de Thou's legal counsel, Henry drew up the Edict of Nantes in 1598, which

41

guaranteed a century of relative freedom of worship for French Protestants and finally brought peace to the traumatized kingdom.

History was de Thou's passion, more than law and politics. He was a bibliophile who amassed a spectacular library of 12,500 volumes—perhaps the finest in France—with the intention of writing a history of the tumultuous events he had witnessed.[3] He took inspiration from chroniclers and panegyrists such as Joachim du Bellay, Paolo Giovio, and Paul Emile, as well as from political historians such as Guicciardini and Philippe de Commines. Among the ancients, he placed Sallust and Tacitus in the "first rank" of historians. He saw impartial, accurate history as a tool for peace and a chance to shed light on the crimes committed by both Catholics and Protestants during the wars. He believed that historical truth would clear the air and help build a stronger state.[4] In the quest for impartiality, de Thou's monumental *History of His Own Time* (1605) showed not only the crimes committed by Protestants but also those committed by the Catholic Church.[5]

Although he was a friend of the French king, had good connections in Rome, and even knew Pope Paul V, historical impartiality in the age of the Counter-Reformation was politically risky. De Thou's *History* was a thorn in the side of his influential friends. At the time it came out, the pope was in a protracted battle with the Venetians—which, as we shall see, ended in the excommunication of the entire Venetian republic in 1606, one year after the publication of the *History*. Thus, the papacy was threatened by and ever more concerned about criticism from within its own ranks. Its instincts were correct, for de Thou had solicited material for his own chapter on the Council of Trent from the arch antipapist and a defender of Venice, Paolo Sarpi.[6] At the same time, de Thou learned that good kings do not always make loyal friends. He encountered harsh criticism back in France, where the crown withdrew its support of the *History*. The French king had given royal permission to publish de Thou's work but became annoyed by the scandal it caused.[7] Despite de Thou's long and faithful service, Henry assigned the powerful Duke de Villeroy to block the printing of the *History* in Rome.[8] De Thou's impartiality became a diplomatic affair.

De Thou lamented to his friend and confidant Jacques Dupuy, "It is quite difficult to tell the truth, as is required by the law of History and as is prescribed by Polybius, while also pleasing the great and powerful."[9] He feared that without the support of Henry, his *History* would meet the same fate as Machiavelli's *The Prince*. Indeed, three years later, in 1609, the Vatican placed the *History* on the *Index of Forbidden Books*. The well-intentioned president of the Paris Parliament became the author of a banned book.[10] Thus, de Thou was forced to work as his own publicity agent, sending copies of the *History* to his numerous correspondents across the international web of the republic of letters, where it was, for the most part, enthusiastically received.[11]

De Thou's work illustrates how the critical tradition had changed by the beginning of the seventeenth century, evolving outside of the sphere of secular royal interests. From inside the political apparatus of the state, de Thou had tried to write an impartial critical political history according to the Tacitist and Polybian rules of accuracy. The republic of letters welcomed the project, while the state reacted defensively. This marks a decisive moment in the critical tradition. While the crown had sponsored the critical historical tradition at the end of the sixteenth century in the hopes of creating a political weapon, it now formed reservations about the tool it helped create.

PAOLO SARPI (1552–1623)
Venetian Republicanism, Gallicanism, and the Critical Tradition

While de Thou's *History* posed the possibility that history could be a political threat, the Venetian Paolo Sarpi crossed the line and showed that methods from the Tacitist and even royal Gallican traditions could be used as political weapons. Inspired by de Thou to write his *History of the Council of Trent* (1619), Sarpi took the humanist tradition of accurate, critical history to a new level; he portrayed the Vatican as an imperial Roman court, full of intrigue and earthly politics.[12] In doing so, he showed that Tacitism and the Gallican, antipapal traditions were the foundation stone of a culture of skepticism.

Sarpi was the defender of Venice's independence from Rome. The interdict crisis of 1606 during which Pope Paul V excommunicated the Venetian republic grew out of a conflict with the church over fiscal and legal jurisdiction. The comparatively secular Venetian republic did not want the church meddling in its legal affairs and collecting much needed revenue from ecclesiastical taxes on the terra firma. Venice rebuffed papal authority, and Pope Paul V responded by excommunicating the entire republic.

A Tacitist, a skeptical scientist, possibly a crypto-Protestant, and often accused of atheism, Sarpi adhered to the ancient Gallican tradition, championed by figures—such as Jean Bodin—who sought to show the legal grounding of the French church's independence from Rome through the study of historical documents. At first glance, Sarpi's adherence to Gallicanism might seem only a circumstance born of the necessities of the interdict; but it was more profound. Gallican scholars were legal historians. They saw the French church as "free" and under the jurisdiction of the monarchy. Like the Venetian struggle, Gallicanism was but a chapter in the ancient, pan-European saga of the struggle between secular and clerical power over the investiture of bishops and the collection of benefices. Medieval thinkers such as William of Ockham and Marsilius of Padua were early defenders of secular independence. This tradition was continued by French jurists and historians who, in response to the Council of Trent in the 1540s, developed a scholarly tradition that placed the authority of the French kings over the French church on a firm, documented, historical basis.[13] Royal Gallican "legists" such as Jean Ferrault and Charles de Grasaille compiled lists of French "regalian rights" over the papal jurisdiction.[14] Donald Kelley has pointed out that the "Gallican tradition involved a rudimentary kind of historicism which, reinforced by humanism, was to become the basis for a distinctive and comprehensive interpretation of European history."[15] Ironically, Gallicanism took the medieval tradition of secular royal dominion to a new level by suggesting that its legitimacy resided in the authority of earthly precedent, not in the will of God.[16] Wielding historical documents, Gallican archivists and lawyers compiled great compendia of documents as authoritative evidence.[17] Historical documentation could be used as a weapon to assert legitimacy in the ongoing battle between the French monarchy and the papacy over the appointment of bishops.[18]

Paolo Sarpi represents a shift toward a politically subversive trend in both the Tacitist and Gallican traditions. Tacitist history could be used as a potent weapon against the church and thus against political authority in general. Tacitism was a historical tool for political criticism and strategizing, while Gallicanism was a historical tradition that sought to undermine papal authority in favor of earthly monarchy. Both traditions were intellectual weapons that relied on mechanisms of textual and political criticism. Sarpi drew from the Venetian republican traditions of independence, mixed government, and constitutional pragmatism—best embodied in Gasparo Contarini's *De magistratibus et republica Venetorum* (1543)—to create a particularly virulent strain of political criticism.[19]

The interdict crisis played out on a European stage, but nowhere were Sarpi's works more popular than in France. There, his *History of the Council of Trent* was a best seller for the whole seventeenth century, first as a sanctioned work and then, later, as a banned book.[20] As was all too often the case in its relations with Rome, the French crown took an ambiguous stance toward Sarpi's history. A book of such critical realism was, without doubt, dangerous; but it was also useful in conflicts over Gallican authority. Sarpi's book revealed the force of critical history. Even a book written in the Gallican tradition could pose a threat to French royal power.

PUBLIC PRUDENCE

Gallicanism, Tacitism, and reason of state were supposed to be pillars of royal authority. Yet at the beginning of the seventeenth century, these three traditions began their slow transformation into a public culture of political criticism. Giovanni Botero's *Della ragion di stato* was, in some ways, an Italian counterpart to Lipsius's *Politica,* published in the same year (1590).[21] A onetime Jesuit, Botero used his work to condemn pure practical, Tacitean, Machiavellian reason of state, while insisting, like Lipsius, that empirical political methods be used for the good and unity of Christendom.[22] However, Botero's public refutation of unmitigated reason of state, along with the clear exposition of its practices, had the effect of advertising pure reason of state to a wide audience. It was in the great tradition of books attacking sin— ironically selling well because they openly discuss the forbidden practices they claim to oppose. His book became an international best seller. It was published at least five times in Italian between 1589 and 1630 and was translated into German, French, Spanish, and Latin.[23]

The most eloquent description of the public explosion of reason-of-state culture at the beginning of the seventeenth century is found in Trajano Boccalini's (1556–1613) political satire *De' Ragguagli di Parnaso* (Reports from Mount Parnassus, 1613), set in a fictitious, pan-European "Court of Apollo" where princes, literati, and political theorists debate about political and moral concerns.[24] As a good Tacitist, Boccalini quoted the Roman historian in almost every report. But as an innovator, he took a step that no one before him dared. He actually made fun of Tacitus. His satire is a stinging indictment of the triumph of Tacitism in early seventeenth-century Europe.[25] When Tacitus is elected the king of the island of Lesbos, his political schemes and maneuverings get him into so much trouble that he is forced to flee the island and return to Parnassus. Tacitus, the master of politics, could fail miserably and even end up on trial.

Even worse than failing, Tacitism risked falling into the wrong hands. Boccalini joked that reason of state, once the reserve of kings, was becoming popular public knowledge.

> A diabolical Craft [sc., reason of state], and publish'd by TACITUS for the use of Princes, but now becomes so universal, that this Author, once esteem'd fit only for Royal Closets, is in every pitiful Scoundrel's hand, so that to the disgrace of an Art so highly esteem'd by great Men, Porters enter into Reason of State, and the World is full of Politick Coblers.[26]

Lipsius and those who followed him had made it clear that using reason of state was only condoned when done for the common good. It was the sole monopoly of the king. If commoners used practical prudence, it would become dangerous, immoral, and even ridiculous. Boccalini was proved prophetic when, in 1627, the Venetian Council of Ten censored his own commentaries of Tacitus for fear that they would publicize the workings of reason of state.[27] Thus, Boccalini initiated the great shift, as Tacitism openly became a threatening, critical movement.

In Italy, the birthplace of Machiavellianism and Tacitism, it had long been known that prudence was a double-edged sword. Guicciardini had remarked, "Cornelius Tacitus teaches those who live under tyrants how to live and act prudently, just as he teaches tyrants ways to secure their tyranny."[28] At the beginning of the seventeenth century, Italian and French political authors stressed the dangers of prudence falling into popular hands. Federico Bonaventura, in his *Della ragion di stato e della prudenza politica* (1601), cautions that while princes need prudence and its "consultative faculty" of strategies and dissimulation, subjects must only follow orders.[29] He argues that subjects must be prevented from employing political prudence; otherwise, the foundations of authority would be threatened. Echoing Boccalini, Ludovico Zuccolo begins his essay *Della ragione di stato* (1621) by warning, "Not only the counselors at court and the doctors of the schools, but even the barbers and the lowest of artisans in their stalls discuss and dispute reason of State and look to understand which things are done by reason of State and which are not."[30]

In *De la sagesse* (1601), Pierre Charron warns that it is dangerous and unnecessary for individuals to use prudence.[31] He maintains that this "extraordinary," immoral form of political action must be reserved for the vital interests of the state. Marcel Gauchet notes that in 1612, Antoine de Laval deplored that reason of state "was on everyone's lips."[32] The great libertine Gabriel Naudé took up Charron's theme of reason of state and public interest in his treatise *Considérations politiques sur les coups d'état* (1639). He considered prudence a state secret. Individuals (*particuliers*), he asserted, should not use prudence like kings, for their affairs are not important enough to warrant immorality.[33] At the same time, he suggested that with the growth of the state's diplomatic bureaucracy, royal agents would need to use prudence in the name of the crown.

As the political apparatus of the state expanded, so proliferated the culture of reason of state. As the century wore on, Tacitus's accessibility expanded. Following the general publishing trends of the seventeenth century, after 1660, French translations of Tacitus became more accessible as great luxury editions shrank to comparatively cheap duodecimo formats, casting off their quality illustrations, wide margins, and expensive bindings. The period between 1660 and 1694 saw the publication of five quarto, five octavo, ten duodecimo, and one sextodecimo editions of translations of Tacitus. While the quarto and octavo editions of the first half of the century could measure up to 26 × 18 cm, those published after 1660 measure only around 15.5 × 9.5 cm. Certain editions published in octavo shrank to sizes more common for duodecimo and sextodecimo editions. These editions were not only smaller but easier to handle and consult. With this physical transformation, the reader's material relationship to Tacitus changed. While large editions of Tacitus did not disappear (they remained on library shelves, as their presence today confirms), smaller French editions became readily available to a wider reading public. Tacitus's books were no longer monumental objects to be opened on the marble tables of royal libraries and military headquarters. They could now be hidden in a pocket or a bag to be read anywhere, even in secret. The threat of popular prudence was indeed material and real, but was there a solution to Guicciardini's paradox? Could the crown control the old tradition of historical criticism in the arena of seventeenth-century politics?[34]

RICHELIEU AND THE IRRESISTIBLE RISE
OF REASON OF STATE

Louis Marin once remarked that there is always a danger when one writes history at the behest of a great prince. If it is too flattering, it becomes ridiculous; if it is not flattering enough, it becomes an insult; and if it contains too many truths, it can pose a threat.[35] As absolutist culture matured in the first half of the seventeenth century, the balance between historical truth and political flattery became ever more delicate. With the ascent to power of Cardinal Richelieu came a golden age of Tacitism and pragmatic political history. Under his patronage, commentaries on Tacitus and works on reason of state proliferated. The ministry of Richelieu marks the triumph of prudential culture, for he was the first to truly realize the Polybian ideal expressed by Machiavelli. Here was a chief minister who admitted to using historical reason of state as a political tool. He collected historical exempla and even wrote his own historical maxims of state in his *Testament politique* (1624). The abbé de Choisy claimed that Richelieu kept a copy of *The Prince* on his night table, and whether or not this story is true, it illustrates the widespread perception that Machiavellian political culture had triumphed in France. While never forsaking religious concerns, Richelieu subscribed to the major tenet of Machiavellian reason of state: the state's best interest was to use utilitarian "reason" to achieve its goals.[36]

Part of Richelieu's arsenal of political tools was printed propaganda. He vigorously published pamphlets and posters in well-organized information campaigns. Of course, this led his opponents to fire off salvos of pamphlets in return. Richelieu relished the arms race. He developed a communications office to counter hostile information campaigns and to disseminate propaganda.[37] The first half of the seventeenth century was a golden age of historical and political information, as Richelieu's state-sponsored propaganda campaigns reached previously unprecedented heights of political print production.[38] As we have seen, he continued Henry IV's program of publishing official editions of the works of Tacitus. He created the Académie Française and hired poets, historiographers, and philosophers, many of whom worked on official versions of Tacitus.

At the same time, this explosion in political literature had unforeseen consequences. The more politics and reason of state were discussed in public, the more possible it became for readers to enter into the critical, political polemic.[39] Recent studies of Richelieu's use of propaganda by Hélène Merlin and Christian Jouhaud have questioned whether he fully understood the ramifications of taking governmental action into the arena of public debate. Jouhaud has noted the irony that the master of reason of state unwittingly promoted the "public use of reason."[40] Although Richelieu persecuted his critics and opponents, he did not develop a censorship machine equivalent to his use of propaganda. The very idea that state-sponsored historical works might be used against the crown seemed to take Richelieu off guard.

In his classic study, *Raison d'état et pensée politique à l'époque de Richelieu* (Reason of State and Political Thought in the Époque of Richelieu), Etienne Thuau identified almost three hundred printed works from the beginning of the seventeenth century concerning reason of state. This number does not include manuscript works or reeditions and is certainly not exhaustive. The age of Richelieu was truly a "Tacitean moment"; not only were the works of Tacitus and Machiavelli widely published, but it seemed that almost every political writer was involved in either praising or condemning prudence and reason of state. But how long could this go on? Eventually the state would have to respond to the threat of public critical culture.

JEAN CHAPELAIN AND COLBERT'S
NEW POLITICS OF HISTORY

The letters of Jean Chapelain (1595–1674) give a measure of how historical policy changed between the ministries of Richelieu and Colbert, as the crown became aware of the menace of critical historical culture. Chapelain made his living as an official state representative in the republic of letters under Richelieu and Colbert. His voluminous correspondence spans the years from 1632 to the year before his death in 1673. He corresponded with his friends in France as well as with foreign scholars whom he contacted for the French state, offering them pensions and commissioning them to write books. Chapelain's early letters show that critical history—even the works of Sarpi— were still considered respectable by a representative of the state if they were not used against the interests of the state.

In a 1632 letter to the academician Auger de Mauléon de Granier (?–1650), Chapelain defines his historical ideal in the terms of Tacitism. He criticizes Cardinal Bentivoglio's *History of the War in Flanders,* which he feels was not politically critical enough. He notes, for example, that Bentivoglio had used Tacitus as his model but that his "judgements" remained within certain proscribed "boundaries," never digging deep enough into the political motives behind Elizabeth I of England's policies toward religion. Therefore, in Chapelain's estimation, Bentivoglio does not equal Francesco Guicciardini and Paolo Sarpi, the modern masters of critical history.[41]

At the same time, Chapelain warns against using history as pure political criticism. He argues that history's primary role is to be "useful for civil life." This means that the criticism and judgments of the "judicious historian" must only be made for the "health, well-being, wealth and aggrandizement of the State." Any historian who uses historical criticism to counter the "good Religion" and the "Republic of the Prince," is a "base" troublemaker.[42] Thus, Chapelain poses a challenge that de Thou would have found impossible. Historical truthfulness would have to be wedded to complete loyalty to the state.

While showing an interest in the critical historical tradition, Chapelain walked a fine line between freethinking scholarship and serving the French state.[43] He was an admirer of Tacitus (whose history he considered to be the finest of all the ancients) and of Galileo. He did not see any conflict between his dedication to truth and to the crown. Yet all this changed in 1661, when Louis XIV and his new minister, Colbert, ascended to power. During the chaos of the Fronde, Chapelain was effectively unemployed. With the arrival of a new regime, he hoped to find a place in royal service. He wrote to Colbert, complaining that his old pension had been discontinued. He also reminded the new minister that he could be of service to the state in his old capacity of royal representative in the republic of letters.[44]

A year later, in November 1662, Chapelain wrote Colbert in response to the minister's proposition to help the crown recruit and direct royal historians. He clearly understood that Colbert had a new project: to muzzle the old political tradition, while sponsoring a new movement of royal panegyric. He offered his services.

> [H]istory should serve only to conserve the splendor of the King's enterprises and to detail his miracles. At the same time, history is like a fruit that is not good out of season. For if it does not analyze the motives of the things it explains, and if it is not accompanied by prudent commentaries, then it is nothing but a pure, undignified relation. . . . However, this sort of history should not be used during the reign of the Prince who is the subject of the history, for if one were to write this history, it would render public the secrets of the Prince's Cabinet; it would warn his enemies, nullify his policy, and betray those who work with him in secret and in the shadow of a profound silence. Therefore, I think that we should produce a history in such a manner that the work is kept hidden until no inconvenient remarks can be used against his Majesty and his allies.[45]

Here was a clear response to the same sort of problem posed by the de Thou affair. Critical history would simply be kept a state secret. True, Chapelain concedes, "real history" is political and analytical. Yet, he maintains, few scholars are capable of both historical accuracy and professional discretion. He worries that it will be impossible to find a trustworthy scholar for writing contemporary political history.[46] He suggests an old approach. Rather than a political historian, why not look for an orator, a highly skilled writer who will "treat the [king's] miracles with great oratory, and panegyrics equaling those of Pliny the Younger for Trajan?"[47] This sort of scholar, he assures Colbert, will be easier to find. Chapelain may have admired Jacques-Auguste de Thou and his struggle to write critical history, but he certainly did not share de Thou's unbending dedication to historical truth.

THE RESPONSE TO TACITISM
Cicero and the Triumphal Return of Panegyric History

The first great propagandist of the modern era, Louis XIV, knew that to build absolute power, he also needed to control historical truth.[48] The critical culture that Richelieu had fostered in hopes of strengthening the state was now seen as subversive in a system where all culture was supposed to serve the glory of the king.[49] Within the state apparatus of culture, Louis sought to cultivate a literary form of history subservient to his political interests. He gave extravagant pensions to the great literary geniuses of his age to write glorious histories of his reign. He assigned Colbert to bring all aspects of cultural production—domestic and foreign—under the umbrella of the interest of the state.

In Colbert, Louis had found his man. The minister's letters reveal his sophisticated approach to carrying out this cultural policy. Building on the work of Richelieu and Mazarin, Colbert personally recruited historians, artists, poets, musicians, and architects to work for the state. The average amount of money spent on pensions for scholars between 1664 and 1674 was eighty-seven thousand pounds a year.[50] While this sum was relatively modest in comparison with other state expenditures (the crown spent a staggering eighty-one million pounds building Versailles between 1664 and 1690), it was still enough to keep hundreds of scholars on the state's payroll. The policy worked. Figures such as the playwright Jean Racine were not in the least ashamed of comparing Louis to Alexander in exchange for gold.[51]

To write his royal histories, Racine did not go into the archives. Instead, he turned to the literary tradition of historiography based on the works of Aristotle, Livy, Lucian, Quintilian, and, most of all, Cicero. He was part of an old humanist school that cast history more "as a problem of literary form and of oratorical grace rather than as one of scientific truth or political inquiry."[52] While Ciceronianism and Tacitism had coexisted since the Italian Renaissance, Cicero's popularity in late seventeenth-century France was in great part a reaction against Tacitism. It was part of Colbert's plan to promote purely eloquent historical propaganda, while outlawing critical political history.

The Ciceronian historiographical tradition served Colbert's purposes.[53] But there was a distinct difference between late seventeenth-century Ciceronians and their predecessors. Beginning in the 1670s, a number of Ciceronian scholars not only praised a literary form of history; for the first time, they also attacked political history and even Tacitism. The Jesuits, who had once spearheaded the royal Tacitist movement, now, in many cases, repudiated Tacitus for Cicero. In his *Instructions sur l'histoire* (1670), the Jesuit father René Rapin (1621–87) supported the cause of royal historiography when he suggested that history was a branch of literature and should be based on the classical rules of oratory.[54] Three hundred years before Hayden White claimed that history was by its very nature fiction, Rapin stated that history could never be scientific. History did have to be "true," but the "truth is not the truth," says Rapin, "unless it is beautiful."[55] He warned against the "excesses" of political history written by Tacitus and his modern heirs, Machiavelli, Paolo Giovio, Davila, and other "Italian and Spanish" authors.[56] He criticizes the use of reflections, maxims, and other rhetorical tools of political commentary and analysis.

For Rapin, the antithesis of good historical language is embodied by the writings of Tacitus, who commits what Rapin considers to be the worst of crimes: his writing is "unnatural" because it is not easily "intelligible."[57] Tacitus assigns the logic of reason of state to the motives behind all the actions he describes. Rapin complains that to "rummage" in the secret intentions of individuals leads only to "conjecture" and to guilty action.[58] He attacks political history, calling it "complicated, poor in words and serious."[59] He condemns technical description of any kind: even Julius Caesar's descriptions of weapons were too serious and lacking in narrative qualities.[60] Anything that is not eloquent was political, immoral, and even dangerous.

Although the Jesuit abbé Pierre Le Moyne (1602–71) was not a fervent anti-Tacitist like Rapin, he, too, warned against the vices of analytical, political history. In his *De l'histoire* (1670), Le Moyne reveals his Ciceronian leanings when he insists that truth be "dressed in the clothing of ornament."[61] Like Rapin, he believed that truth was subject to a number of conditions. Truth, he maintains, has to be "limited by conscience, honor, fear of scandal and public virtue."[62] Furthermore, truth must be presented according to the rules of religion and birth; it is subject to "decorum, morality and good taste."[63] "Eloquence," he says, "is the very fabric [*étoffe*] of history." The greatest threat to eloquent history comes in the form of historical exempla used to create sententiae. He warns against maxims cluttering narrative. Ciceronian history sought not to coexist with Tacitism but rather to banish it from history, into the exile of the sinful world of politics.[64]

Forty years after Le Moyne, another Jesuit, Gabriel Daniel (1649–1728), a royal historiographer and the author of a *Histoire de France* (1713), attempted to mix erudite methods with a sober interpretation of Ciceronian eloquence. While he was a restrained Ciceronian, he, too, warned against the danger of the old pedagogical, Tacitean form of history. He maintained that the greatest menace to eloquence was maxims, sentences, and commonplaces, which he believed to harm the necessary "natural simplicity" of historical narration.[65] He argued that one should never write history by separating sentences from the body of the text itself.[66] Worse than sentences is political commentary. Nothing, maintains Daniel, is more affected than a historian giving his political opinion as if he were a "Conseiller d'État."[67] He considered a number of historians guilty of using the political, Tacitean style, among them the famed Florentine Guicciardini; the Paduan Arrigo Caterino Davila (1576–1631), author of *The Civil Wars in France* (1630); and the Frenchman Antoine Varillas (1626–96), author of a contentious *History of Heresy* (1682), as well as a number of political histories.[68]

Daniel, Rapin, and Le Moyne represent a new trend to rehabilitate old Ciceronianism in response to the growth of politically critical history. Colbert had clearly succeeded in inspiring a new trend in historical rhetoric. Now he set out to revive the Gallican archival tradition within the bosom of the state, under a shroud of secrecy.

AN AGENT IN THE STACKS *Denis II Godefroy (1615–81)*

One can only marvel at the subtlety of Colbert's awareness of the culture of politics. Although he banned public critical history, he still valued it as a political weapon.[69] Thus, he sought to set right the situation that had been out of control since the days of de Thou and Sarpi, by bringing the old archival tradition into the fold of the French state. While it is not clear whether Colbert ever read the work of Jean Du Tillet, he attempted to revive the royal Gallican tradition of collecting archival documents for uses, just as Du Tillet had recommended at the end of the sixteenth century. He sought the help of Dom Mabillon and his document-hunting Benedictine monks, and he hired a good archivist to find and collect politically relevant documents from the Chambre des Comptes in Lille. His objective in Lille was to turn these documents into secret weapons in legal, territorial quarrels by using them as surprise legal documentation or as propaganda. To put his plan into action, he called on Denis II Godefroy, a historian from an ancient archivist family whose members had worked in the royal archives since the sixteenth century.

The Godefroy family was the incarnation of Du Tillet's royal archivist tradition. Denis II's father, Théodore Godefroy (1580–1649), was a member of the famed Calvinist Godefroy family from Geneva and had been baptized by the Protestant leader Théodore de Beza. Théodore Godefroy converted to Catholicism on his arrival in Paris at the beginning of the seventeenth century. He thus easily entered into the humanist elite then close to the throne. Théodore was an associate and friend of the Dupuy brothers, who received the first official charge to organize the royal archives with the goal of establishing the rights of the crown, both territorially and in relation to the Catholic Church. He participated in the distinguished humanist *académie* that met at Jacques Dupuy's house on the rue de La Harpe between 1617 and 1646.[70] He worked with members of the great parliamentary family Harlay de Champvallon, as well as with Jacques-Auguste de Thou. He received lucrative offices, all related to his archival skills.[71] Louis XIII named Godefroy royal historiographer in 1613, Director of the Inventory of the Royal Archives in 1615, and sent him to catalog the archives of the contentious duchy of Lorraine in 1634.[72] Between 1637 and his death in 1649, he worked as the ambassadorial counselor and secretary in Cologne and then at the Congress of Münster (beginning in 1643), where he apparently died in 1649 from "hard to digest German meats."[73]

Louis XIII himself was said to have chosen Godefroy due to his archival expertise.

> For the care and great studied knowledge of the diverse, important negotiations that have been made in Europe for a long time and for having collected a number of treaties formerly made to be employed by [His Majesty's] extraordinary ambassadors who found themselves where peace was being negotiated between His Majesty and his allies, and on the other side, the emperor and King of Hungary, the King of Spain and their allies . . .[74]

Godefroy's skills lay not only in finding and organizing political documents but also in interpreting them and understanding their logic. What the king sought was a scholar who had the critical-reading skills to recognize historical documents that had political value.

The Godefroy family's extraordinary archival skills also caught Colbert's attention. He commissioned Théodore's son, Denis II, who had been a royal historiographer under Louis XIII, to go to Lille to curate and organize the archives. By the standards of the time, Godefroy was a lucky man. In 1668 he became Director of the Chambre des Comptes of Lille. He was the most highly paid historian in France and probably in the world, for Colbert provided him with a series of pensions totaling 13,600 pounds per annum.[75]

The archives in Lille were of critical importance to the French monarchy. In 1667 Louis invaded Flanders. He sought to legitimize his territorial aggressions through the old claim of the French crown to the duchy of Burgundy, whose ancient archives housing medieval treaties and feudal and ecclesiastical contracts were in Lille. With his annexations and territorial claims, historical documents more than ever translated into political power and legitimacy. The goal was to figure out which documents best historically illustrated the legitimacy of the king's claims in the Netherlands.

Colbert's choice of Denis Godefroy shows how the humanist historical culture of the sixteenth century had successfully infiltrated the new state apparatus. Godefroy's work in Flanders was a crucial part of the immense propaganda and legal campaigns that accompanied Louis's invasions. At the same time, Colbert was in the process of rationalizing government finance. He needed to know the history not only of the royal tax administration but also of every possible source of royal income. Part of Godefroy's mission was to find, protect, and organize important documents concerning royal rights and finances, such as the foundations of monasteries.[76]

Inasmuch as he was a document hunter and an archivist, Godefroy was a traditional humanist and a Gallican. Both in practice and through family ties, he was a direct product of Du Tillet's royal chartist tradition, brought to fruition by the Dupuy brothers and his father, Théodore Godefroy. Yet whereas Jean Du Tillet maintained a relative aristocratic independence in relation to the king, Godefroy was a hired hand. There was no hint of Sarpi's virulently critical, Venetian strain of Gallicanism. Denis II was not paid to write history. He was supposed to figure out which documents were potentially useful and get them to Colbert. The precious collection of documents that he sent to the royal library consisted of 182 volumes of collected documents from as early as the year 1000. It contained "peace treaties, princely marriages and dowries, wills, common laws, the privileges of provinces and towns, foundations, donations, engagements, acquisitions, ecclesiastical matters, finances, domains and fiefs and political documents and correspondences."[77]

Denis II was not entirely satisfied with his purely archival role. A good humanist, he did not just want to find documents; he also wanted to read them, write about them, and publish them. In 1664 he anonymously published a collection of archival documents called *Recueil des traités de confédération et d'alliance entre la couronne de France et les princes et états étrangers, depuis l'an MDCXXI jusques à présent; avec quelques autres pièces appartenantes à l'histoire.* His preface advertises the value of his collection of treaties as being useful for understanding the workings of secret princely prudence.

> These Treaties are like the center into which converge all the deliberations that take place in the private Counsels: And it is here that is revealed the most sublime Political prudence of the great Men who govern the World.[78]

In the Tacitist tradition of Du Tillet, Godefroy believed that his practices were the basis for developing political prudence through the teaching of a political reading of historical treatises. Yet this does not explain why he published his *Recueil* in Holland, outside the jurisdiction of his royal master.

Godefroy kept closeted a hidden secret: he was a frustrated Tacitist.[79] In a manuscript note written to himself, he outlines his plan to write a history of France.[80] In a rather wistful personal tone, Godefroy describes his frustration as a compiler. With clear reference to Lipsius and in contrast to Rapin, he claims to want to change his "old, long and boring narrative" into a "brief and pure" style. At the end of each extract, he intended to put the name and the exact source reference from where it was taken.[81] After these brief and verified extracts, Godefroy intended to formulate "political maxims."[82] The work was to be divided into three parts, "Extracts, Maxims and Discourses"—all in the same volume. His unfulfilled longing was to write a commentary to make his historical documents useful for politics.[83]

In a letter dated November 23, 1667 (a copy of which is in the same packet of documents as the manuscript note just cited), Godefroy wrote to Colbert begging for support for this project. He calls it a history of "the most worthy and the glorious plans and beautiful actions of Louis XIV" and his predecessors.[84] His claim that the project would take advantage of his underutilized skills clearly refers to his hopes to emerge as a political critic. This last point had an effect on Colbert, for he packed off Godefroy to Lille with a handsome salary and with strict orders to stay in the archives. Colbert had no need for another historian, and Godefroy was no master of eloquence. He was useful collecting the raw, documentary materials of political power. Colbert's orders were explicit: Godefroy's mission was to "collect and guard the titles and archives of the Chambre des Comptes."[85] Colbert had poets and Ciceronians to write history for the public. Denis would never realize his Tacitist dream.

COUNTERINTELLIGENCE
Amelot de La Houssaye Exposes Godefroy's Documents

Like his father, Denis II died in the service of his king. He was buried in Lille in June 1681, unable to obtain his dying wish to pass on his office in Lille to his sons, Denis III and Jean.[86] The younger and more successful of the two, Jean, managed to finally obtain his father's old office in the Chambre des Comptes in 1684, winning the prestigious office of Procureur du roi au Bureau des Finances in 1693.[87] Despite his brother's noted laziness, Jean managed to appoint Denis III to the office of counselor guard of the books of the Chambre des Comptes in 1688.[88] Thus, another generation of Godefroys entered into royal service in the archives. Yet with Colbert's death in 1683, the greater part of the royal patronage that had sustained the Godefroy family was lost. Perhaps due to Louis's expensive military ventures or perhaps due to a lack of understanding, Colbert's successors did not continue his vast cultural program.[89] The government scaled back its archival projects and its pensions for royal historiographers. Denis II's sons continued their father's project to publish a collection of French treaties with foreign countries, but with no government support.[90]

To sustain their archival work, Jean and Denis III were forced to turn the Lille archival project into a commercial venture. They turned to the royal printer Frédéric Léonard for patronage. Léonard was a successful entrepreneur. His investment in the Godefroys meant that he expected something in return. He at least kept his promise to publish the first grand collection of treaties from Lille, but he took credit for the project. Léonard boasted to have worked for "eighteen years" on the project, generously noting that while he "amassed" the collection, it would be unjust to forget the Godefroy family, who "provided all the Treaties" in question.[91] The four-volume compilation *Recueil des traitez de paix faits entre les rois de France et tous les princes de l'Europe depuis le règne de Charles VII* was first published in a regal folio edition in 1693, preceded by an abridged duodecimo pocket edition, entitled *Préliminaires des traitez faits entre les rois de France et les rois de l'Europe* (1692). The *Préliminaires* (published in 1691, 1692, 1693, 1699, and 1700) consists primarily of a long critical essay by Léonard's old friend and employee Amelot de La Houssaye which later appeared in the *Recueil*. The goal of Amelot's "Observations historiques et politiques sur les traitez des princes" was to expose Léonard's document collection in an original light.

Léonard was not just a rapacious businessman; he was also a brilliant humanist publisher. Where Colbert had wanted to keep the collection secret for the purposes of reason of state, Léonard sought to publish the treatises specifically to reveal the workings of the state.[92] He claimed that his project was "new" and "important" in that it would expose to an "intelligent public" what was normally a secret for government ministers and ambassadors.[93] Amelot's pocket edition of 1692 allowed normal readers easy access to what had hitherto been royal, exclusive knowledge.

> So that it will be a book, that everyone will be able to carry in their pocket, one will read it willingly, due to the novelty of the project, and due to the importance of the material itself; for the Recüeil [in folio] can only be read in the Cabinet, considering the large size of the four volumes that compose it; where this book offers itself Conveniently, in one's carriage, or on a voyage, while walking, and everywhere else.[94]

At all levels, Amelot's *Préliminaires* and Léonard's subsequent *Recueil* countered the spirit of Colbert's plan and fulfilled Denis II's dream of creating an analytical work in the style of Du Tillet and Lipsius. Rather than collecting historical documents for the secret analysis and use of the government, Léonard and Amelot's joint project was a remarkable work of criticism and a full frontal attack on monarchical dissimulation. Not just accessible, it was a guide to deciphering political, historical documents for understanding how princes use reason of state and prudence. In his introduction, Amelot writes that the study of treaties is useful not only to members of government but also to the public. He explains that to truly understand government, one must learn to read historical documents as does a minister.

> But if the science of making Treaties has few disciples, it is because it is a profession, which, due to its importance, and the difficulties it incurs, only appeals to people of superior genius, who are gifted with an exquisite prudence, and with long experience; that is not to say, that those, who are not capable of negotiating themselves, or who do not take part in Government, cannot usefully employ their time reading Peace Treaties, and the Memoirs of Ambassadors. For there are thousands of things in History, that one cannot understand, unless one has the knowledge of Treaties, and of that on which they are founded; and many Historians talk into the air when they discuss Princely disputes, since they are not informed of the conventions, capitulations, and transactions, that Princes make among themselves. Now, since History is the principal occupation of the greater number of the *gens du monde,* no matter which profession they might be of, the robe, or the sword; one must conclude, that the reading and intelligence of the Treaties of Princes is absolutely necessary to them, to understand the diverse points of History, which are not sufficiently worked out by Historians, and to discern which side is in the right in quarrels, which Princes have every day between themselves concerning their Treaties. For although they know how to give their own meaning to the articles upon which they infringe, (on this point Maurice, the Elector of Saxony, reproached Charles V, that he thought he was dealing with an Emperor, and not with a Legist) people of good understanding will see through the bad faith of the Prince, who breaks his word, by collating glosses, or interpretations, with the litigious article.[95]

This text is not only subversive; it is startlingly innovative. Amelot and Léonard propose to publish documents to which only government ministers and the prince had previously had access, with the express goal of revealing royal hypocrisy. The documents, along with Amelot's observations, reveal the mechanics of princely dissimulation and the governmental decision-making process. Much like Machiavelli's call for the critical reading of history in the *Discourses,* Amelot de La Houssaye proposes a critical reading of hitherto secret documents. He repeats Machiavelli's credo that the reading of history is the basis for political criticism. Yet Amelot takes his project one step further. The documents he discusses are nominally secret and currently relevant. The *Recueil* was an open invitation to peer into the contemporary workings of the state.

By its cover, one would think that the *Recueil* is yet another great tome produced in the Gallican, absolutist tradition. But Léonard and Amelot were not employed in a Gallican endeavor. They were neither lawyers nor humanist members of the academic establishment. They were part of a more ambiguous group of marginal humanists who worked behind the scenes of intellectual production, and they managed to publish a truly subversive handbook of political criticism in Louis XIV's Paris.

4. IN THE WORKSHOP OF POLITICS
Amelot de La Houssaye and the
Methods of Unmasking Venice

The rue St. Jacques is one of the oldest streets in Paris. It begins in front of Notre Dame and the Île de la Cité and leads directly south through the Left Bank. In ancient Lutetia, it was the main road to Rome, and later of course, to Santiago de Compostela. By the sixteenth century, it was the printers' street, teeming with bookshops, printers, apprentices, authors, and scholarly editors; the Sorbonne was just a block away. This street made Paris one of the great centers of print culture in early modern Europe, along with Venice and Amsterdam.[1] Today, the warehouselike business offices of modern printing houses pale in comparison with the teeming wood-beamed workshops of old Europe.[2] These shops were not just offices, stores, and printing centers; they were intellectual workshops filled with scholars who earned their bread and butter as hired hands in close proximity to shop owners and printers who, in the great humanist printing tradition of Aldus Manutius, were often accomplished scholars in their own right.[3]

The life of Amelot de La Houssaye was set on the rue St. Jacques. He lived on the faubourg de St. Jacques, the continuation of the rue St. Jacques, a fifteen-minute walk south, past the university and the great church of Val de Grâce, outside the medieval walls of Paris on the way to the abbey of Port Royal. During the late 1670s and early 1680s, Amelot regularly walked to work down the faubourg, toward the center of Paris, to the bookshop of his friend Frédéric Léonard, the king's own printer, under the shop sign of the Écu de Venise.[4] On some days, after work, Amelot would continue north, crossing the Seine on the Petit Pont, going over the Île de la Cité by the parvis de Nôtre Dame, then taking the Pont Nôtre-Dame. He would cross the place de Grève at the Hôtel de Ville and make his way up the rue du Renard into the labyrinthine center of medieval Paris, where the Pompidou Center today stands in a great pit that was once the stomach of medieval Paris. Where the coiled entrails of the Pompidou Center hang over the rue Beaubourg begins the rue Geoffroy L'Angevin. Retaining its medieval aspect, this dark, narrow street in the Marais curves with the inexplicable purposefulness of ancient, pre-Haussmannian Paris. Amelot sometimes lived on this street, in the house of Charles Herbin, master of requests for the royal administration.[5]

During the early 1670s, Amelot would often spend the night at the Herbin house. In fact, one court document attests to the fact that a witness spotted Amelot there wearing only his underwear as he helped administer the sacraments to Herbin, a fact that Amelot did not entirely deny.[6] He admitted that he was a "close friend" of the Dame Marguerite Herbin, née Léonard, the daughter of Amelot's friend Frédéric Léonard, the royal printer.[7] In the suit brought against Amelot and "la fille Léonard," the Herbin family claimed that while their brother slowly died of epilepsy, Amelot all but moved into the house as he and the printer's daughter entered into an adulterous relationship. On some afternoons, Amelot and Marguerite were seen driving through Paris in Herbin's coach, while the old accountant lay in his bedroom, apparently twitching and drooling away the last miserable days of his life.

In an age when popes and bishops unrepentantly had children and kings built palaces for their mistresses, such sexual libertinism was hardly unusual. Indeed, Amelot and Marguerite were acquitted of the charge of adultery with the help of the influential père Léonard. But more than a story of libertine morality, this anecdote reveals a fascinating aspect in the history of authorship and politics. It opens a window into a marginal literary world where a revolution in political culture was taking place. The print-shop floor became the setting for the rebirth of the Tacitist movement, which Colbert had sought to suppress. Here, Amelot and Léonard set out to transform the Tacitean and Machiavellian traditions. Mixing the tools of the pedagogical reading tradition of Tacitist history with an editorial strategy of popularization, Amelot and Léonard transformed the critical Tacitist tradition for a new market at the end of the seventeenth century. They turned works that "unmasked" the mechanics of royal government and the strategies of reason of state into publicly accessible, commercially viable books that taught the methods of political criticism to the reading public. They brought to the ancient traditions of compilation and commentary a graphic consciousness—an awareness of the importance of printing and a willingness to harness its strategies and techniques for the revolutionary project of publishing criticism.

In 1671 Amelot returned to Paris from Venice, fired from the diplomatic corps. With few professional options and his reputation tarnished, he descended into a marginal literary world of correctors, compilers, translators, and editors—far from the gilded dome of the Collège des Quatre Nations and the Académie Française, where the great authors of the seventeenth century worked with generous royal pensions. The rue St. Jacques was a proto–Grub Street.[8] Though it was not exactly a literary underground, its inhabitants were marginal players in the world of classical humanism, making their often meager livings from their learned skills.[9]

At a rather difficult moment in his career—professionally disgraced and with no income—Amelot came to work for the royal printer Frédéric Léonard on the rue St. Jacques. Trial documents reveal that Amelot played an essential role in Léonard's shop. In her defense testimony, Marguerite Léonard stated that Amelot was an "old friend" of her father who "drank, ate and slept" at his shop while "making and composing works for her father, as, she noted, he was doing presently."[10] When accused of illicitly going alone to Amelot's personal residence on the faubourg St. Jacques, Marguerite claimed to have gone to bring him notebooks and to help him with Italian and Latin translations.[11]

While he corroborated Marguerite's testimony, Amelot revealed a more nuanced picture of his own role in Léonard's shop. He claimed to have lived in Léonard's shop while writing works for Léonard. More than an editor, he was an in-house Tacitist. A sort of low-paid Lipsius, he compiled historical texts and collections of maxims, commented on works of politics, and revived the ancient tradition of translating and commenting on Tacitus that had been dormant for almost forty years. The old culture of Machiavellianism and Tacitism had thrived in close proximity to the crown, in the chambers of Gallican legal scholars, and in the erudite collections of humanist historians and translators; it now resurfaced in the greasy back room of a printing shop.

Unlike the great French Tacitists who preceded him, Amelot did not receive a royal pension. He earned his money creating political books. His raw materials were the traditional works of historical criticism, which he now marketed as a popular, accessible product. It was the first conscious attempt to transform the royal, Gallican tradition of political historiography into a truly public phenomenon. Obviously, the books of Machiavelli, the great Tacitists, and other political historiographers had been accessible on an open market. Yet as Justus Lipsius had said in the introduction to his critical edition of Tacitus, the historical methods of prudence were to be used only by kings. When Amelot and Léonard started reediting the great works from the critical tradition, they did so with the specific intention to show nonroyal readers how to use humanist historical erudition to analyze contemporary politics. Indeed, they envisioned exposing the secret sphere of the state and possibly creating a new public space for political criticism.

PUBLISHING THE SECRETS OF VENETIAN DECADENCE
The Invention of a Genre

In his quest to create a modern historical method in the mid-nineteenth century, the great German historian Leopold von Ranke turned to the archives. Seeking to systematize earlier historiographical practices, he insisted that to write truthful history—"wie es eigentlich gewesen"—historians would need to base their accounts on authentic documents.[12] In the Venetian archives, Ranke found the building blocks for his "scientific" historiography of politics. He believed that documents such as ambassadorial "relations" unmasked the "truth" of politics. Venetian archives came to represent not only the tradition of scientific history but also a culture of political unmasking. Filippo de Vivo writes, "The veneration of documents as veritable historical sources revealed to the historian truths otherwise hidden by the ruses of princes and their servants."[13] Nineteenth-century republicans saw the revelation of historical documents as a basis for political liberty. Lord Acton praised Ranke's historical method as a pillar of freedom.[14]

While Ranke, Michelet, and Acton went to the Venetian archives to understand the secret workings of government, their approach and the claim that historical truth was related to political liberty were hardly revolutionary.[15] Archival research had long been connected with the cultures of republican and even royal liberty. Leonardo Bruni saw the archives of the Florentine republic as a source for strengthening republican liberty, and Gallican legists had long seen the analysis of authentic documents as a basis for proving the liberties of the French church. Like their Florentine cousins, Venetian civic historians also turned to their own archives to prove the legitimacy of their political liberty.[16] The first great modern practitioner of "political unmasking" was Paolo Sarpi. His *History of the Council of Trent* sought to defend the interests of Venice by unmasking the motives and corruption of the papacy. At the same time, Sarpi and the Venetians did not hesitate to publicly circulate historical documents as propaganda in their quest to expose the political motivations of the papacy.[17]

While working as a secretary in Venice, Amelot got the idea to use this tradition in an entirely new way. When the ambassador to Venice, de Saint André, discovered Amelot's alleged theft of secret documents in Lisbon, he relieved his secretary of ambassadorial duties and allowed him to spend his time at the St. Mark's Library. As a foreigner, Amelot had the unusual privilege of doing documentary research in the archives of the great republic for two years, until the President de Saint André's return to Paris in 1671. Clearly not suited to the discretion demanded of an ambassadorial secretary, Amelot found his true, critical calling in the archives. He appropriated the Venetian historiographical tradition but turned it against its master. In a great twist of irony, Amelot founded the dark legend of Venetian tyranny by turning the critical method of Paolo Sarpi, the great Venetian protector, against Sarpi's cherished republic. On his return to Paris from Venice in 1671, Amelot de La Houssaye began the process of writing his own *History of the Government of Venice,* based on archival research and extracts of Sarpi's work.

At the most basic level, Amelot's *History of the Government of Venice* was the outgrowth of his checkered career. He was making a living with the only assets and skills he had. Perhaps as a student of the Jesuits or as an ambassadorial secretary, or maybe in the bookstalls of Venice, Amelot had learned to find politically useful historical documents and analyze them.[18] Influenced by his experience in the diplomatic underworld of Venice, he mixed the practices of royal Gallicanism and Tacitism with the street sense of a thief. It was Amelot's singular achievement to weave his education and personal experiences into the basis of a new critical methodology. In the *History of the Government of Venice,* he not only attempted to write a Tacitist book; he also set out to innovate on the tradition. If the great Tacitists had built a redoubtable weapon of royal politics, Amelot now set out to transform Tacitism by clearly creating a political methodology for the common reader. By teaching the reader to interpret archival documents, he would not only unmask the methods of political reason of state in the public arena; he would create a critical instrument with exceptional lasting power.

The *History of the Government of Venice* was first published in Paris in 1676 by Frédéric Léonard. Amelot dedicated the work to Louis XIV's rising war minister, the marquis of Louvois. He promised Louvois that his book would reveal the true political maxims of the Venetians for the first time. He advertised the difficulty of such a project: "Venice is a place where the secrets of government are impenetrable to Foreigners, and particularly to Ambassadors, and to all other Ministers, to whom they speak with only gestures and signs." The Venetian government was particularly secretive, he claimed, for it was "covered by a veil of appearances, and pretexts far removed from reality."[19]

Here, for the first time, was a book that offered to unveil the secrets of Venetian government and distill them into easy-to-use political maxims. The offer, of course, was old; it was the very essence of royal Tacitism and Machiavellianism. But the theme of Venetian secrets was new, and the topos of modern decadence was revolutionary, a development of Machiavelli's own study of corruption, decline, and fall in his *History of Florence* (1520–21). Venice, Amelot asserted, was a decadent state. The *History of the Government of Venice* revealed the secret mechanics of how governments fail. A scholar could make no greater attack on a government. Like Rome, the Venetian state was corrupted and ruined by its territorial ambitions.[20] It was not simply a bad system that had overstepped its rights, he insisted; it was a good system that failed due to its citizens' lack of virtue.

To explain the reasons for this grandiose decline, Amelot turned to the trusted analytical tools of the Aristotelian, Thomist tradition. With direct reference to Gasparo Contarini, he framed the unmasking of government in the terms of the ancient corporeal analogy of the state. He would dissect the workings of the Venetian government and assign each office of government a part of the body.[21] But while Contarini used his description of Venetian government to celebrate its myth, Amelot sought to tear it down.[22] In the first two sections of the second volume of his *History*—"The Principle Causes of the

Decadence of the Venetian Republic" and "Mores and General Maxims of the Venetian Nobility"—Amelot lays out the secret reasons for Venice's decline.[23] Following Contarini, he compares Venice to the ancient republic of Sparta. Like Sparta's ephors, the Venetian Council of Ten is a secretive supreme court that maintains balanced government. But whereas Contarini had made this comparison to celebrate the stability of the Venetian political system, Amelot uses it to explain the demise of the two republics and, in doing so, uses Venetian republicanism as a model for political decadence. Not only had Venice declined due to its territorial ambitions and slow deliberations; using a theme from Tacitus and Suetonius, Amelot correlates Venetian political decline with a crisis of political virtue in the ruling elite.[24] He calls the Venetian nobility "perfidious, treacherous, guilty of ingratitude, envy, venom, treachery, dissimulation, a hatred of foreigners," and, finally, "licentiousness and vice."[25] Here was all the drama of Tacitus's Rome.

Just as, during the Enlightenment, Montesquieu and Gibbon were to use decadence and decline as the critical topoi that undermined monarchy and religion, Amelot continued the work of Machiavelli and, with great prescience, unsheathed the accusation of decadence as the greatest criticism that could be made of a state.[26] Before Montesquieu made his cultural comparisons in the *Persian Letters,* Amelot showed that modern governments could be compared with ancient ones. By putting "universal" maxims by Tacitus in the margins, Amelot suggested that Venice could be used as an exemplum like Athens and Rome and that, as Bodin had suggested, modern political cultures could be compared. These elements of political criticism would become staples of the idiom in the eighteenth century. Both Montesquieu and Gibbon owned copies of the *History of the Government of Venice* in their libraries. We know that Montesquieu cited it in *De l'esprit des loix* (1748). Note the similar title of Montesquieu's work *Considérations sur les causes de la grandeur des Romains et de leur décadence* (1734). Whether or not Montesquieu and Gibbon used the *History of the Government of Venice* as a source for their own studies, Amelot's *History* led the charge of political criticism at the end of the seventeenth century.

THE FACTS OF POLITICS *The Uses of
Venetian Historical Documents*

Along with the novelty of Venetian secrets and the theme of decadence, Amelot also proposed a new and improved methodology for unmasking. He attached the accusation of political decadence to a systematic apparatus for exposing historical documents. To recognize decadence, or how a government loses its virtue, one must use the old lens of historical erudition to peer into the entrails of the state. The metaphor and the method were classic, but the claim was extravagant and essentially subversive. History would not be used to heal the state as an arm of parliamentary or royal statecraft, as thinkers such as François Hotman and Bodin had recommended during the sixteenth century.[27] Amelot showed through his own example that a simple individual, armed with the tools of erudition and reading, could attack a sick state and weaken it through the understanding of its flaws. It was a paradigmatic moment in the history of critical culture.

Whereas Sarpi used irony and innuendo to unmask the political workings of the papacy, Amelot looked for a more commercial and easily usable approach. Before Pierre Bayle, he offered historical erudition as a tool to show the reader how to understand the workings of politics. Moreover, he told a classic tale with innovative technology. A humanist precursor to Robert Graves's *I, Claudius,* Amelot's history recounted the tale of tyranny from Tacitus's *Annals;* but like a Renaissance playwright, Amelot set his piece in Venice with a host of new special effects based on the exposition of "authentic" documents. He boasts in his preface:

> In a way that, if the subject is not exactly new, I can at least say, without praising myself, that the manner in which I treat it is completely new. However, this is not, Reader, the main reason for which I want to recommend my Work, for it is also so due to the wealth of materials that I used, which are Letters, Memoirs, and Ambassadorial Relations that were given to me; the ancient Annals of this Republic from which I took examples and facts, that I provide; and principally the instructions that I took from the very place where, for three years, I had the honor to be employed in Venice [sc., the French Embassy]; which is the primary reason for this book, without such employ, I would never have written.[28]

To the force of political immediacy was matched a potent claim of veracity. While Sarpi divulged the secrets of government by telling a story, Amelot upped the ante by divulging secrets through the presentation of original documents. Maxims distilled from real sources would carry indubitable potency. By examining documents concerning the Council of Ten, he would extract the most "delicate maxims of the Republic, and the most hidden mysteries of its domination, *dominationis arcana* (Tacitus, *Annals,* 2.)."[29]

Amelot used as a selling point the fact that the *History of the Government of Venice* was a textual toolbox for the analysis of Venetian politics. It is comprised of narrative writing, marginal commentary, semi-plagiarized passages, compiled primary documents, Tacitean maxims, glossaries, and tables. The last section of the first volume and almost the entire second volume are comprised of compilations of reproduced primary documents and historical texts. Addressing his Gallican readers, Amelot maintained that original documents would aid in understanding the supremacy of royal jurisdiction over that of the pope.

Having already spoken in the other Parts of this History of the Quarrels of the Republic of Venice with the Popes, I thought that I would render a service to the Public, in providing a Relation of the Controversy, between these Patricians and Pope Paul V for the defense of their authority; And a Translation of two little Treatises on the Interdict published by the Doctors of Venice; of the Monitorius of this Pope against the Senate; and the Protestation of the Senate against this Monitorius, with a Circular Letter written to the Cities of the Venetian State; all the documents that I have judged worthy of the curiosity of *honnêtes-gens,* and that I believe are even more agreeable, for they defend the common Cause of all Princes, against the pretensions and the enterprises of the Jurisdiction of the Court of Rome.[30]

Amelot's clever offer mixed elements from Gallicanism with Sarpi's own critical technique. Amelot hoped that his history would carry the force of an original document. He called his book a "simple relation"[31]—a faithful, eyewitness account of the true workings of the Venetian state. In opposition to Colbert's policy that public history be entertaining and supportive of the state, Amelot's goal was to reveal what he considered to be the political truth in the plainest terms possible.[32] It is possible that Amelot had René Rapin in mind when he scoffed, "Eloquence is the job of a grammarian."[33] In Amelot's estimation, a real historian tells the "bony" truth.[34] Like an ambassador giving a relation, Amelot claimed to speak with the directness of a "witness" to the institutions of the state and to the wisdom that can be extracted from them.[35] Thus, exemplarity and historical accuracy were joined through the idea of prudence.

PUBLISHING POWER: *The Uses of Relations*

Amelot was conscious that his practice was part of the diplomatic tradition of the ambassadorial relation—or, in Venetian terms, the *relazione.*[36] Relations were the purest form of reason of state: they were firsthand observations recorded by an ambassador, who either sent them or presented them in person to the Venetian Senate.[37] In some cases, they contained political analysis and an attempt to understand the motives behind political observations. The Venetians were considered to have perfected political observation in the *relazioni,* which came to be seen as one of their political strengths.

During the sixteenth century, relations—veritable and false—were commonly printed and circulated all over Europe as a nascent form of the news, competing with manuscript *nouvelles à main* (news sheets). They told of politics and of royal policy. For the most part, they were pure narrative accounts of events, with no analysis. The controversial doctor and publisher Théophraste Renaudot (1586–1653) was the first in France to market rela-

tions.[38] Beginning in 1631, he published the *Gazette,* where he printed relations, government reports, treaties, and other official documents. Printing
relations turned them into news; the *Gazette* was the documentary ancestor to
the newspaper. Cardinal Richelieu supported Renaudot's publication and
used it as an arm of propaganda. The Paris Parliament, however, saw a threat
in Renaudot, who practiced free medicine for the poor as well as publishing
state information. After the death of Richelieu, Renaudot was put on trial,
and his operations were closed down. The Paris Parliament and, later, Colbert made it clear that they did not like state documents being published
unless it was to directly support their own political authority.

Amelot was no stranger to the culture of diplomatic relations: one of his
primary functions as secretary would have been to copy down the relations of
his ambassadorial master. In 1676 he published the *Relation du conclave de
MDCLXX,* an eyewitness account of the process by which the College of
Cardinals chose a successor to Pope Clement IX. In this printed pamphlet,
Amelot writes a documented political commentary in which he looks over the
proceedings, points to various actors, and explains who they are, what they
are doing, and why. Bringing his experience in writing relations to the *History of the Government of Venice,* he cites a number of printed relations—such
as a relation made to the Senate in 1648 in which Giovanni Battista Nani
unveils the motives of Anne of Austria.[39] More often, his marginal notes refer
to manuscript relations and manuscript annals from the Venetian archives, as
well as to eyewitness relations made directly to him. In the case of one manuscript source, he gives an excerpt: on page 108, he refers to "une Rélation
MS. que j'ai vuë" and then provides a long paragraph from it to back his
claim.

His methodology is simple: excerpts from historical texts, boiled down to
the bare, explanatory facts, will have the same informative qualities as a true
relation.[40] Thus, he includes a number of translated historical texts that he
considers to have the value of relations. In the primary text of volume 1 of his
History, he reproduces long descriptive passages from Gasparo Contarini's
De magistratibus et republica Venetorum (1543) concerning Venetian voting
procedure.[41] In the section entitled "La Relation du différend du Pape Paul
V. et la République de Venise," he gives an abridgement of Sarpi's *Dell'Inquisitione nella Città, e Dominio di Venetia* (1639), mixed with passages from
Andreus Morosini's *History of Venice,* all of which he calls "relations."[42] He
paraphrases a number of printed treaties, which he also considers the raw
material of political analysis. Amelot's presentation of sources was not fundamentally different from that of later antiquarians such as Bernard de Montfaucon, who with the same erudite zeal as Swift's academicians of Lagado,
claimed that by literally "handing over examples," his book contained the
"entirety of classical Antiquity."[43] The title of de Montfaucon's history of

classical monuments—*Antiquity Explained and Represented in Figures*—is a just description of what Amelot did with his own texts.[44] His work claims to contain a total collection of Venetian historical exempla.

Amelot had succeeded in creating a vast tapestry of compiled, archival documents in the quest to make his history useful. As a Tacitist and a commercial author, however, he needed to prove that these modern documents were useful beyond the limited sphere of Venetian politics. To do this, he demonstrated that Venetian history was a crucible for all politics because it mirrored ancient Greek and Roman political institutions.

> If I have often compared the Magistrates of Venice to those of Sparta and Rome, this was not to search for foreign ornaments to my History, much as it might need them, but rather to show that the Republic of Venice has borrowed from these two others, and has made good use of them; which is a mark of its rare prudence. . . . And furthermore, I have followed the example of Polybius, who made the same sort of parallels between the Carthaginians and the Romans, and with other nations. But there is the following difference, that his comparisons take up entire pages, while I am able to make mine in just three words, excepting two cases, that of the Doge and the Kings of Sparta; and the other being the Ephores with the Council of Ten.[45]

The comparison with Polybius was an essential point about method (and possibly a reference to Machiavelli). Amelot was not only writing a comparative work; he was also showing his reader how to do erudite analysis. His margins are filled with short references to classical works alongside his descriptions of Venice. His notes form a running "proof" of the universal value of the historical exemplum of Venice. There are 124 references to works of classical authors, 84 of which are to Tacitus.[46] These references are in the same form as the contemporary references, with name of author, work, and section or chapter. Not only did Venice's politics grow directly out of the ancient tradition; the *History of the Government of Venice* showed that universal political lessons could be drawn from modern exempla.

Here was a new and improved Tacitism. It was immediate, based on relatively current events and a living government. A good Tacitist could extract maxims from modern historical sources. Like Lipsius, Amelot did not just present a series of maxims; rather, he put his references to Tacitus in the margins of his Venetian history to show how to read history with a political eye. No longer did the publication of the methodology of reason of state happen by accident or by double entendre. Instead, publication was the entire purpose of Amelot's work. He gave reason-of-state literature new life, but this critical approach was risky. The *History of the Government of Venice* was like *The Prince;* it sold copies, but it was considered immoral, improper, and even dangerous. Eventually, it landed Amelot in the Bastille. The French authorities clearly realized the threat of Amelot's enterprise. With the *History of the Government of Venice* came the unwanted Renaissance legacy of the history of reason of state.

FACING THE FACTS *Amelot Defends the* History of the Government of Venice

The *History of the Government of Venice* could not have been published without Frédéric Léonard's support. Amelot needed a patron to subsidize the expensive printing of his compilation. In fact, he probably would not have been able to take on such a project without a guarantee of prior funding. The virulence of the work made it a risky venture for any printer, but Léonard was in a good position to take such a risk.[47] He was a royal printer and also an official printer to the clergy, with a commercially successful catalog. Nonetheless, it is hard to understand why he would have invested in such a project. He clearly did not need the money. We can only assume that in his dealings with Amelot, Léonard was not purely interested in profit but also personally invested in publishing the tools of political criticism. The *History of the Government of Venice* did have some obvious strengths for the French market. At one level, it supported French policy by attacking Venetian republicanism. It also served as a useful tool to advertise Gallican liberties. Indeed, it received a royal license to be published, and Louvois evidently accepted the book's dedication. In the end, it was edited five times between 1677 and 1695 and was translated into English and Italian.

While Léonard had correctly assessed the commercial potential of the book, he underestimated the Venetian reaction to the work. The publication of original political documents entailed risks, and an open attack against the Venetians begged a response. The Venetians rightly perceived the project as a threat. A manuscript rough draft of the *History* in the Biblioteca Marciana suggests that they were aware of the work in advance, somehow obtaining this early copy—which also suggests Amelot wrote the draft in Venice. At the moment the book hit the market stalls early in the year 1677, the Venetian procurator of the Senate, Giovanni Battista Nani (1616–78)—author of the famous *History of Venice* and other relations cited by Amelot—demanded that Amelot be jailed. The Venetian ambassador Nicolas Contarini not only complained to the French government; he publicly bragged that he would bring Amelot's severed head back to Venice and offer it to the Senate.[48] Although the Venetians never obtained Amelot's head, they did manage to have him thrown into the Bastille for six weeks.[49] While the French authorities had sanctioned the book, it was clearly not worth a diplomatic row. Amelot was expendable.

Why would the Venetians consider the *History* such a threat? They could have publicly refuted the book, while allowing Sarpi's supportive texts to circulate. Was a history book worth a diplomatic imbroglio? Amelot's critical vision of Venice came at a delicate time for both Venice and the French king. Pope Paul V had issued his 1606 interdict in response to the republic's open challenge to papal authority concerning the succession of the bastard son of the duke of Ferrara. It had also broken the understanding that only the church could judge its own in bringing legal actions against two lecherous ecclesiastics, Scipione Sarceno and Marcantonio Brandolini.[50] At the beginning of their decline, the Venetians, led by Paolo Sarpi, resisted and eventually overturned the interdict, weakening the hand of the pope and leaving relations tense between the two Italian powers.[51]

Despite their victory over Rome, Venice's position had considerably weakened by 1668, when Amelot arrived as secretary to the ambassador. The war of Candia (Crete), between Venice and Turkey, which had lasted forty-three years, had come to an end that same year. It was a devastating loss for the Venetians, who, portraying the war as the last great crusade against "the Turk," emptied their coffers, lost many men, and, most important, abandoned by the French, lost their last and most significant trading post in the eastern Mediterranean. When the *History of the Government of Venice* was published in 1676, the memories of Candia were still fresh. The Venetian ambassador's strong reaction to the book must be understood in this context.

The French crown, initially favorable, was less concerned than the Venetians about the book even after having jailed Amelot. Despite Amelot's arrest, they continued licensing the *History of the Government of Venice* for publication. As well as publishing subsequent editions of the book, Léonard also allowed Amelot to make additions to it. The *History of the Government of Venice* was a long-term project on which both protagonists worked over the years. The second, 1677 edition contains minor corrections but also an entirely new text at the end of the book, the "Memoir to Serve as a Defense of the History of the Government of Venice," a violent attack against the Venetians. In this text, Amelot vents his bile, accusing the Venetians of historiographical hypocrisy. He claims that they should have been more tolerant of the book since all the information in the book came from Venetian sources: "If the Venetians would take the trouble to leaf through their own manuscript Chronicles that are in their Library of St. Mark, they would find the same documents that I found, that offend them so much in my history."[52] He maintains that the very use of "truth" as a guide to historical writing was a method developed by the Venetians themselves.[53] He notes that Nani had defined the historian as an "absolute dictator" who had the right and the responsibility to preside at the "tribunal of Fame," with jurisdiction to judge, condemn, and absolve kings and commoners alike.[54] Did this only apply to the Venetians, Amelot asked? Amelot maintains that Nani's own published relations used the language of reason of state to criticize monarchical government.[55] Why, then, asked Amelot, should he himself not analyze republican government the same way?[56] If the *History of the Government of Venice* has been banned, so, he argued, should be Venetian histories such as that by Nani, for their critical styles are the same.[57] The implication of Amelot's argument was that the Venetians should look on his history as a compliment, for political criticism was, after all, a Venetian tradition. Thus, Amelot openly admitted that he was transforming state-sponsored critical culture into an arm of political subversion.

Léonard not only printed the "Memoir"; he also reedited the *History of the Government of Venice* a third time, in 1685, with yet more corrections given to him by Amelot.[58] Léonard softened Amelot's tone in this subsequent reedition. In a hand-annotated copy of the 1677 edition of the *History*, Amelot made hundreds of corrections and added entirely new sections to the text, some of which were understandably caustic remarks directed at the Venetian ambassador. Léonard incorporated these manuscript notes into the revised 1685 edition, but without the more inflammatory, anti-Venetian passages.[59] Amelot had Léonard's support and clearly benefited from his sense as a commercial publisher. In any case, even after Amelot's arrest and his adulterous affair with Marguerite, the subversive author and the royal printer continued to work together. By any standards, this was a successful professional relationship. Yet as touching as Léonard's support for Amelot was, some essential questions about their relationship remain. Why would an ambitious printer hire a known thief and let him live in his house? Why would he sponsor risky and expensive printing runs of a banned book? Amelot and Léonard continued to publish critical works, not always with commercial success. Under the circumstances, their main inspiration could hardly have been financial. Rather, Amelot and Léonard's main goal appears to have been to publish critical works. Before the eighteenth century and even before Bayle began his *Dictionary*, Amelot and Léonard set out to create the basis of a critical movement.

5. HOW TO READ A SUBVERSIVE
Decoding Reason of State of the Self

Amelot learned a hard lesson with the *History of the Government of Venice:* if you publish an original work of political criticism with your name printed on the title page, you may risk prison or even worse. Was it possible in Amelot's time to publish politically critical works while avoiding censorship and retribution? Amelot's response to the problem came from a stock practice of humanist authorship: he would use dead authors to write new books. Amelot's books might get banned, but it was less likely that he would be jailed for publishing the works of established authors, particularly authors who had been dead a long time. Of course, Amelot did not invent the method of writing ancient history to criticize the present. This was an implicit function within the Tacitean tradition. In 1683 he published critical translations of sections from Tacitus's *Annals,* Machiavelli's *The Prince,* and Paolo Sarpi's *History of the Council of Trent.*

Since the nineteenth century, Amelot's critical editions have been overlooked by historians of political philosophy—considered mere translations. Even today, dealers of rare books sell Amelot's versions of Tacitus as works "by Tacitus." But these works are far more complex than simple translations. Amelot wrote his own philosophy between the lines (or, rather, under them, in the margins of his books), transforming their meaning. To understand the full significance of Amelot's versions of Tacitus, Machiavelli, and Sarpi, we must look behind his authorial masks to understand what these books actually said. By doing so, we get a clearer understanding of what readers read when they opened the cover of *The Prince* at the end of the reign of Louis XIV and during the Enlightenment.

THE NEW LIPSIUS

Modern historians of political philosophy rightfully see 1660 as an essential cutoff date for Renaissance political thought, with the end of the libertine political movement and the great age of reason-of-state literature.[1] Gabriel Naudé was in some ways the last true representative of the Renaissance humanist *politique* tradition that began with Bodin and de Thou. He was secretary to the Roman Cardinal Bagni and a professional librarian. He turned to Lipsian Tacitism to formulate a new theory of princely prudence, and he wrote his own reason-of-state manual with examples from the ancients. Naudé's talents were still in demand at the end of the Fronde, and he worked as Cardinal Mazarin's personal librarian. But with Mazarin's eventual victory during the Fronde, the long period of chaos that began during the Religious Wars and continued into Louis XIV's minority abated. With new political stability, reason-of-state literature and the humanists who produced it faded from the scene.

Naudé died in 1657, and his brand of political humanism effectively disappeared with him. Louis took real power in 1661, but he did not hire a humanist advisor. This was a significant departure from precedent. From the time of François I, French kings had copied their Italian counterparts and surrounded themselves with Renaissance humanist counselors, scholars, and librarians. But Louis XIV saw no need for a Jean Du Tillet, a de Thou, or a Naudé. Reason of state, the primary political element of humanist politics, was born of the necessities of the wars and uprisings of the sixteenth and early seventeenth centuries. Louis saw no need to embrace reason-of-state culture. Perhaps he thought it dangerous—or simply useless. In any case, it appeared that the humanist political tradition had reached the end of its life cycle.

Once popular works, Machiavelli's *The Prince* and Paolo Sarpi's *History of the Council of Trent* were rarely printed in French after Louis XIV's ascent to power in 1661. Granted, it was possible to obtain these works in older French editions, but, clearly, the demand of the earlier part of the century was drying up. In terms of printing, the beginning of the seventeenth century was a Machiavellian moment. According to the *Catalogue général* of the Bibliothèque Nationale, at least thirty-five editions of three French translations of *The Prince* appeared between 1553 and 1664. The doctor Guillaume Cappel is credited with the first French translation of *The Prince* (1553), followed by Gaspard d'Auvergne (1553) and Jacques Gohory (1571).[2] Gaspard d'Auvergne's translation became the standard edition, published in a compiled edition of Machiavelli's works, *Discours de l'estat de paix et de guerre de messire Nicolas Macchiavelli . . . sur la première décade de Tite-Live, traduict d'italien en Françoys, plus un livre du mesme auteur intitulé: Le Prince* (1571). With several variations, this compilation was published at least thirty times until 1637. By the midcentury, however, only one edition of *The Prince* was printed in 1664, when the sieur de Briencour published the first French translation of *The Prince* since 1640. Although it was not included in the French police's list of banned books, this edition was never reedited. Only three French editions of the *Discours* appeared between 1637 and 1692. This contrast between the turn of the sixteenth century and the second half of the seventeenth century is striking.

On a smaller scale, the same trend is perceptible in the French translation of the works of Paolo Sarpi. Giovanni Diodati's French translation of the *History of the Council of Trent* was published at least seven times between 1621 and 1665.[3] But as with Machiavelli, after a last edition in 1665, there were no further editions. Louis's literary prohibition worked. During his reign, reason-of-state works slowly disappeared, replaced by historical memoirs, translations of classical authors, and official histories, such as Samuel Guichenon's *Histoire généalogique de la royale maison de Savoie* (1660), which sought only to back up Louis's territorial claims.[4]

The flagship of international humanism, once lauded as the theoretical basis of royal statecraft, Lipsian Tacitism faded from the scene. Best sellers of the Renaissance, Tacitus and Lipsius lost their privileged place in the bookstalls of Paris. From 1582 to the beginning of Colbert's government in 1661, at least thirty-two editions of eleven different translations of Tacitus or of Tacitean maxims appeared in print. However, from 1661 to Colbert's death in 1683, twelve editions of Tacitus appeared, ten of which were reprints of Nicolas Perrot d'Ablancourt's translations of Tacitus from the 1650s. The two others were by Puget de La Serre.[5] Most significant, new Lipsian editions of Tacitus were rare. A great pan-European best seller of the first half of the seventeenth century, Lipsius's *C. Cornelii Taciti opera omnia quae exstant* (1581) went through more than eighteen reeditions between 1581 and 1650, at least four of which were printed in France.[6] Lipsius's critical Tacitus was replaced by Perrot d'Ablancourt's eloquent, literary translation devoid of maxims and commentary.[7] The only trait that Perrot d'Ablancourt's Tacitus shared with older editions was that it, too, was dedicated to a king, Louis XIII. But it marked the last time Tacitus would be represented as a royal historian in France. The Sun King neither commissioned nor accepted a translation of Tacitus. Thus, the Roman historian lost his exclusive entrée into the cabinet of the French monarch.

For a literary entrepreneur such as Amelot de La Houssaye, the dearth of political works in mid-seventeenth-century France presented a potential opportunity. There was an opening in the market. But anyone hoping to fill this void would have to face the essential problem confronted by political literature of the ancien régime: how to write political criticism in an age of censorship or in an age without strong political opposition. The great historian of libertinism René Pintard once complained of the difficulty of studying seventeenth-century freethinkers who dissimulated the true motives of their writings with ambiguities and contradictions. These thinkers were mysterious even to their contemporaries. Anyone who could "decode" their writings, he noted, would provide a great service to the history of ideas, for their hidden messages were the link that connected "the Ancients to Montaigne and the great Italians of the Renaissance, who prepared the way for Bayle and Fontenelle."[8] Leo Strauss famously described this problem of literary dissimulation in his classic work *Persecution and the Art of Writing* when he challenged historians of ideas to read between the lines.

> [I]f an able writer who has a clear mind and a perfect knowledge of the orthodox view and all its ramifications, contradicts surreptitiously and as it were in passing one of its necessary presuppositions or consequences which he explicitly recognizes and maintains everywhere else, we can reasonably suspect that he was opposed to the orthodox system as such and we must study his whole book all over again, with much greater care and much less naïveté than before.[9]

The art of surreptitious writing described by Pintard and Strauss was particularly characteristic of baroque historiography. Political veils and masks were described, but this practice in turn masked the true subversive motives of the author, who masked himself to expose others.[10] To dissimulate one's own motives while showing the reader how to read through the motives of others was the greatest achievement of Machiavellian practices of authorship. In France, where Louis XIV and Colbert went to great lengths to stifle free speech, criticism had to function within the sanctioned stage props of political literature, perceptible only to those whose eyes were trained to see through the multiple layers of classical references and the thick references of double entendre. If Amelot de La Houssaye wanted to continue what he began in the *History of the Government of Venice,* he would need his own surreptitious strategy.

In the fall of 1677, after six weeks in jail, Amelot was free and working again. He returned to Frédéric Léonard's shop, where he earned his bread as a simple corrector. For six years, between 1677 and 1683, he did not publish anything. Either he did not think it wise to do so, or he was censored. Whatever the reason, in 1683, after the death of Colbert, he emerged from his professional cocoon as a corrector in Léonard's shop. It seems plausible that there was a correlation between the two events. We know that the new administration, dominated by the marquis of Louvois as minister of war, did not share Colbert's interest in cultural politics. Perhaps it was not concerned with the literary works of a gadfly author, or maybe Amelot had better contacts with this new ministerial clique. Evidence suggests that Amelot had good relations with Louvois's family, the Le Telliers.[11] He may even have been protected by Louvois himself, to whom he dedicated the *History of the Government of Venice.* In any case, in 1683 he felt that he could again take the risk of publishing critical works.

After what seems to have been a period of probation, one would have expected Amelot to avoid publishing seditious books. However, in 1683 Amelot published his first translation of Tacitus. It was an interesting choice for an author with a subversive history and a jail record. As we have seen, Tacitus was not only the most popular classical historian of the seventeenth century; he was also, until the death of Richelieu, the official classical historian of the Bourbon monarchy. In choosing to translate Tacitus, Amelot hoped to limit his risks of censorship. His translation of and commentary on extracts from the sixth book of Tacitus's *Annals*, entitled *Tibère: Discours politiques sur Tacite*, was first printed in Amsterdam in 1683, by the heirs of Daniel Elzevier. The title page of the book tells us that this was done "at the expense of Frédéric Léonard." Amelot and Léonard published the book out of the reach of the French censors, and Amelot took the precaution of using a pseudonym, "sieur de La Mothe-Josseval d'Aronsel," of which the first part is an anagram of Amelot's name and the second of his birthplace, Orléans.[12] It seems doubtful that such meager precautions would have fooled the police lieutenant, La Reynie. Yet in 1684 *Tibère* was reedited twice, without a pseudonym and in Paris by Frédéric Léonard. The title page of one of the editions (in quarto) says that it was printed in Amsterdam but "sold" in Paris in the boutique of Frédéric Léonard. Once it was clear that *Tibère* had not offended the censors, Amelot and the entrepreneurial royal printer brought the book back to Paris, where it was profitably reedited four times in two years. They had succeeded, and Amelot found his literary niche: he would write with the books of others.

Emboldened by the success of *Tibère*, which obtained a royal publishing privilege, Amelot published two more critical translations in Amsterdam in the same year, his new translations of Machiavelli's *The Prince* and of Paolo Sarpi's *History of the Council of Trent*.[13] Together, Tacitus, Machiavelli, and Sarpi represented the critical tradition from Rome to the Florentine Renaissance and the Venetian baroque. They were the pillars of a tradition respectively celebrated by Italian humanists, French kings, English revolutionaries, Dutch republicans, and French libertines. In publishing these works, Amelot made a bold statement: despite the risks, he was going to revive the old critical tradition.[14]

There were many forms of political defiance in France during the ancien régime. Peasants caused insurrections, nobles revolted, merchants refused to pay taxes, and even after the Revocation of the Edict of Nantes in 1685, some people refused to renounce the outlawed Protestant religion. Amelot's act of defiance was to publish a new commentary on Tacitus. In the preface, his first public statement since the Venetian scandal, he declared himself the new Justus Lipsius. It seems an odd choice, for as we have seen, Lipsius's works were synonymous with the absolutist humanist culture embraced by the early Bourbons. What was it about imitating Lipsius that constituted an act of opposition? By identifying with Lipsius, Amelot embraced the ambiguity of the Tacitist tradition and the central paradox in the practice of exposing the methods of political secrecy. This was the true beginning of Amelot's career. He would transform Lipsius's dual authorial practice into a tool of criticism.

By commenting on authors such as Tacitus, he shed the responsibility of primary authorship, rendering the content of his books more ambiguous and harder to censor.

Lipsius originally envisioned prudence as a tool of public service and royal utility. Prudence—or, possibly, immoral political action—was meant to be exclusively for the prince. It was immoral for private individuals, such as courtiers, to use the methods of reason of state, for they could not be trusted to have the best interests of the res publica in mind. The people, for their part, could not pose a threat, for Lipsius had implied that they are driven by passions and thus incapable of reason and secrecy.[15] Indeed, Amelot was the new Lipsius in the sense that he, too, would extract political maxims and comment on them. What was subversive in this is that Amelot did not write for the prince. His ideal of public utility was to expose princely prudence to the largest possible audience. The title *Tibère* hints at his intentions. Since Botero's study of Tiberius in *Della ragion di stato* (1590), Tiberius had been associated with the art of tyranny. Nicolas Caussin put it best in his Christian, anti-Machiavellian critique *De regno Dei* (1650), where he called tyranny the *Tiberianae artes*.[16] Thus, by its very nature, Amelot's study of Tiberius was a portrait of tyranny.

TACITUS *The Lens of Personal Prudence*

Ostensibly, *Tibère* is a commentary on Tacitus and a historical examination of the reign of the emperor Tiberius. "But if you remark," Amelot writes in his preface, "that the basis of the material concerns all Princes in general, then this book is no longer about the reign of Tiberius, but rather about the art of reigning in general."[17] In other words, Amelot was not only writing about the past; he was also writing about the present. If Louis XIV wanted to be the new Augustus, it was, in turn, only a short step to compare him to Tiberius.

Attached to the preface of *Tibère* is an extraordinary historical essay about reason of state, comprised of commonplaces by ancient and modern authors. It not only reveals Amelot's own definition of the idea of reason of state but also is a key for understanding how to read *Tibère*. Here, Amelot explains why the reader would need to understand the motives of the prudent prince: "Several people having asked me what exactly Reason of State is, which I discuss so often in this Book, they have advised me to explain here for the instruction of many other people, who might be asking the same question."[18] While reason of state is necessary for the aggrandizement of the state, Amelot repeats over and over that it goes against individual interests, law, and rights. He cites Tacitus's definition of reason of state as *dominationis arcana,* or "the secrets of domination," implying that reason of state fosters political domination, not civic good.

I readily admit that Reason-of-State derogates Common-Law, or, as some say, Civil-Law: *Minui jura,* said Tiberius, *quoties gliscat potestas.* But one must admit reciprocally, that this derogation, or contravention, was only ever introduced, and is only used by Princes, for the greatest common good, which is the conservation, or the aggrandizement of the State, of which the interest is almost always incompatible with that of Particulars.[19]

This passage reveals how Amelot masks his own motives by contradicting himself. Reason of state might be necessary, but it goes against the interests of individual citizens. In another passage, he calls reason of state "rude and mean" [*rude et fâcheux*], "unjust and violent," and, again, contrary to the interests of "Particular individuals."[20] Was this essay intended to reveal reason of state, to critique it, or both? Clearly, Amelot did not want to make the censor's job easy.

Whereas the preface to *Tibère* is cryptic, the main text is a more obvious critique of reason of state and political tyranny. Amelot attacks the duplicity of princes—their methods of retaining power through misinformation, violence, propaganda, and other methods. The text is a litany of the abuses of power and the dangers of a capricious autocrat. Watch out for the silent prince, Amelot warns on page 20, for he is plotting revenge. The king's court was not a theater of glory but, rather, a machine of submission: "The more a Prince takes away his Subjects' liberty, the more he showers them with false appearances, so that soon they accept them in the place of reality itself."[21] This maxim must have had particular resonance at the very moment when Louis XIV had moved into Versailles. The man who only one year later would publish the best-selling *L'Homme de cour* writes, "Flattery is the inseparable companion of servitude, and the best friend of Tyranny."[22] He goes so far as to accuse gluttonous princes of representing the corruption of their own regimes.[23] This was no small accusation to make under a Bourbon king who ate in public and was a notorious gourmand.

Finally, Amelot repeats his refrain: while reason of state is a political necessity, it is also a crime and a vice.[24] Surely we can read between the lines. This is no manual for a docile and wellborn courtier but, rather, an attack on absolutist royal power and on courtly flattery itself. The message is a complex syllogism: princes use reason of state; reason of state harms personal interests; Amelot's book reveals the workings of reason of state; thus, Amelot's book will help the reader protect his or her personal interests. Amelot had made his intentions difficult to identify, but any skilled reader wanting to use *Tibère* as a guide to understanding the dangers of living under a tyrant would be able to do so.

Tibère was a more successful literary venture than was the *History of the Government of Venice.* Amelot's strategy of publishing the work in Amsterdam under a pseudonym worked, for the book won a publishing license in

France. Amelot must have felt some satisfaction at having managed to legally publish an attack on monarchical tyranny in Louis XIV's Paris without state retribution. Added to that, the book was a relative editorial success. Frédéric Léonard published two editions of the book in Paris in 1684 and another in 1685. Emboldened, Amelot published his second Tacitean handbook, called *La Morale de Tacite: De la flatterie,* in 1686. *Tibère* had established the dangers of tyranny; *La Morale* was a follow-up study. It was a portrait of the untrustworthy courtier and his particular method of prudence. The first page of *La Morale de Tacite* illustrates Amelot's method of writing political criticism under the guise of translating the ancients. He uses a translation of Tacitus as an attack on monarchical absolutism and court society. The first page sets the critical, openly republican tone for the entire book. Under a tyrannical regime, contends Amelot, virtue wilts, and only flattery flourishes.

DECORA ingenia, gliscente adulatione, deteruntur.* *Tacitus Annalium* I. (*The text says:* Non defuere decora ingenia, donec gliscente adulatione detererentur). Good souls become dull and degenerate, when it is neither permitted to speak, nor to write, without flattering.

THERE is no need for any Commentary, other than that of Tacitus himself. Many Authors, he says, have given us the history of the first seven centuries of the Roman Republic, of the time when one was able to write with so much eloquence, and liberty. However, since the battle of *Actium,* when it was necessary to abandon all power to a sole person, to have peace, the *grands esprits* soon become eclipsed[a]. And the reason for this that he gives in another passage, is, that Domination having taken the place of Equality, which is the soul of Republics, all studied to please and to humor the Prince[b], to acquire honors, to the point that one could no longer move upwards, except by degrees of servitude[c]. Now, the fact is that servitude and flattery are inseparable companions[d]. And it was in relation to the shameful flatteries of the Senate, that Tiberius so often wrote, *O great slaves*[e]! Pliny the Younger, whom I often cite, due to the conformity of his maxims with those of Tacitus, whom he made examine his writings, speaking of the books of his Uncle, apologizes for eight of them, which were neither of the same style, nor the same force as the others, due to the fact that he composed them during the time of Nero, under whom the servitude did not permit one to write with liberty[1]. And in another letter he says, that he saw a reign under which the Senate had become mute, and even dazed, from having so long been forced to stay silent[2].

NOTES

[a]Of the former period, the 820 years dating from the founding of the city, many authors have made studies, and when they had to record the transactions of the Roman people, they wrote with equal eloquence and freedom.

After the conflict at *Actium,* when it became essential to peace, that all power should be centered in one man, these great intellects passed away. *Hist.* I. ᵇStripped of equality, all looked up to the commands of the sovereign. *Ann.* I. ᶜThe readier they were to be slaves, the higher they were raised to wealth and promotion. *Ibidem.* ᵈBecause flattery involves the shameful connotation of servility, where as malignity wears the false appearance of honesty. *Hist.* I. ᵉTradition says that Tiberius would rise in eager rivalry to propose shameful and preposterous motions. As often as he would leave the Senate, he would say to himself: How ready these men are to be slaves! *Ann.* 3. I. Eight miscellaneous books written in the last years of Nero, when servility made any sort of free or higher studies dangerous. *Epist.* 5. *lib.* 3. 2. We saw the Senate, but the Senate trembled and was silent, when it was dangerous to say what one wanted. We senators, we participated in the evil, for many years we saw it and were a part of it, during which time, our spirits were dulled, broken and shattered for the future. *Epist.* 14. *lib.* 8. *He speaks of Domitian. And in his Panegyric to Trajan, he calls this servitude of the Senate,* the mute and passive assent of necessity.²⁵

Speaking through the medium of citations from Tacitus and Pliny the Younger, Amelot states that under the domination of tyranny, great thinkers and politicians degenerate into servile flatterers, and great writers must change their styles to mask their true intentions. He discusses the example of Pliny the Elder, who was forced to change the style of eight of his books so as not to run the danger of offending Nero. He implies that only under the "egalitarianism" of "republics" can one retain one's dignity and speak freely. This was not only a historical insight but also a veiled confession to the reader: Amelot will have to disguise his own intentions, and the reader in turn will have to read his book accordingly.

If there were any doubts about Amelot's subversive intentions, *La Morale* surely dispelled them. The book's definition of the idea of prudence was, at one level, a radical break from Machiavelli and Lipsius. In a complete reversal of one hundred years of reason-of-state theory, Amelot equated prudence not with effective government but, rather, with individual survival and defense against the state itself.

In his commentary on a passage from the fourth book of the *Annals,* he compares the cases of two courtiers, Lepidus and Thrasea. The first example shows how Lepidus used courtly prudence not only to survive but also to soften the capricious death sentences meted out by Tiberius.²⁶ When Lepidus heard that Lutorius Priscus had been sentenced to death for writing several disrespectful verses, he spoke out in public, saying that he could not believe that Tiberius could have approved of such a disproportionate sentence. Priscus was executed when Tiberius was away on a campaign. However, when the emperor heard of Lepidus's comments, Amelot claims that Lepidus managed to "pique" Tiberius's sense of honor. When the emperor returned, he commended Lepidus, scolded the Senate, and was for a time clement in many of his decisions.

Thrasea, in contrast, was imprudent. When hearing of how the praetor Antistius had written a satire at Nero's expense, Thrasea exclaimed that the time of cruel reigns was over and that despite his insolence, Antistius should be spared and exiled to an island. Nero granted Thrasea's wish but was irritated that Thrasea would dare to speak for him. Nero commented that he hoped that Thrasea loved him as much as he loved justice. Several years later, Nero had Thrasea killed. The lesson to be learned from these exempla is that while Lepidus and Thrasea were equally virtuous (and Tiberius and Nero equally capricious), Lepidus was the more prudent of the two courtiers, for not only did he make his voice heard, but he also survived. Thrasea was perhaps a better and braver man, but Lepidus was a better subject, for he knew how to accommodate himself to the times.

> Lepidus's moderation is a good testimony that there can be great men, I mean, people impenetrable to flattery, and to injustice under the domination of the most wicked Princes; and that there has never been a century so sterile in virtue, that has nonetheless provided such good examples. Prudence takes us down a path that leads neither to the precipice of liberty, nor to the abyss of servitude. Prudence is neither free nor servile; it maintains a character, with which it injures neither Majesty, nor Justice; prudence renders unto Caesar that which is Caesar's, which is obedience and respect; and to God that which is God's, that is, all that is demanded by a good conscience.[27]

This is an explanation of how to preserve one's dignity in an age of tyranny through a new kind of prudence based on individual interest. But it is not an end-all. Amelot implies that the ultimate goal of prudence is political liberty and that truthful political history is the only possible way to reach republican liberty.

> Flattery and History will never get along together, for one is devoted to lying and the other to the truth; one fools Princes, and the other instructs and even reforms them. The great and powerful fool themselves if they believe that their reputations are protected by suppressing books that reveal their faults. To burn books, is to light the curiosity to read them. . . . It is easy for the great to take revenge on historians, for they have the power to take their lives; but they shall never have the final authority over History, which is immortal and has all posterity for its judge.[28]

Clearly, the author of the *History of the Government of Venice* was not condoning flattery. Instead, he was explaining how to use history and prudence as a shield of personal defense against tyranny. This was not revolutionary talk; it was a call for a culture of criticism in the face of undisputed power.

Amelot's works on Tacitus are the clearest example of the first stage of what Marcel Gauchet calls the "mirror of reason of state." First, the crown uses reason of state; then, in turn, the public uses a reading of reason of state—its literary reflection—to criticize the political power of the state; this ultimately leads to conflict and to competition over the power monopoly. Gauchet describes the spread of Tacitist and Machiavellian manuals during the ministry of Richelieu (1629–42) as "a mass movement of Machiavellism."[29] As the state became more "rationalized" and "secular" in its self-justification and as its methods of power were publicly discussed and contested, it created an inevitable movement toward "political publicity."[30] "This fundamental tension," Gauchet notes, "between the opacity of the function of the State and the decoding of its mystery" is the very basis of modern political democracy.[31] Yet this so-called mass movement was neither a political movement nor an ideology of opposition. Its effects were nuanced and are therefore harder to measure with the tools of the history of philosophy. No French reason-of-state theorist attacked Louis personally or questioned his legitimacy. *Tibère* and *La Morale de Tacite* do not represent the growth of an opposition party. Instead, they were successful attempts to spread Tacitist and Machiavellian political culture and thus spark a worldview of individualist, skeptical criticism.

Amelot's Tacitus was meant to sow the seeds of political doubt and an ethos of self-interest, leading to what Anna Maria Battista calls the "separated," or alienated, individual of the seventeenth century.[32] Battista maintains that the absolutist state's attempt to claim divine legitimacy while openly turning to secular, prudential methods of power ultimately failed as the public became skeptical and disenchanted.[33] While seventeenth-century intellectuals accepted the brute political monopoly of the Leviathan, they nonetheless responded with a new apolitical ethic of personal survival separate from the collective interest of the corporate and communitarian ethos of the Middle Ages.[34] If the state had no real moral or sacred claim to power, what, then, kept the individual from seeking personal profit and private tranquility at the expense of the state?[35] Thus, Battista explains that the collective critical epiphany of personal political self-interest constituted an evolutionary step that led toward the eighteenth-century calls for political democracy. The seventeenth century was not simply the century of the sycophantic courtier or of Pascal the pessimist: it was also the age of a mercenary, utilitarian individualist with a good Jesuit education.

The process of political disenchantment and the rise of a new historical culture of individual self-interest were strongly anchored in the Machiavellian, Tacitist/Lipsian traditions. Amelot de La Houssaye was the central figure in this transformation. He single-handedly developed a program of publishing the reading practices of reason of state, not for princes, but for a general public. His goal was a cultural revolution that would turn prudence into a reason of state of the self. Along with two successful works of Tacitean criticism, he reedited *The Prince* and the *History of the Council of Trent.* He had yet to publish a defining work on individual prudence. He would find his opportunity in a little-known Spanish Jesuit book that he called *L'Homme de cour.*

THE SPANISH ORACLE OF PERSONAL PRUDENCE

Before Amelot began his program of popularizing prudence, Spanish Jesuits taught prudence to their soldiers of God.[36] Alongside a blossoming of the arts and philosophy in the Spanish Golden Age, the inquisitorial Catholic orthodoxy of the Counter-Reformation and an increasingly centralized absolutist state tracked down dissidents and minorities with a zeal born of the crusader's racial obsession with *limpieza de sangre,* or "purity of blood."[37] Spain's vast multiethnic and religious empire had been built on the back of slavery, over which church and crown attempted to force a mask of orthodox unity. Its strategies of self-protection and adaptation sprang from the impossibility of strict adherence to the demands of the Counter-Reformation. How could one conform effectively in Spain's sophisticated imperial court, where daily demands so often pushed the individual off the path of moral righteousness? As elsewhere, the Jesuits responded to this problem with the theory of casuistry, the art of bending religious morality to fit exceptional, unavoidable circumstances.[38] While they rejected Machiavelli, Jesuits nonetheless permitted vice in the name of expediency, particularly in the affairs of the church. It was a truly cynical act, for it implied an admission that the world was indeed a cruel and unjust place.[39] According to this view, the individual would need to bridge this earthly gap between fallen humanity and God with an attempt at self-perfection beyond the strict moral precepts of religion, and God could hardly be angry if humankind used every possible tool for self-improvement. Although tailored to a spiritual end, a basic element of Machiavellian culture thus entered a practical, everyday culture.

Indeed, Loyola's soldiers of God had to be practical. In stark opposition to the hermetic scholasticism of the universities, which had so alienated such figures as Luther and Erasmus, Jesuits insisted on worldly results. They were at war with Protestants (often in conflict with their own church), and before them stood the pagan peoples of the new Spanish world empire, a sea of souls, slaves, and gold-hungry émigrés. Their weapon was modern—faith through humanism. It was a response to the ravages of doubt that had been brought on in part by textual criticism. Not only would they deny new interpretations of the Bible; they would argue about them and fight textual criticism with more textual criticism. Jesuits were teachers consciously molded in the Renaissance tradition of Latin studies. Their manifesto demanded discipline and study, which they preached across the world with their study program the *ratio studiorum,* which began in the second half of the sixteenth century. As successful as they were in combating heresy, the Jesuits adopted dangerous tools that risked backfiring. They taught moral casuistry along with critical reading methods, and in a great balancing act, they embraced Tacitus while rejecting Machiavelli.[40]

A masterpiece of Spanish Jesuitical literature, Baltasar Gracián's *Oráculo manual y Arte de prudencia* (Oracle manual and art of prudence) was first published in Spain in 1647, when Louis XIV was only nine years old.[41] It would become the most famous and widely circulated of modern treatises on prudence and the second most published Spanish work after *Don Quixote.*[42] Gracián's manual was a cross between the personal behavioral manuals of the Christian Renaissance and Jesuit casuistry.[43] A good Jesuit, Gracián claimed to reject Machiavelli and derided reason of state as "reason of stable," but he still adopted Lipsius's attempt to create a moral version of "watered-down" Machiavellian prudence.[44] True to Machiavelli's definition of prudence, Gracián's *Oráculo* focuses on the methods for attaining success, which he equates with virtue.[45] The book is a list of Tacitean and Machiavellian personal maxims for practical life: "Live practically"; "Know how to use your enemies"; "Learn to Dissimulate Your Intentions."

Rather than Lipsius's civil utilitarianism, Gracián's new art of prudence aimed at individual, personal success. Maxims 99, 130, and 220 recommend "dissimulation" in order to "gain profit." Taking a line right out of *The Prince,* the *Oráculo* maintains that while virtue and honesty are no doubt ideal, "the times" have rendered them impractical. The "prudent man" knows what virtue and honesty are and would like to practice them; however, the sad state of current affairs (that old Machiavellian refrain) obliges prudent, defensive action. In maxim 220, Gracián cites the great commonplace that Machiavelli took from Cicero's *De officiis* and turned around, "When you cannot cover yourself with the skin of a lion, use that of a fox."[46] When surrounded by one's personal enemies, one must take the "detour of artifice" to fight them.[47] Thus, the prudent person must neither lie nor tell the truth (931); instead, he must know how to "manipulate the truth" (210).[48] The final chapter of the *Oráculo* is entitled "Finally, Be a Saint." Here was a masterful monument of Jesuit casuistry and perhaps the most elegant attempt since Aristotle's *Nicomachean Ethics* to reconcile pure practicality with spiritual fulfillment.[49]

The *Oráculo* was not an initial editorial success. It seems doubtful that Gracián envisioned a wide audience beyond his native Aragon and the Spanish court, for although the first printing of the work was overseen by his friend Don Juan de Lastanosa, a great Aragonese humanist and aristocrat, it was a limited edition, and original copies were rare. It was reprinted a second time in Madrid in 1653 and a third time in Amsterdam in 1659, and it was anonymously translated in a single Italian edition in 1670, but the Spanish work was not widely accessible to the European readership of the republic of letters, fluent in Latin and increasingly versed in French.[50]

Of course, this was not the end of the *Oráculo*. Like the works of Tacitus, Gracián's work would have many lives. From the beginning, the *Oráculo* was a product of the sort of Lipsian editorial practices that encouraged appropriation, commentary, and rewriting. While Gracián was the author of the maxims in the *Oráculo,* Don Juan de Lastanosa wrote the preface and claimed to have compiled it from Gracián's papers and to have given it its title. In other words, Gracián wrote the text, but Don Juan created the book. Gracián had lauded Lastanosa as a "great genius," a collector of "marvels," and a protector of the "memory of Antiquity."[51] Indeed, Lastanosa was no ordinary editor. He was a high Aragonese nobleman, a humanist, and a renowned collector of antiquities who owned one of the greatest seventeenth-century libraries of Aragon, for which the catalog is still in existence.[52] It is assumed that Gracián used this very collection to write his works. Like any good humanist library, it contained editions of maxims from Tacitus.[53] At the beginning of the seventeenth century, Spain—even more than France—had known an explosion of political editions of Tacitean maxims. These varied and often anonymous works peppered Lastanosa's collection alongside the great Spanish works of pragmatic political thought by Antonio de Herrera, Saavedra Fajardo, Emmanuel Sueyro, and Juan Suarez.[54] The mixture of political treatises, humanist manuals, and works of maxims in this collection suggests that the owner of this library was interested in the reading practices that characterized Tacitean humanism. Significantly, the collection contained Sacchini's *Reading with Fruit,* with its practical reading methods similar to those recommended by Tacitists. Lastanosa's was a Lipsian library.[55] Lipsius was the best-represented author there, with nine books (far more than any other), including his complete works and some Spanish translations. Gracián's works grew from this world of Aragonese Jesuit humanism, and they were, in part, an outgrowth of the Tacitean, Lipsian tradition. They showed the deep and complex relationship between court society and humanist, Jesuit traditions.[56]

L'HOMME DE COUR

If Amelot had been interested in the mechanics of prudence and in how to teach them to a wide audience, the *Oráculo* was the perfect book to realize his ambitions, for in Amelot's version of Gracián's work, Neo-Stoicism, antiquarianism, reason of state, and Tacitism were boiled down into a political ethos for a new age. He published his version of the *Oráculo* in 1684, under the title *L'Homme de cour* (The man of the court), a phrase Gracián never used. More than any other work, Amelot's *L'Homme de cour* earned him international fame. Dedicated to Louis XIV, it was reprinted at least nine times before Amelot's death in 1706 and was translated into English, German, Italian, Polish, and Russian. During the second half of the seventeenth century, Gracián and Amelot's combined literary creation signified a new chapter in the history of prudence, for this work became the most effective vehicle for popularization of the methods and practices of reason of state. In essence, it was a new work, and along with its new, French title, it found a new significance. Building on Norbert Elias's characterization of the work as the "first manual of court psychology," Roger Chartier sees Amelot's book as a reflection of a new competitive court society in which courtly social rationality served to calculate human relations and prestige.[57] He places *L'Homme de cour* in a schema of the "process of civilization," in which individual behavior slowly became more controlled and calculated. According to Chartier, behavioral control and dissimulation are the most important elements in Amelot's *L'Homme de cour*.[58] Through this method of personal sociology, the individual learns to hide inner thoughts or emotions. This "contained," domesticated self is the basis of Elias's genealogy of the modern individual.

Certainly, Amelot's work represents wide fascination with the courtly "fetish of prestige." But, as Chartier points out, its intended audience was ambiguous. If one reads *L'Homme de cour* in the context of Amelot's other publications between 1683 and 1686, it emerges less as a simple tool of self-control and dissimulation than as a guide to reading and social behavior. It is a lens through which to view the mechanics of social power used by kings and courtiers alike. Whereas *Tibère* revealed the workings of tyranny and *La Morale* examined the relationship between tyranny and courtly flattery, *L'Homme de cour* taught individual reason of state and the methods to see through it.

When reading Lastanosa's preface to Gracián's *El Discreto* (1646), Amelot was fascinated by its ambiguous Lipsian nature. Who, he asked, was the author of Gracián's works, Gracián or Lastanosa?[59] Amelot had found a kindred spirit in Lastanosa, whose prefaces he cites in his preface to *L'Homme de cour*. Like Lastanosa, Amelot announces that he, too, will name and rearrange Gracián's work, giving it new meaning: "I have changed its Title to that of the *Homme de cour,* which, besides the fact that it is less ostentatious and less hyperbolic, better explains the quality of the Book, which is a sort of Rudiment of the Court and of Political-Code."[60] This book is only for courtiers, he assures the reader. Yet, as in *La Morale de Tacite,* Amelot contradicts himself in his preface, tipping off the reader that even the title of his work must be read critically. *L'Homme de cour,* he says, "is a Man-of-the-Cabinet, who only whispers in the ear." He adds, "one must be very fine not to let anything escape." In Amelot's view, Gracián is an unintelligible author;

his works were written "not to be understood."[61] The implication of Amelot's argument is that the reader will clearly have to be careful and critical, for in the court and in books, things are not always what they seem.

Amelot cites Lastanosa's introduction to the *Discreto*, in which the nobleman warns of the danger of "reason of state of the self." Lastanosa explains that the countess of Aranda had complained that Gracián's works would make public the maxims of prudence to the lowest "plebeyo."[62] But Lastanosa assures the reader that this is not the case—that the "sublime" and "arcane" nature of the "materials" will ensure that Gracián's writings will remain "mysterious."[63] Amelot agreed that only the truly sophisticated reader would be able to decipher Gracián's manual. That is precisely, he claims, why his version has been designed to clarify the book for a wide audience.

> The knowledgeable Countesse of Aranda (Dona Luisa de Padilla), whose name has been set in writing by six immortal pens, worried that such important matters, which are only appropriate for true Heros, would become common by the printing of this book; so that the most lowly bourgeois could obtain for one ecu things, which due to their excellence, should never be found in such hands. . . . In this way, although the Works of Gracián are printed, they are not really common, for in buying them, one does not buy the means to understand them. Everyone can see the feast that he serves, but few can partake of it: perhaps he only wanted to whet everyone's appetite. For, as he himself says, to write only for a skillful audience, is to hook the bait for the general public, for that is what each person hopes to be, and feels the desire to become.[64]

Amelot's goal was to undo the mystery of Gracián's manual. He cites a passage from Lastanosa's introduction to Gracián's *El Héroe* (1646): "Here in this book, you will have a Reason-of-State of yourself [Raison-d'État de vous même], and a compass that will guide you to rise through the door of Excellence."[65] This is Amelot's final insistence. The *Oráculo*, or *L'Homme de cour*, is a manual for a "reason of state of the self." Amelot's handy, annotated edition with a table and glossary of maxims has made the book easy to use. Readers need not feel intimidated by this work, for it has been mapped out for them. In the end, Amelot says, Gracián is "the perfect Tacitus," and Tacitus, as Amelot has already told us, is a tool to be used against tyrants. Thus, *L'Homme de cour* was the perfect tool to collapse the boundary between private and public prudence.

But it was not enough for Amelot to tell his readers to use personal reason of state. He had to do for individuals what early Tacitists did for kings: he had to make them into textual critics. Thus, along with his strategy of reediting great works of political criticism, Amelot also needed to teach his readers how to apply a critical eye to the reading of Tacitus, history books, and even social behavior. To do this, he would turn to the ancient tradition of political commentary and criticism and take them to heights unknown before the advent of Bayle's *Dictionary*. Much as Protestants had reformed the reading of the Scriptures, Amelot now sought a popular reformation in political reading.

6. THE MACHIAVELLIAN REFORMATION
Critical Technologies of Reading
and the Culture of Personal Prudence

From its ascendancy in late antiquity, the Catholic Church regulated which books were to form its holy canon, who had the right to read them, and how to read in general. As passionate as St. Augustine felt about reading, his *Confessions* represent the church's long obsession with limiting the reading of the faithful. Turn away from Aristotle and books of futile secular learning, Augustine ordered, and focus on faith alone.[1] Augustine's books became the staples of medieval reading, and his paradoxically Ciceronian treatise *De doctrina Christiana* set the rules for the reading of sanctioned Christian texts.[2] But Augustine closed many great books to the readers of the Middle Ages. Despite the early dynamism of Augustinian hermeneutics and St. Jerome's vision of faith as an act of reading, the later scholastic tradition was prone to be formulaic.[3] In many cases, reading consisted of memorizing endless deductive syllogisms that worked as trustworthy proofs of interpretive orthodoxy. To aid students in the mastery of vast amounts of literature, new technologies of reading and interpretation flourished, as practices of note taking, textual organization, and compilation developed in the fertile ground of the monastic scriptorium. Ironically, these technologies of reading could serve as interpretive controls, guiding the reader while nonetheless facilitating the dissemination of information. In any case, schoolmen sought to protect dogma by forbidding unsanctioned reading. In *The Name of the Rose*, Umberto Eco's psychopathic scholastic monk, the venerable Jorge, quotes the last lines of the last book of the New Testament—Revelation—to justify shutting away and finally burning his monastery's collection of classical texts.

For I testify unto every man that heareth the words of the prophecy of this book. If any man shall add unto these things, God shall add unto him the plagues that are written in this book; and if any man shall take away from the words of the book of this prophecy, God shall take away his part out of the book of life, and out of the holy city, and from the things which are written in this book.[4]

While no doubt dramatic, this is a stark warning to all readers of the Scriptures.

In part, Renaissance humanism changed this puritanical tradition of censorship. While humanist pedagogy remained a mind-numbing experience of serial memorization, humanist critical-reading practices nonetheless complicated the smooth passage of dogma from official priests to the faithful. In some cases, humanism turned readers into individual critics, using philology not to bolster the monolith of the Scriptures but to understand them as dynamic historical products.[5] From the very beginning, the humanist revolution in reading practices shook the foundations of the church and the concept of authority.

Indeed, reading was at the very basis of the Reformation that split Christendom. Martin Luther was not just a religious dissenter; he was a reformer of reading—although after the bloody peasant uprisings in 1524, he questioned his own popular program of sacred reading that spread the basic practices of textual interpretation.[6] When he set out, in 1529, to translate the Bible into German vernacular, his goal was to render the Scriptures into a language that common people could read and understand.[7] While he was not truly a humanist critic, Luther was a student of Erasmus, the greatest reader of the Renaissance and a radical reformer of religious reading practices. The master and, by association, the student were products and propagators of the pious reading practices that spread in the northern Netherlands in the fourteenth and fifteenth centuries, promoted by Erasmus's teachers, the Brethren of the Common Life, who saw Bible reading and humility as the foundations of Christian salvation. The Brethren believed that people needed to read the Scriptures effectively to save their souls. This movement of Christian pedagogy was the spark that began the northern Renaissance and later lit the stage of the Protestant Reformation.

The Reformation, the Counter-Reformation, and the cataclysmic wars they inspired were, in part, conflicts over the culture of reading. The Catholic Church struggled to preserve its role as a textual guide and interpreter for the believer. The Bible was in Latin, the language of a small, educated elite. When the church issued the *Index of Forbidden Books,* in 1564, one of its major concerns was to ban vernacular translations of the Bible and guarantee the church's monopoly on reading.[8] Latin and textual criticism were the high walls that kept rabble and subversives from attacking Rome's authoritative reading of the Scriptures. In 1546 the fourth session of the Council of Trent announced:

No one relying on his own skill shall—in matters of faith and morals . . . wresting the sacred Scriptures to his own senses, presume to interpret the said sacred Scripture contrary to that sense which holy mother Church—whose it is to judge of the true sense and interpretation of the holy Scriptures—hath held and doth hold; or even contrary to unanimous consent of the Fathers.[9]

The pope's gatekeepers were trained textual interpreters, and to attain salvation, the believer had to pay the gatekeeper. This angered Luther. Protestants protested against the church's monopoly on scriptural interpretation by publishing vernacular versions of the Bible during the 1530s. If salvation came through personal reading, then certain strains of Protestantism implied more widespread reading. Followers of Calvin and Zwingli believed that individuals had to cultivate their own relationships with God and that, to do this, they needed to hold the Bible in their own hands and read it themselves.[10]

One hundred years later, in the face of this cultural revolution, the seventeenth-century church still saw reading as a reserve for the chosen few. The heritage of the Council of Trent was about retaining textual control, not providing access.[11] In *The Sanctuary Closed to the Profane, or The Bible Defended against the Vulgar* (1651), Nicolas Le Maire confidently maintained the old line that "one of the most important practices of the Church . . . consists in concealing the mysteries from the unworthy and distancing the profane from the sanctuary."[12] In other words, the church needed to keep the faithful from interpreting—or even reading—the Bible on their own terms, without firm, authoritative guidance. Yet this fundamental principle of religious authority was increasingly a source of conflict within the French Catholic Church. While Louis XIV's independent-minded confessor, Fénélon, believed that pious readers should be docile and uncritical, there were other French Catholics—Jansenists and Gallicans—who did not accept the ultimate interpretive authority of Rome or of its select elite.[13] The Jansenist monks of Port Royal designed a more accessible liturgy, and important Gallican prelates such as Achilles de Harlay de Champvallon, who translated Tacitus for Anne of Austria, supported pastoral missions that promoted reading and writing.[14] What better way was there to limit Roman authority—freeing the French from the ultramontane yoke—than by teaching the tools of salvation, reading and writing? Yet Louis XIV himself counterattacked against the popularization of Bible reading, pressuring the papacy to publish the *Unigenitus Bull* (1713), which condemned Jansenism and affirmed that the Scriptures be read only under the strict guidance of the church.

In retrospect, it seems extraordinary that as late as 1713, Louis and the church believed that they could turn the tide of personal reading that had been furthered by the explosive invention of the printing press and the rise of humanist reading and personalized piety. It was a losing battle. Not only did the movement of personal reading spread, but seventeenth-century Bible scholars promoted a new and sophisticated textual criticism that threatened the Scriptures' status as an infallible text.[15] Baruch Spinoza led the first effective charge of atheism when he attacked the historical veracity of miracles.

Through a critical reading of the Scriptures, he argued that the Bible was a purely historical text, produced only as a tool for the maintenance of power and authority.[16] The full force of philology reared its hydra head as critics transformed the tools of humanism into the basis of atheism. By the mid-seventeenth century, Catholic scholars counterattacked Protestantism and Spinozist atheism with their own brand of Bible criticism. Most notably, Richard Simon's *Critical History of the Old Testament* (1678) looked to undermine the Protestant claim that salvation could be attained *sola scriptura,* through personal reading alone.[17] The Scriptures, he showed, were full of imperfections and tricky allegories; thus, without a "divinely inspired interpreter," one could never hope to find the true path to salvation. "La seule et véritable Écriture se trouve dans l'Église," (The only true Writing is found in the Church) for the very nature of biblical truth, he maintained, was not the Bible but the church itself.[18] However, Simon's creative defense of the church's authority backfired, for both Protestants and Catholics alike considered his critical approach dangerous.[19] Not surprisingly, Rome banned Simon's commentaries and condemned him for having cast doubt on the veracity of the Scriptures and for subjecting them to rationalist modes of verification.

COMMENTARY *From Sacred Reading to Political Criticism*

The practice of textual commentary, the central facet of humanist reading and criticism, had long been a staple of medieval scholastic scholarship. From the twelfth century onward, university education consisted of a professor reading aloud his own commentary on a holy book in a *lecture*—meaning, literally, "a reading." Students would then copy these lectures into their own notebooks, which as we have seen in the case of commonplaces, were the essential tool of reading. Here they also wrote their own commentaries of major texts, which in Latin were called *lectura.*[20] These practices were not only part of the apparatus of learning; they were also the foundation of a major learned industry within the church. University-trained scholars made their mark—and sometimes their living—by publishing commentaries on the Bible, patristic works, and legal, medical, and other texts. These glosses were lenses attached to the primary texts, which acted as built-in interpretive guides. Medieval scholars worked to handle and mediate the huge amount of manuscript information amassed by scribes and scholars. They were the first to create the modern textual technologies of criticism, the study guides to commentary, which were designed to digest the information overload of the late Middle Ages.[21] Cistercian monks worked tirelessly to create the interpretive frameworks for managing manuscripts, frameworks essential for commentary. They organized manuscript texts through sections, headings, indexes, tables, concordances, summaries, and abridgments.[22] By rationalizing textual presentation, they created a physical, textual framework to aid the reader in critical analysis.

At the end of the sixteenth century, when the monotonous mantras of scholasticism receded into a distant echo in the halls of the universities, the practice of commentary remained strong, forming the practical basis of humanist studies. Classical humanists turned commentary back against scholasticism, filling their margins not with deductions but, in the best cases, with accurate historical emendations, corrections, source references, and proofs.[23] This was a crucial link between religious modes of textual mediation and intervention and a new secular world of human and natural knowledge.[24] As we have seen, Renaissance lawyers, such as Jacques Cujas and Jean Bodin, seeking to establish political and legal authority, emended the legal code through extensive philological commentaries and exegesis. By transforming what had been in many cases a religious hermeneutical practice, they were continuing and expanding the scope of what Lorenzo Valla had begun in 1440 in his revolutionary textual commentary *Declamation on the Donation of Constantine.* Indeed, as in the case of Valla's work, glosses could become primary texts of their own.[25] One of the premier best sellers of the Renaissance, Erasmus's *Adages* (1500), was a vast series of commentaries, extracts, and maxims.[26] Its editorial success illustrated that secondhand texts—commentaries and extracts—were a favorite of a reading market that had been formally trained in the art of extraction and compilation.[27]

Thus, historical philology and critical-reading practices evolved out of textual commentary. As Anthony Grafton shows in his history of historical epistemology, *The Footnote* (1997), the marginal emendations of philology crossed reading practices with a culture of proof and gave birth to the modern footnote, the cornerstone of the edifice of modern scholarly knowledge. Philology replaced the anonymous collections and commentaries of the Middle Ages with the individual mediations and interventions of Renaissance readers. Within the humanist political tradition, Tacitism was the primary repository of practices of commentary. Carlus Paschalius and Lipsius used gloss to help readers extract and understand the "fruit" of Tacitus's text, and they were followed by generations of Tacitists across Europe. Tacitism was the political equivalent of the religious reading tradition, and more than any other tradition, it turned politics into a set of discursive, interpretive practices.

If Amelot de La Houssaye wanted to be the new Lipsius, he, too, would have to read and write like a good humanist and a skilled Bible critic. The Jesuit-trained corrector was prepared for this task, but if he wanted to expose the mechanics of tyranny by creating a new genre of personal reason-of-state literature, he would have to tweak the old practice of commentary, pushing it toward pure expositional pedagogy.[28] His marginal notes would have to clearly show his reader how to read historical texts to gain personal, political wisdom. If religion could be made personal through personal reading, could the same be done to secular history? Was it possible to create a private, individual realm of historical and political reading and criticism? Amelot clearly thought so, and he set about creating a textual apparatus to achieve this political reformation. He would have to create a perfect gloss of political revelation to teach his readers to read in the critical manner described by Machiavelli. Once and for all, he intended to fulfill the challenge laid out in the introduction to Machiavelli's *Discourses* and show that humanist reading practices could be used as a tool for political criticism.

In his groundbreaking study of the culture of Tacitism, Jürgen von Stackelberg called Amelot de La Houssaye a "Tacitomaniac."[29] Amelot's works had so many marginal references to Tacitus that his practice reached the heights of a mania—a mad optic through which Amelot saw political authors. Indeed, Amelot often saw Tacitus where he was not. In the margins of Amelot's version of *The Prince* are written eighty-eight maxims from Tacitus that Amelot claimed had inspired Machiavelli. No one has ever proven whether these claims are accurate. But to call Amelot a Tacitomaniac obscures the significance of his achievement, for despite his methodical enthusiasm, he had not lost control of the Lipsian practices of commentary and annotation. Rather, he had harnessed them for an intricate exercise in writing between the lines. Amelot wrote his marginal notes in *The Prince* not simply to prove that Machiavelli was the heir to Tacitus; he did it to illustrate the correct, critical way of reading Machiavelli. In doing so, he went beyond Lipsius to create a technological apparatus with which to teach his readers to see through the dissimulations of the prince, an apparatus that he hoped would nail down the meaning of Machiavelli on the side of political critics. Where Protestants had taught Bible reading for personal piety, Amelot would now teach reading for secular personal prudence in the public sphere. His goal was political reformation, and the text he chose to use as a weapon was, appropriately, Machiavelli's *The Prince*.

During his internal exile in Frédéric Léonard's print shop between 1677 and 1683, Amelot had come up with a new and more effective editorial approach to publishing political criticism. Like any first model, the *History of the Government of Venice* had some obvious glitches. It was a long work, filled with various secondary texts, commentaries, entirely separate works, and pamphlets. Therefore, it was unwieldy and often unclear. More than a book, it was really a portfolio of documents, and despite Amelot's glossaries and operating directions, it was still hard to use. The *History of the Government of Venice* was both too complicated and too blunt at the same time. Indeed, the book had landed him in the Bastille. Amelot needed to streamline his new authorial practice and protect himself.

Drawing on a rich arsenal of discursive and editorial practices, Amelot now developed a strategy to create critical editions out of the works of other authors. He produced new versions of works by Tacitus, Machiavelli, Sarpi, and Gracián. By writing commentaries, Amelot realized his political philosophy. These authors would provide large portions of text—the fuel of criticism—while also shielding Amelot from clear authorial responsibility. He would then create critical editions out of these existing works. An early modern precursor to a postmodern author, he hoped not to be seen as the author of his own works. He used methods from humanist reading and correcting, manuscript editing, and commercial printing to construct his textual apparatus for political criticism.[30] Like a theater director, his first act of creation was choosing which work to use. Machiavelli's *The Prince* was the premier book of political criticism. In choosing to reedit it, Amelot declared himself the standard-bearer of French political criticism.

REFORMING MACHIAVELLI

One of the great mysteries of the history of political philosophy is whether Machiavelli was a monarchist or a republican. When Machiavelli states in chapter 18 of *The Prince* that "a prudent ruler cannot keep his word,"[31] it is impossible to tell for sure whether this is counsel for princes or an unmasking of tyrannical methodology. Machiavelli—in true form—never publicly debated *The Prince*, which was not published in his lifetime. No matter what his intentions were, once his book was published in Rome five years after his death in 1532, its meaning remained ambiguous. For at least 250 years, between the Renaissance and the Enlightenment, Machiavellians and anti-Machiavellians, monarchists and Jesuits, and Calvinists and republicans wrote numerous treatises addressing the question. The only way to decipher Machiavelli's intentions was to read his text carefully, and even then, skilled readers came to opposing conclusions about its meaning. This tradition continues to this day.

It is easy to imagine why Richelieu and Rousseau read *The Prince* in different ways. One was the seventeenth-century master of royal absolutism, the other an Enlightened and impoverished former Calvinist, a pioneering visionary of popular democracy. As such, they represent opposing poles of European reading traditions and two conflicting ages of politics. But perhaps their differing interpretations of Machiavelli were not solely the products of their own personal worldviews. Indeed, it is possible that Richelieu and Rousseau were not reading the same book. No one has ever asked if the French edition of *The Prince* of 1600 is the same as that of 1683 or that of 1760. Were these the same static texts, or were they distinct books with their own meanings? The editions of *The Prince* found in Montesquieu's personal library at La Brède illustrate that different editions of *The Prince* could present opposing interpretations. His collection contains three different editions of *The Prince,* from 1600, 1613, and 1684.[32] The editions are neither rare nor particularly fine. What distinguishes them is that each one is a different edition by a different translator or editor. The 1600 edition contains anti-Machiavellian commentaries, while Amelot de La Houssaye's 1684 edition is a defense of Machiavelli. Montesquieu was not a bibliophile; he was a historian of ideas and, above all, a well-trained reader. He took into account important editorial differences often ignored by modern historians of political theory. He knew that there were many different editions of *The Prince* and that some had distinctly different meanings. One assumes that he read his copies of *The Prince* as distinctly different versions of the same book.

Like many commentators before him, Amelot's goal in publishing *The Prince* was to lift the veil of the book's traditional ambiguity. His reading would irrevocably push Machiavelli into the corner of political subversion. Published in Amsterdam by Henry Wetstein, Amelot's version of *The Prince* was a commercial success. It was reedited by Wetstein at least five times before his death in 1706—twice in 1683; once in 1684, 1686, and 1694—and was reedited more than fifteen times in the eighteenth century. These were exclusively small duodecimo editions, published cheaply, presumably in large daily printing runs of between eight hundred and twelve hundred or fifteen hundred copies. Beyond the bold statement of translating and commenting on *The Prince,* Amelot's preface is an extraordinary defense of Machiavelli, which claims that Machiavelli has been misunderstood as a friend of tyranny, when, in fact, his only goal was to criticize and expose the sins of absolute monarchs. The lone protector of the critical tradition, Amelot was the only Frenchman openly defending Machiavelli in late seventeenth-century Paris. It is hard to tell if this was an act of courage or folly. In any case, Amelot had joined his destiny to that of the great master of secular political science.

That Machiavelli's critics had misunderstood him only proved the need for a clarifying exegesis. Amelot argued that Machiavelli, like Tacitus, was a difficult author, impossible to truly understand without a proper guide, well trained in the art of extracting sentences of political wisdom out of the text.

> Since Machiavelli is an author who is neither used by, nor accessible to many people, one should not be surprised if the Vulgar is so prejudiced against him. I say prejudiced. Because all those who censure him, you will find, will admit that they have never read him: and that others who say that they have read him, never truly understood him, as it clearly appears from the literal sense that they assign to certain passages, which real *Politiques* know how to interpret in another way. . . .[33]

Was there a correct way to read Machiavelli? Amelot does not clearly say, but if one pieces together the context of what he says, it is clear that Amelot is trying to teach the reader to read Machiavelli as a tool for political criticism. In his possibly ironic dedication to the Medici grand duke of Tuscany, Amelot asserts that Machiavelli is useful for his maxims of reason of state, in particular because he "borrowed most of them from Tacitus."[34] As we know from *Tibère,* published in 1683 (only months before *The Prince*), Tacitus is a lens for understanding tyranny. From the preface, we can deduce that Amelot saw Machiavelli as a tool for personal prudence.

A FRUITFUL READING OF TACITUS

The foundation stone of the Reformation was the personal vernacular Bible. Because it was affordable, many readers could purchase it, and because it was small, it could be read anywhere. Popular piety was about this personal access to the text, and it implied a level of appropriation. Traditionally, appropriation meant making the text one's own through textual intervention and memorization. With a personal copy of a book, a reader could make manuscript annotations, commenting on a work or noting passages of personal interest for future reference. In his *Ways of Reading Fruitfully,* the Jesuit Francesco Sacchini recommends numerous methods for annotating printed works, particularly the Bible. He offers a series of manuscript symbols to use in texts to serve as guides to memory.[35]

> I believe that it is more useful to write in the exterior margins of the page an abridgment of that which is the most beautiful in the text; if one does it with intelligence, one can, in a short hour, be reminded of all that is most important in a voluminous book.
> There are those who have the habit of writing certain arbitrary marks, to indicate different things that offer themselves up as worthy of being collected; this method has its advantages, and takes its approach from that of the ancients. Suidas tells us how Suetonius wrote a work from markings that he found in ancient books; in [Diogenes] Laertes, one can see the role these markings once played in Plato, some to designate phrases, others to indicate beautiful sentences; just like the signs written to show accord with certain dogmas, and other signs to show what one needed to correct, or to reject.[36]

Sacchini justifies this interventionist form of reading by placing its origins in ancient practices. Suetonius, Aristarchus, Cicero, Origen, and St. Jerome all used annotations in texts as interpretive guides. Following the ancients, Sacchini argues, the modern reader should also use annotations to navigate the giant historical compendia produced by compilers. While Jerome explained how Origen had used horizontal lines in the margin to note a passage of interest, Sacchini, for his part, thought it best to write a cross to mark a moral sentence and an "O" for a remarkable phrase.[37]

Annotating a text had advantages beyond making a printed text easier to navigate. Sacchini noted that once a book was marked, the reader could skip through its pages and extract the most useful passages, or the "fruit" of the text, in order to compose compilations, as Erasmus had famously done in the *Adages*.

> It is from [writing extracts] that come the books called *Variantes,* ancient lessons, mélanges, the most curious collections, summaries, compilations, *journaux* and other similar books. If these books are made by someone else's hand, they are useful, but how much more useful they would be if we made them ourselves![38]

Once works were prepped with notes, the reader could go back, find and extract the passages of interest, and recompose them into new independent works. Of course, Sacchini was careful to insist that these practices be used only on sanctioned holy works, noting that critical active reading was dangerous if used outside the proscribed boundaries of orthodoxy.

Amelot had been exposed to multiple traditions of humanist annotation. Instilled with the Jesuit ideal of textual intervention, he had practiced these skills professionally as an editor in Frédéric Léonard's shop, but good Tacitist that he was, he did not hesitate to use them in the realm of secular philosophy. Annotation and commentary were the stock practices of his trade. Now he would turn them toward his project of personal prudence. He would use the old technique of annotating in order to create a manageable, personal version of Machiavelli's *The Prince*.

Probably while perusing the bookstalls during his time in Venice, Amelot purchased a critical edition of the works of Tacitus, *C. Corn. Tacitus, et in eum M. Z. Boxhornii et H. Grotii observationes* (1645).[39] Adding to the printed annotations of Van Boxhorn and Hugo Grotius, Amelot filled this book with hundreds of his own manuscript notes and commentaries and with an extensive system of numerical reference markings. These annotations are found on more than 90 percent of Tacitus's text, turning Tacitus's book into a personal notebook. They show precisely how Amelot used an amplified, systematic version of traditional humanist reading practices to create an innovative hermeneutical framework for extracting political information from Tacitus. He hoped to teach his readers how to use his own textual method for extracting political wisdom.

Amelot not only used crosses and "O's"; he created an extensive system of numerical annotations. Almost every page is covered with numbers, which are found sometimes on the printed text itself but mostly in the margins. He wrote numerical annotations not only on the text but on the index as well.[40] On average, each page contains fifteen numerical annotations. By multiplying the average fifteen numerical annotations a page times the 668 pages of the principal text, we come to a presumed total of 10,020 numerical annotations. This was not a mania; it was a pseudoscience.[41]

Amelot's numerical annotations serve as reading guides to navigating the text, cross-referencing between similar subjects and words. A numerical annotation is usually found in the margin of a line of text. Often, the particular word being referenced is underlined with black ink or red pencil; then, in the margin across from it, the same word is found with the corresponding page number in the margin.[42] In some cases, to aid in matching the numerical reference with the intended word, the marginal reference has a letter, a cross, or a symbol written next to it, which corresponds to the same symbol written next to a word in the printed text.[43] Amelot's use of this manuscript corrector's print practice gives the impression that he considered his annotations to be permanent additions to the printed text—additions that would facilitate future use of the book as an easy reference manual.[44] In effect, Amelot had created a new book out of his old, 1645 edition of Tacitus's *Works*.

For Amelot, Tacitus's text was a tool chest of examples, which he reordered in the fashion of a commonplace book. Rather than simply translating Tacitus's works, Amelot maneuvered around the text with the aid of his manuscript signposts, translating some words, but mostly, as we shall see, looking for examples that he could use as maxims and illustrations. Amelot's numerical annotations act like a computerized cross-referencing system, unifying the five different books in his edition of Tacitus's *Works* into a single source of maxims. His annotations give his edition the quality more of a primitive CD-ROM than of a compact Venetian book.

Not just a source of references, Amelot's homemade manual, filled with personal notes and moral messages, also had the intimate dimension of a personal Bible. He clearly used it for moments of personal inspiration. In the margins of the "Index scriptorum," Amelot writes, "L'histoire nous aprend à mesurer les afaires au tems, et le tems aux afaires" (History teaches us to measure events by the times, and the times by events). Equally, on the first page of the *Annales,* we see a moral note—quoted ironically enough from the Ciceronian René Rapin—that Amelot appears to have written to himself: "As soon as one involves oneself with writing, one must place oneself above opposition and fear, to have the force to always write the truth."[45] Here, hewn from the original text with Lipsian precision, was a manual for personal prudence. More important, here is the key moment when Amelot transformed a private reading, his hand-annotated copy of Tacitus, into a public object—his version of *The Prince.*

RE-PRESENTING *THE PRINCE*

Not simply a private reader, Amelot was a secular evangel who attempted to reveal the mechanics of criticism to his readers much like reformers in Geneva had done with the Bible a century earlier. To spread his critical gospel, he still had to transform his personal reading of Tacitus's maxims into a public "lecture." *The Prince* would serve as a canvas on which he would superimpose and reveal his personal, critical reading. First, his notes in *The Prince* seek to prove that Machiavelli was the heir to Tacitus.

> Now since Machiavelli has, for the most part, borrowed them [his political maxims] from Tacitus, the Master and oracle to Princes, I have cited the passages of this author, so that one can touch with their finger, [the fact that] Machiavelli is nothing but his disciple, and his interpreter.[46]

Second, Amelot uses his notes to simulate his ideal critical reading for the reader. They not only constitute a step-by-step interpretive guide that shows how to read Machiavelli as Tacitus; they also work as historical proofs of the validity of Machiavellian prudence.

> Outside of several Notes, taken from the other Works of Machiavelli, and the Histories of Nardi and Guicciardini, I have placed under the text diverse passages from Tacitus, which serve as proof, confirmation, or example, to what Machiavelli says. And this makes a sort of concordance between these two Authors, by which one will see that one can neither approve, nor condemn one without the other; such that if Tacitus is worth reading for those, who need to learn the art-of-governing, Machiavelli is no less; one teaching how the Roman Emperors governed, and the other how one governs today.[47]

Amelot's translation of *The Prince* (1683) is annotated on a grand scale. There are 442 concordances with Tacitus; thirty with Machiavelli's other works; nine with Pliny the Younger; six with Paterculus; six with Nardi; six with Gracián; three with the Bible (with Exodus, Psalms, and Kings, respectively); two each with Commines, Gaspard d'Auvergne, Guicciardini, Plutarch, Seneca, and Virgil; and one each with Bocaccio, Cicero, Diogenes, La Rochefoucauld, Mézeray, Sallust, Sarpi, Thucydides, the Chevalier de Temple, Livy, and Xenophon. There are sixty-nine general notes concerning questions of translation and detailed historical explanations. All the cited passages are quoted in their original and in French, and many are briefly discussed.

The references to Tacitus come directly out of Amelot's Tacitean manual. Much like an adult teaches a child how to write by taking the hand of the child and tracing the forms of letters, Amelot wanted to take his readers step-by-step through the critical process. Thus, he wrote his footnotes to *The Prince* to coax his readers through the text, teaching them to read exactly like he had done. On page 6, we find one such footnote.

Car, au dire de Paterculus, l'on encherit toujours sur les premiers exemples. *Non enim ibi consistunt exempla undè cœperunt, sed quamlibet in tenuem recepta tramitem latissimè evagandi sibi viam faciunt.* (Hist. 2.) Qu'une mutation en entraine toujours d'autres aprês soi, Tacite en donne de beaux éxemples. *Libertatem et Consulatum L. Brutus instituit. Dictatura ad tempus sumebantur. Neque Tribunorum Militum Consulare jus diu valuit. Non Cinne, non Sulla longa dominatio: et Pompeii Crassique potentia cito in Cæsarem: Lepidi, atque Antonii arma in Augustum cessere.* (Ann. 1.) C'est à dire: Brutus fit succeder la Liberté et le Consulat à la Roiauté. Et quelque fois on créoit un Dictateur, mais son pouvoir finisoit aussitot que le peuple étoit hors de danger. Les Décemvirs ne durérent pas plus de deux ans. Les Tribuns des Soldats prirent la place des Consuls, mais ne la gardérent pas longtems. La domination de Cinna, ne la Dictature de Silla ne furent pas de longue durée. La puissance de Crassus et de Pompée fut bientôt réunie en la personne de César, et l'autorité de Lepidus et d'Antoine en celle d'Auguste. Voila un enchainement de mutations. En voici un autre. *Sulla Dictator abolitis vel conversis prioribus, cùm plura addidisset, otium ei rei haud in longum paravit. Statim turbidis Lepidi rogationibus, neque multo post Tribunis reddita licentia quoquò vellent populam agitandi. Jamque non modò in commune, sed in singulos homines lata quaestiones. . . . Exin continua per vigintii annos discordia, non Mos, non Jus.* (Ann. 3.) C'est-à-dire: Le Dictateur Sulla changea, ou abolit les Loix de Gracchus et de Saturninus, pour établir les siennes. Mais elles furent de peu de durée. Car Lepidus et les Tribuns recommencérent bientôt à semer des broüilleries parmi le peuple, en sorte qu'on faisoit autant de réglemens, qu'il y avoit d'hommes. . . . Et depuis, il n'y eut ni droit, ni coutume, par l'espace de vingt ans, que durérent les dissensions du peuple et du Sénat.

The first Latin citation is on page 3 of the Juntas et Baba copy. In the margin beside the text, a reference to the page number "103" is written twice. If the reader turns to page 103, a second Latin citation is found, with the number "3" written in the margin next to its first line.[48] Thus, the reader follows the references in the same logic as they are annotated in Amelot's copy of Tacitus.

In the twenty-five examples of multiple thematic extracts from Tacitus in the footnotes of *The Prince,* twenty can be found to have numerical cross-references in the Juntas et Baba copy.[49] Thus, in reading *The Prince,* the reader is taken through Amelot's own reading of his homemade handbook. According to Amelot, if Machiavelli comes from Tacitus, here is the way to read both authors. Equating Machiavelli with Tacitus sends a clear message: Machiavelli, too, could be used for personal prudence and for unmasking tyranny. This was not a particularly republican Machiavelli; rather, it was a personal Machiavelli suited to "raison d'État de soi-même."

This new version of *The Prince* was clearly different from that of the beginning of the century. Amelot's extracts from Tacitus influenced the meaning of *The Prince* by emphasizing its critical possibilities. In note I on page 61, Amelot emphasizes the idea that excessive authority was dangerous. By matching his French translation of Machiavelli with a Latin quote from Tacitus, Amelot guides the reader toward interpreting the text in a very different way than if the text stood alone: "But ever since, the Duke [Cesare Borgia] feared that such excessive authority would become odious I. *Nec unquam satis fida potentia, ubi nimia est,* says Tacitus (Hist. 2.)."[50] He does the same thing in the following note on the same page, transforming Machiavelli's description of Cesare Borgia, the duke Valentino's strategy to deflect criticism of his atrocities by executing the responsible minister into a lesson about the perverse nature of princes and their vile ministers.

> And as he saw that the rigors of the past had brought down hatred on him, he decided, one morning, to assassinate Remiro [his evil henchman] by cutting him up, and to display the pieces of his Body on the Piazza di Cesena, nailed to the stake, with a bloody knife nearby, to show to the people, that the Cruelties committed, did not come from him, but from the natural violence of his Minister. 2. It is the normal practice of Princes to sacrifice, sooner or later, the instruments of their cruelty. *Scelerum Ministros,* says Tacitus of Tiberius, *ut perverti ab aliis nolebat: ita plerumque satiatus, veteres et prægraves adflixit.* (Ann. 4.) *Levi post admissum scelus gratia, dein graviore odio.* (Ann. 14.).[51]

Amelot casts Machiavelli not as a villain but as a critic of despotism. Clever publisher that he was, he knew that by claiming *The Prince* to be based almost entirely on the most popular classical historian of the age, he was equating Machiavelli with the historian embraced by generations of Bourbon kings.

TACITIST FOOTNOTES AND THE
PRUDENTIAL READING OF HISTORY

What Amelot did to Machiavelli, he also did to Sarpi, Gracián, and La Rochefoucauld. He Tacitized them, possibly using his manual. His editions of all these authors contain numerous references to Tacitus, and in each case, he claimed that he had created new critical editions to illustrate how to read these older works in a new way. Five years after *The Prince*, Amelot transformed La Rochefoucauld into a manual for reading history with a political eye and extracting maxims for political prudence. Earlier, in 1686, in his "Discours critique," published as a prefatory text to *La Morale de Tacite,* Amelot had claimed that La Rochefoucauld's *Mémoires contenant les brigues pour le gouvernement à la mort de Loüys XIII, et de la guerre de Paris* (1662)[52] was a commentary on the works of Tacitus, applied to the period of Anne of Austria's regency.[53] He called La Rochefoucauld's memoirs a "relation" and La Rochefoucauld a perfect modern Tacitus: "I say without hesitation, that there has never been anything written in our language, which so resembles the character of Tacitus."[54]

As with Machiavelli, Amelot "proves" that La Rochefoucauld's maxims have been taken from Tacitus, by pairing three pages from the *Brigues* with corresponding maxims from Tacitus.[55] Eight passages extracted from La Rochefoucauld are paralleled with eleven concordances from Tacitus, which are found at the bottom of the page in the form of lettered source references.[56] One such parallel gives a sense of the distinctly critical flavor of the maxims he has chosen: "concord and power are incompatible in the same place: Arduam eodem loci potentiam et concordiam esse. *Ann.* 4."[57] La Rochefoucauld's authority is enhanced by that of Tacitus, rendering his work all the more "useful" as a source of applicable political prudence.

Two years after the first version of the "Discours critique," Amelot published his own Tacitean edition of La Rochefoucauld's *Brigues* under the title *Mémoires de la minorité de Louis XIV* (1688), realizing on a grand scale what he had briefly discussed in his "Discours." The text contains 345 footnoted concordances with Tacitus; nine with Paterculus; three with Pliny; and one each with Florus, Livy, and Sallust. Once again, Amelot wanted not only to prove the Tacitean genealogy of La Rochefoucauld but also to show his reader how to transform this primary historical document into a tool of personal prudence.

> It is to give some proofs that I have taken the time to put at the bottom of each page extracts from the Latin text of Tacitus, to show the conformity of his maxims with those of our Author.[58]

Amelot wrote his critical, historical notes to verify the applicability of La Rochfoucauld's work to current politics. Forty-nine historical notes in the margins either explain historical events mentioned by the text (e.g., giving their date) or give source references. On page 189, where Machiavelli is mentioned by La Rochefoucauld, Amelot adds a corresponding source reference in the margin. On pages 231 and 234, Amelot cites *La Vie de M. de Turenne* (1676) as a corroborative source for facts presented by La Rochefoucauld.[59] Thus, Amelot deftly joined the Lipsian sententious tradition with the old humanist pragmatic tradition of de Thou. He used Tacitus as a guide for reading contemporary history, then extracted modern examples from contemporary history to teach political prudence.

THE MATERIAL RHETORIC OF SUBVERSION
Pierre Bayle Reads Amelot

Michel de Certeau famously remarked that readers behave like poachers.[60] They enter into a textual territory (sometimes trespassing), and once there, they take what they want. The author, like a landowner, is rarely on hand to oversee the illicit hunt for information and its free interpretation—acts that are, by their very private nature, clandestine and uncontrollable. A Jesuit, de Certeau knew that readers made texts into their own creations by their personal readings. De Certeau's metaphor of the poacher could have been inspired by Carlo Ginzburg's celebrated study of the subversive miller Menocchio; the miller read sacred texts in a personal and critical way that threatened the church, which eventually burned him for his interpretations.[61] The Inquisitors were the "gamekeepers" of the vast theological reserve of the church, and they knew that without supervision, trespassing readers would find forbidden meaning in books.

It was surely his ability as a high-end textual poacher that made Pierre Bayle the most fascinating literary figure of the end of the seventeenth century. Significantly, the man who would be remembered as the most important philosopher of his day cast himself, first, not as an author of philosophy but as a reader and critic. Beginning in 1684, Pierre Bayle worked as a professional reader, publishing his groundbreaking scholarly journal *Nouvelles de la république des lettres*. In his monthly set of book reviews, Bayle was a human information bank, collecting works from across Europe and reviewing those that he considered particularly significant, summarizing their arguments and citing particular passages. At their most fundamental level, literary reviews have an aspect of poaching, for through the mediums of summary and critique, reviewers are able to synthesize and assign particular meanings to the works that they read. Yet Bayle did not just poach works. In the spirit of humanism, he also collected and re-presented information he deemed salient. Drawing from his expansive readings, Bayle began to collect the notes and references that he would spin together into the tapestry-like construction of his *Dictionary*.

While the metaphor of the poacher aptly characterizes the general practice of reading, it does not fully describe the complexities of humanism, for humanist readers were more like trespassing butterfly collectors than brutal game thieves. Pierre Bayle did not poach information solely for clandestine consumption. His ultimate objective was to display his poached materials to the public. In the end, Bayle's *Dictionary* is like a museum of specimens, hung together on pages much like the thematic shelves or rooms of a museum, collected and presented with the same obsessive lepidopteran pleasure so passionately evoked by Vladimir Nabokov.

This collage of information, taken in its entirety, was a bold statement of its own and became, twenty-five years after its first publication, the first best seller of the Enlightenment. The underpinning of Bayle's philosophy was to take as much evidence as possible from critical readings, put it all together, and find the contradictions and consistencies that allow the reader to undermine accepted truths. Bayle characterized this textual practice as "compilation" and was very conscious of how "commentaries" and extracts could compliment the writing of a primary narrative.[62] In the preface to the *Dictionary*, he writes,

> I have divided my narration into several Parts: one is purely Historical, a succinct Narration of Facts: the other is a great Commentary, a melange of Proofs, and of Discussions, to which I add the Censure of several Errors, and sometimes even a tirade of Philosophical Reflections: in short, enough variety to believe that in one place or another, each kind of Reader will find that for which they are looking.[63]

In this passage, Bayle justly describes what Henri-Jean Martin calls the art of the *mise en page*,[64] or the setting of texts on a page, and the *mise en livre*, the arrangement of various texts into a compilation. The passages Martin describes in modern terms were second nature to Bayle and to generations of humanists who were experts in critical, textual technology. Writing could be done through collages and compilations. Authors—the producers of meaning—worked by arranging these materials to fit their own discourse. Bayle crossed the style of the Tacitean, legal historical tradition with practices of antiquarianism.[65] He had a clear strategy for teaching the reader how to apply "proofs" to historical facts: "One must present proofs, and then one must examine them, confirm them and analyze them. In one word, this is a Work of Compilation."[66]

Lawrence Lipking has aptly termed Bayle's practice an "inductive model" of "perpetual commentary."[67] With a dose of anachronism, we can call this ancient practice "material rhetoric," for Bayle was simply writing by rearranging preexisting materials on a page. Bayle had a rhetorical agenda, and with it he bypassed the rhetorical critics of his time, leaving eloquence, arriving at induction, and constructing on the page itself a model of material rhetoric in which to house his narrative of proofs. But contrary to Lipking's assertion that Bayle was the "father of the Enlightenment,"[68] it is necessary to avoid the treacherous sands of hindsight and consider Bayle's material model of criticism in the historical context in which it functioned. Bayle was, above all, a seventeenth-century thinker, who, as the editor of the *Nouvelles*, scanned the scholarship of his time, looking for methods with which to construct his historical palace of doubt and proof. It is through Bayle's reviews in the *Nouvelles*, written seven years before he began the *Dictionary*, that we can understand the origins of Bayle's revolutionary model of commentary. Bayle was treading on well-worn paths, and while journeying through the forbidden territories of seventeenth-century textual criticism, he spied a veteran information collector, Amelot de La Houssaye.

In the July 1684 issue of the *Nouvelles de la république des lettres*, Pierre Bayle wrote a review of *L'Homme de cour*, his first review of a work by Amelot. He used the occasion to provide a brief overview of Amelot's publishing career, and he noted that he had read all of Amelot's works. Bayle's reviews of Amelot's works are useful at two levels. First, they tell us what Bayle thought of Amelot's works and how he read them. Second, because these were book reviews, they also show what Bayle thought that his own readers should take away from any given book. They reveal that Bayle read in a different way than modern historians of philosophy. He was attuned to Amelot's authorial strategies and to the methods Amelot used to transform books by other authors into his own creation. Bayle focused not only on what Amelot's books said but also on his prefaces and on how he used commentary and annotation.

Of course, Bayle was only following the readers' directions laid out by Amelot in the prefaces to his works. Following textual cues, Bayle read Amelot's works as an ongoing project, with each work complimenting the next. Although he never specifically reviewed *Tibère*, which appeared before Bayle started writing the *Nouvelles,* he was aware that this work contained a detailed manual on how to read Amelot's critical editions. Today, it is not the custom for scholarly authors to create innovative textual frameworks to present their research. Granted, some scholars produce CD-ROMS, and others offer up long annexes of primary materials. Some even create Web sites to make accessible their research and to give links to related materials. Yet today's pedagogical media apparatus is not always as complex as the textual technologies used by humanist authors. For them, the printed page had rich possibilities. Surely the page of Bayle's *Dictionary* is more complex and practical than any CD-ROM. Today, no book editor would allow an author of a book of political theory to design a unique page setting, with complex systems of annotation and a detailed user's manual in the place of a preface. It is also unlikely that they would publish a book made up almost entirely of detailed source references and commentaries. Yet critical, textual technology was on the cutting edge of intellectual culture during the seventeenth century, and, therefore, it interested Bayle. It was what Léonard sought to publish, and it was what concerned Amelot when writing his flagship translation of Tacitus, *Tibère,* in 1683.

Amelot's introduction to *Tibère* contains a set of directions that explain not only his Lipsian discursive method but also how to read the book itself. The first lines of the preface describe the practice of Tacitism, the art of extracting political maxims from the text of Tacitus to apply them to practical politics.

> For I have almost always compelled myself to comment on [Tacitus] with
> his own works, taking as an incontestable maxim, that the Commentator
> must never borrow from other enlightened sources [*lumières*], except from
> the very spirit of the Author on whom he is commenting, especially when it
> concerns someone who excels above all others, as does Tacitus in the realm

of Politics. Thus my Commentary is also a sort of Concordance of the best Axioms and Aphorisms of Tacitus, as is obvious when one looks at the passages that are in all the margins of this book. There one will also find passages from Pliny the Younger, to whom I refer all the more willingly since he was Tacitus's Companion in studies, and they served as Master to each other.[69]

Amelot tells his reader that to use Tacitus's text for political secrets, one must not only read the primary text but also closely follow the notes in the margins, which are the "key" to a political understanding of the work.

> For since the design, the order, and the words are of my fashioning, the precepts and the teachings which are aimed at Princes, their Ministers, and their Courtiers are almost all from Tacitus, as you will see, by the multitude of passages that I have put in the margins, which will serve as a key for entering into the highest mysteries of his Politics.[70]

If we ourselves examine pages from *Tibère*, we see the complex workings of Amelot's material rhetoric (figs. 5a and 5b). At the top of the page is found the original Latin passage from Tacitus, in large font, no longer than a phrase or a paragraph. Underneath, in italics, is Amelot's translation. Then, in smaller, normal font is Amelot's commentary, often constructed from other maxims from Tacitus, which can go on for pages. In the margins in small font are found numerous historical notes and maxims taken from Tacitus and other authors. Thus, following an ancient practice, Amelot annotated passages from Tacitus with other passages from Tacitus.[71]

In his second translation of Tacitus, *La Morale de Tacite* (1686), Amelot felt he needed to explain to the reader how to use his new system, so the reader would know beforehand how to maneuver the complex page.

> I end in warning the reader, that all the passages by Tacitus [in the margins] are marked by letters of the alphabet, and those by Pliny the Younger and Paterculus, by numbers; and the French notes by stars; . . . so that my text serves to elucidate my notes, and my notes reciprocally serve my text.[72]

More than simply a preface, which acted as a guide, Amelot also included analytical tools to help the reader navigate and personalize the text, making it an easy-to-use political reference manual. At the end of the *La Morale*, he includes a "Recapitulation of Sentences and Maxims of Tacitus concerning Flattery," a collection of fifty-seven maxims taken from all of Tacitus's works.[73] Amelot gives the reference from which each passage is taken by listing the work of Tacitus and chapter number. At the same time, he gives page references where the reader will find examples of the same subject. The reader can choose a thematic maxim from Tacitus and then find it developed

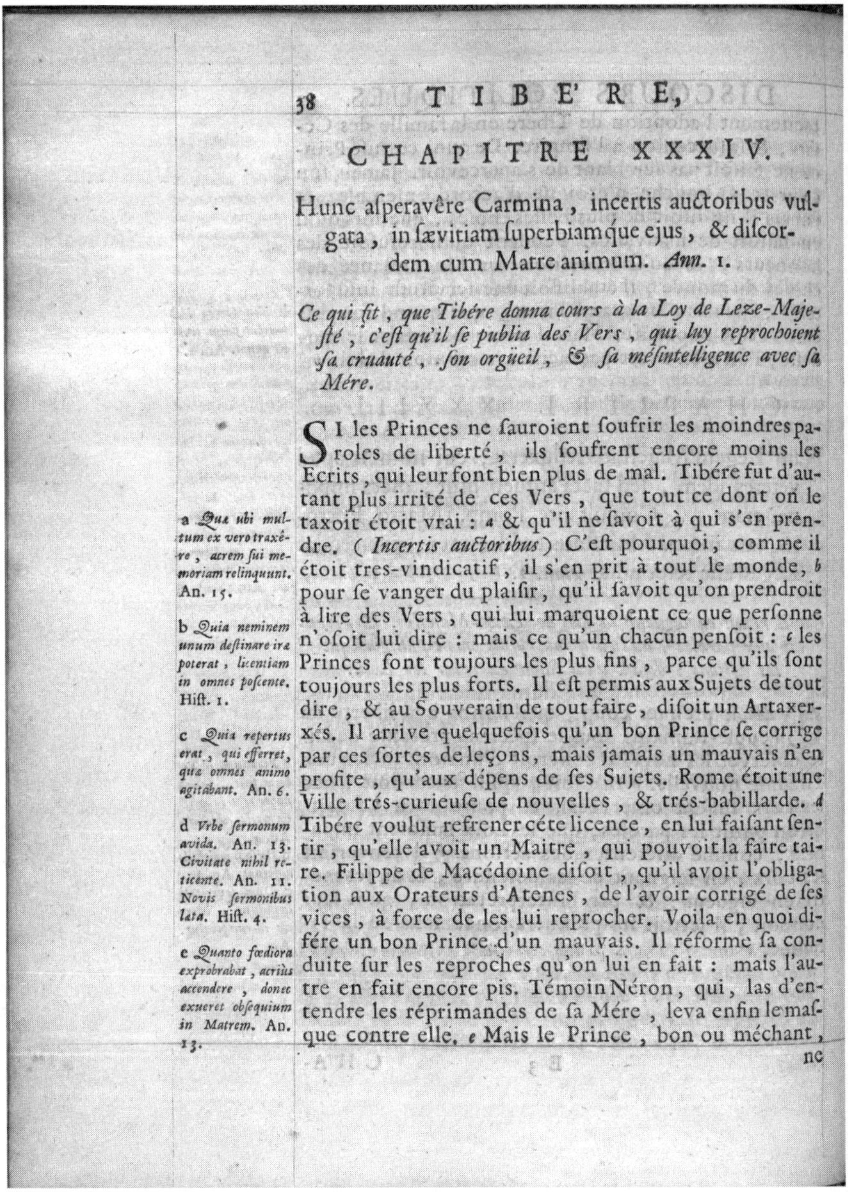

CHAPITRE XXXIV.

Hunc afperavêre Carmina, incertis auctoribus vulgata, in fævitiam fuperbiamque ejus, & difcordem cum Matre animum. *Ann.* 1.

Ce qui fit, que Tibére donna cours à la Loy de Leze-Maje-fté, c'eft qu'il fe publia des Vers, qui luy reprochoient fa cruauté, fon orgüeil, & fa méfintelligence avec fa Mére.

S I les Princes ne fauroient foufrir les moindres paroles de liberté, ils foufrent encore moins les Ecrits, qui leur font bien plus de mal. Tibére fut d'autant plus irrité de ces Vers, que tout ce dont on le taxoit étoit vrai : *a* & qu'il ne favoit à qui s'en prendre. (*Incertis auctoribus*) C'eft pourquoi, comme il étoit tres-vindicatif, il s'en prit à tout le monde, *b* pour fe vanger du plaifir, qu'il favoit qu'on prendroit à lire des Vers, qui lui marquoient ce que perfonne n'ofoit lui dire : mais ce qu'un chacun penfoit : *c* les Princes font toujours les plus fins, parce qu'ils font toujours les plus forts. Il eft permis aux Sujets de tout dire, & au Souverain de tout faire, difoit un Artaxerxés. Il arrive quelquefois qu'un bon Prince fe corrige par ces fortes de leçons, mais jamais un mauvais n'en profite, qu'aux dépens de fes Sujets. Rome étoit une Ville trés-curieufe de nouvelles, & trés-babillarde. *d* Tibére voulut refrener céte licence, en lui faifant fentir, qu'elle avoit un Maitre, qui pouvoit la faire taire. Filippe de Macédoine difoit, qu'il avoit l'obligation aux Orateurs d'Atenes, de l'avoir corrigé de fes vices, à force de les lui reprocher. Voila en quoi difére un bon Prince d'un mauvais. Il réforme fa conduite fur les reproches qu'on lui en fait : mais l'autre en fait encore pis. Témoin Néron, qui, las d'entendre les réprimandes de fa Mére, leva enfin le mafque contre elle. *e* Mais le Prince, bon ou méchant,

a Quæ ubi multum ex vero traxê-re, acrem fui memoriam relinquunt. An. 15.

b Quia neminem unum deftinare iræ poterat, licentiam in omnes pofcente. Hift. 1.

c Quia repertus erat, qui efferret, quæ omnes animo agitabant. An. 6.

d Vrbe fermonum avida. An. 13. *Civitate nihil re-ticente.* An. 11. *Novis fermonibus læta.* Hift. 4.

e Quanto fœdiora exprobrabat, acriùs accendere, donec exueret obfequium in Matrem. An. 13.

ne

Fig. 5. Abraham-Nicolas Amelot de La Houssaye, *Tibère: Discours politiques sur Tacite* (Amsterdam: Héritiers de Daniel Elzevier, 1683), pp. 38–39. (Courtesy of Annenberg Rare Book and Manuscript Library, University of Pennsylvania.)

ne doit jamais tolérer les Libelles difamatoires, d'autant que, sous couleur de le reprendre, ils font à ses
Sujets une leçon de mépris & de desobéissance. Et
c'est ce que vouloit dire le Roi Cléomenés en répon-
dant à celui qui disoit, que les Rois devoient être de-
bonnaires. Oui, si cela ne les fait pas méprifer. Au-
gufte receut en bonne part un billet, que Mécénas lui
fit aler de main en main dans le Sénat, contenant ces
mots, *fors d'ici, Boureau.* Car céte correction ne paf-
foit qu'à lui, & c'étoit une leçon de clémence, que
le tems demandoit, & qui lui difoit, que la cruauté
n'étoit pas de faifon pour un Prince, qui ne faifoit
que commencer de regner. *f* Il fut le premier, qui
comprit les Libelles dans la Loi de Leze-Majefté : *g*
& Tibére y comprit auffi les paroles, & même des paroles, qui ne bleffoient, ni lui, ni fa Mére, témoin
Cremutius Cordus, à qui il fit un crime d'avoir loué
Brutus & Caffius. *h* Et quoique l'on n'eût jamais oüi
parler de chofe pareille, il vouloit faire accroire, que
c'étoit une Loi établie par fon Pére, dont il n'ofoit,
difoit-il, enfreindre les Ordonnances. *i*

*f Atrocior, quàm
novo regno condu-
ceret. An. 11.*
*g Primus Augu-
ftus cognitionem de
famofis libellis fpe-
cie legis ejus tracta-
vit. An. 1.*
*h Sed neque hæc in
Principem, aut
Principis parentem,
quos Lex Maje-
ftatis amplectitur.
An. 4.*
*i Neque fas Tiberio
infringere dicta e-
jus. An. 1.*

CHAPITRE XXXV.

Egens, ignotus, inquies, dum ocultis libellis fævi-
tiæ Principis adrepit, mox clariffimo cuique peri-
culum faceffit, potentiam apud unum, odium apud
omnes adeptus, dedit exemplum, quod fecuti, ex
pauperibus divites, ex contemptis metuendi, per-
niciem aliis, ac poftremùm fibi invenêre. *Ann.* 1.

*Hiffon, de pauvre, inconnu, & défefperé qu'il étoit, s'infi-
nua dans l'efprit ombrageux du Prince par des rapports fe-
crets, & heurta depuis les plus grands de Rome : & apuïé
d'un feul contre la haine de tous les autres, il aprit à plu-
fieurs un fecret, qui de pauvres & méprifés les rendit ri-
ches & redoutables, puis les entraina dans le précipice,
où ils avoient pouffé les autres.*

Un

in *La Morale*. Following this section is a collection of "Sentences and Precepts by Pliny the Younger, for Princes, and Courtiers."[74] Readers of *La Morale de Tacite* get not only a Tacitean manual of flattery but also an extra set of courtly maxims. In language, commentary, and formal presentation, Amelot set the way readers should read the book, by thematically directing them through the text with the maxims as a guide.

The question is, did Amelot's critical technology work? Did the audience he had in mind read the way he wanted? In the June 1686 issue of the *Nouvelles*, Bayle reviewed *La Morale de Tacite*, calling it one of the best works he had ever seen on Tacitus.[75] In the review, Bayle examined Amelot's preface, went over his system of notes and annotations, and analyzed the *mise en page*. Bayle followed the directions and read the work precisely as Amelot intended. In this work, Amelot had put his translation of Tacitus next to that of the famous midcentury translator Perrot d'Ablancourt, to illustrate the difference of his "political" translation. As we saw in chapter 1, Bayle's review notes this along with the form of the page and Amelot's use of commentary and maxims in the margins.[76] Most important, Bayle understood Amelot's critical, political project. Having read Amelot's long prefatory "Discours critique" and commentaries, Bayle characterizes the work as an indictment of modern court culture. He notes that flattery has become excessive in all branches of society and that political culture, like the church, is in need of a "reformation."[77] Flattery led the Romans, he says, away from republican liberties toward "prostituting themselves to their Emperors."[78] He paraphrases the long passage about Lepidus and Thrasea and notes that the examples that Amelot gives will act as an antidote to the "venom" of flattery and will work to "heal our century."[79]

> One thing that everyone can agree on about this ancient Historian [Tacitus], is that his Histories are the image of the behavior of all Princely Courts, and with this, one can easily respond to those who complain that his Works are a School of pernicious politics, for it is just to imagine that a thing that has spread everywhere and in all the centuries is so deeply embedded in the corrupt nature of man, that it would have the same relevance whether or not Tacitus had written about it. His maxims of State have almost become a necessary evil, and those who condemn them when they are but private men, have no qualms about becoming their most loyal followers when they are called to work in the Ministries of government.[80]

Each of Bayle's reviews quotes Amelot's prefaces and explains how he has used his notes to alter and redirect the meaning of the work. In his review of *L'Homme de cour*, Bayle notes that Amelot has changed the title of the work and added a long preface, three hundred maxims, notes, concordances, and entirely new passages from Gracián's other works.[81] He quotes Amelot quoting Lastanosa and agrees that the most important aspect of this work is that it will promote "reason of state of the self." In his 1687 review of Amelot's version of *The Prince*, the first thing Bayle remarks is that "[t]he notes that he has joined to the main text have strongly contributed to the success of this translation, and the Preface is particularly useful."[82] Finally, he agrees with Amelot's assertion that *The Prince* reveals tyranny rather than buttressing it.

> It is surprising that there have been so few people who believe that Machiavelli only teaches Princes that which they have taught him to write. It is the study of the world, and the observation of what happens there, and not a hollow Mediation of the Cabinet of the Prince, that acts as Master to Machiavelli. Let one burn his books, another refute them, another translate them, that one comments on them, he will, in spite of it, be no more and no less influential in relation to government.[83]

Thus, through Amelot, Tacitus and Machiavelli became critical protagonists in Bayle's *Dictionary*, which devotes long chapters to Tacitus, "the first among historians," and to Machiavelli. In the Tacitus chapter, Bayle mentions Amelot's 1690 translation of the *Annals*, *Tacite: Les six premiers livres des Annales*, published at the same time Bayle was writing the *Dictionary*, whose *mise en page* it most resembles (fig. 6). In the chapter on Machiavelli, the section dedicated to *The Prince* is a reprint of Bayle's own review from the *Nouvelles* of Amelot's version, where Bayle, through Amelot, calls for a rehabilitation of Machiavelli. Thus, Amelot's strategy worked to an extent he could never have imagined. For his own illicit readings had been poached by Bayle and re-presented on the pages of the *Dictionary*. Any reader who turned to the chapters on Tacitus and Machiavelli would be referred to Amelot's works. Under the guises of Tacitus and Machiavelli, Amelot had been picked up by Bayle and swept into the eighteenth century.

Bayle was not the only seventeenth-century reader to carefully note and follow Amelot's textual user's guide. In the more orthodox *Journal des sçavans*, Adrien Baillet also reviewed *La Morale de Tacite*. He compliments the use of brief, but original, examples, and he notes the contrast of different texts on the page and the use of maxims. Yet Baillet, whose officially sanctioned *Journal* was published in Paris, could not afford the subtle reading of Bayle. For him, this was a book that warned princes against the "poison" of flattery.[84]

Amelot clearly knew that readers were interested in his page settings, for in the preface to his final translation of Tacitus, *Tacite*, he assures his reader that while some people had claimed he was recycling his notes and commentaries, *Tacite* indeed contained new commentaries and notes.

> Someone having warned me, that it was said in "le monde," that the historical and political Notes that serve as a commentary to my translation, were

deſte de Prince 6 du Sénat f.

Tout ce qui eſt arivé de bonheur ou de malheur à l'ancienne République a été raconté par de célébres Ecrivains 7 : Et Auguſte même n'a pas manqué de beaux eſprits, pour écrire ſon hiſtoire, avant que la néceſſité de flater, qui croiſſoit 8 *de jour en jour*, les eût abatardis. Lorſque Tibére, Caligula, Claudius & Néron, regnoient, la crainte *de les ofenſer*, feſoit écrire des menſonges ; mais dés qu'ils furent morts, la haine

Ou n'a pas manqué d'habiles gens, pour écrire ſon hiſtoire, juſqu'à ce que la flaterie prenant la place de la liberté, eût émouſſé la pointe des eſprits,

Les faits de Tibére, de Caligula, de Claudius & de Néron, ont été raportez fauſſement durant leur vie, parce qu'on les craignoit ; & ſiniſtrement aprés leur mort, parce que l'on ſe laiſſa emporter à la haine récente. Ou ont été déguiſez durant leur vie, parce qu'on les craignoit ; & envenimez aprés leur mort, parce qu'on les haïſſoit.

6 Un Prince nouveau doit toujours s'abſtenir des titres odieux : car outre que l'autorité n'eſt pas dans les titres, ceux qu'il accepte ſont juger des bonnes ou mauvaiſes diſpoſitions, qu'il aporte au gouvernement. Il eſt naturel de croire, qu'un Prince, qui prend volontiers un titre, qui choque ſes Sujets, ne ſe ſouciera guére d'être aimé, & fera ſon capital de la maxime, *Oderint, dum me tuant*. Le Pape Paul II. fit concevoir une tres-mauvaiſe opinion de ſon Pontificat, dés le jour de ſon éxaltation, pour avoir voulu prendre le nom de *Formoſe*, parce qu'il étoit fort bien fait. Et véritablement, la vanité, qu'il en tiroit, fut cauſe, qu'il fit beaucoup de choſes indécentes à un Pontife, car, au raport de Platine, il ſe fardoit & ſe paroit comme une femme.

7 Ceux, qui ne racontent que les choſes, qui font honneur à leur patrie, & ſupriment les autres, ſont de bons Citoïens, mais de tres-mauvais Hiſtoriens.

> *Dum patriam laudat, dum damnat Poggius hoſtes,*
> *Nec malus eſt civis, nec bonus hiſtoricus.*

Selon Tacite, l'Hiſtoire eſt toujours mieux écrite par les Républiquains, que par les Sujets de Monarchie, parce que la flaterie eſt peu en regne dans les Républiques.

8 La flaterie croît à meſure que la domination s'afermit. Elle commença ſous le regne d'Auguſte, mais elle fut au comble ſous celui de Tibére. Pour voir le progrés énorme, qu'elle fit en peu de tems parmi les Ecrivains, il n'y a qu'à conférer l'Hiſtoire de Paterculle avec celle de Tite-Live. Celui-ci a écrit en Républiquain, & l'autre en Roïaliſte. Si Auguſte apelloit Tite-Live *Pompéïen*, il auroit aſſurément apellé Paterculle *Tibérien*.

NOTES HISTORIQUES.

Peuple, mais peu aprés il y en eut quatre, & par ſucceſſion de tems ils furent multipliez juſqu'à dix, ſans qu'aucun Noble pût éxercer cête charge. Ce qui ne s'obſerva pas dans la ſuite. C. Licinius Stolo & Sextius Lateranus empéchérent durant cinq ans l'élection des Conſuls, & par ce moïen le Sénat fut contraint d'admétre les Plébeïens au Conſulat, qui leur fut conféré la première fois en la perſonne de Sextius & de Licinius. Silla, ennemi juré du Peuple avoit fort abatardi ces Tribuns, mais aprés ſa mort ils reprirent toute leur autorité.

f Prince du Sénat] Il n'avoit aucune ſupériorité ſur les Sénateurs, qui lui étoient égaux en tout, excepté la preſſéance : & pour cête raiſon Dion l'apelle πρόκϱιτος γεϱυσίας, i. e. le premier du Sénat. Ce titre étoit en uſage ſous l'ancienne République. Le premier, qui en fut honoré, fut Fabius Ambuſtus, environ l'an de Rome 435. Les Conſuls étoient plus que le Prince du Sénat, car ils étoient les Princes du Peuple.

Fig. 6. Abraham-Nicolas Amelot de La Houssaye, *Tacite: Les six premiers livres des Annales* (Paris: Martin, Boudot & Martin, 1690), p. 4. Ironically, this extraordinary page setting looks much like those common to medieval manuscript commentaries, though of course the content and the internal logic are radically different. (Courtesy of Rare Books Division, Department of Rare Books and Special Collections, Princeton University Library.)

nothing but a reedition of my notes from Tibère, I feel obliged to declare here, that they are as different as my version of Tacitus is different from that of d'Ablancourt. And I am confident that anyone who would like to take the trouble to compare one Commentary to the other, will have to admit that I have produced yet another work.[85]

Tacite was the culmination of Amelot's project to write through the work of other authors. Its pages contain the most complex *mise en page* of any of his works, with commentaries called "Notes critiques et historiques" at the bottom of the page and even in boxes in the middle of the primary text. Here, according to the author, was a complete "critical," "historical" version of the first six books of the *Annals*.

Perhaps the most striking illustration of Amelot's success as a textual poacher is that his new versions of old works were translated into other languages. Amelot's notes and commentaries were international, best-selling material. An English translation of *Tacite* carefully retained Amelot's original *mise en page* and prominently advertised his notes, to which were added the notes of the English publicist Henry Savile (*The Annals and History of Cornelius Tacitus: His Account of the Antient Germans, and the Life of Agricola, Made English by Several Hands, with the Political Reflections and Historical Notes of Monsieur Amelot de La Houssaye, and the Learned Sir Henry Savile* [1698]). His version of *The Prince* was particularly popular in Italy, where it was published on the clandestine presses at the imaginary "Cosmopoli" at least three times—in 1745, 1768, and 1769—"con la prefazione e le note istoriche e politiche di Mr. Amelot de La Housaye."

Of all Amelot's works, *L'Homme de cour* was his most popular, and it was the work he had most transformed, giving it a new title and adding to and rearranging Gracián's original work. Perhaps also due to the fact that the original *Oráculo* was hard to find, most translations of *L'Homme de cour* were made from Amelot's version, rendering the work more than ever "by Amelot." The title page of a 1687 English translation reads *The Modern Courtier, or the Morals of Tacitus upon Flattery, Paraphras'd and illustrated with Observations by Amelot de La Houssaye, Newly done out of French.* An Italian version of 1718 remarked that the work had been translated twice: "Tradotto dal Spagnuolo nel Francese Idioma et comentato dal Signor Amelot de La Houssaye."

Amelot had succeeded not only in reviving the critical tradition of Tacitus and Machiavelli but also in transforming it. As Bayle's *Dictionary* shows, Amelot's antityrannical, personal vision of reason of state triumphed, and he succeeded in spreading his own subversive version of the Machiavellian reading method. But Amelot's success still does not make it easy to characterize his political significance. Was Amelot a republican, and were his re-creations of Tacitus and Machiavelli republican works? In *Tacite,* the notes tucked around his primary text give a taste of his sympathies.

4. Republican Government is always odious to neighboring Princes and Kings, for it gives their Subjects a perspective of liberty, and renders their servitude insupportable, and sometimes gives them the ticklish temptation to deliver themselves from it. 5. Today there is no form of flattery left to be invented, for the human spirit has worn itself out in that respect. The coming centuries will have an obligation to ours, for they will need to look at our century if they want to avoid making the same errors that will lead them to infamy.[86]

These lines surely reveal sympathy for republicanism and contain a veiled reference to Holland, without really showing a clear republican ideology. The police knew this. Amelot was not a revolutionary; instead, he was "fâcheux aux rois," a thorn in the side of royalty—in short, a critic.

Amelot had developed a technology and a way of reading that, as Bayle said, reformed politics. Bayle clearly thought that political reformation followed spiritual reformation, and his comment reveals to what extent he understood the cultural ramifications of the popularization of reason of state. In the marginal textual trenches of Amelot's commentaries, we find the first sprouts of a new political age. In the 1760s, Rousseau's *Confessions* would clearly enunciate the relationship between personal reading and political reformation, when he declared that reading had been the tool that freed him from servitude and liberated his republican spirit.[87] Of course, Rousseau achieved his enlightenment without the trained method of a humanist, the very thing to which he was opposed. The essence of Rousseau's reading revolution was that reading could be passionate and that emotion and sensibility could be transferred through the page. Rousseau would never read like Lipsius. Yet there was a link between Amelot and L'Ami Jean-Jacques. When Rousseau read *The Prince,* it was very likely Amelot's version of it, which was reedited in Voltaire's compilation *L'Antimachiavel,* published in 1740 and reedited at least fifteen times before 1765. Surely it is no accident when, in the *Social Contract,* Rousseau declares that "*The Prince* is the book of republicans."[88] We hear echoes of *Tibère* when Rousseau insists that the interests of monarchs go against the interests of the people and when he cites Tacitus to define royal political science.[89] Amelot was no revolutionary; rather, he was the guardian of the critical tradition, which he reshaped and prepared for a new political age. He was something of a prophet, for the coming century would take the critical tools Amelot had preserved and resuscitate them as the republican virtues he found so lacking in his own sterile age of flattery.

7. AN ENLIGHTENED PRINCE READS MACHIAVELLI, AND A *PHILOSOPHE* PUBLISHES *THE PRINCE*

I n 1739, one year before ascending the throne, Frederick II, future king of Prussia, the most famous royal reader of the Enlightenment, set out to refute Machiavelli with a commentary on *The Prince*. Wanting a model on which to base his refutation, Frederick read Amelot de La Houssaye's translation of the first books of Tacitus's *Annals, Tacite: Les six premiers livres des Annales* (1690).

> I revealed to someone my Design to refute Machiavelli, and this someone assured me that I was wasting my time since one could find in the political Notes by Amelot de la Houssai [*sic*] on Tacitus a complete refutation of the political Prince. I therefore read Amelot and these Notes, but I found nothing of what I had been told, these are Maxims of the very Dangerous and Detestable politics that I refute. . . .[1]

With *Tacite*, Frederick the Great was confronted with the old ambiguity of reason-of-state culture. While his friend had seen Amelot's works as a refutation of the treacherous prince, Frederick saw him as a promoter of treachery and, perhaps, of republicanism. He now expanded his project. Frederick sought to refute both Machiavelli and Amelot de La Houssaye.[2]

Frederick's commentary on Machiavelli represents his own brand of Protestant-inspired royal despotism. Like Voltaire, he defended the interests of monarchy but insisted that royal government be highly moral. For him, Machiavelli represented a radical tradition of immoral political tyranny from the Renaissance, a political parallel to Spinoza.

> Machiavelli's *The Prince* is for Morals what the Work of Spinoza is for matters of Faith. Spinoza weakened the basis of Faith, and tried nothing less than to overthrow the edifice of Religion; Machiavelli corrupts Politics, and undertakes to destroy the precepts of healthy Morals.[3]

On the surface, the work that came to be known famously as the *Antimachi-avel* (1740) was an essay on political morality. Like a number of anti-Machi-avellians before him, Frederick's goal was to fight immoral politics: "I dare to take the defense of humanity against this monster who wants to destroy it; I dare to oppose reason and justice to inequity and crime. . . ."[4] However, publishing *The Prince* had always been a complex affair, and in refuting Amelot's Machiavelli with a new critical edition, Frederick unwittingly helped create a work that allowed Amelot's version to be widely published throughout the eighteenth century and beyond.[5]

In the first years of their friendship, and seeking to please his royal friend and admirer, Voltaire offered to publish Frederick the Great's refutation, anonymously, as the king requested.[6] Clearly, it was not appropriate for Frederick, a king, to publish his own work. In the spirit of Don Juan de Lastanosa and Amelot, Voltaire did not just publish his master's manuscript—he also revised it, gave it its subtitle (an *Essai de Critique*), consciously created a *mise en page,* and added an introduction and his own notes.[7] Corresponding with the publisher Jean Van Duren in The Hague, Voltaire oversaw both the order of the texts in this work and their presentation on the page, consciously piling different texts together. He told the Dutch editor that he wanted his preface to precede that of Amelot so that it would announce "the economy [*l'oeconomie*] of the entire book."[8] Like an ancient castle onto whose foundations generations of inhabitants tacked their own subsequent additions, this new, critical edition of *The Prince* was a textual hodgepodge—a buildup of seventy-five years of readings and criticisms. Voltaire now occupied this castle, and he intended to make his mark.

The 1740 edition contains Voltaire's preface; Amelot's preface; translation of *The Prince* and notes; and, finally, Frederick's preface and commentary, which was, at his request, printed in the margins, alongside the passages he refutes. Amazingly, Voltaire retained the original form of Amelot's very particular edition, with its preface and the precise layout of Amelot's notes. Using a page format similar to that of *La Morale de Tacite,* Voltaire left Amelot's notes at the bottom of the page and in the side margins and placed Frederick's commentaries next to and around Amelot's translation of and notes on Machiavelli. With its different commentaries and prefatory texts, the book looked a lot like old humanist editions of Tacitus. Here was an enlightened critique of a seventeenth-century version of a sixteenth-century humanist text.

While Voltaire wanted to add his own authorial character to the book, he never expected that Van Duren had plans of his own. Before Voltaire and Frederick could make the revisions they wanted, the Dutchman began publishing the *Antimachiavel* and collecting royalties without permission.[9] Van Duren was not the only publisher to profit from this new version of Machiavelli. Between 1740 and 1741, at least eleven editions of the *Antimachiavel* appeared in The Hague, Amsterdam, Brussels, Copenhagen, Göttingen, and London. Most of these copies were cheap bootlegs. The king and the philosopher were furious. Their new version of *The Prince* had slipped out of their hands, taking on a life of its own in the illicit markets of the republic of letters.

While Frederick lamented the loss of authorial control, Voltaire seemed more concerned about pleasing his master than personally profiting from the work. That the book was circulating freely in Europe did not seem to worry him, for he clearly wanted this new version of *The Prince* to circulate. The whole point of the book was to fight the publication of *The Prince* with the publication of its refutation. Voltaire's short preface is a tirade against Amelot de La Houssaye, in which he agrees with his Prussian patron that *The Prince* is political "poison"[10] Voltaire argued that, even worse, it was a poison that had become "too public."[11] Therefore, he hoped that the *Antimachiavel* would act as a "public antidote." Taking Richelieu's old approach, he would fight publication through public refutation.

Voltaire could not contain his disdain for Amelot: "a man who, having been an Ambassadorial Secretary, never learned the secret of how to stay out of poverty, understands badly, in my opinion, reason of state."[12] Voltaire heaped contempt on the Lipsian humanist political tradition and, most notably, on the tradition of publicizing practical prudence. Connecting Amelot to Lipsius, he felt that Justus Lipsius and those who followed him were nothing but propagators of a "disastrous [*funeste*] vision of humanity."[13] Lipsius had no character, maintained the philosopher of Ferney: who could respect a man who changed religion three times? Moreover, argued Voltaire, since Lipsius's *Politica* was a book for emperors and princes, while Amelot's version of *The Prince* suggested opposition to monarchy, certainly Amelot could not claim to be the heir to Lipsius. Voltaire found it impossible to defend Machiavelli.

> In the end, la Houssaye pretends that Machiavelli hated tyranny; probably all men detest it, but it is very cowardly and awful to hate it while teaching it.[14]

Here was a man who advocated assassination and poisoning as political tools.[15] Voltaire insisted that no reasonable mind could accept such a mountain of contradictions.

Voltaire's preface to Frederick's *Critical Essay on Machiavelli* is crucial for understanding the transformation of the humanist critical tradition of the sixteenth and seventeenth centuries into the new moral criticism of the Enlightenment. Though he grasped the contradictions of Amelot's project, Voltaire, the elitist monarchist, neither completely understood nor accepted it. He considered the very idea of co-opting humanist, absolutist political culture for political subversion sneaky and dishonorable. Indeed, Voltaire had nothing but contempt for the idea and culture of prudence, royal or personal. Given his admiration for Bayle, Voltaire's disdain for the old reason-of-state tradition seems out of touch with the possibilities of the humanist critical tradition.

Voltaire never had to contend with Louis XIV, and by the time he published his preface, he was living in Potsdam under the protection of Frederick the Great. By the mid-eighteenth century, the French monarchy had loosened what had been, half a century earlier, a comparably tight hold on political discourse. Censors such as Malesherbes actually helped publish seditious philosophical works. There was no need for a Lepidus if the Thraseas of the world could operate without fear of deadly retribution. Surely Voltaire wanted political criticism, but not the sly dissimulations of the seventeenth century. What he had in mind were his own *coups médiatiques,* the witty public jibes he aimed at those he considered inhumane or stupid, which, in turn, brought him great notoriety. Yet by publishing his new version of *The Prince,* Voltaire guaranteed the survival of Amelot's old, critical reading. It would be edited at least eighteen times during the eighteenth century—in French and in English, German, Italian, and Spanish. It was through this refutation that *The Prince* became publicized, as cheap editions flourished for the first time.

Like Renaissance kings before them, many philosophers rejected the immoral element of Machiavellian politics, while gladly accepting the Machiavellian method. Much like the act of clarifying butter, they cooked criticism until the old dissimulating, immoral prudence bubbled up, then they scooped it off the top, leaving only the potent, purified tool of reading history for examples to be used in practical, political life. Thus, there was one aspect of prudence that many eighteenth-century thinkers embraced. While the philosophers rejected the immorality of prudence and reason of state, they retained the idea and culture of criticism, this time to be used as a tool of morality. Indeed, a new historical consciousness based on archival historical research emerged as a primary tool of political criticism and contestation against the royal, historical edifice. Many philosophers swallowed parts of the old critical tradition of reason of state and tried to wash down the often acerbic by-products of prudence with the aged, Ciceronian sweet wine of political morality.

A CRITIQUE OF PURE PRUDENCE

The rejection of courtly prudence—of dissimulation and treachery in the name of effectiveness—is one of the recurring themes in the work of many philosophes. It was a central issue on which early philosophes and those from the later part of the century agreed. As we know, Voltaire hated reason of state and later called prudence a "sotte vertu."[16] Diderot, defining prudence in the *Encyclopédie* (1762), only reluctantly admitted the need for a purely pragmatic philosophy of action.[17] Echoing the ancients, Diderot insisted that prudence be tempered by a quest to do good.

> [Prudence] *the virtue which makes us take measures to arrive at an end,* I suppose that this implies a *praiseworthy* or *reasonable* end: the ends giving value to all of our actions, how can there be merit in knowing how to achieve a goal that does not merit achievement?[18]

In a clear rejection of the old Lipsian reason of state, in which political expediency for the good of the state was sanctioned, Diderot's definition insists on the primacy of good over political utilitarianism.

> There is . . . a great difference between prudence and bad faith; and although in this corrupt century, one gives them the same name, the wise can easily distinguish between them. Real prudence is not a matter of learning rules to shake off the yoke of virtue and honor. . . . A great heart, in whatever state it finds itself, always takes virtue as a guide. A crime is always a crime, and nothing makes it lose its darkness.[19]

There is no moral relativity in this definition; a crime is a crime no matter what its purpose. More like Cicero than Aquinas, Diderot criticizes reason of state, for he says that individuals as well as nations have rights and that no one should exempt themselves from the laws of "honor" and "probity." In this estimation, reason of state without morals is thus a motor of oppression for the powerful against the weak.[20] The result was not the heavenly city but, rather, shades of Roman republican virtue.

While Diderot rejects immorality in politics, he nonetheless defends critical political culture in his long entry entitled "Critique."[21] There, Diderot defines criticism as a textual, scientific and historical method of finding truth and discerning "progress."[22] Diderot considers Tacitus the first among critical historians.[23] He maintains that moral criticism comes from an examination of history and the political use of history;[24] that it helps avoid flattery and make kings good; and, most of all, that it is the basis of "republican citizenship."[25] It is, he argues, the moral guide to reading history.

> By this, History, in its moral component, is a sort of labyrinth where the opinion of the reader is constantly misled; the reader thus needs a guide: now this guide should be a critic capable of distinguishing truth from opinion, rights from authority, duty from interest, even virtue from glory itself; in short to reduce man as he is, to the condition of citizen; the condition which is the basis of laws, the rule of morals, which no man in society should ever have the right to escape.[26]

Diderot maintains that real critics, such as Montaigne and Montesquieu, have the truth on their side, for through reason, they defend "the interests of humanity."[27]

So, at one level, old humanism faded, but at another, more subtle level, it triumphed. Philosophes did not believe that they could re-create ancient Rome, but they did want to employ Tacitean and Ciceronian political virtue. They endeavored to use critical readings of historical evidence as a basis for discerning political truth and historical authority. Thus, the Machiavellian *technē* of political observation, reading, and analysis slowly permeated European political culture, until it became an autonomous authority during the eighteenth century.

The persistence of humanist political critical culture is evident in Diderot's definitions of "politique" and "Machiavelisme." While he adhered to the basis of the classic definition of "politique" as the governance of the state, he made a clear departure from the traditional humanist definition by equating politics with political criticism. In his 1685 *Dictionary*, Pierre Richelet, citing Naudé, had defined politics in terms similar to those of Lipsius.

> POLITICS. It is the art of governing States. The aim of politics is to establish a nascent State, and to conserve the State which is established, to support those which do not have strong foundations and to stop them from falling into decadence. Prudence is the soul of politics.[28]

While Diderot agreed that politics was about governance and prudence, he disagreed that "prudence was the overturning of all moral virtues" for the defense of the state, as Richelet had defined prudence. Diderot's definition insists that "politics" means not only governing the state but also criticizing it. His definition contains a brief history of political philosophy, in which four authors—Bodin, Gracián, Boccalini, and Machiavelli—make up his political pantheon.[29] It is a subtle selection—the pragmatic, Gallican, Tacitist tradition in a nutshell. This passage is really the first intellectual history of the critical tradition. Diderot notes Bodin's erudition and mastery of "all the arts and sciences," as well as the value of his political maxims.[30] He admires the "ingenious fashion" by which Boccalini "criticizes vices." He questions whether Machiavelli was trying to teach vice or to expose it: "When Machiavelli wrote his treatise on the prince, it was as if he was saying to his fellow citizens, *carefully read this book. If ever you accept a master, it will be as I depict it; here is the ferocious beast to which you abandon yourselves.*" Thus, Machiavelli's ideas were bad, but the Machiavellian method was good, and this method was based in the fact that Machiavelli "possessed history."[31] Certainly Diderot celebrated Machiavelli, not as a tool for governance, but, rather, as shield against bad governance.

Of *L'Homme de cour,* Diderot underlines the importance of the idea of "reason of state of the self." Not only does he mention Amelot's translation of *L'Homme de cour* and cite his introduction, but he notes that this work is important precisely because it publicizes prudence. He cites Bayle's review of *L'Homme de cour* in the *Nouvelles,* where Bayle cites Amelot's quote of the countess of Aranda, who, as we have seen, warned that "by the printing of this book . . . the least bourgeois could obtain for one ecu things, which due to their excellence, should never be found in such hands." It was the publication of prudence—the basis of Amelot's entire project—that Diderot found significant enough to put into his short list of essential political books. Through this brief history, Diderot recentered the definition of politics away from the concept of politics purely as state governance, focusing instead on the modern tradition of politics as political—and possibly public—or individual criticism.

TACITUS'S TRIUMPH

Diderot was not the only philosopher to look for a moral, though critical, version of humanist politics. A new breed of eighteenth-century Tacitists were using the Roman historian as a literary tool for attacking political immorality and understanding human nature.[32] Their reading of the *Annals* centered not on political effectiveness, political stability, or cynicism but, rather, on Tacitus's critique of politics, which they perceived as the first step toward political reform and progress. The royal Bourbon historian was now the inspirer of Montesquieu, d'Alembert, and Rousseau.

Indeed, Montesquieu not only read Tacitus; his library contained a copy of Amelot's *Tibère.*[33] It is impossible to tell if he ever read Amelot's version of Tacitus, for he never annotated this work. It seems likely that he did read it, for it is the only French edition of Tacitus in his collection, and we know he read other works by Amelot. In any case, later prominent philosophers focused on Tiberius as a model of tyranny. Their Tacitus was that of Amelot.

Amelot's last translation of Tacitus, *Tacite: Les six premiers livres des Annales* (1690), which contains his "Discours critique" on the history of Tacitism and extensive notes, was posthumously published in 1709 and 1724 and, notably, in 1731, when François Bruys (1708–38) reedited it in an expanded edition. Bruys not only found and published the remaining seven unpublished chapters of Amelot's critical translation of Tacitus' *Annals;* he also added his own translation of the rest of the works of Tacitus, consciously imitating Amelot's commentaries in creating a joint edition of Tacitus's complete works. Like Lipsius, Bruys had worked as the librarian to a Dutch nobleman, converted to Protestantism, and later abjured and returned to Catholicism.[34] In his preface, Bruys marries morality to criticism by equating

Tacitean historical and political criticism with Christian honesty. Situating himself as Amelot's heir, he attacks the Ciceronian historiography of Rapin and talks of the need to follow the example of Bayle, thus illustrating the connection between the Tacitist tradition and Bayle.[35] Bruys boasts that he has received encouragement from important figures to continue Amelot's project.[36] He has tried, he claims, to imitate the method of commentary of Amelot, an "illustrious political thinker."[37] Like Amelot, he never openly admits to espousing a political ideology. Instead, in following Amelot's Tacitism, he claims to be a critic of tyranny.

> I appear a bit Republican in my Political Notes; but one would be mistaken to conclude that I disapprove of Monarchical Government. I know too well its advantages: I only blame Tyrants and Tyranny.[38]

Bruys illustrates how Amelot's version of Tacitus fit the critical interests of the new age, repackaged as a tool for political morality. Indeed, Montesquieu could have easily agreed with Bruys, for the former was no republican but was opposed to monarchical tyranny.

Tacitus not only appealed to early radicals. By the midcentury, new translations of Tacitus abounded. Notably, Rousseau tried his hand at translating the *Histories,* in order to "learn how to write."[39] D'Alembert called Tacitus's writings "le premier et le plus vrai des romans philosophiques" (the first and the most veritable philosophical novel).[40] In 1753, d'Alembert published his own translation of "morsels from Tacitus," which concerns the reign of Tiberius.[41] Headings of extracts in the notes—"The Cruelty of the Master," "Eyes Fixed on the Ground," or "The Path of Servitude Was Narrow and Slippery"—reveal his interest in the subject of tyranny.[42] In 1768, the abbé de La Blétterie's translation had much the same focus. Reminiscent of Amelot's earlier work, he entitled his translation *Tibère: Les six premiers livres des Annales de Tacite.* His goal was to reveal the most perverse aspects of politics and the "bizarre composition of a despot."[43]

> In the course of twenty-two years, of which I translated the history, one follows the progress of despotism. One watches it march first by slow steps, as if testing the terrain; then it advances more rapidly; arriving finally at its height, always under the veil of republicanism, always abusing according to the letter of the law in order to destroy its spirit.[44]

La Blétterie held Amelot's translation in low esteem, but he valued Amelot's political notes: "In this compilation of maxims and insights for the most part borrowed from Spanish authors, among many common things, one sometimes finds pure gold."[45]

If Amelot did not occupy a central place in the eighteenth-century French Tacitist movement, he at least had given it its start by producing the first

French translations published at the beginning of the eighteenth century. While many philosophers scorned his dissimulated, ambiguous criticism, Amelot's *Tibère* found its way into Montesquieu's library. Amelot had cultivated Tiberius as the effective figure to criticize tyranny; now Tiberius had come to the fore and was being used publicly as a foil for republicans.

THE CRITICAL SOCIETY

The Machiavellian, Tacitist tradition of political criticism survived into the eighteenth century through Amelot's mediation. But what were the political uses of historical evidence and history? In an exemplum of Kant's equation of Enlightenment with the "public use of reason," Daniel Roche has shown how historical culture based on erudition and philological criticism drove the rationalist tendencies of the philosophers.[46] The central question for Roche is the process by which the "academic erudition of the Lumières, descended from humanism," managed to escape from the basic function of backing royal power.[47] The historical roots of this shift are found in the work of Amelot and in the larger framework of the history of Gallicanism and legal culture. When Amelot published his *Préliminaires des traitez faits entre les rois de France* in 1692, his goal was to extricate history from the royal power monopoly and publish it into the open market. Amelot maintained that by publishing historical treaties with a critical reader's guide, he would help "people of good understanding . . . see through the bad faith of the Prince."[48]

Amelot's call to critical arms was a key moment in the process of political disenchantment. It was the first shot in the battle over the systematic public revelation of a rich archival, historical culture that had to a great extent been developed and shrouded in the complex information culture of the secret sphere of the state. We know now that eighteenth century politics was dominated by a great struggle over authority between the crown and the French parliaments. This struggle centered mainly on the question of feudal aristocratic rights. Montesquieu and the count de Boulainvilliers, legally challenged royal absolutism by publishing works of history and, later in the 1750s, through parliamentary remonstrances seeking to show that the crown had usurped the feudal rights of the aristocracy, thus establishing an illegal tyranny.[49]

Their case was made in legal terms, and their evidence was archival, feudal documentation. The genealogy of the tradition could not be clearer. These were the very documents initially organized by Du Tillet, the parliamentary registrar; collected by Peiresc,[50] Godefroy, and the Benedictines; and which Colbert had worked to keep under the crown's control, for they showed who legally had the right to collect taxes on certain lands. The archival evidence presented in parliamentary remonstrances was of much the same character as the materials used in the crown's conflict with Rome over administration of the Gallican church. In his rush to control historical archives, it was almost as if Colbert presaged the coming historical battle of the eighteenth century.

By the eighteenth century however, the crown had lost its relative monopoly over the use of archival documents. Royal historical institutions such as the Académie Française and the Petite Académie were not exclusively manned by allies of the crown. The culture of these royal academies slowly permeated the growing ranks of provincial academies and private salons that began springing up in France even before the death of the Sun King in 1714. Daniel Roche has illustrated how provincial academicians believed that an understanding of the history of their regions was a source of understanding the "nation" itself and could also serve as protection against the encroachment of absolutist royal power. Both provincial and Parisian academicians came to believe that archival history was the "école du vrai citoyen" or the school of the true citizen.[51] Whether they were for or against the crown, these academies became spaces of critical liberty, where members were allowed to express their own opinions openly based on critical, source-based historical research.[52]

This was the publication of the historical culture and consciousness of prudence that Amelot had advocated in the *Préliminaires*. If, as Roche maintains, these noble historians—in particular, Mabillon and the Benedictine monks—were the direct descendants of the erudite tradition, then these "republicans of letters," as he so aptly calls them, had appropriated one of the primary intellectual tools of royal political power.[53] Among those who openly opposed the crown was Durey de Meinières, one of the presidents of the Paris Parliament. He imitated the Godefroys and worked to create his own extensive historical archive to use as ammunition for remonstrances. His vast collection contained thousands of manuscript folios and cartons (Du Tillet's old *layettes*), and he expanded his collection by purchasing old archives of great parliamentary figures from the seventeenth century, such as that of Omer Talon.[54] As much as they were building a "collective memory," as Keith Baker puts it, parliamentary archivists were also building and spreading the raw practices of criticism by reading and using historical documents as active tools of public politics.[55] If good citizens were supposed to be good historians, then, like kings and ministers, they, too, would have to become good textual, political critics. By doing so, they would take Tacitism and critical history to a level beyond that used even by Sarpi.

Equally damaging to royal power was the crown's own response to the great barrage of historically documented remonstrances that the Paris Parliament hurled at Louis XV in the 1750s. These official documents were based on claims of rights derived from archival documents, and at the same time they were sent to the king, they were also published in the open market. In response to parliamentary claims, the crown turned again to the archives to protect its royal interests. Although from a parliamentarian family, the archivist and royal historiographer Jacob-Nicolas Moreau (1717–1804) realized that by losing control of historical documentation, the crown had lost control of political discourse.[56] Hired by the minister Etienne de Silhouette as the head of the Cabinet des Chartes in 1759, Moreau was to form a new administrative library for the defense of the royal cause through the collection of historical documents.[57]

Moreau not only wanted to create his own archival arsenal; he also sought to publish many of these documents for readers who were by now well trained in the analysis of feudal documents, presumably so they could understand the crown's claims through their own readings. The fifty thousand documents he eventually amassed would be used to rebut remonstrances and bolster the authority of a once divine monarchy.[58] The antithesis of the secretive Colbert, Moreau set about establishing a royal archive for use in the public sphere. In an unintended way, by organizing and then publishing historical documents, he only poured oil on the fires of criticism and situated royal authority in the realm of human history. Without mystical authority and a strict monopoly on historical truth and the archives, old legal absolutism could hardly stand up against the critical onslaught of the first historically conscious generation. It was a supreme moment of disenchantment and was the culmination of the process begun by Gallicans who attempted to ground royal authority on historical precedent. In Joseph de Maistre's mystical schema of monarchy, this struggle over historical authority was a fatal error for French kings who for so many centuries had been anointed at Reims with holy oil brought from heaven by a dove.[59]

CONCLUSION

Amelot de La Houssaye died in 1706, the same year as Pierre Bayle, in the house of a friend and benefactor, the abbé Henri de Fourcy. Despite his once influential position at the heart of Parisian publishing, Amelot left behind no catalog of what was surely an extensive personal library. Instead, his books became a part of de Fourcy's collection and, in a fitting end, were sold as part of the abbé's library in 1737. The man who earned his living writing through the books of others now disappeared, his books swallowed up by another library. Even in death, Amelot's textual presence was masked behind someone else's identity. This was, of course, Amelot's plan. Like Balzac's Père Goriot, Amelot had found advantageous spouses for his textual children, and although he died in impoverished obscurity, his books would enjoy great success after his death, wedded to the destinies that he had helped shape of Tacitus, Machiavelli, Contarini, and Gracián.

If Bayle is seen as the father of the Enlightenment, Amelot was surely its prophet. He identified, shaped, and published the cultural components that later transformed the court society into the critical society of the Enlightenment. It seems amazingly ambitious that Amelot believed that his books would spread critical historical culture, but in the end, he was right. He saw the keys to political liberty through the act of publishing criticism of Tacitus and Machiavelli and analysis of historical information. Beyond the longevity of the books he published, he could not have known that his plan would work and that his vision of a culture of a "reason of state of the self" would be realized on a grand scale. The act of reading history critically, in public, would become a major cultural force in eighteenth-century politics.

Yes, the philosophes did new things unimagined by Renaissance humanists. They extended the Newtonian revolution beyond the natural sciences. They adopted the natural rights theories of Hobbes and Locke to criticize nonrepresentative government; they questioned organized religion, and some even advocated atheism; and they created a theory of human rights.[60] Yet there was an essential continuity between humanist scholarly practices, royal political culture, and the philosophers' quest to build a universal culture and to develop mythologies around the cultures of secular truth, criticism, and progress. The Renaissance sense of the past and its reading and textual practices, which Machiavelli and numerous kings had harnessed for politics, were passed through the seventeenth century and refashioned into tools for political contestation, reform, progress, and even revolution. Of course, these tools could still be used for tyranny, and the old internal conflict of critical culture remained. Napoleon read Amelot's *History of the Government of Venice* and took detailed notes on the passages concerning the mechanics of government and voting.[61] Yet he hated Tacitus, for he knew the danger of widespread, public political criticism for kings and emperors.

"Censure freely," Jeremy Bentham said.[62] Kant not only agreed; free and public criticism was the very basis of his definition of Enlightenment. The old critical tradition had broken free. Thus, the Enlightenment was a chapter in the book of humanism—a transformative epilogue in which the historical consciousness of Valla and of Machiavelli spread. Gibbon's critical masterpiece *The Decline and Fall of the Roman Empire* became indicative of the spirit of the age. Gibbon was clearly the apotheosis of the Tacitean tradition, a new Sarpi who went far beyond Amelot's study of decadence in the *History of the Government of Venice,* who perhaps unwittingly undermined the fundaments of Christianity itself. The public sphere did not emerge as a consequence of late seventeenth-century and eighteenth-century culture and institutions but, rather, grew out of a secret sphere, developed in the sixteenth century at the heart of the royal state and ultimately lost by the crown through its own cultivation and through the ensuing process of revelation brought about by its critics. So we see clearly for the first time that the Enlightenment did not invent criticism; it emancipated and published the old royal tradition of politics, which grew from the winding roots of the Machiavellian method. But this is not the end of the story, for the publication of political criticism did not lead directly to a utopian golden age or to the unmitigated triumph of public opinion but, rather, set the stage for a long-term conflict between the secret sphere of the state and the public sphere of criticism. This permanent state of tension is the legacy of humanism and the very heart of modern republicanism. It will only stop when the critical spirit dies out.

Notes

Chapter 1

1. Joseph de Maistre, *Les Soirées de Saint-Petersbourg, ou entretiens sur le gouverne-ment temporel de la Providence* (Lyon: J. B. Pélagaud, 1850), quatrième entretien, pp. 231–45.

2. Peter Gay, *The Enlightenment: An Interpretation* (New York: Vintage Books, 1968), vol. 1, pp. 31–58. On Gibbon and Enlightenment thinkers in general and their attempt to create a historical science of government, see J. G. A. Pocock, *Barbarism and Religion: The Enlightenments of Edward Gibbon, 1737–1764*, vol. 1, (Cambridge: Cambridge University Press, 2001–3), pp. 4, 72–134.

3. Paul Hazard, *La crise de la conscience européenne* (Paris: Arthème Fayard, 1961), p. ix.

4. This definition in text for reason of state comes from Maurizio Viroli, *From Poli-tics to Reason of State: The Acquisition and Transformation of the Language of Politics, 1250–1600* (Cambridge: Cambridge University Press, 1992), p. 4. On the history of reason of state, see Friedrich Meinecke's classic *Machiavellism: The Doctrine of Raison d'État and Its Place in Modern History*, trans. D. Scott (London: Routledge and Kegan Paul, 1957). For a useful overview, see Peter Burke, "Tacitism, Scepticism, and Reason of State," in *The Cambridge History of Political Thought*, ed. J. H. Burns and Mark Goldie (Cambridge: Cambridge University Press, 1991), pp. 479–98. For the German context, see Michael Stolleis, "Machiavellismus und Staatsräson: Ein Beitrag zu Conrings Politis-chem Denken," in *Hermann Conring (1606–1681): Beiträge zu Leben und Werk*, ed. Michael Stolleis (Berlin: Dunker and Humblot, 1983), p. 208. Most studies of Machiavel-lian political theory do not examine the second half of the seventeenth century. Etienne Thuau's important work *Raison d'État et pensée politique à l'époque de Richelieu* (Paris: Armand Colin, 1966) stops after the reign of Louis XIII, as does René Pintard's *Le liberti-nage érudit dans la première moitié du XVIIe siècle* (Paris: Boivin, 1943). Other relevant contextual literary histories—such as Jean Jehasse's *La Renaissance de la critique: L'essor de l'humanisme érudit de 1560 à 1614* (Saint-Etienne: Publications de l'Université de Saint-Etienne, 1976), William F. Church's *Richelieu and Reason of State* (Princeton: Princeton University Press, 1973), and Marc Fumaroli's already classic, *L'âge de l'éloquence* (Paris: Albin Michel, 1980)—also ignore the later part of the seventeenth century. Also see Anna Maria Battista's *Alle origini del pensiero politico libertino: Montaigne e Charron* (Milan: Giuffrè, 1966). From the Cambridge school of the history of political thought, Q. R. D. Skinner's *The Foundations of Modern Political Thought*, 2 vols. (Cambridge: Cambridge University Press, 1978), also stops before the reign of Louis XIV, as does Viroli's *Politics to Reason of State* and Richard Tuck's *Philosophy and Government, 1572–1652* (Cam-bridge: Cambridge University Press, 1993). Two notable examples of histories of libertine

thought during the reign of Louis XIV are J. S. Spink's *French Free-Thought from Gassendi to Voltaire* (London: Athlone Press, 1960). On this topic, see also the useful work by Lionel Rothkrug, *Opposition to Louis XIV: The Political and Social Origins of the French Enlightenment* (Princeton: Princeton University Press, 1965), p. 385. Although not a standard history of political ideas, one of the most useful works for tracing the circulation and influence of libertine works under Louis XIV is Henri-Jean Martin's monumental thesis *Livre, pouvoirs et société à Paris au XVIIe siècle 1598–1701*, 2 vols. (Geneva: Droz, 1984); see vol. 2 in particular. On the idea of a shift from "black" to "red" Tacitism, see Giuseppe Toffanin, *Machiavelli e il Tacitismo: La politica storica al tempo della Controriforma* (Naples: Guida, 1972), pp. 149–209.

5. On humanist republican virtue in the seventeenth century and during the Enlightenment, see J. G. A. Pocock, *The Machiavellian Moment: Florentine Political Thought and the Atlantic Republican Tradition* (Princeton: Princeton University Press, 1975); Martin van Gelderen, "Holland und das Preußentum: Justus Lipsius zwischen niederländischen Aufstand und Brandenburg-preußischem Absolutismus," *Zeitschrift für Historische Forschung* 23 (1996): pp. 29–56.

6. H. T. Mason, *Pierre Bayle and Voltaire* (Oxford: Oxford University Press, 1963), p. 3.

7. Daniel Mornet, "Les enseignements des bibliothèques privées (1750–1780)," *Revue d'Histoire Littéraire de la France* 17 (1910): p. 460.

8. Reinhart Koselleck, *Critique and Crisis* (Oxford: Berg, 1988); *Kritik und Krise: Ein Beitrag zur Pathogenese der Bürgerlichen Welt* (Freiburg: Verlag Karl Alber, 1959); *Le règne de la critique* (Paris: Éditions de Minuit, 1979). The original German and French editions are different. For an analysis of Koselleck's place in Enlightenment historiography, see Giuseppe Ricuperati, "Illuminismo e settecento dal dopoguerra ad oggi," in *La reinvenzione dei lumi: Percorsi storiografici del novecento,* ed. Giuseppe Ricuperati (Florence: Olschki, 2000), pp. 214–19. Blandine Barret-Kriegel shows links between Renaissance philology, seventeenth-century erudition, and the Enlightenment in her monumental work *Les historiens et la monarchie,* 4 vols. (Paris: Presses Universitaires de France, 1988); see vol. 2 in particular.

9. Anthony Grafton, *Defenders of the Text: The Traditions of Scholarship in an Age of Science, 1450–1800* (Cambridge: Harvard University Press, 1991), pp. 37–38. Also see John W. Aldridge, *The Hermeneutic of Erasmus* (Richmond, Va.: John Knox Press, 1966), pp. 98–126.

10. Koselleck, *Critique and Crisis,* p. 88.

11. Ibid.

12. Ibid., p. 89. On the connection between modern political historiography and eighteenth-century thought, see Arnaldo Momigliano, *The Classical Foundations of Modern Historiography* (Berkeley: University of California Press, 1990); also see his chapter "Gibbon's Contribution to Historical Method" in *Contributo alla storia degli studi classici* (Rome: Edizioni di Storia e Letteratura, 1955), pp. 195–211. For a classic reading of how English historical criticism grew out of humanism, see Joseph Levine, *Humanism and History: The Origins of Modern English Historiography* (Ithaca: Cornell University Press, 1987). The idea that humanist scholarly practices helped shape the critical philosophies of the Enlightenment is central to the work of Anthony Grafton: see *Defenders of the Text,* pp. 1–22; *The Footnote: A Curious History* (Cambridge: Harvard University Press, 1997), pp. 94–121. For a recent study of the connection between humanism and the critical philosophy of the Enlightenment, see Pocock, *Barbarism and Religion,* vol. 1, pp. 121–34.

13. Koselleck, p. 88.

14. Ibid. On the relationship between humanism and critical political reasoning, see Richard Tuck's examination of humanism and Dutch republicanism in *Philosophy and*

Government, pp. 154–201. For another, more detailed study of Dutch humanism, republicanism, and political theory, see Martin van Gelderen, *The Political Thought of the Dutch Revolt, 1555–1590* (Cambridge: Cambridge University Press, 1992), pp. 182–87.

15. The paradox that the crown helped foster critical history, which then became subversive, is the central thesis of Christian Jouhaud's *Les pouvoirs de la littérature histoire d'un paradoxe* (Paris: Gallimard, 2000), p. 156.

16. Carl Schmitt, *Politische theologie: Vier Kapitel zur Lehre von der Souvränität* (Berlin: Dunker and Humblot, 1922), translated by George Schwab into English as *Political Theology: Four Chapters on the Concept of Sovereignty* (Cambridge: MIT Press, 1985), p. 36.

17. Pocock, *Barbarism and Religion*, vol. 1, p. 121.

18. Ira Wade has done a literary examination of how elements of the philosophy of the Renaissance and the ancien régime influenced eighteenth-century thinkers by looking backward at the reception of ideas: see *The Intellectual Origins of the French Enlightenment* (Princeton: Princeton University Press, 1971).

19. For the best overview of the contextual language approach to the history of philosophy and how ideas create influence, see Q. R. D. Skinner, " 'Social Meaning' and the Explanation of Social Action," in *Meaning and Context: Quentin Skinner and His Critics,* ed. James Tully (Princeton: Princeton University Press, 1988), pp. 79–96. On the opposition of discourse and circulation approaches to intellectual history, see Robert Darnton, *The Forbidden Best-Sellers of Pre-Revolutionary France, 1769–1789* (New York: W. W. Norton, 1996), pp. 169–80. Also see Darnton, "Two Paths through the Social History of Ideas," in *The Darnton Debate: Books and Revolution in the Eighteenth Century,* ed. Haydn T. Mason (Oxford: Voltaire Foundation, 1998), pp. 251–94.

20. Peter Burke defines this term and outlines basic approaches in *The Social History of Knowledge from Gutenburg to Diderot* (Cambridge: Polity Press, 2000).

21. Robert Darnton, "In Search of the Enlightenment: Recent Attempts to Create a Social History of Ideas," *Journal of Modern History* 43 (1971): 132.

22. Adrian Johns has worked toward complicating the canon in *The Nature of the Book: Print and Knowledge in the Making* (Chicago: University of Chicago Press, 1998).

23. Marcel Gauchet, "L'état au miroir de la raison d'État: La France et la chrétienité," in *Raison et déraison d'État: Théoriciens et théories de la raison d'état aux XVIe et XVIIe siècles,* ed. Yves-Charles Zarka (Paris: Presses Universitaires de France, 1994), pp. 193–244. Also see—for a reprint of this chapter and for a collection of essays dedicated to it and to the study of reason of state in seventeenth-century France—Christian Jouhaud, ed., special issue, *Cahiers du Centre de Recherche Historique* 20 (1998): pp. 103–29.

24. On the paradox of the simultaneous rise of absolute power and the tools for dismantling it in the context of a general history of religion, see Marcel Gauchet, *Le désenchantement du monde: Une histoire politique de la religion* (Paris: Gallimard, 1985), pp. 52–80. On the question of the relationship between the state, the public, and publishing, as well as for a history of the idea of the "public" in medieval and early modern France, see Hélène Merlin, *Public et littérature en France au XVIIe siècle* (Paris: Belles Lettres, 1994), pp. 59–112.

25. On the difference between the notion of the public during the seventeenth and eighteenth centuries and the *theatrum mundi* of the Baroque practice of dissimulation and theatrical public personas, see Roger Chartier, *The Cultural Origins of the French Revolution* (Durham: Duke University Press, 1991), p. 33. Also see Hélène Merlin's extremely useful history of the idea of the public in relation to the idea of the state, the *corpus mysticum* of the crown, society, and the individual in France between the sixteenth and eighteenth centuries (*Public et littérature,* pp. 13–112), as well as her reading of absolutism and theater, *L'absolutisme dans les lettres et la théorie des deux corps: Passions et politique*

(Paris: Honoré Champion, 2000), pp. 7–47. On the idea of a burgeoning literary public sphere, or *champs littéraire*, see Alain Viala, *La naissance de l'écrivain* (Paris: Éditions de Minuit, 1985); see also Pierre Bourdieu's study of the same questions during the nineteenth century, *Les règles de l'art: Genèse et structure du champ littéraire* (Paris: Seuil, 1992). For an in-depth study of the same questions, see Christian Jouhaud, "Histoire et histoire littéraire: Naissance de l'écrivain," *Les Annales* 4 (1988): pp. 849–66.

26. On Amelot de La Houssaye, see Jürgen von Stackelburg, *Tacitus in der Romania: Studien zur literarichen Rezeption des Tacitus in Italien un Frankreich* (Tübingen: Max Niemeyer, 1960), pp. 189–208; Pierre-François Burger, "Deux documents sur Amelot de La Houssaie," *Dix-Septième Siècle* 131 (1981): pp. 199–202; Suzanne Guellouz, "Du bon usage des textes liminaires: Le cas d'Amelot de La Houssaie," *Littéraires Classiques* 13 (1990): pp. 261–75; Terence Allott, "Undermining Absolutism: The Disguised Critique of Amelot de La Houssaie," *Seventeenth Century* 7 (1992): pp. 71–81; Jacob Soll, "The Hand-Annotated Copy of the *Histoire du gouvernement de Venise;* or, How Amelot de La Houssaie Wrote His History," *Bulletin du Bibliophile* 2 (1995): pp. 279–93; Jacob Soll, "Amelot de La Houssaie and the Tacitean Tradition in France," *Translation and Literature* 6 (1997): 186–202; Jacob Soll, "Amelot de La Houssaie (1634–1706) Annotates Tacitus," *Journal of the History of Ideas* 2 (2000): pp. 167–87. In this book, I spell the name *Houssaye* with a *y* rather than an *i*. Amelot's only known manuscript signature—signed with a *y*—is found in the front flyleaf of his personal edition of Tacitus in the Bibliothèque Nationale: *C. Corn. Tacitus, et in eum M. Z. Boxhornii et H. Grotii observationes* (Venice: Juntas and Baba, 1645), Réserve of the Bibliothèque Nationale de France, Rés. J. 2353. I discuss this book in "Amelot de La Houssaie Annotates Tacitus" and in chapter 6 of the present book.

27. Soll, "Amelot de La Houssaie Annotates Tacitus," pp. 183–87.

28. On the French crown's attempt to keep historians from writing critically, see Jouhaud's insightful work *Les pouvoirs de la littérature,* especially pp. 150–250.

29. Arnaldo Momigliano, "Tacitus and the Tacitist Tradition," in *Classical Foundations of Modern Historiography,* p. 130.

30. Pierre Bayle extensively read Amelot's work over the years and corresponded with him on at least one recorded occasion: see Emile Gigas, *Choix de la correspondance inédit de Pierre Bayle, 1670–1706* (Copenhagen: G. E. C. Gad, 1890), pp. 128–30. Bayle reviews or mentions the following works by Amelot in the *Nouvelles de la république des lettres,* 6 vols. (Amsterdam: Henri Desbordes, 1684–88): the *Histoire du gouvernement de Venise* and the *Histoire du concile de Trente* (March 1684, p. 456); the *Histoire du concile de Trente* (October 1685, p. 1180); the *Traité des bénéfices* (January 1686, p. 111); *La Morale de Tacite* (June 1686, p. 623); *Le Prince* (January 1687, p. 99). The *Mémoires de la minorité,* published anonymously, is also reviewed (January 1688, p. 72), although Bayle is unaware of Amelot's authorship.

31. Carlo Ginzburg, *Il formaggio e i vermi: Il cosmo di un mugnaio del'500* (Turin: Einaudi Editore, 1976), translated into English by John and Anne Tedeschi as *The Cheese and the Worms: The Cosmos of a Sixteenth-Century Miller* (Baltimore: Johns Hopkins University Press, 1980).

32. *L'Histoire du concile de Trente* (Amsterdam: G. P. and J. Bleau, aux dépens de la Compagnie, 1683), with subsequent editions in 1686 (two editions) and 1699; *Le Traité des bénéfices* (Amsterdam: Henri Wetstein, 1685), with subsequent editions in 1687, 1690, 1699, 1706, 1765. *Histoire des Uscoques* (Paris: Veuve Louis Billaine, 1682), with a subsequent edition in 1684.

33. An extraordinary best seller, Amelot's critical translation of Machiavelli's *The Prince* was twice published in Amsterdam by Henri Wetstein in 1683. It was published three more times during the seventeenth century, in 1684, 1686, and 1694. Amelot's pref-

ace, translation, and commentaries were reedited with Voltaire and Frederick II's *Anti-machiavel* (La Haye: Jean Van Duren, 1740). Amelot's texts were reproduced with the *Antimachiavel* six times in 1740, five times in 1741, and once each in 1742, 1743, 1750, 1759, 1789, 1790, 1793, 1834, 1848, 1941, 1948, and, finally, 1960.

34. At least ten editions of *L'Homme de cour* were published between 1684 and 1808, making it a best seller for more than one hundred years. Amelot's translation has been reedited for more than three hundred years. It has appeared eight times since 1924 and was a best seller of the 1990s, with editions in 1924 (two editions), 1972, 1980, 1990, 1993, 1995, and 1997.

35. Editions of the *Mémoires de la minorité de Louis XIV* appeared in 1688, 1689, 1690, 1700, 1723, and 1754; editions of the *Réflexions, sentences et maximes morales* appeared in 1711, 1725, 1743, 1746, 1754, 1765, and 1777 (two editions).

36. Amelot's *Mémoires historiques, politiques, critiques et littéraires* was published twice in 1722 and 1731, twice in 1737, and once in 1742. Jean-Pierre Niceron considered this work a forgery: see *Mémoires pour servir à l'histoire des hommes illustres de la république des letters* (Paris: Briasson, 1727–45), vol. 35, p. 120–31.

37. Amelot's *Tibère: Discours politiques sur Tacite* was published in 1683, 1684 (two editions), 1685, 1686, and 1688; *La Morale de Tacite* in 1686 (four editions); *Tacite: Les six premiers livres des Annales* in 1690 (two editions), 1692, 1709, 1724, and 1731.

38. These were published in 1681, 1688 (two editions), 1691, and 1693.

39. As we shall see, Voltaire dedicated a large portion of his preface to Frederick II's *Antimachiavel* (1740) to criticizing Amelot's preface to *The Prince*, which was, oddly, included in the *Antimachiavel* along with Amelot's translation and extensive notes. Geoffrey Keynes's *The Library of Edward Gibbon* (London: St. Paul's Bibliographies, 1980) lists Gibbon's library as containing an edition of the *Histoire du gouvernement de Venise* (1754), Amelot's critical edition of La Rochefoucauld's *Mémoires de la minorité de Louis XIV* (1754), Amelot's critical edition of the *Lettres du Cardinal d'Ossat* (1732), and an edition of Amelot's translation of Sarpi's *Histoire du concile de Trente* (1736). Montesquieu cites the *Histoire du gouvernement de Venise* in *De l'esprit des loix* (Geneva: Barrollot and Fils, 1748), book 5, chap. 8, nn. e and i. Muriel Dodds gives several examples of passages on Venice from chapter 5 of the *Esprit* that Montesquieu takes directly from Amelot: *Les récits de voyages: Sources de l'Esprit des lois de Montesquieu* (Paris: Honoré Champion, 1929), pp. 35–39. Louis Desgraves's *Catalogue de la bibliothèque de Montesquieu* (Geneva: Droz, 1954) lists a number of notable works by Amelot, including the first edition of *L'Homme de cour* (1684) with Montesquieu's manuscript annotations. Other works in the library of La Brède include (in the order given in the catalog) Amelot's translation of Sarpi's *Traité des bénéfices* (1685), another unmarked edition of *L'Homme de cour* (1685), Amelot's translation of Machiavelli's *The Prince* (1684), Amelot's translation of and commentary on Tacitus entitled *Tibère: Discours politiques sur Tacite* (1683), the *Histoire du gouvernement de Venise* (1676), Amelot's translation of Sarpi's *Histoire du concile de Trente* (n.d.), and Amelot's critical edition of La Rochefoucauld's *Mémoires de la minorité de Louis XIV* (1710). Pasquale Villari discusses a copy of Amelot's translation of *The Prince* that is located in the Vatican library and is filled with manuscript annotations by Queen Christina of Sweden, who appears to have closely read Amelot's commentaries: see *The Life and Times of Niccolò Machiavelli*, trans. Linda Villari (London: T. Fisher, 1892), vol. 1, p. 211. See also Napoleon Bonaparte, *Manuscrits inédits*, ed. Frédéric Masson and Guido Biagi (Paris: Société d'Éditions Littéraires et Artistiques, 1907), pp. 338–49. Napoleon took his notes from the 1695 and 1740 editions of the *Histoire du gouvernement de Venise*. See Soll, "Amelot de La Houssaie Annotates Tacitus," p. 169, n. 12.

40. For a characterization of censorship under Louis XIV as particularly strict, see Anne Sauvy, *Livres saisis à Paris entre 1678 et 1701* (La Haye: Martinus Nijhoff, 1972),

p. 1. On the crown's control of printing, see Martin, *Livre, pouvoirs et société,* vol. 2, pp. 662–756.

41. On the influence of Tacitus and other ancient historians on modern critical historiography, see Arnaldo Momigliano, "Les études classiques aux XIXe et XXe siècles: Leur place dans l'histoire des idées," in *Entretiens sur l'Antiquité Classique* 26 (1979): pp. 127–57, translated and reedited as "The Place of Ancient Historiography in Modern Historiography," in Arnaldo Momigliano, *Settimo contributo alla storia degli studi classici e del mondo antico* (Rome: Edizioni di Storia e Letteratura, 1984), pp. 13–36. Also see, in general, Momigliano's *Classical Foundations of Modern Historiography.* The question of how critical history evolved from late Renaissance to Enlightenment is notably examined in Grafton, *Footnote.* On the connection between Montesquieu's historical method and that of the Tacitean tradition, see Chantall Grell, *L'histoire entre érudition et philosophie: Étude sur la connaissance historique à l'âge des Lumières* (Paris: Presses Universitaires de France, 1983), pp. 171–72.

42. On Amelot's relationship to the abbé de Fourcy during his later years, when Amelot actually resided at de Fourcy's house in the Marais, see the preface to the posthumous edition of Amelot's critical edition of La Rochefoucauld's *Réflexions, sentences et maximes morales* (Paris: Etienne Ganeau, 1711). Amelot's library was mixed in with—and thus sold during the dispersal of—de Fourcy's. Some of Amelot's personal editions are mentioned in the *Catalogue des Livres de M. ***** (Henri de Fourcy), dont la vente se fera en détail le Lundy 13. May 1737. et jours suivans, depuis deux heures de relevée jusqu'au soir, rüe de Joüy dans le Cul-de-sac de Fourcy* (Paris: Gabriel Martin, 1737).

43. Gerhard Oestreich emphasizes the dependent connection between Renaissance scholarly practices and the development of early modern political philosophy: see his classic *Neostoicism and the Early Modern State,* ed. Brigitta Oestreich and H. G. Koenigsberger, trans. David McKlintock (Cambridge: Cambridge University Press, 1982), pp. 2–9.

44. "Mémoire sur les vies, les moeurs du sieur Amelot, historien, renvoyé par le Roy à M. de Seignelay" (hereafter "Le Roy à Seignelay") and "M. de la Reinie sur le sieur Amelot," Archives Nationales de France, KK 601, fols. 141, 137. On these documents, see the critical reprint by Burger in "Deux documents sur Amelot de La Houssaie," pp. 199–202.

45. "Le Roy à Seignelay," fol. 141.

46. There is no evidence that Amelot was a spy. Therefore, it is difficult to hypothesize to whom and why he was selling documents. On spy activities in Venice and Amelot de La Houssaye, see Paulo Preto, *I servizi segreti di Venezia* (Milan: Il Saggiatore, 1994).

47. "Le Roy à Seignelay," fol. 141.

48. Amelot's first works reflect this mix of talents. In 1670, Amelot's first book appeared, a printed summary (without preface or notes) of the trial of the Jews of the city of Metz, *Abrégé du procès des Juifs de Metz* (Paris: Frédéric Léonard, 1670). A standard anti-Semitic accusation of Jewish child killing, this text appears to have been printed for commercial reasons by the royal printer and edited by his in-house copyist and translator, Amelot de La Houssaye, who is credited as the "author." Six years later, Amelot's name appears on a diplomatic relation of strong Gallican character published by Léonard, *La Rélation du conclave de MDCLXX* (Paris: Frédéric Léonard, 1677).

49. On the tradition of the in-house corrector and editor, see Mary A. Rouse and Richard H. Rouse, *Authentic Witnesses: Approaches to Medieval Texts and Manuscripts* (Notre Dame: University of Notre Dame Press, 1991), pp. 427–47. On the connection between correctors, scholarly editors, and printing shops, see James S. Hirstein, *Tacitus' Germania and Beatus Rhenanus (1485–1547): A Study of the Editorial and Exegetical Contribution of a Sixteenth-Century Scholar* (Franfurt am Main: Peter Lang, 1995).

50. For a detailed account of how the *Histoire du gouvernement de Venise* was written, see Jacob Soll, "Hand-Annotated Copy."

51. "Le Roy à Seignelay," fol. 142. On Amelot's term at the Bastille, see F. Funck-Brentano, *Les lettres de cachet à Paris* (Paris: Imprimerie Nationale, 1903), p. 673. Amelot was incarcerated from April 2 to May 15, 1676.

52. On the various editions of the *Histoire,* see Soll, "Hand-Annotated Copy," p. 228.

53. My own research at the Bibliothèque Nationale de France, at the British Library, and in the National Union Catalogue has unearthed five editions in French of the *Histoire* between 1676 and 1695. On Drouyn's calculations of the number of editions of the *Histoire,* see François Ravaisson, *Archives de la Bastille: Documents inédits; Règne de Louis XIV 1675–1686* (Paris: A. Durand and Pédone-Lauriel Libraires, 1876), pp. 93–94, especially the "Note de l'abbé Drouyn" (p. 94): "Amelot de La Houssaie est l'auteur de l'*Histoire du gouvernement de Venise,* qui parut au trois mars 1676, et qui fut supprimée au mois d'avril suivant, à l'instance de Justiniani, alors ambassadeur à Venise, ce qui n'empêcha pas Léonard de l'imprimer une deuxième fois dans la même année, avec un supplément contenant une relation de l'interdit de Venise et la traduction de plusieurs écrits publiés, au nom de la république contre le monitoire du pape Paul V. Cette seconde édition attira une seconde suppression, et cette suppression fit encore plus de bruit que la première, à cause des emportements de l'ambassadeur Contarini, successeur de Justiniani, contre l'auteur, qui fut cause qu'en moins de trois ans il se fit 22 autres éditions de cette *Histoire du gouvernement de Venise,* en Hollande, en Angleterre, où elle fut traduite en anglais, par un secrétaire de mylord Falconbridge, gendre de Cromwell; en Allemagne, en Piémont et en Espagne, où elle a été traduite en castillan." The importance of the *Histoire* can also be measured by the fact that it was put on the Vatican *Index of Forbidden Books* the very year it was published: see *Index librum prohibitorum* (Rome: Typis Vaticanis, 1901), p. 43.

54. Amelot also published two critical texts related to the *Histoire du gouvernement de Venise:* a translation of Alfonse de la Cueva's *Squitinio della Liberta Veneta: L'Examen de la liberté originaire de Venise* (Rastisbonne: Jean Aubri, 1677) and a translation of Sarpi and Minucci's *Histoire des Uscoques* (Paris: Veuve Louis Billaine, 1682). Both these texts are integrated into the 1740 edition of the *Histoire du gouvernement de Venise* (Lyon: Jacques Certe).

55. For seventeenth- and eighteenth-century examples of the in-house editor, see Ann Goldgar, *Impolite Learning: Conduct and Community in the Republic of Letters, 1680–1750* (New Haven: Yale University Press, 1995), pp. 45–48.

56. On Amelot's life in Léonard's printing shop, his work habits, and his adulterous relationship with Léonard's freethinking daughter, Marguerite, see Soll, "Hand-Annotated Copy," which outlines the original documents from the lawsuit concerning the affair: "Requête de Pierre Herbin," Bibliothèque Nationale de France, MS fr. 8122, microfilm 5570, 12 pages; "Factum," Bibliothèque Nationale de France, MS Thoisy 94, fols. 84–85; "Request servant de défenses par attenuation pour dame Marguerite Léonard, veuve de M. Herbin . . . ," Bibliothèque Nationale de France, MS fr. 2454, fol. 1.

57. Amelot de La Houssaye, *Tibère: Discours politiques sur Tacite* (Paris: Frédéric Léonard, 1684), pp. 2–3 of the preface: "Pour moi, Lecteur, je serois assés empêché de vous dire précisément ce que c'est que mon Ouvrage, quoique je sache bien ce que c'est. Et véritablement, il est dificile de lui donner un nom, qui lui convienne. Car si vous considérés seulement le titre, ou le texte des Chapitres, c'est une pure traduction d'autant de passages de Tacite; si vous regardés au contenus des Chapitres mêmes, c'est un Commentaire Politique, et Historique, sur ses Oeuvres; si vous observés, que Tibère est toujours le principal sujet de chaque Chapitre, c'est en partie l'Histoire, en partie l'Examen de son regne, depuis le commencement jusqu'à la fin: à raison dequoi le Livre est intitulé

TIBERE. Mais si vous remarqués, que le fond de la matière concerne tous les Princes en général, ce n'est plus le regne de Tibère, mais l'Art-de-regner. Enfin, si vous éxaminés les instructions, et les Maximes d'Etat, qui sont répandües par tout le corps de l'Ouvrage, vous trouverés que c'est un abregé, et comme un élixir de toutes les Oeuvres de Tacite, plutôt qu'un Commentaire sur les six premiers Livres de ses Annales. De sorte qui je puis dire de mon ouvrage, aussi-bien que Juste-Lipse de son Livre de la *Doctrine Civile,* que l'invention et la forme en sont telles, qu'il est vrai de dire, que tout est de moi, et que rien en est."

58. Justus Lipsius, *Politicorum sive ciuilis doctrinae libri sex* (Leiden: Plantin, 1589), pp. 2–3 of the "Ad lectorem de consilio et forma nostri operis."

59. On the relationship of Tacitus to the Bourbons and the Académie Française, see Soll, "La Houssaie and the Tacitean Tradition," p. 189.

60. I take these terms from Henri-Jean Martin, *Mise en page et mise en texte du livre manuscrit* (Paris: Editions du Cercle de la Librairie, 1991).

61. Amelot de La Houssaye, "Dedication to the Grand Duke of Tuscany," in *Le Prince de Nicolas Machiavel* (Amsterdam: Henry Wetstein, 1683), p. 5r. On the dependence of Amelot's concordances on traditional Renaisance commonplace reading practices, see Soll, "Amelot de La Houssaie Annotates Tacitus," pp. 169–78.

62. On the relationship between the form and meaning of books, see Donald F. McKenzie, *The Bibliography and Sociology of Texts* (London: British Library, 1985), pp. 3–9, 38. On the development of the concept of authorship in the social context of seventeenth-century France, see Viala, *La naissance de l'écrivain.* On the idea of "la production du sens" and the idea of an author "appropriating" the text of another, see Roger Chartier, *L'ordre des livres* (Aix-en-Provence: Alinea, 1992), pp. 35–67. For a reading of McKenzie and Chartier in the context of commentary, see E. Tribble's extremely useful work *Margins and Marginality: The Printed Page in Early Modern England* (Charlottesville: University Press of Virginia, 1993), pp. 1–10. For a further analysis of the qualification of the definition of authorship by the study of scholarly practices of annotation, see William H. Sherman, *John Dee: The Politics of Reading and Writing in the English Renaissance* (Amherst: University of Massachusetts Press, 1995), pp. 53–59. For an overview of Fredson Bowers's method, see the first chapter of his *Textual and Literary Criticism* (Oxford, Clarendon Press, 1972).

63. This reading of McKenzie comes in part from Roger Chartier's preface to the French translation: Donald F. McKenzie, *La bibliographie et la sociologie des livres* (Paris: Editions du Cercle de la Librairie, 1991), p. 6.

64. Peter Burke, "Tacitism," in *Tacitus,* ed. T. A. Dorey (London: Routledge and Keegan Paul, 1969), p. 158.

65. On the idea of "paratexts," see Gérard Genette, *Seuils* (Paris: Seuil, 1987). In the first edition of his translation of Gracián, Amelot gives a dedication to Louis XIV (27 pages), a preface (11 pages), a table of maxims (24 pages), and the text, which is annotated by eighty-three concordances with Tacitus and various other commentaries; finally, the principal text is followed by a "recapitulation of precepts" (13 pages) and another list of maxims (4 pages). On Amelot's appropriation of Gracián's *Oráculo manual y Arte de prudencia,* see Roger Chartier, "Trajectoires et tensions culturelles de l'Ancien Régime," in *Les formes de la culture: Histoire de la France,* ed. André Burguière and Jacques Revel (Paris: Seuil, 1993; 2nd ed., 2000), vol. 3, pp. 25–142.

66. These practices of the *mise en livre* of "paratexts" are most prominent in the *Histoire du gouvernement de Venise.* Volume 1 of the 1685 edition of the *Histoire* contains a dedication (8 pages), a preface (15 pages), a table of chapters (1 page), and the primary text (420 pages). Volume 2 contains the primary text (20 pages); maxims (32 pages); a glossary (44 pages); corrections (1 page); the *Mémoire pour servir à la défense de l'Histoire du gou-*

vernement de Venise (16 pages); a translation of the *Examen de la liberté originaire de Venise (Squitinio della Liberta Veneta)* by A. de la Cueva, containing de la Cueva's dedication and Amelot's preface (128 pages); Amelot's commentary on the *Examen* (24 pages); and the *Harangue de Louis Hélian* (33 pages).

67. On this traditional Tacitean authorial strategy, see Burke, "Tacitism," p. 163. For a fascinating account of how Charles I interpreted Isaac Dorislaus's Tacitean lectures as a criticism of the crown, see A. T. Bradford, "Stuart Absolutism and the Utility of Tacitus," *Huntington Library Quarterly* 46 (1983): pp. 148–49.

68. Bayle, *Nouvelles de la république des lettres,* July 1684, pp. 521–22: "M. Amelot est consommé dans l'étude de la Politique, et ne manque ni de l'esprit necessaire à penetrer les pensées d'un grand sens, ni des manieres de s'exprimer qui conservent la force de cette espece de pensées. Tous les livres qu'on a de luy ont eu beaucoup de succés. L'Histoire du Gouvernement de Venise, et celle des Uscoques sont de ses premiers Ouvrages. Il publia trois livres à Amsterdam l'année passée qui luy font beaucoup d'honneur, sçavoir le Prince de Machiavel, l'Histoire du Concile de Trente de Fra-Paolo, et des Discours Politiques sur Tacite. . . . Quant à son *Homme de Cour* qui vient de paroître, on peut s'assûrer qu'il plaira à toutes personnes de bon goût, car c'est comme la *Quintessence* de tout ce qu'un long usage du monde, et une Reflexion continuelle sur l'esprit et le cœur humain, peuvent apprendre pour se conduire dans une grande Fortune."

69. Bayle even took pleasure in figuring out which works Amelot wrote under a pseudonym. He correctly suspected that the abbé de Saint-Marc was Amelot: "J'avois toujours cru que le Traité des Benefices traduit de l'Italien du P. Paul par l'Abbé de S. Marc, etoit une production de M. Amelot de la Houssaïe: cependant je ne voulus pas le dire lors que je parlai de cette version dans les Nouv. de Janvier 1686. rien n'empeche presentement que je ne l'asseure, puis que la 2. edition de cet Ouvrage paroîtra avec le nom propre de ce Traducteur" (*Nouvelles de la république des lettres,* January 1687, p. 100).

70. Bayle, *Nouvelles de la république des lettres,* June 1686, p. 631.

71. On Renaissance textual and literary practices, see Ian Maclean, *Interpretation and Meaning in the Renaissace: The Case of Law* (Cambridge: Cambridge University Press, 1992), pp. 12–66.

72. Bayle, *Nouvelles de la république des lettres,* October 1685, p. 1180: "Le débit de la première (édition de l'Histoire du concile de Trente) a si bien instruit le Public de l'importance de ce travail, de l'utilité des notes, et de la beauté de la Préface où l'on voit régner un esprit qui a de la force, qu'il seroit superflu d'en rien dire."

73. For a later example of what La Reynie's literary police became, see Robert Darnton, "A Police Inspector Sorts His Files: An Anatomy of the Republic of Letters," in Robert Darnton, *The Great Cat Massacre, and Other Episodes in French Cultural History* (New York: Vintage Books, 1985), pp. 145–89.

74. "Le Roy à Seignelay," fol. 143.

75. Ibid.

76. Ibid. Lieutenant La Reynie's report on Amelot gives the same description of the danger of Amelot's authorial strategy, suggesting, however, that Amelot be tolerated and even manipulated by French authorities, for fear that he, like Bayle, might escape to a foreign country where enemy regimes would make it easier for Amelot to attack the French monarchy.

77. Bayle, *Nouvelles de la république des lettres,* October 1685, p. 1180.

78. These words are J. K. Coyle's in the preface to his *Augustine's De Moribus Ecclesiæ Catholicae: A Study of His Work, Its Composition, and Its Sources* (Fribourg: University Press, 1978), p. v.

79. I am referring to the concept of Max Horkheimer and Theodor W. Adorno: see *Dialectic of Enlightenment,* trans. John Cumming (New York: Herder and Herder, 1972).

80. Peter Burke, *The Renaissance Sense of the Past* (New York: St. Martin's Press, 1969). On parallels between historical culture, medicine, and natural philosophy, see Nancy Siraisi "Anatomizing the Past: Physicians and History in Renaissance Culture," *Renaissance Quarterly* 53 (2000): 1–30; "History, Antiquarianism, and Medicine: The Case of Girolamo Mercuriale," *Journal of the History of Ideas* 64 (2003): pp. 231–51. Also see Jacob Soll, "Healing the Body Politic: French Doctors, History, and the Birth of a Nation, 1570–1634," *Renaissance Quarterly* 55 (2002): 1259–86.

81. Herbert Butterfield, *The Statecraft of Machiavelli* (London: G. Bell, 1940), pp. 59–61.

82. Michel Foucault, "What Is Enlightenment?" in *The Foucault Reader,* ed. Paul Rabinow (New York: Pantheon Books, 1984), pp. 42–43.

83. Ibid., pp. 43–44. On Immanuel Kant's definition of the Enlightenment as a mode of perpetual, public criticism, see his *Foundations of the Metaphysics of Morals and What Is Enlightenment?* Ed. and trans. Lewis White Beck (New York: Liberal Arts Press, 1959), pp. 85–92.

84. Peter Gay (*The Enlightenment,* vol. 1, p. 17) points out that for the philosophes, their own critical practices were kept sharp by constantly criticizing their own works.

85. On Bayle's textual method and philosophy of doubt, see Grafton, *Footnote,* p. 195.

Chapter 2

1. Anthony Grafton, "The Humanist as Reader," in *A History of Reading in the West,* ed. Gugliemo Cavallo and Roger Chartier, trans. Lydia G. Cochrane (Amherst: University of Massachusetts Press, 1999), p. 180.

2. Ernst Cassirer, *The Myth of the State* (New Haven: Yale University Press, 1946), p. 134.

3. Niccolò Machiavelli, *The Discourses,* ed. Bernard Crick, trans. Leslie J. Walker (London: Penguin Books, 1970), pp. 98–99.

4. Skinner, *Foundations,* vol. 1, p. 208.

5. Ibid.

6. Cassirer, *Myth of the State,* p. 155. See also Felix Gilbert, *Machiavelli and Guicciardini: Politics and History in Sixteenth-Century Florence* (Princeton: Princeton University Press, 1965), pp. 158–59.

7. Butterfield, *Statecraft of Machiavelli,* p. 59. See also Anthony Grafton and Lisa Jardine, "Studied for Action: How Gabriel Harvey Read His Livy," *Past and Present* 129 (1991): 32.

8. Timothy Hampton, *Writing from History: The Rhetoric of Exemplarity in Renaissance Literature* (Ithaca: Cornell University Press, 1990), pp. 31–80.

9. Gilbert, *Machiavelli and Guicciardini,* pp. 153–54.

10. Nicolai Rubenstein, "The Beginning of Niccolò Machiavelli's Career in the Florentine Chancery," *Italian Studies* 9 (1956): pp. 72–91.

11. Skinner, *Machiavelli* (Oxford: Oxford University Press, 1981), pp. 28–29; Johann Macek, "La *Fortuna* chez Machiaveli," *Le Moyen Age* 77 (1971): pp. 305–28.

12. Gene Brucker, *The Civic World of Early Renaissance Florence* (Princeton: Princeton University Press, 1977), p. 290.

13. Skinner uses the word *revolution* in *Machiavelli,* p. 39. On the general, intellectual history of the idea of "wisdom"—or *sapientia*—during the Renaissance, see Eugene Rice, *The Renaissance Idea of Wisdom* (Cambridge: Harvard University Press, 1958); see also Hans Baron's reading of Rice in "The Secularization of Wisdom and Political Humanism in the Renaissance," *Journal of the History of Ideas* 21 (1960): pp. 131–50. On prudence as a political "technique," see Leopoldo Eulogio Palacios, *La prudencia politica*

(Madrid: Instituto de Estudios Politicos, 1945), p. 111. For a study of the idea of prudence in Machiavelli's works and its originality, see Eugene Garver, *Machiavelli and the History of Prudence* (Madison: University of Wisconsin Press, 1987), p. 11.

14. Werner Jaeger, *Aristotle: Fundamentals of the History of His Development,* trans. R. Robinson (Oxford: Clarendon Press, 1934), p. 81. Also see W. K. C. Guthrie, *A History of Greek Philosophy,* 6 vols. (Cambridge: Cambridge University Press, 1981), vol. 6, pp. 345–46. On Aristotle's concept of prudence and its relationship to history, see Eric Voegelin, *Anamnesis,* ed. and trans. Gerhart Niemeyer (Notre Dame: University of Notre Dame Press, 1978), pp. 61–70. For a recent reading of Aristotelian prudence, see Vittorio Dini, "Phronesis: Scienza politica, virtù esistenziale," in *Il governo della prudenza: Virtù dei privati e disciplina dei custodi* (Milan: Franco Angeli, 2000), pp. 79–101. G. J. Dalcourt points out the ambiguity between the practical and ethical dimensions of Aristotle's definition of *phronesis:* see "The Primary Cardinal Virtue: Wisdom or Prudence," *International Philosophical Quarterly* 3 (1963): p. 59. Dalcourt's article provides a very brief overview of definitions of prudence from Plato to Aquinas. See also Pierre Aubenque, *La prudence chez Aristote* (Paris: Presses Universitaires de France, 1963), p. 34. For Plato's definition of *phronesis,* see his *Philebus,* trans. H. N. Fowler (London: Heinemann, 1962), pp. 232–45. Also, on Aristotle's recentering of *phronesis* to the worldly sphere, see Guthrie, *History of Greek Philosophy,* vol. 6, p. 346.

15. Aristotle, *Nicomachean Ethics,* trans. H. Rackham (London: Heinemann, 1968), 6.8.5 (p. 351), 6.12.10 (p. 369), 6.13.3 (p. 371). On Aristotle's definition of "good" and on his ethics of prudence, see Dini, *Il governo della prudenza,* p. 96.

16. Butterfield, *Statecraft of Machiavelli,* 22. For a later formulation of this idea, see Gilbert, *Machiavelli and Guicciardini,* pp. 155, 158, 171, 239.

17. Polybius, *The Histories,* vol. 1, trans. W. R. Paton (London: W. Heinemann; New York: G. P. Putnam's Sons, 1922–27), pp. 35, 7–8, 99. On Polybius's reception during the Renaissance, see Arnaldo Momigliano, "Polybius' Reappearance in Western Europe," in *Essays in Ancient and Modern Historiography* (Middletown, Conn.: Wesleyan University Press, 1987), 79–98. On the humanist resurrection of Polybius and his popularity in sixteenth-century France, see Carlotta Dionisotti, "Polybius and the Royal Professor," in *Tria corda: Scritti in onore di Arnaldo Momigliano,* ed. E. Gabba (Como: Edizioni New Press, 1983), pp. 197–98. On the classical use of exempla in historical writing, see Carlo Ginzburg, "Montrer et citer," *Le Débat* 56 (1989): pp. 45–47. For a description of *enargeia* in relation to source citation, see Michael Wintroub, "The Looking Glass of Facts: Collecting, Rhetoric, and Citing the Self in the Experimental Natural Philosophy of Robert Boyle," *History of Science* 35 (1997): pp. 190–92.

18. Polybius, *Histories,* 12.25b (vol. 1, p. 371).

19. Cicero, *De officiis,* trans. Walter Miller (Cambridge: Harvard University Press, 1913), 2.9.34 (p. 202).

20. On the idea of *gubernaculum* ("the holding of the tiller of government"), see Pocock, *Machiavellian Moment,* p. 25. Also see C. H. McIlwain's treatment of the concept in his *Constitutionalism Ancient and Modern* (Ithaca: Cornell University Press, 1958), pp. 77–78, cited by Pocock, *Machiavellian Moment,* p. 25.

21. Cf. Cicero, *De officiis,* 1.8–9.41–42 (pp. 45–47). On Machiavelli's twisting of Cicero, see Skinner, *Machiavelli,* p. 40; also see Skinner, introduction to *The Prince,* by Niccolò Machiavelli, ed. Quentin Skinner and Russel Price (Cambridge: Cambridge University Press, 1988), pp. xix–xx; Viroli, *Politics to Reason of State,* pp. 146–47. See also N. Wood, "Machiavelli's Concept of *Virtù* Reconsidered," *Political Studies* 15 (1967): pp. 159–72.

22. Machiavelli, *The Prince,* pp. 61–62. In the original, Machiavelli uses the term *signor prudente:* see *Il Principe* (Rome: A. Blado, 1532), p. 23.

23. For an excellent study of absolutism and its relationship to the new science, see James E. King, *Science and Rationalism in the Government of Louis XIV, 1661–1683* (Baltimore: Johns Hopkins University Press, 1949). It should be noted that the single seventeenth-century French translation of the *Nicomachean Ethics* translates *phronesis* as "prudence": *La Morale d'Aristote,* trans. M. Catel (Toulouse: Pierre Bosc, 1644).

24. J. P. Somerville, "Absolutism and Royalism," in *The Cambridge History of Political Thought, 1450–1700,* ed. J. H. Burns and Mark Goldie (Cambridge: Cambridge University Press, 1991), pp. 347–73. In a recent article, Julian Franklin revises his reading of Bodin's theories of sovereignty and seeks to remove any doubt that Bodin envisioned an independent, absolute monarchy: "Sovereignty in Bodin's Account of Law," in *Historians and Ideologues: Essays in Honor of Donald R. Kelley,* ed. Anthony T. Grafton and J. H. M. Salmon (Rochester: University of Rochester Press, 2001), pp. 40–47.

25. Louis XIV, *Mémoires pour l'instruction du Dauphin,* ed. Pierre Goubert (Paris: Imprimérie Nationale, 1992), p. 67.

26. On the limits of Louis XIV's absolutism, see A. Lossky, "The Absolutism of Louis XIV," *Canadian Journal of History* 19 (1984): pp. 1–15.

27. Ernst H. Kantorowicz, *The King's Two Bodies: A Study in Medieval Political Theology* (Princeton: Princeton University Press, 1957), p. 218.

28. On the cosmology of medieval politics and society, see Arthur O. Lovejoy, *The Great Chain of Being: A Study of the History on an Idea* (Cambridge: Harvard University Press, 1936), pp. 99–182; W. H. Greenleaf, *Order and Empiricism in Politics: Two Traditions of English Political Thought, 1550–1700* (Oxford: Oxford University Press, 1964), p. 144; S. K. Heninger, *Touches of Sweet Harmony: Pythagorian Cosmology and Renaissance Poetics* (San Marino, CA: The Huntington Library Press, 1974), pp. 325–52; Rothkrug, *Opposition to Louis XIV,* pp. 7–24; Pierre Duhem, *Medieval Cosmology: Theories of Infinity, Place, Time, Void, and the Plurality of Worlds,* ed. and trans. Roger Ariew (Chicago: University of Chicago Press, 1985).

29. Gauchet, *Le désenchantement du monde,* pp. 64–70. Also see Vittorio Dini, "La prudenza da virtù cardinale a regola di comportamento: Rra ricera del fondamento ed osservazione empirica," in *Sagezza e prudenza: Studi per la ricostruzione di un'antropologia in prima età moderna,* ed. Vittorio Dini and Giorgio Stabile (Naples: n.p., 1983), pagination not available. Rothkrug (*Opposition to Louis XIV,* pp. 51–85) makes the same argument. Wilhelm Kühlmann illustrates the rise of rational, political criticism within the late humanist tradition in Germany in particular: see *Gelehrtenrepublik und Fürstenstaat: Entwicklung und Kritik des deutschen Späthumanismus in der Literatur des Barockzeitalters* (Tübingen: Max Niemeyer, 1982), pp. 319–63.

30. Gauchet, "L'état au miroir de la raison d'état," pp. 199–204; also see Marcel Gauchet, "État, monarchie, public," *Cahiers du Centre de Recherche Historique* 20 (1998): pp. 9–18. For a classic study of the ideas of *sapientia* and *prudentia* in the Western tradition, see Eugene Rice, *Renaissance Idea of Wisdom;* for a useful study of *sapientia,* see A. Levi, *The French Moralists* (Oxford: Clarendon Press, 1964), pp. 74–111. See also Pocock, *Machiavellian Moment,* especially pp. 3–31. On the literary culture of prudence, see Mario Santoro, *Fortuna, ragione e prudenza nella civiltà letteraria del cinquecento* (Naples: Ligouri Editore, 1977); Victoria Kahn, *Rhetoric, Prudence, and Skepticism in the Renaissance* (Ithaca: Cornell University Press, 1985); Victoria Kahn, *Machiavellian Rhetoric from the Counter-Reformation to Milton* (Princeton: Princeton University Press, 1994). For a more historical study of the idea of prudence in the work of Machiavelli, see Garver, *Machiavelli;* Ian Maclean, "From Prudence to Policy: Some Notes on the Prehistory of Policy Sciences," in *Guest Lectures* (Nijmegen: Katholieke Universiteit, 1993), pp. 5–27. Also see Dini's *Il governo della prudenza.*

31. For the early studies of reason of state, see Giuseppe Ferrari, *Histoire de la raison*

d'état (Paris: Michel Lévy Frères, 1860); Meinecke, *Machiavellism;* Gaines Post, *Studies in Medieval Legal Thought: Public Law and the State, 1100–1322* (Princeton: Princeton University Press, 1964), pp. 241–309. On the history of the term *ratio status*, see Rodolfo de Mattei, *Il problema della "Ragion di stato" nell'età della controriforma* (Milan: Riccardo Ricciardi, 1979), pp. 24–39. The classic history of the idea of reason of state in early seventeenth-century France is Thuau's *Raison d'état et pensée politique.* See that work and Oestreich's *Neostoicism and the Early Modern State* for political and cultural context. See also Roman Schnur, ed., *Staatsräson: Studien zur Geschichte eines politischen Begriffs* (Berlin: Dunker and Humblot, 1975); Michael Stolleis, *Staatsraison, Recht und Moral in philosophischen Texten des späten 18. Jahrhunderts,* Monographien zur Philosophischen Forschung 86 (Meisenheim am Glan: Verlag Anton Hain, 1972); Michael Stolleis, "Arcana imperii und Ratio status: Bemerkungen zur politischen Theorie des frühen 17. Jahrhunderts," *Studien an d. Herzog-August-Bibliothek* 39 (1980): pp. 5–34. For a bibliographical study of works concerning reason of state up until the early 1980s, also see Michael Stolleis, "L'idée de la raison d'état de Friedrich Meinecke, et la recherche actuelle," in *Raison et déraison d'état: Théoriciens et théories de la raison d'état aux XVIe et XVIIe siècles,* ed. Yves-Charles Zarka (Paris: Presses Universitaires de France, 1994), pp. 11–39. Also see Stolleis's influential series of essays in *Staat und Staatsräson in der frühen Neuzeit: Studien zur Geschichte des öffentlichen Rechts* (Frankfurt am Main: Suhrkamp, 1990). See Zarka's useful collection that contains Gauchet's important "L'état au miroir de la raison d'état," pp. 193–244. For a short history of the idea of reason of state, see Michel Senellart, *Machiavellisme et raison d'état* (Paris: Presses Universitaires de France, 1989); see also Peter Burke's useful overview "Tacitism, Scepticism, and Reason of State." Also see Christian Lazzari and Dominique Reynié, eds., *Le pouvoir de la raison d'état* (Paris: Presses Universitaires de France, 1992). In particular, see Lazzari's chapter "Le gouvernement de la raison d'état" (pp. 91–134), p. 131. On the rise of reason of state at the beginning of the seventeenth century, see Viroli, *Politics to Reason of State,* pp. 266–80; also see Tuck, *Philosophy and Government,* pp. 31–64; G. Borrelli, *Ragion di stato e leviantano: Conservazione e scambio alle origini della modernità politica* (Bologna: Il Mulino, 1993). Christian Jouhaud's collection "Miroirs de la raison d'état," special issue, *Cahiers*—a series of commentaries and reactions to Gauchet's work—contains a particularly original series of studies of reason of state.

32. On the rise of a political information science in the nineteenth and twentieth centuries, see Alain Dewerpe's chapter on "l'érudition d'État" in *Espion: Une anthropologie historique du secret d'état contemporain* (Paris: Gallimard, 1994), pp. 224–64.

33. Also see Carlo Borghero, *La certezza et la storia* (Milan: Franco Angel, 1983).

34. On the relationship between historical mythmaking and the state, see Filippo de Vivo, "Dall'imposizione del silenzio alla 'Guerra delle Scriture': Le pubblicazione ufficiali durante l'Interdetto del 1606–1607," *Studi Veneziani* 41 (2001): pp. 179–213.

35. U. Rossi Merighi, ed., *Segreto di stato tra politica e amminitrazione* (Naples: ESI, 1994); M. Ricciardi, "Appunti su segreto di stato e principio di transparenza," *Politico del Diritto* 24 (1993): pp. 35–50.

36. Daniel Mornet, *Les origines intellectuelles de la Révolution française 1715–1787* (Paris: Armand Colin, 1933); Chartier, *Cultural Origins;* Darnton, *Forbidden Best-Sellers,* pp. 78–79.

37. Gauchet, "L'état au miroir de la raison d'état," p. 235. Also see Christian Jouhaud, "La tactique du lierre: Sur 'L'état au miroir de la raison d'état' de Marcel Gauchet," in *Cahiers,* pp. 39–47.

38. See Chartier, *Cultural Origins,* pp. 16–17, 20–36; Darnton, *Forbidden Best-Sellers,* pp. 171–72.

39. Jürgen Habermas, *The Structural Transformation of the Public Sphere: An*

Inquiry into a Category of Bourgeois Society, trans. Thomas Burger and Frederick Lawrence (Cambridge: MIT Press, 1989), p. 27.

40. Keith Baker has noted that Habermas fails to take into account the importance of opposition to the crown during the *ancien régime:* see *Inventing the French Revolution: Essays on French Political Culture in the Eighteenth Century* (Cambridge: Cambridge University Press, 1990), p. 171. For a historical rereading of Habermas's theory of the public sphere and the place of literature and literary culture in the formation of a "public" in France, see Merlin, *Public et littérature,* pp. 24–112.

41. See King's study of Louis XIV's "system of inquiry" in *Science and Rationalism,* pp. 116–46. See also Vittorio Dini, "Pubblico/privato: Sovranità, segreto e governo," in *Il governo della prudenza,* p. 105.

42. This question is a political approach to Richard Popkin's classic philosophical take in *The History of Skepticism from Erasmus to Spinoza* (Berkeley: University of California Press, 1979).

43. Pierre Mesnard, *L'essor de la philosophie politique au XVIe siècle* (Paris, J. Vrin, 1951), pp. 538–43; G. Cardascia, "Machiavel et Jean Bodin," *Bibliothèque d'Humanisme et Renaissance* 3 (1943): pp. 129–67; Church, *Richelieu and Reason of State,* p. 50.

44. On Machiavelli's influence in France, see Anna Maria Battista, *Politica e morale nella Francia dell'età moderna* (Geneva: Name, 1998); see p. 112, n. 6, for a bibliography of works on Machiavelli in France.

45. On the uses of political history during the Counter-Reformation and the religious wars, see A. Enzo Baldini, "Le guerre di religione francesi nella trattatistica italiana della ragion di stato: Botero e Frachetta," special issue, *Dal machiavellismo al libertinismo: Studi in memoria di Anna Maria Battista, Il pensiero politico* 22 (1989): pp. 301–24; Giorgio Spini, "The Art of History in the Italian Counter Reformation," in *The Late Italian Renaissance,* ed. Eric Cochrane (London: MacMillan, 1970), p. 95.

46. The classic work on the cosmography of the Middle Ages is Lovejoy's *Great Chain of Being,* pp. 99–182; for an erudite study of the order of the medieval cosmos, see C. S. Lewis, *The Discarded Image: An Introduction to Medieval and Renaissance Literature* (Cambridge: Cambridge University Press, 1964).

47. Skinner, *Foundations,* vol. 2, p. 300.

48. According to Gauchet (Le desenchantement du monde, p. 66), the transformation of royal power into a practice of empiricism represents the beginning of the process of political desecularization leading to modernity. Also see Greenleaf, *Order and Empiricism,* 66.

49. Soll, "Healing the Body Politic," pp. 12–23.

50. John L. Brown, *The Methodus ad facilem historiarum cognitionem of Jean Bodin: A Critical Study* (Washington, D.C.: Catholic University of America Press, 1939); Leonard F. Dean, "Bodin's *Methodus* in England before 1625," *Studies in Philology* 39 (1942): pp. 160–66; J. Gilissen, ed., *La preuve: Recueils de la Société Jean Bodin pour l'histoire comparative des institutions* 17 (1965); Julian Franklin, *Jean Bodin and the Rise of Absolutist Theory* (Cambridge: Cambridge University Press, 1973); Julian Franklin, *Jean Bodin and the Sixteenth-Century Revolution in Law and History* (Westport, Conn.: Greenwood Press, 1977); Donald Kelley, "The Development and Context of Bodin's Method," in *Jean Bodin: Verhandlungen der Internationalen Bodin Tagung,* ed. Horst Denzer (Munich: C. H. Beck, 1973), pp. 123–50; J. H. M. Salmon, "Francois Hotman and Jean Bodin: The Dilemma of Sixteenth-Century French Constitutionalism," *History Today* 23 (1973): pp. 1–7; Philippe Desan, "Jean Bodin et l'idée de méthode au XVIe siècle," *Corpus* 4 (1987): pp. 3–18; Marie-Dominique Couzinet, "Jean Bodin: État des lieux et perspectives de recherches," *Bulletin de l'Association d'Étude sur l'Humanisme, la Réforme et la Rénaissance* 21 (1995): pp. 11–36; Marie-Dominique

Couzinet, *Histoire et Méthode à la Renaissance: Une lecture de la Methodus de Jean Bodin* (Paris: J. Vrin, 1996); Also see Ann Blair, "Humanist Methods in Natural Philosophy: the Commonplace Book," *Journal of the History of Ideas* 53 (1992): pp. 541–51; *The Theater of Nature: Jean Bodin and Renaissance Science* (Princeton: Princeton University Press, 1997), pp. 69–70.

51. On the paradox of Bodin as both a medieval witch-hunter and a pioneer of rationality, see Gay, *The Enlightenment*, vol. 2, p. 298. Also see Donald Kelley, *The Foundations of Modern Historical Scholarship: Language, Law and History in the French Renaissance* (New York: Columbia University Press, 1970), p. 114. Also see Kelley's "The Rise of Legal History in the Renaissance," *History and Theory* 9 (1970): p. 180.

52. Jean Bodin, *Method for the Easy Comprehension of History*, ed. and trans. Beatrice Reynolds (New York: Columbia University Press, 1945; New York: W. W. Norton, 1969), p. 69. I have modified Reynolds's translation. Significantly, the original Latin sentence uses the word *prudentiae*. See Jean Bodin, *Oeuvres philosophiques de Jean Bodin,* ed. and trans. Pierre Mesnard (Paris: Presses Universitaires de France, 1951), p. 134. In the *Methodus (Method*, p. 31), Bodin cites book 6 of Aristotle's *Nicomachean Ethics* as a source for understanding how to develop complex government.

53. *Method for the Easy Comprehension of History,* p. 70.

54. Ibid., pp. 54, 57.

55. Ibid., pp. 43–49.

56. Ibid., p. 20. Bodin was a pioneer of historical methodology, but his documentary criticism was primitive by period standards. See Grafton, *Defenders of the Text,* pp. 98–100.

57. *Method for the Easy Comprehension of History,* pp. 2–3.

58. Ibid., p. 2.

59. Donald Kelley, "Murd'rous Machiavel en France: A Post-mortem," *Political Science Quarterly* 85 (1970): p. 521. London A. Fell, *Origins of Legislative Sovereignty and the Legislative State,* vol. 3, *Bodin's Humanistic Legal System and Rejection of "Medieval Political Theology"* (Boston: Oelgeschleger, Gunn and Hain, 1987). Also see Battista, *Pensiero politico libertino,* pp. 7–50.

60. Jean Bodin, *Les six livres de la république* (Paris: Livre de Poche, 1993), p. 48.

61. See J. H. M. Salmon, "The Legacy of Jean Bodin: Absolutism, Populism, or Constitutionalism?" *History of Political Thought* 17 (1996): pp. 500–522.

62. Donald Kelley, "Jean Du Tillet, Archivist and Antiquary," *Journal of Modern History* 38 (1966): pp. 337–54.

63. Jacob Soll, "Empirical History and the Transformation of Political Criticism in France from Bodin to Bayle," *Journal of the History of Ideas* 64 (2003): p. 304.

64. Jean Du Tillet, sieur de la Bussière, *Recueil des roys de France, levrs covronne et maison,* 2 vols. (Paris: Jean Houzé, 1607).

65. Elizabeth A. R. Brown, "Jean Du Tillet et les archives de France," *Histoire et Archives* 2 (1997): pp. 29–63.

66. Du Tillet, *Recueil des roys de France,* vol. 2, p. 244.

67. Kelley, *Foundations,* p. 222.

68. Du Tillet, *Recueil des roys de France,* vol. 2, p. 219. Du Tillet's reorganization of the royal archives is described and illustrated with reprints of original documents in H. Omont, "Jean Du Tillet et le trésor des chartes (1562)," *Bulletin de la Société de l'Histoire de Paris* 31 (1904): pp. 79–81.

69. Du Tillet, *Recueil des roys de France,* vol. 1, p. 2 of the dedication to Charles IX.

70. Ibid., vol. 1, p. 1 of the dedication.

71. Ibid.

72. On Lipsius, see, in general, Oestreich, *Neostoicism and the Early Modern State;*

J. L. Saunders, *The Philosophy of Renaissance Stoicism* (New York: Liberal Arts Press, 1955); José Ruysschaert, *Juste Lipse et les Annales de Tacite: Une méthode de critique textuelle au XVIe siècle* (Turnhout: Brepols Press, 1949); Mark Morford, "Tacitean *Prudentia* and the Doctrines of Justus Lipsius," in *Tacitus and the Tacitean Tradition*, ed. T. J. Luce and A. J. Woodman (Princeton: Princeton University Press, 1993), p. 138; Mark Morford, *Stoics and Neostoics: Rubens and the Circle of Lipsius* (Princeton: Princeton University Press, 1991); Jacqueline Lagrée, *Juste Lipse et la restauration du stoïcisme. Étude et traduction des traités stoïciens de La Constance, Manuel de philosophie stoïcienne, Physique des stoïciens* (Paris: J. Vrin, 1994). For an account of Lipsius's sources, see Lagrée's "Avant propos" to *Le Politiques: Livre IV de Juste Lipse* (Caen: Presses Universitaires de Caen, 1994), p. 7. Martin van Gelderen shows that while Lipsius was popular across Europe, he was most popular in France: "Holland und das Preußentum," p. 40. For a study of how Lipsius created his manual of political wisdom with techniques from the commonplace tradition, see Jan Wasznik, "*Inventio* in the *Politica*: Commonplace-Books and the Shape of Political Theory," in *Lipsius in Leiden: Studies in the Life and Works of a Great Humanist*, ed. K. Enenkel and C. Heesakkers (Voorthuizen, Holland: Florivallis, 1997), pp. 141–62. Also see Pierre-François Moreau, ed., *Le stoïcisme au XVIe et au XVIIe siècle* (Paris: Albin Michel, 1999), especially pp. 77–139. The best overview of Lipsius's significance is by Anthony Grafton: "Portrait of Justus Lipsius," *American Scholar* 56 (1987): pp. 382–390, reprinted in *Bring Out Your Dead: The Past as Revelation* (Cambridge: Harvard University Press, 2001), pp. 227–43. For the latest reading of modern scholarship on Lispsius, see Peter Miller, "Nazis and Neo-Stoics: Otto Bruner and Gerhard Oestreich before and after the Second World War," *Past and Present* 176 (2002): pp. 144–86, especially p. 148, n. 11. To date, the most complex work on the Tacitist tradition and Lipsius' place in it is volume 3 of Pocock's *Barbarism and Religion* (Cambridge: Cambridge University Press, 2003).

73. On Tacitus as a stand-in for Machiavelli, see Toffanin, *Machiavelli e il Tacitismo*, pp. 149–70; and Stackelburg, *Tacitus in der Romania*, pp. 63–93.

74. The classic biography of Tacitus is Sir Ronald Syme's *Tacitus* (Oxford: Clarendon Press, 1958).

75. Burke, "Tacitism," pp. 149–53.

76. Momigliano, "Tacitus and the Tacitist Tradition," in *Classical Foundations of Modern Historiography*, p. 117.

77. On the question of Lipsius's attitudes toward the necessities of princely power and morality, see Oestreich, *Neostoicism and the Early Modern State*, pp. 8–9, 63. On Machiavelli's influence in sixteenth- and seventeenth-century France, see Albert Cherel's erudite, but sometimes dated, *La pensée de Machiavel en France* (Paris: L'Artisan du Livre, 1935). The best overview is Thuau's *Raison d'état et pensée politique;* also see Stackelburg, *Tacitus in der Romania*, pp. 63–93.

78. Wasznik, "*Inventio* in the *Politica*," pp. 141–62; Arnaldo Momigliano, "Tacitus and the Tacitist Tradition," in *Classical Foundations of Modern Historiography*, pp. 123–24; André Stegmann, "Le Tacitisme: Programme pour un nouvel essai de définition," in *Machiavellismo e Antimachiavellismo nel cinquecento* (Florence: Olschki, 1970).

79. I take this translation from Mark Morford, "Tacitean *Prudentia*," p. 138.

80. Michel de Montaigne, *Essais* (Paris: Garnier Frères, 1962), vol. 1, book 26, p. 158: "ce docte et laborieux tissu." See Burke, "Tacitism, Scepticism, and Reason of State," p. 485.

81. Justus Lipsius, *Politicorum sive ciuilis doctrinae*, pp. 2–3 of the "Ad lectorem de consilio et forma nostri operis."

82. Ibid.

83. Burke, "Tacitism, Scepticism, and Reason of State," pp. 484–85.

84. Burke, "Tacitism," p. 162.

85. On the different textual practices of Tacitism, see Burke, "Tacitism, Scepticism, and Reason of State," pp. 486–87.

86. Grafton and Jardine, "Studied for Action," pp. 32–33. Also see Fabio Todeschi, " 'Lector Scepticus': La recezione della tradizione scettica e formazione del publico in area tedesca 1680–1750," Ph.D. diss., European University Institute, Florence, 1998.

87. Anthony Grafton, "Teacher, Text, and Pupil in the Renaissance Classroom: A Case Study from a Parisian College," *History of Universities* 1 (1981): pp. 37–70.

88. See Aldridge, *Hermeneutic of Erasmus,* in general; Charles Trinkaus, *In Our Image and Likeness: Humanity and Divinity in Italian Humanist Thought* (London: Constable, 1970); Erika Rummel, "God and Solecism: Erasmus as a Literary Critic of the Bible," *Erasmus of Rotterdam Society Yearbook* 7 (1987), pp. 54–72; Kathy Eden, *Hermeneutics and the Rhetorical Tradition: Chapters in the Ancient Legacy and Its Humanist Reception* (New Haven: Yale University Press, 1997), pp. 64–101.

89. Terence Cave, *The Cornucopian Text: Problems of Writing in the French Renaissance* (Oxford: Clarendon Press, 1979); Jean Céard, "Les mots et les choses: Le commentaire à la Renaissance," in *L'Europe de la Renaissance: Cultures et civilizations,* ed. Jean-Claude Margolin and Marie-Madelaine Martinet (Paris: J. Touzot, 1988), pp. 25–36; Nancy Streuver, *The Language of History in the Renaissance: Rhetoric and Historical Consciousness in Florentine Humanism* (Princeton: Princeton University Press, 1970), pp. 82–143; Paul Grendler, *Schooling in Renaissance Italy: Literacy and Learning, 1300–1600* (Baltimore: Johns Hopkins University Press, 1989).

90. Francesco Sacchini, *De ratione libros cum profectu legendi libellus, deque vitanda moribus noxia lectione, oratio Francisci Sacchini* (Sammieli: F. Du Bois, 1615), p. 53.

91. Durey de Morsan translated Sacchini's work with the title *Moyens de lire avec fruit* (La Haye: Guillot, 1786).

92. On the culture of collecting, see Lisa Jardine, *Worldly Goods: A New History of the Renaissance* (London: MacMillan, 1996); Paula Findlen, "Possessing the Past: The Material World of the Italian Renaissance," *American Historical Review* 103 (1998), p. 89. Also see Blair, "Humanist Methods"; "Reading Strategies for Coping with Information Overload ca. 1550–1700," *Journal of the History of Ideas* 64 (2003): pp. 11–28. Also see, in general, Anthony Grafton and Nancy Siraisi, eds., *Natural Particulars: Nature and the Disciplines in Renaissance Europe* (Cambridge: MIT Press, 1999). On the general concept of the commonplace, see Ann Moss, *Printed Commonplace-Books and the Structuring of Renaissance Thought* (Oxford: Clarendon Press, 1996), p. 7; Francis Goyet, *Le sublime du "Lieu Commun": L'invention rhétorique dans l'antiquité et à la Renaissance* (Paris: Honoré Champion, 1996).

93. Moss, *Printed Commonplace-Books,* p. 27.

94. Moss, *Printed Commonplace-Books,* pp. 134–85. On the concept of Roman *educatio* in the Renaissance and the formation of the perfect elite citizen, see Anthony Grafton and Lisa Jardine, *From Humanism to the Humanities: Education and the Liberal Arts in Fifteenth- and Sixteenth-Century Europe* (London: Duckworth, 1986), 5. Also see R. Kolb, "Teaching the Text: The Commonplace Method in Sixteenth-Century Biblical Commentary," *Bibliothèque d'Humanisme et Renaissance* 49 (1987): pp. 571–85; Grafton, "Teacher, Text, and Pupil," p. 39. On pedagogy and commonplaces in general, see Moss, *Printed Commonplace-Books,* pp. 134–85.

95. See the translation of Desidirius Erasmus's *Institutio principis Christiani* (1516), *The Education of a Christian Prince,* trans. Neil M. Cheshire and Michael J. Heath, and ed. Lisa Jardine (Cambridge: Cambridge University Press, 1997). On manuals of royal education, see Isabelle Flandrois, *L'Institution du Prince au début du XVIIe siècle* (Paris:

Presses Universitaires de France, 1992); Michel Senellart, *Les arts de gouverner: Du regimen médiéval au concept de gouvernement* (Paris: Seuil, 1995).

96. For a characterization of Catholic and Protestant attitudes toward using commonplaces to render the Bible accessible to students, see Moss, *Printed Commonplace-Books*, p. 141. For another exemple of Protestant uses of commonplaces from the Scriptures, see Kolb, "Teaching the Text," pp. 571–85.

97. On the teacher extracting commonplaces for students, see Grafton, "Teacher, Text, and Pupil," p. 39. On pedagogy and commonplaces in general, see Moss, *Printed Commonplace-Books*, pp. 134–85.

98. Carlus Paschalius, *C. Cornelii Tacitii equitis romani ab excessu divi Augusti Annalium libri quatuor priores, et in hos observationes C. Paschalii cuneatis* (Paris: Aldus, 1581). For Momigliano's study of this work, see "The First Political Commentary on Tacitus," *Journal of Roman Studies* 37 (1947): pp. 91–101.

99. Momigliano, "First Political Commentary," pp. 50–51.

100. The idea of commentators of Tacitus forming maxims to make his text "usable" and "applicable" for royal readers who did want to get lost in the labyrinth of Tacitus's text is outlined in Bradford, "Stuart Absolutism," pp. 131–33.

101. These large margins may also be due to the fact that the Aldine edition is a characteristically beautiful luxury edition in folio. With the margins removed, the printed text can easily fit onto a smaller page.

102. Cambridge University Library, no. Q.8.2.

103. Michel Senellart, "Le stoïcisme dans la constitution de la pensée politique: *Les Politiques* de Juste Lipse (1589)," in *Le stoïcisme au XVIe et au XVIIe siècle*, ed. Pierre-François Moreau (Paris: Albin Michel, 1999), p. 119.

104. Justus Lipsius, *Les six livres des politiques, ou Doctrine civile de Justus Lipsius, où il est principalement discouru de ce qui appartient à la principauté*, trans. Charles Le Ber (La Rochelle: H. Haultin, 1590); *Les politiques ou doctrine civile . . . avec Le traité de la constance . . . reveus et augm. d'annotations en marge*, trans. Simon Goulart (Tours: G. Montreul and J. Richer, 1594).

105. Lazzari and Reynié, *Le pouvoir de la raison d'état*, pp. 119–28. Also see Battista, *Pensiero politico libertino*, p. 54. On the context of Charron's thought, see Henri Busson, *La pensée religieuse française de Charron à Pascal* (Paris: J. Vrin, 1933).

106. Lazzari and Reynié, *Le pouvoir de la raison d'état*, 119–28.

107. Pierre Charron, *De la sagesse*, ed. Amaury Duval (Geneva: Slatkine, 1964), vol. 2, p. 493.

108. Ibid., vol. 2, p. 487: "Ceste matiere est excellement traictée par Lipsius, à la maniere qu'il a voulu: la moüelle de son livre est ici."

109. Ibid., vol. 2, p. 283.

110. Ibid., vol. 2, p. 287.

111. Ibid., vol. 2, p. 295.

112. Adam Theveneau, *Advis et notions* (Paris: Toussaincts du Bray, 1608), pp. 3–5.

113. Adam Theveneau, *Morales* (Paris: Toussaincts du Bray, 1607), p. 320.

114. Ibid., pp. 322–23.

115. Ibid., p. 333.

116. Rodolphe Le Maistre, *L'Institution du Prince: Ensemble La Sagesse des Anciens* (Paris: Michel Sonnius, 1613), p. 4r.

117. Ibid., p. 22: "La Prudence, qui est la perfection de L'Homme, n'est pas héréditaire: elle vient par l'Expérience des choses et par l'Instruction."

118. Ibid., p. 21.

119. Ibid., p. 7.

120. Rodolphe Le Maistre, *Le Tibère Français, ou les six premiers livres des Annales de*

Cornelius Tacitus (Paris: Robert Estienne, 1616), pp. aij verso and aiij recto of the dedication.

121. Ibid., p. aij verso.

122. Ibid., p. aiiij recto.

123. Ibid.

124. Norbert Elias, *Über den Prozess der Zivilisation: Soziogenetische une psychogenetische Untersuchungen* (Basel: Haus zum Falken, 1939; 2nd ed., 2 vols., Frankfurt: Suhrkamp, 1981). See the English translation, *The Civilizing Process: The History of Manners,* trans. Edmund Jephcott (New York: Urizen Books, 1978), pp. 60–84. For a more detailed examination of the rationalization of princely behavior, see the excellent French critical edition of Elias's *La société de cour,* trans. Pierre Kamnitzer and Jeanne Etoré, with a preface by Roger Chartier (Paris: Flammarion, 1985), pp. 115–54. See Roger Chartier's study of courtly rationality, "Trajectoires." The classic study of French manners and culture in the ancien régime is Maurice Magendie's *La politesse mondaine et les théories de l'honnêteté en France au XVIIe siècle, de 1600 à 1660* (Paris: Alcan, 1925).

125. Soll, "Healing the Body Politic."

126. Soll, "La Houssaie and the Tacitean Tradition," p. 187. This number is probably greater. See Thuau, *Raison d'état et pensée politique,* pp. 33–54.

127. Henri-Jean Martin, *Livres, pouvoirs et société,* vol. 2, pp. 583–85; Roger Chartier, *Lectures et lecteurs dans la France de l'Ancien Régime* (Paris, Seuil, 1987), pp. 88–89.

128. On the foundation of the Académie Française, see L'abbé A. Fabre, *Chapelain et nos deux premières Académies* (Paris: Perrin, 1890).

129. They were Claude Fauchet (1530–1601), Jean Baudoin (1590–1650), François de Cauvigny (1588–1648), Rodolphe Le Maistre (?), Marie de Jars de Gournay (1566–1645), Louis Giry (1595–1655), Achilles de Harlay de Champvallon (?–1671), Perrot d'Ablancourt (1606–64), and Jean Puget de La Serre (1600–1665). The anonymous "P.D.B.," Etienne de La Planche (dates unknown), and Ithier Hobier (?–1644) were not in any major way connected with the king. See the bibliography in the present book for the principal translations by these authors.

130. They were de Cauvigny, Le Maistre, de Jars de Gournay, Giry, and d'Ablancourt.

131. They were de La Planche, Baudoin, Giry, Hobier, and d'Ablancourt.

132. They were Fauchet, de Cauvigny, de Jars de Gournay, and Giry.

133. The two who for certain held the position were Fauchet and Puget de La Serre. Perrot d'Ablancourt was barred from the post by Louis XIV due to his Protestantism.

134. Ithier Hobier was treasurer of the navy in the Levant and later president of the treasurers of the Généralité of Bourges. Marie de Jars de Gournay was also the adopted daughter and confidant of Montaigne.

135. Rodolphe Le Maistre, *Les oeuvres de Tacite,* 2nd ed. (Paris: J. Dugast, 1636).

136. Nicolas Perrot d'Ablancourt, *Oeuvres de Tacite* (Paris: A. Courbé, 1658), p. 1 of the dedication.

137. Achilles de Harlay de Champvallon, *Les oeuvres de Corneille Tacite,* 3rd ed. (Paris: Veuve de Jean Camusat, 1645), p. 2.

Chapter 3

1. Grafton, *Footnote,* pp. 133–38.

2. Ibid., p. 10.

3. The relationship between de Thou's library and his *Histoire* is outlined by Antoine Coron in, " 'Ut prosint aliis'; Jacques-Auguste de Thou et sa bibliothèque," *Histoire des bibliothèques françaises* (Paris: Promodis, 1988), vol. 2, p. 105.

4. Grafton, *Footnote,* p. 133.

5. The manuscript was not printed immediately. For an early printed edition, see

Jacques-Auguste de Thou, *Iac. Augusti Thuani Historiarum sui temporis libri CXXV,* 11 vols. (Paris: H. Drouart, 1609–14).

6. Peter Burke, introduction to *The History of Benefices and Selections from the History of the Council of Trent,* by Paolo Sarpi, ed. and trans. Peter Burke (New York: Washington Square Press, 1967), pp. xix–xx.

7. "Pièces concernant l'Histoire de J. A. de Thou," in Jacques-Auguste de Thou, *Histoire universelle* (La Haye: Henri Scheurleer, 1740), vol. 1, p. 373, "Extrait d'une lettre de Henri IV, à M. de Bethune, son Ambassadeur à Rome," May 4, 1604.

8. Ibid., p. 374, "Extrait d'une lettre de M. de Villeroy à M. de Bethune, Ambassadeur de France à Rome," 1604.

9. Ibid., p. 342, "Lettre de M. de Thou à M. Dupuy, à Rome," July 1606: "Il est bien difficile de dire la verité, comme la loy de l'Histoire le requiert et qu'elle est prescrite par Polybe, et pouvoir plaire aux Grands."

10. Samuel Kinser, *The Works of Jacques-Auguste de Thou* (The Hague: Martinus Nijhoff, 1966), p. 22. Despite papal censorship, de Thou managed to print various editions of his *History.* After the assassination of Henri IV in 1610 by a Catholic fanatic, he even managed to reintroduce himself at court. His historical enterprise was not wholly disastrous, for although his *History* caused him political worries until he died in 1617, it nonetheless won him the admiration of humanist Europe.

11. Grafton, *Footnote,* pp. 135–38, especially p. 136, n. 23.

12. On Sarpi, Tacitus, and the tradition of critical history, see Peter Burke, introduction to *The History of Benefices,* ix–xli. For the political context of Sarpi's work, see William J. Bouwsma, *Venice and the Defense of Republican Liberty: Renaissance Values in the Age of the Counter Reformation* (Berkeley: University of California Press, 1968). The standard intellectual biography of Sarpi is David Wootton's *Paolo Sarpi: Between Renaissance and Enlightenment* (Cambridge: Cambridge University Press, 1983).

13. J. H. M. Salmon, "Clovis and Constantine: The Uses of History in Sixteenth-Century Gallicanism," *Journal of Ecclesiastical History* 41 (1990): pp. 584–605.

14. Kelley, *Foundations,* p. 159. Kelley defines the term *legist* as a "lawyer who wrote on the king's behalf."

15. Ibid., p. 160.

16. Ibid., p. 174.

17. Ibid., p. 218.

18. Salmon, "Clovis and Constantine," p. 591.

19. Bouwsma, *Venice,* pp. 144–55.

20. Sauvy, *Livres saisis à Paris,* p. 212.

21. On Botero and reason of state, see Enzo Baldini, ed., *Botero e la "Ragion di stato"* (Florence: Olschki, 1992); *Aristotelismo politico e ragion di stato* (Florence: Olschki, 1995). The 1992 book contains Baldini's extraordinary "Bibliografia Boteriana," which includes not only Botero's works but also works on Botero and reason of state from the seventeenth century to the present (pp. 503–53). Also see Baldini, "Le guerre di religione francesi."

22. Tuck, *Philosophy and Government,* pp. 65–67.

23. Burke, "Tacitism, Scepticism, and Reason of State," pp. 479–83.

24. Viroli, *Politics to Reason of State,* pp. 257–67; Tuck, *Philosophy and Government,* p. 101.

25. Skinner, *Foundations,* vol. 1, p. 188.

26. Trajano Boccalini, *Advices from Parnassus, in two centuries, with the Political touchstone, and an appendix to it, Written by Trajano Boccalini, To which is added, a continuation of the Advices, by Girolamo Briani . . . All tr. from the Italian by several hands, Rev. and cor. by Mr. Hughes* (London: Printed by J. D. for D. Brown, 1706), chap. 86, p. 158.

27. Tuck, *Philosophy and Government,* p. 101.

28. Francesco Guicciardini, *Ricordi,* ed. Nicolai Rubenstein, trans. Mario Domandi (Phildelphia: University of Pennsylvania, 1965), 18, p. 45.

29. Cited by Brendan Dooley, *A Social History of Skepticism: Experience and Doubt in Early Modern Culture* (Baltimore: Johns Hopkins University Press, 1999), pp. 25–26.

30. Ludovico Zuccolo, *Della ragione di stato,* in *Politics e moralisti del seicento: Strada, Zuccolo, Settala, Accetto, Brignole Sale, Malvezzi,* ed. Benedetto Croce and Santino Caramelle (Bari: Laterza and Figli, 1930), p. 25.

31. Pierre Charron, *De la sagesse* (Bordeaux: S. Millanges, 1601), book 3, chap. 3.

32. Gauchet, "L'état au miroir de la raison d'état," p. 195.

33. Gabriel Naudé, *Considérations politiques sur les coups d'état,* ed. Louis Marin (Paris: Les Editions de Paris, 1988), p. 88.

34. Christian Jouhaud, *Les pouvoirs de la littérature,* pp. 156, 158.

35. Louis Marin, *Le portrait du roi* (Paris: Éditions de Minuit, 1981), p. 59. The ancients had, of course, developed a science to deal with this problem. See Sabine Mac-Cormack, *Art and Ceremony in Late Antiquity* (Berkeley: University of California Press, 1981).

36. Armand du Plessis, Cardinal de Richelieu, *Testament politique,* ed. Françoise Hildesheimer (Paris: Société de l'Histoire de France, 1995), book 2, chap. 2, pp. 245–47.

37. Alfred Soman, "Press, Pulpit, and Censorship in France before Richelieu," *Proceedings of the American Philosophical Society* 120 (1976): pp. 439–63.

38. On the culture of propaganda under Richelieu, see Christian Jouhaud, *La main de Richelieu ou le pouvoir cardinal* (Paris: Gallimard, 1991).

39. The relationship between publication and political skepticism is examined by Dooley in *A Social History of Skepticism,* pp. 1–7.

40. Jouhaud, *Les pouvoirs de litterature,* pp. 191–231; also see Jacob Soll, "Empirical History," p. 308.

41. Jean Chapelain, *Lettres,* ed. Philippe Tamizey de Larroque (Paris: Imprimerie Nationale, 1880–1883), vol. 1, p. 15.

42. Ibid., p. 16.

43. Chapelain lists his favorite ancient historians on pp. 336 and 519 of vol. 1 of his *Lettres.* He speaks of Galileo with praise on p. 310.

44. George Collas, *Un poète protecteur des lettres au XVIIe siècle, Jean Chapelain, 1595–1674* (Paris: Perrin, 1912). Also see Orest Ranum's classic *Artisans of Glory: Writers and Historical Thought in Seventeenth-Century France* (Chapel Hill : University of North Carolina Press, 1980), pp. 188–96.

45. Chapelain, *Lettres,* vol. 2, p. 275: "Je viens à l'histoire qu'avec beaucoup de raison vous avez jugée, Monsieur, un des principaux moyens pour conserver la splendeur des entreprises du Roy et le détail de ses miracles. Mais il est de l'histoire comme de ces fruits qui ne sont bons que gardés et pour arrière-saison. Si elle n'explique point les motifs des choses qui y sont racontées, si elle n'est pas accompagnée de réflexions prudentes et de documents, ce n'est qu'une relation pure, sans force et sans dignité. De les y employer aussy, durant le règne du Prince qui en est le sujet, cela ne se pourroit sans exposer au public les ressorts du Cabinet, donner lieu aux ennemis de les prévenir ou de les rendre inutiles, et trahir ceux qui auroient des liaisons avec luy, lesquelles ne subsistent que par le secret et à l'ombre d'un profond silence. Ainsi, j'estime que si vous faites travailler à l'histoire de Sa Majesté en la manière qu'elle doit estre que pour tenir l'ouvrage caché jusques à ce que les inconvénients remarqués ne puissent préjudicier à ses affaires et à ses alliés."

46. Ibid., p. 275.

47. Ibid., p. 276. Chapelain refers to Pliny's *Panegyricus,* delivered in the fall of the

year A.D. 100, when Emperor Trajan made Pliny consul. See Pliny, *Panegyricus,* trans. Betty Radice (Cambridge: Harvard University Press, 1969).

48. On Louis XIV's use of history as an arm of propaganda, see Ranum, *Artisans of Glory,* pp. 6–9.

49. Marc Fumaroli, "Histoire et mémoires," in *Chateaubriand mémorialiste: Colloque du cent ciquantenaire 1848–1998,* ed. Jean-Claude Berchet and Philippe Berthier (Geneva: Droz, 2000), p. 17.

50. Jean-Baptiste Colbert, *Lettres, instructions et mémoires* (Paris: Imprimerie Impériale, 1861–73), vol. 5, pp. 451–98.

51. Also see Ranum, *Artisans of Glory,* p. 280.

52. See Spini, "The Art of History," p. 95.

53. Ranum, *Artisans of Glory,* p. 153.

54. René Rapin, *Instructions pour l'histoire* (Paris: Sebastien Marbre-Cramoisy, 1677).

55. Ibid., p. 39.

56. Ibid., p. 94.

57. Ibid., p. 5.

58. Ibid., pp. 70, 96.

59. Ibid., p. 96.

60. Ibid., pp. 79–80.

61. Pierre Le Moyne, *De l'Histoire* (Paris: A. Billaine, 1670), pp. 200–204.

62. Ibid., p. 111.

63. Ibid., pp. 127–29.

64. On the tension between empiricism and eloquence, see Brendan Dooley, *"Veritas Filia Temporis:* Experience and Belief in Early Modern Culture," *Journal of the History of Ideas* 60 (1999): pp. 502–3.

65. Gabriel Daniel, *Histoire de France* (Paris: Jean-Baptiste Delespine, 1713), vol. 1, pp. 22–25.

66. Ibid., vol. 1, p. 25.

67. Ibid., vol. 1, p. 3.

68. Arrigo Catarina Davila, *Historia delle guerre civili di Francia* (Venice: T. Baglioli, 1630); Antoine Varillas, *Histoire de l'hérésie de Viclef, Jean Hus et Jérôme de Prague, avec celle des guerres de Bohême qui en ont esté les suites* (Lyon: J. Certe, 1682). It should be noted that Varillas nonetheless received a pension from Colbert.

69. On Colbert's vast project of collecting politically useful manuscripts, see Léopold Delisle, *Histoire générale de Paris. Le Cabinet des Manuscrits de la Bibliothèque Impériale* (Paris: Imprimerie Impériale, 1868), vol. 1, pp. 440–44.

70. Pintard, *Le libertinage érudit,* pp. 91–92.

71. Ibid., p. 113.

72. D. C. Godefroy-Menilglaise, *Les savants Godefroy: Mémoires d'une famille* (Paris: Didier, 1873), pp. 112–13.

73. Ibid., p. 114.

74. Ibid., p. 135, cited from "Instructions d'Ambassade datées du 12 mai 1637": "par soing et grande estude la cognoissance de diverses négociations importantes qui sont faictes dans l'Europe depuis long temps et mesme recueilly plusieurs traitez cy devant faits pour estre employé près de ses ambassadeurs extraordinaires qui se trouveront où la paix se traictera entre S. M. et ses alliez d'une part et l'empereur et Roy d'Hongrie, le Roy d'Espagne et les leurs d'autre. . . ."

75. Godefroy received two royal pensions, at thirty-six hundred and two thousand pounds. He received a five-hundred-pound pension from the clergy and four hundred

pounds from the princes of Longueville, who continued to pay him his father's pension. Colbert also paid him eight thousand pounds for his work in Lille, although this pension was three years in arrears when Godefroy died in 1681 (Godefroy-Ménilglaise, *Les savants Godefroy*, p. 183).

76. Godefroy-Ménilglaise, *Les savants Godefroy*, pp. 274, 385.

77. Ibid., pp. 160–61.

78. Denis II Godefroy, *Recueil des traités de confédération et d'alliance entre la couronne de France et les princes et états étrangers, depuis l'an MDCXXI jusques à présent; avec quelques autres pièces appartenantes à l'histoire* (Amsterdam: P. Van Dyke, 1664), p. 1 of the "Avertissement": "Ces Traités sont comme le centre auquel aboutissent toutes les deliberations qui se prennent dans les Conseils privez: Et là se descouvre la plus sublime prudence Politique de ces grands Hommes qui gouvernent le Monde."

79. Perhaps the greatest erudite family in French history, the Godefroys not only organized the documents of the king; they also organized their own working documents—their research notes, unpublished works, and correspondences. The fifteen large notebooks stored in the library of the Académie Française contain invaluable information concerning the work habits and methods of five generations of the Godefroy family. In Denis II's case, the documents are particularly significant, for they reveal a contrast between his ideal of history and his professional, state-sponsored work.

80. Bibliothèque de l'Institut, Fonds Godefroy, no. 287, fol. 1. Entitled "Mémoire touchant un nouveau dessein de l'histoire de France depuis St. Louis I," the note appears to date from 1665, a year after the publication of the *Recueil* and three years before Godefroy took up office in Lille.

81. Bibliothèque de l'Institut, Fonds Godefroy, no. 287, fol. 2, "Advis pour le Recueil des anciens Historiens de France."

82. Ibid., fol. 1.

83. Ibid., fol. 1.

84. Ibid., fols. 4–8, Godefroy to Colbert, November 23, 1667: "les plus dignes des glorieux desseins et belles actions de Louys XIV."

85. "Lettre au Sieur Godefroy, historiographe à Lille, 5 mars, 1669," in Colbert, *Lettres*, vol. 5, p. 274.

86. Godefroy-Menilglaise, *Les savants Godefroy*, p. 166.

87. Ibid., pp. 273–78.

88. Ibid., p. 239.

89. Barret-Kriegel, *Les historiens*, vol. 1, p. 215.

90. Denis II envisioned this project in the 1660s but never realized it. See Barret-Kriegel, *Les historiens*, vol. 1, pp. 169–70.

91. Frédéric Léonard, *Recueil des traitez de paix faits entre les rois de France et tous les princes de l'Europe depuis le règne de Charles VII* (Paris: Léonard, 1693), p. 4 of the "Avertissement."

92. Godefroy-Ménilglaise, *Les savants Godefroy*, p. 165. The Colbert family kept much of the Godefroy collection in their private possession, finally selling it back to the Bibliothèque Royale in 1732 for the staggering sum of one hundred thousand ecus. Godefroy-Ménilglaise notes that the Colberts thus made a fortune by selling to the king that which was rightfully his.

93. Léonard, *Recueil des traitez*, p. 1 of the "Avertissement."

94. Amelot de La Houssaye, *Préliminaires des traitez faits entre les rois de France et tous les princes de l'Europe* (Paris: Frédéric Léonard, 1692), P. I of the "Avertissement": "Que comme ce seroit un livre, que chacun pouvoit porter dans sa poche, on le liroit volontiers, à cause de la nouveauté du project, et de l'importance de la matière en elle-

même; que le Recüeil ne se pourroit lire dans le Cabinet, vû la grosseur des quatres volumes, qui le composent; au lieu que celui-ci se livroit Commodément, en carosse, en voyage, à la promenade, et par tout ailleurs."

95. Ibid., pp. 1–5 of the "Observations historiques et politiques sur le traitez des princes." Here is the entire passage: "Il y a si peu de gens qui sachent bien à quoi sert la lecture ou l'étude des Traitez, qui se sont entre les Princes, qu'il est besoin d'en dire ici quelque chose, avant que de parler des Traitez mêmes, pour desabuser tous ceux qui croient, que céte sorte d'étude est nécéssaire, qu'aux Ministres, aux Secretaires, et aux Conseillers d'État, ou qu'aux Ambassadeurs, aux Plenipotentaires, et enfin à ceux qui aspirent au maniment des afaires publiques, lesquels sont toûjours en très petit nombre dans les Monarchies, où tout dépend du Choix et de la Volonté du Prince. Mais si la science de faire de Traitez a peu de disciples, parce que c'est un métier, qui, à cause de son importance, et des difficultez qui s'y rencontrent, ne convient qu'à des personnes d'un génie supérieur, d'une prudence exquise, et d'une longue expérience; ce n'est pas à dire, que ceux, qui ne sont pas capables de négocier eux-mêmes, ou qui n'ont point de part au Gouvernement, ne puissent employer utilement leur temps à lire des Traitez de Paix, et des [2] Mémoires d'Ambassadeurs. Car il y a mille choses dans l'Histoire, où l'on n'entend rien, faute d'avoir connoissance des Traitez, sur lesquels elles sont fondées; et beaucoup d'Historiens raisonnent en l'air sur les différends des Princes, à faute d'être informez des conventions, des capitulations, et des transactions, que ces Princes ont fait entre eux. Or, comme l'Histoire fait la principale ocupation de la pluspart des gens du monde, de quelque profession qu'ils soient, de robe, ou d'épée; il faut conclure, que la lecture et l'intelligence des Traitez des Princes leur est absolument nécéssaire, pour entendre divers points d'Histoire, qui ne sont pas sufisament débroüillez par les Historiens, et pour discerner de quel côté est le bon droit dans les querelles, que les Princes ont tous les jours ensemble au sujet de leurs Traitez. Car bien que ceux-ci sachent donner le sens qu'ils veulent aux articles, auxquels ils contreviennent, (sur quoi Maurice, Electeur de Saxe, reprochoit à Charle-quint, qu'il avoit cru traiter avec un Empereur, et non pas avec un Légiste) les personnes de bon entendement ne laissent pas de découvrir la mauvaise foi du Prince, qui manque à sa parole, en conférant la glose, ou l'interpretation, avec le texte de l'article litigieux. C'en est assez dit sur les Traitez en général; il faut parler maintenant du Recüeil, que l'on donne au public."

Chapter 4

1. On the world of printing in seventeenth-century Paris, see, in general, Georges Lepreux, *Gallia typographica: Série parisienne; Livre d'Or des Imprimeurs du Roi* (Paris: Honoré Champion, 1911), vol. 1. See also Henri-Jean Martin, *Livre, pouvoirs et société*, vol. 1, pp. 32–47, 296–467; vol. 2, 639–44, 699–728. See, further, Elizabeth Eisenstein, *Grub Street Abroad: Aspects of the French Cosmopolitan Press from the Age of Louis XIV to the French Revolution* (Oxford: Clarendon Press, 1992); Jean-Dominique Mellot, *L'édition rouennaise et ses marchés, vers 1600–vers 1730* (Paris: École des Chartes, 1998), pp. 61–110.

2. Johns (*The Nature of the Book*, pp. 108–36) gives a sense of this labyrinthine world.

3. On the tradition of humanism and printing, see Martin Davies, *Aldus Manutius: Printer and Publisher of Renaissance Venice* (London: British Library, 1995).

4. "Requête de Pierre Herbin," Bibliothèque Nationale de France, MS fr. 8122, microfilm 5570 (hereafter "Requete de Pierre Herbin"), p. 1; Lepreux, *Gallia typographica*, vol. 1, p. 307.

5. "Requête de Pierre Herbin," p. 1.

6. Ibid., p. 3: "ledit Amelot descendit de la Chambre de ladite Défenderesse sur les trois heures du matin, pour voir administrer les Sacremens audit défunt sieur Herbin, et

l'on remarqua qu'il avoit les jambes et pieds nus." For a full account of this affair and of Amelot's life with the Léonards, see Soll, "Hand-Annotated Copy," pp. 283–86.

7. "Requête de Pierre Herbin," pp. 5–6.

8. Eisenstein, *Grub Street Abroad,* chaps. 3 and 5.

9. I am comparing the rue St. Jacques with Robert Darnton's later descriptions in *The Literary Underground of the Old Regime* (Cambridge: Harvard University Press, 1982), chap. 1.

10. "Requête de Pierre Herbin," p. 6.

11. Ibid., p. 9.

12. Leonard Krieger, *Ranke: The Meaning of History* (Chicago: University of Chicago Press, 1977), p. 1. For a similar concept of Ranke's significance, see Felix Gilbert, *History, Choice and Commitment* (Cambridge: Belknap Press, 1977), p. 43.

13. Filippo de Vivo, "Quand le passé résiste à ses historiographes: Venise et le XVII siècle," *Cahiers du Centre de Recherches Historiques* 28–29 (2002): p. 228.

14. John Pemble, *Venice Rediscovered* (Oxford: Clarendon Press, 1995), pp. 73–74.

15. Peter Burke, "Ranke the Reactionary," in *Leopold von Ranke and the Shaping of the Historical Discipline,* ed. Georg G. Iggers and James M. Powell (Syracuse: Syracuse University Press, 1990), p. 37.

16. Gino Benzoni and Tiziano Zanato, eds., *Storici e politici veneti del cinquecento e del seicento* (Milan: Riccardo Ricciardi, 1982); Elizabeth Gleason, "Reading between the Lines of Gasparo Contarini's Treatise on the Venetian State," *Historical Reflections/ Refléxions Historiques* 1 (1988): pp. 252–70.

17. Filippo de Vivo, "Le armi dell'ambasciatore: Voci e manoscritti a Parigi durante l'interdetto di Venezia," in *I luoghi dell'imaginario barocco,* ed. Lucia Strappini (Naples: Liguori Editore, 1999), pp. 189–201; "Dall'imposizione del silenzio."

18. On travel, document collection, and knowledge culture, see, in general, Justin Stagl's very fine *A History of Curiosity: The Theory of Travel, 1550–1800* (Chur, Switzerland: Harwood Academic Publishers, 1995).

19. Amelot de La Houssaye, *Histoire du gouvernement de Venise* (Paris: Frédéric Léonard, 1685), p. 7 of the dedication: ". . . vous verrez, comme dans un fidèle miroir, toutes les plus délicates maximes des Vénitiens. Je souhaiterois, qu'elle fût moins imparfaite, mais j'espère, que vous en excuserez tous les défauts, et que vous en loüerez peut être l'entreprise, qui étoit d'autant plus difficile, que Venise est un lieu, où le secret est impénétrable aux Etrangers, et particulièrement aux Ambassadeurs, et à tous les autres Ministres, à qui l'on ne parle que par gestes et par signes. Outre que l'on ne voit presque rien dans ce Gouvernement, qui ne soit couvert d'une nouée d'aparences, et de prétextes bien éloignez de la vérité. Pour moi, j'ai tâché de la dire par-tout, et vous le reconnoîtrez sans peine, MONSEIGNEUR, Vous qui la dites toujours, et qui savez si bien discerner d'avec le mensonge."

20. Ibid., p. 545.

21. Ibid., pp. 6–7.

22. Elizabeth Gleason, *Gasparo Contarini: Venice, Rome, and Reform* (Berkeley: University of California Press, 1993); Myron Gilmore, "Myth and Reality in Venetian Political Theory," in *Renaissance Venice,* ed. John R. Hale (London: Faber, 1974), p. 434.

23. *Histoire du gouvernement de Venise.* These two sections are found on pp. 543–638 (1685).

24. Ibid., pp. 543–45.

25. Ibid., pp. 563–86.

26. Pocock, *Barbarism and Religion,* vol. 1, p. 90.

27. Soll, "Healing the Body Politic," pp. 1–2, 6–9.

28. *Histoire du gouvernement de Venise* (1685), pp. 2–3 of the preface: "De sorte que,

si le sujet n'est pas nouveau, je puis dire au moins, sans me loüer, que la manière dont je traite est toute nouvelle. Ce n'est pas pourtant, Lecteur, par où je pretens rendre mon Ouvrage plus recommendable, car il l'est bien davantage par la bonté des matériaux, dont je me suis servi, qui sont les Létres, les Mémoires et les Rélations des Ambassadeurs, que l'on m'a communiquées; les anciennes Annales de céte République, d'où j'ai tiré les éxemples et les faits, que je raporte; et principalement les instructions, que j'ai eu lieu de puiser à la source même, Durant trois ans que j'ai eu l'honneur d'être employé à Venise; qui est la première cause de cet Ouvrage, auquel sans cela, je n'eusse jamais mis la main."

29. Ibid., pp. 9–11: "Pour la même raison, j'ai tâché de tirer le Conseil-de-Dix au naturel, estimant, que ce portrait seroit d'autant plus agréable, que l'on y verroit en racourci toutes les plus délicates maximes de la République, et les mistères les plus cachez de sa domination, *dominationis arcana*.* (Marge: Tac. Ann. 2.). Et je ne crains pas, que personne m'acuse de haine ni d'aigreur contre les Vénitiens, (que je n'ai aucun sujet de haïr) puisque je n'ai rien avancé que sur de bons Mémoires, et que j'ai pour garans leurs propres Historiens, plusieurs Ambassadeurs, et la Foi publique, qui métent la mienne à couvert. D'ailleurs comme ces Républicains, ainsi que le reste des hommes, sont mêlez de bien et de mal, je n'ai point supprimé, ni même exténué leurs loüanges et la gloire de leurs belles actions, lors que le fil de mon discours me les a presentées. De sorte que je crois avoir satisfait le devoir d'un Historien, qui n'aiant point d'autre but, que d'instruire, ne doit rien dissimuler, mais dire ingénûment la vérité, sans se soucier ni d'ofenser, ni de plaire, suivant le conseil de Lucien."

30. Ibid., pp. 355–56. In the fourth part of the *Histoire du gouvernement de Venise*, Amelot rewrites Sarpi's *Discurso dell'origine, forma, leggi ed uso dell'ufficio dell'Inquisitione nella Città, e Dominio di Venetia* (Venice: n.p. 1639), calling it a "Rélation du diférend du Pape Paul V. et de la Republique de Venise." Amelot expresses his belief that presenting the original documents alongside Sarpi's original, but rewritten, history will allow the reader to understand better the idea of the supremacy of royal jurisdiction over that of the pope. The *Histoire du gouvernement de Venise* (1677) also reproduces five original texts: "Bref d'Excommunication du Pape Paul V. contre les Vénitiens" (pp. 352–59); "Protestation du Sénat de Venise contre le Monitoire de Paul V." (pp. 359–62); "Letre du Sénat de Venise, écrite aux Recteurs, Consuls, & Communautez des Villes, et des autres Lieux de son Etat" (pp. 362–70); "Revocation de la Protestation du Sénat contre le Monitoire" (p. 371); "Traité de l'Interdit du Pape Paul V" (pp. 372–450). Also, bound in every edition of the *Histoire* are the *Examen de la liberté originaire de Venise* (*Il Squitinio della Libertà Veneta*) by Alphonse de la Cueva and the *Harangue de Louis Hélian Ambassadeur de France prononcé en présence de l'Empereur Maximilien etc., en l'An 1510* (both texts are printed in the same edition, first published in Ratisbonne in 1677 and then in Amsterdam in 1695 by Pierre Mortier). Also present is another separate work, Amelot's translation of the *Histoire des Uscoques,* begun by Minuccio Minucci, the archbishop of Zara, and continued by Sarpi; it was first published in 1606 in Venice. These works act like gigantic footnotes to a text that is already heavily annotated. It also contains further commentaries and the "catalogue des Maisons nobles de Venise," as well as a detailed "table des matières."

31. Ibid., p. 56.

32. Colbert sent his son, the marquis of Seignelay, to Venice in 1671 expressly to write a "relation" concerning the government, art, and the arsenal. Of course, this relation was secret. See Jean-Baptiste Colbert, Marquis de Seignelay, *L'Italie en 1671: Relation d'un voyage du marquis de Seignelay, suivie de lettres inédites à Vivonne, Du Quesne, Tourville, Fénelon, et précédée d'une étude historique* (Paris: Didier, 1867).

33. *Histoire du gouvernement de Venise* (1685), p. 14 of the preface.

34. Ibid., p. 3.

35. Ibid., p. 1.

36. For a brief characterization of the function and form of Venetian ambassadorial *relazioni*, see Donald E. Queller, "The Development of Ambassadorial Relazioni," in *Renaissance Venice*, ed. John R. Hale (London: Faber, 1974), pp. 174–96. The great collection of *relazioni* is in Luigi Firpo, ed., *Relazioni Ambasciatori Veneti*, 13 vols. (Turin: Fondazione L. Firpo, 1975).

37. Antoine Furetière's *Dictionnaire universel* (Rotterdam: A. & R. Leers, 1690) defines a "relation" as either observations made by a voyager or a testimony made by a public figure or in a court of law.

38. For an example of Renaudot's compilation of newsletters, see Théophraste Renaudot, *Pièces Historiques contenant les Couriers, Mercures, Relations, et autres semblables Observations curieuses sur l'Estat et gouvernement de France, comme il est en la présente année, 1649, C'est comme une notice générale pour servir de fondement à toute l'Histoire du temps* (Paris: Sebastien Martin, 1649). On Renaudot, see Howard M. Solomon, *Public Welfare, Science, and Propaganda in Seventeenth-Century France: The Innovations of Théophraste Renaudot* (Princeton: Princeton University Press, 1972); Pierre Clair, "L'information au quotidien: Discours politique et vision du monde dans le Mercure François et quelques autres gazettes," in *L'état Baroque: Regards sur la pensée politique de la France du premier XVIIe siècle*, ed. Henri Méchoulan (Paris: J. Vrin, 1985), pp. 301-33. Also see Jean Sgard, ed., *Dictionnaire des journalists 1600-1789* (Grenoble: Presses Universitaires de Grenoble, 1976), p. 312.

39. *Histoire du gouvernement de Venise* (1685), p. 7 of the "Défense." These *relazioni* are available in Luigi Firpo, *Relazioni Ambasciatori Veneti*, vol. 6, pp. 424-73; for the relation in question, see p. 440.

40. See the *Histoire du gouvernement de Venise* (1685), p. 355.

41. The passage on voting procedure is found on pp. 22–26 of Gasparo Contarini, *The Commonwealth and Government of Venice*, trans. Lewes Lewkenor (London: John Windet, 1599)—an English version of *De magistratibus*.

42. Andreus Morosini, *Historia Veneta ab anno M.D.XXI. vsque ad annum M.DC.XV.* (Venice: Antonium Pinellum, 1623).

43. Jonathan Swift, *Travels into Several Remote Nations of the World by Lemuel Gulliver* (London: Benjamin Motte, 1726), vol. 2, pp. 75–76.

44. Bernard de Montfaucon, *L'antiquité expliquée et représentée en figures* (Paris: F. Delaulne, 1719), vol. I, p. xij.

45. *Histoire du gouvernement de Venise* (1685), pp. 12–13.

46. On the varying editions of the *Histoire du gouvernement de Venise*, see Soll, "Hand-Annotated Copy," pp. 279-93.

47. On the idea of political literature coming from within the crown's sphere of control, see Robert Schneider's review essay "Political Power and the Emergence of Literature: Christian Jouhaud's Age of Richelieu," *French Historical Studies* 25 (2002): pp. 357-80.

48. "Mémoire pour servir à la défense de l'Histoire du gouvernement de Venise," bound at the end of the book in post-1685 editions of the *Histoire du gouvernement de Venise*, p. 1.

49. Funck-Brentano, *Les lettres de cachet à Paris*, p. 673.

50. Bouwsma, *Venice*, p. 346.

51. On the conflict of the Venetian interdict, see Bouwsma, *Venice*, chaps. 7–9.

52. "Mémoire pour servir à la défense," p. 13.

53. Ibid., p. 2.

54. Ibid. Amelot quotes Nani's dedication to the doge Domenico Contarini in Giovanni Battista Nani, *Historia della Republica Veneta* (Venice: Combi and La Nou, 1668),

vol. 1, p. 4 of the dedication: "In fatti l'Historico, assumendo Dittatura assoluta, anzi autorità piu che humana, sopra i tempi, le persone, e le attioni, presiede alla Fama, misura il merito, penetra l'intentioni, svela gli arcani; e con arbitrio indistinto sopra i Ré, et i plebei, Guidice de' Secoli corsi, e Maestro dell' avvenire, assolue, ò castiga; inganna, ò instruisce." Numerous editions of Nani's *History* were published in French in 1679, following the publication of the *Histoire du gouvernement de Venise* in 1676: Giovanni Battista Nani, *Histoire de Venise,* trans. L'abbé Tallement (Paris: Louis Billaine, 1679–80).

55. "Mémoire pour servir à la défense," p. 13: "Il y a une Rélation imprimée de l'Ambassade Extraordinaire de M. Nani en France, où il parle ainsi du Roiaume. *Vi hò incontrato inesplicabili calamità, et i popoli er ano indotti ad una infelicissima sorte, di pagare molto più di quello ritarre potevano dalla cultura de'terreni, e dalle continaute fatiche, non restandoli altro di libero che' l soffiato, perche l'aria è il più gratuito elemento della Natura, sopra' l quale l'humana inventione e sottigliezza non per anche hà saputo rinvenir dominio leggi, ed imposte.* Ce qui en bon langage veut dire, que le Roi tiranise ses Sujets, et métroit des imposts jusques sur l'air et le Soleil, s'il pouvoit. Qui est la maxime ordinaire des Républicains, pour décrier le Gouvernement des Rois, et par ces impostures rendre le leur plus tolérable à des Sujets, qui gémissent sous un peuple de Tirans." While this particular document by Nani is not reproduced in Firpo's *Relazioni Ambasciatori Veneti,* it is found in Giovanni Battista Nani, *Relazione de Francia fatta al senato veneto dapo l'ambasciata straodinaria a quella corte e letta in senato il 3 febrajo 1661, dal. cav. Gio. Battista Nani, ora la prima volta interamente publicata dal Marchese Giuseppe Melchiorri* (Roma: Tipografica della Minerva, 1844).

56. Benzoni (p. xcv) takes a brief, but insightful, look into the observations made by Amelot, which irritated the Venetians the most.

57. "Mémoire pour servir à la défense," p. 16.

58. On plasticity of printed books, see Elisabeth L. Eisenstein, "Le livre et la culture savante," in *Histoire de l'édition française,* ed. Roger Chartier and Henri-Jean Martin (Paris: Promodis, 1982), vol. 1, p. 577.

59. Soll, "Hand-Annotated Copy," p. 291.

Chapter 5

1. See chap. 1, n. 4.

2. Cappel's version does not appear to have been reedited. I have not established whether Cappel's version definitively predated that by d'Auvergne.

3. Paolo Sarpi, *Histoire du concile de Trente,* trans. Giovanni Diodati (Geneva: E. Gamonet, 1621).

4. Fumaroli, "Histoire et mémoires," p. 20.

5. Puget de La Serre dedicated his rather thin and anodyne *Maximes politiques de Tacite, ou la Conduite des gens de cour* (Paris: J. Ribou, 1664) to Marin, a royal counselor and intendant of finances. As Puget's title implies, his Tacitus was not an oracle of princes but a guide for courtiers, cut down into simple maxims. Italians such as Scipione Ammirato—who wrote the *Discorsi sopra Cornelio Tacito* (Florence: F. Giunti, 1594)—had been producing works of courtly aphorisms from Tacitus since the sixteenth century, but in France, this represented a significant change.

6. After 1650, new editions of Lipsius's *Tacitus* were no longer published. His *Politica* was no longer published after 1630. Jean Baudoin published a lone translation of the *Politica,* entitled *Le Prince parfait et ses qualitez les plus éminentes, avec des conseils et des exemples moraux et politiques tirez des oeuvres de Juste-Lipse et des plus célèbres autheurs anciens et modernes . . .* (Paris: Cardin Besongne, 1650). A translator of Tacitus and Seneca, as well as multiple Spanish works, Baudoin was perhaps the most "Lipsian" of the early seventeenth-century French authors.

7. Perrot d'Ablancourt's translation of the *Annals* (Paris: La Veuve de Jean Camusat, 1640) was reedited six times between 1640 and 1688, while his translation of Tacitus's *Works* (Paris: A. Courbé, 1658)—the *Catalogue général* of the Bibliothèque Nationale suggests that their might be a 1650 first edition—went through at least thirteen editions before 1693.

8. Pintard, *Le libertinage érudit,* pp. ix–x. On the baroque tradition of authorial dissimulation, see Burke's introduction to *The History of Benefices,* p. XXXV. On the development of political dissimulation and the Baroque in seventeenth-century Italy, see Rosario Villari, *Elogio della dissimulazione: La lotta politica nel seicento* (Rome: Editori Laterza, 1987). For an original and highly informed historical overview of dissimulation in early modern culture, see Perez Zagorin, *Ways of Lying: Dissimulation, Persecution, and Conformity in Early Modern Europe* (Cambridge: Harvard University Press, 1990); see also Jean-Pierre Chrétien-Goni, "*Institutio arcanae:* Théorie de l'institution du secret et fondement de la politique," in *Le pouvoir de la raison d'état,* ed. Christian Lazzari and Dominique Reynié (Paris: Presses Universitaires de France, 1992), pp. 135–89. Also see Gianni Vattimo, ed., *La filosofia tra pubblicità e segreto* (Rome: Laterza, 1994); Louis Marin, "La logique du secret," *Traverses* 30–31 (1984): pp. 60–69; Lucien Bély, *Espions et ambassadeurs au temps de Louis XIV* (Paris: Fayard, 1990); Dewerpe, *Espion,* pp. 56–116. For a study of the culture of secrecy and spying in Venice, see Preto, *I servizi segreti,* in general. For a recent set of literary studies on secrecy in the seventeenth century, see Jean-Pierre Cavaillé, *Dis/simulations: Jules-César Vanini, François La Mothe Le Vayer, Gabriel Naudé, Louis Machon et Torquato Accetto; Religion, morale et politique au XVIIe siècle* (Paris: Honoré Champion, 2002).

9. Leo Strauss, *Persecution and the Art of Writing* (New York: Free Press, 1952; 3rd ed., Chicago: University of Chicago Press, 1988), p. 32.

10. On the tradition of history used as a tool for unmasking, see Burke, *The Renaissance Sense of the Past,* pp. 89–104.

11. He dedicated a number of his works to members of the Le Tellier family or their entourage: the *Histoire du gouvernement de Venise* and the *Examen de la liberté originaire de Venise* are both dedicated to Louvois, the *Traité des bénéfices* to Michel Le Tellier, *La Morale de Tacite* to Boucherat, and *Tacite: Les six premiers livres des Annals* to the duc de La Feuillade; a manuscript copy of his translation of Sarpi's *Histoire du concile de Trente* made its way into the personal collection of Harlay de Champvallon, archbishop of Reims (Bibliothèque Nationale de France, MS 8375). All three of these figures had connections to the Le Tellier family.

12. Burger, "Deux documents sur Amelot de La Houssaie," p. 199.

13. Neither of these works ever received permission to be published in France.

14. Cherel (*La pensée de Machiavel,* pp. 158–64) notes that Amelot was the only overt Machiavellian writing during the reign of Louis XIV.

15. Lipsius, *Les politiques ou doctrine civile,* pp. 79–81.

16. Nicolas Caussin, *De regno Dei* (Paris: D. Bechet, 1650), p. 152.

17. Amelot de La Houssaye, *Tibère: Discours politiques sur Tacite* (Amsterdam: Héritiers de Daniel Elzevier, 1683), p. 4 of the preface.

18. Ibid., p. 8.

19. Ibid.: "J'avoüe bien que la Raison-d'Etat déroge au Droit-Commun, ou, comme parlent les autres, au Droit-Civil: *Minui jura,* disoit Tibére, *quoties gliscat potestas.* Mais il faut avoüer réciproquement, que céte dérogation, ou contravention, n'a été introduite, et n'est en usage parmi les Princes, que pour un plus grand bien, qui est la conservation, ou l'agrandissement de l'Etat, dont l'intérest est presque toujours incompatible avec celui des Particuliers."

20. Ibid., p. 1 of the "Addition."

21. Ibid., p. 53.
22. Ibid., p. 112.
23. Ibid., p. 68.
24. Ibid., p. 188.
25. Amelot de La Houssaye, *La Morale de Tacite,* 1st ed. (Paris: Veuve Martin and Boudot, 1686), pp. 2–3. The errors in the Latin text are printed in Amelot's version. This passage is shown in figs. 3a and 3b.

"DECORA ingenia, gliscente adulatione, deteruntur.* *Tacitus Annalium* 1. (*Le texte porte:* Non defuere decora ingenia, donec gliscente adulatione detererentur). Les bons esprits s'émoussent et s'abatardisent, quand il n'est plus permis de parler, ni d'écrire, sans flater.

IL n'y faut point d'autre Commentaire, que celui de Tacite même. Beaucoup d'Auteurs, dit il, nous ont donné l'histoire des sept premiers siècles de la République Romaine, du tems de laquelle on écrivoit avec tant d'éloquence, que de liberté. Mais depuis la bataille d'*Actium,* qu'il falut abandonner toute la puissance à un seul, pour avoir la paix, les grans esprits s'éclipse bientôt[a]. Et la raison qu'il en rend dans un autre endroit, est, que la Domination aiant pris la place de l'Egalité, qui est l'ame des Républiques, chacun s'étudioit à plaire et à complaire au Prince[b], pour s'élever aux dignitez, où l'on ne pouvoit plus monter, que par les degrez de la servitude[c]. Or, est-il, que la servitude et la flaterie sont les deux compagnes inséparables[d]. Et c'étoit à l'ocasion des flateries honteuses du Sénat, que Tibère s'écrioit si souvent, *O les grans esclaves*[e]! Le Jeune-Pline, que je citerai souvent, à cause de la conformité de ses maximes avec celles de Tacite, à qui il faisoit éxaminer ses écrits, parlant des livres de son Oncle, en excuse huit, qui n'étoient pas du même stile, ni de la même force que les autres, sur ce qu'il les avoit composez du tems de Néron, sous qui la servitude ne permétoit pas d'écrire avec liberté[1]. Et dans une autre létre il dit, qu'il a vû un regne, sous lequel le Sénat étoit devenu muet, et même hébété, à force de garder le silence"[2].

NOTES

[a]Post conditam Urbem DCC. et XX. prioris ævi annos multi auctores retulerunt, dum res populi Romani memorabantur pari eloquentia ac libertate. Postquam bellatum apud Actium, atque omnem potestatem ad unum conferri pacis interfuit, magna illa ingenia cessere. *Hist.* I. [b]Omnis exuta æqualitate, jussa principis aspectare. *Ann.* 1. [c]Quanto quis servitio promptior, opibus et honoribus extollerentur. *Ibidem.* [d]Quippe adulationi fœdum crimen servitutis inest. *Hist.* I. [e]Cùm fœda et nimia censerent, quoties Curia egrederetur, eloqui solitum: O homines ad servitutem paratos! *Ann.* 3. I. Dubii sermonis octo scripit sub Nerone novissimus annis, cùm omne studiorum genus paulò liberius et erectius periculosum servitus fecisset. *Epist.* 5. *lib.* 3. 2. Prospeximus Curiam, sed Curiam trepidam et elinguem, cùm dicere quod velles periculosum esset. Jam senatores, jam participes malorum, multos per annos vidimus tulimúsque, quibus ingenia nostra in posterum quoque hebetata, fracta contusa sunt. *Epist.* 14. *lib.* 8. *Il parle de Domitien. Et dans son Panégirique de Trajan il apelle céte servitude du Sénat,* mutam ac sedentariam assentiendi necessitatem."

26. Amelot de La Houssaye, *La Morale de Tacite,* pp. 57–60.
27. Ibid: "La modération de Lepidus est un bon témoignage, qu'il y peut avoir de grans hommes, je veux dire, des gens impénétrables à la flaterie et à l'injustice, sous la

domination même des plus méchans Princes; et qu'il n'y a jamais eu de siécle si stérile de vertu, qui n'en ait donné de bons éxemples. La prudence fait aler par un chemin, qui ne méne ni au précipice de la liberté, ni à l'abisme de la servitude. Elle n'est ni libre, ni servile; elle garde un tempérament, par où elle ne blesse, ni la Majesté, ni la Justice; elle rend à César ce qui apartient à César, c'est-à-dire, l'obéissance et le respect; et à Dieu ce qui est à Dieu, c'est-à-dire, tout ce qu'éxige la conscience."

28. Ibid., p. 68: "La Flaterie et l'Histoire ne sauroient jamais s'accorder ensemble, car l'une est toute dévouée au Mensonge, et l'autre à la Vérité; l'une trompe les Princes, et l'autre les instruit et les désabuse. . . . Les Grans se trompent bien, quand ils s'imaginent, que leur réputation est à couvert par la supression des livres, qui découvrent leurs défauts. Brûler les livres, c'est alumer la curiosité de les lire, au-lieu que les laisser courir, c'est en dégoûter ceux qui les lisent, et ôter la demangeaison de les lire à ceux, qui ne les ont pas lûs. Il est facile aux Grans de se vanger des Historiens, parce qu'ils ont le pouvoir de leur ôter la vie; mais ils ne sauroient éxercer leur autorité contre l'Histoire, qui est immortelle, et a toute la postérité pour juges."

29. Gauchet, "L'état au miroir de la raison d'état," p. 196.

30. Ibid., p. 198.

31. Ibid., pp. 243-44.

32. Anna Maria Battista, "Morale 'privée' et utilitarisme politique en France au XVIIe siècle," in Lazzari Christian and Dominique Reynié, eds., *Le pouvoir de la raison d'état*, pp. 191-230.

33. Ibid., p. 214.

34. Ibid., p. 208.

35. Ibid., p. 209.

36. On the plethora of princely advice books written by Jesuits in seventeenth-century Spain, see Donald Bleznick, "Spanish Reaction to Machiavelli in the Sixteenth and Seventeenth Centuries," *Journal of the History of Ideas* 19 (1958): pp. 542-550. On Loyola and Jesuit "worldly" spirituality, see Alain Guillermou, *St. Ignace de Loyola et la Compagnie de Jésus* (Paris: Seuil, 1960), pp. 158-60.

37. On the historical context of the *Oráculo manual,* see Benito Pelegrín, preface to *Manuel de poche d'hier pour hommes politiques d'aujourd'hui,* by Baltasar Gracián, ed. and trans. Benito Pelegrín (Paris: Hallier, 1978), pp. 13-18.

38. Ibid., pp. 23-25; Zagorin, *Ways of Lying,* p. 154. M. Z. Hafter's *Gracián and Perfection: Spanish Moralists of the Seventeenth Century* (Cambridge: Harvard University Press, 1966) also describes this phenomenon in relation to the idea of prudence (p. 3). On Jesuit moral reasoning, see A. R. Jonsen and S. Toulmin, *The Abuse of Casuistry: A History of Moral Reasoning* (Berkeley: University of California Press, 1988), pp. 139-51.

39. Pelegrín, preface to *Manuel de poche,* p. 21.

40. Bleznick, "Spanish Reaction to Machiavelli," p. 546.

41. In the introduction to his English translation of the *Oráculo manual,* L. B. Walton claims that no known copy of this edition survives: see *The Oracle: A Manual of the Art of Discretion,* ed. and trans. L. B. Walton (London: J. M. Dent and Sons, 1953), p. 43. However, it is mentioned in the authoritative *Biblioteca nueva de los escritores Aragoneses* by Don Felix de Latassa (Pamplona: Joaquin de Domingo, 1799), vol. 3, p. 269. All quotes from the *Oráculo* will come from the first edition of *L'Homme de cour* (Paris: La Veuve Martin and Boudot, 1684); some will be identified by maxim number, which is standard in all modern reeditions of Amelot's translation.

42. On the Spanish reception of the *Oráculo,* see the introduction to M. Romera-Navarro's critical edition of the *Oráculo manual y arte de prudencia* (Madrid: Revista de Filologia Española, 1954), pp. i-xxxix; for an updated modern study, see Pelegrín, preface

to *Manuel de poche,* pp. 65–68. Also see Robert Birely, *The Counter-Reformation Prince: Anti-Machiavellianism or Catholic Statecraft in Early Modern Europe* (Chapel Hill: University of North Carolina Press, 1980), p. 190.

43. Pelegrín, preface to *Manuel de poche,* p. 65. See also K. Heger, *Baltasar Gracián: Estilo lingüístico y doctrina de valores* (Zaragoza: Catedra Gracián—Institución Fernando El Católico, 1960), pp. 119–44.

44. On the diffusion of Gracián's works and his political thought, see the pamphlet by Francisco Maldonado entitled *Baltasar Gracián como pesimista y político* (Salamanca: Imprenta y Libreria de Francisco Nuñez Izquierdo, 1916). On Gracián's works in general and their significance in the wider field of Baroque Spanish literary culture, see Alphonse Coster's classic *Baltasar Gracián, 1601–1658* (Paris: Revue Hispanique, 1913). For somewhat outdated, but still useful, scholarship on Gracián, see the anonymously edited collection of international essays *Homenaje à Gracián* (Zaragoza: Institución Fernando el Católico, 1958). For more modern scholarship on Gracián, begin with Pelegrín's *Éthique et esthétique du Baroque: L'espace jésuitique de Baltasar Gracián* (Arles: Actes Sud, 1985). On the difficulty in deciphering Gracián, see T. L. Kassier, *The Truth Disguised: Allegorical Structure and Technique in Gracián's Criticon* (London: Tamesis Books, 1976). Aurora Egidio has emerged as a leading Gracián scholar: see *La rosa del silencio: Estudios sobre Gracián* (Madrid: Alianza Editorial, 1996); *Las caras de la prudencia y Baltasar Gracián* (Madrid: Editorial Castalia, 2000); *Humanidades y dignidad del hombre en Baltasar Gracián* (Salamanca: Ediciones Universidad de Salamanca, 2001). For superficial studies on Gracián in France, see "Baltasar Gracián: Selección de estudios, investigación actual y documentación," special issue, *Suplementos: Materiales de Trabajo Intelectual* 37 (1993): see especially Andrée Mansau, "Recepción/traducción de Gracián en Francia," pp. 87–93; Suzanne Guellouz, "Gracián en la Francia del Siglo XVII," pp. 97–104.

45. Hafter, *Gracián and Perfection,* p. 128.

46. Cicero, *De officiis,* 1.13.14 (p. 42); Machiavelli, *The Prince,* pp. 61–62.

47. Baltasar Gracián, *Oráculo manual y arte de prudencia,* maxim 220: "Quando no puede une vestirse la piel del león, vistase la de la vulpeja. Saber ceder al tiempo es exceder. El que sale con su intento nunca pierde reputación. A falta de fuerça, destreça; por un camino o por otro, o por el real del valor o por el atajo del artificio. Más cosas ha obrado la maña que la fuerça, y más vezes vencieron los sabios a los valientes que al contrario. Quando no se puede alcançar la cosa entra el desprecio." Amelot's version is the following: "*Se couvrir de la peau du renard, quand on ne peut pas se servir de celle du lion* (Maxime de Lisander qui disoit, qu'il faloit coudre la peau du renard: ou manquoit celle du lion). Sçavoir céder au tems, c'est excéder. Celui, qui vient à bout de son dessein, ne perd jamais sa réputation. L'adresse doit supléer à la force. Si l'on ne sauroit aler par le chemin roial de la force ouverte, il faut prendre la route détournée de l'artifice. La ruse est bien plus expéditive que la force. Les sages ont plus souvent vaincu les braves, que les braves les sages. Quand une entreprise vient à manquer, la porte est ouverte au mépris."

48. Baltasar Gracián, *Oráculo manual y arte de prudencia,* maxim 130: "*Hazer, y hazer parezer.* Las cosas no passan por lo que son, sino por lo que parecen. Valer y saberlo mostrar es valer dos vezes: lo que no se ve es como si no fuesse. No tiene su veneración la razón misma donde no tiene cara de tal. Son muchos más los engañados que los advertidos; prevelezé el engaño y júzganse las cosas por fuera. Ai cosas que son mui otras de lo que paracen. La buena exterioridad es la mejor recomendación de la perfección interior." Amelot's translation is the following: "*Faire, et faire paroitre.* LES choses ne passent point pour ce qu'elles sont, mais pour ce qu'elles paroissent être. Savoir faire, et le savoir montrer, c'est double savoir. Ce qui ne se voit point, est comme s'il n'étoit point. La Raison même perd son autorité, lors qu'elle ne paroît pas telle. Il y a bien plus de gens trompés, qué d'habiles gens. La tromperie l'emporte hautement, d'autant que les choses

ne sont regardées que par le dehors. Bien de choses paroissent tout autre qu'elles ne sont. Le bon extérieur est la meilleure recommandation de la perfection intérieure."

49. On the relationship between aphorisms and skepticism, see Egidio, *Humanidades y dignidad*, pp. 47–58. For a remarkable study of Gracián's influence and the relevance of his prudential theory in modern wartime German culture, see Helmut Lethen, *Cool Conduct: The Culture of Distance in Weimar Germany* (Berkeley: University of California Press, 2002).

50. The very rare first Italian edition is an anonymous translation, *Oracolo manuale e arte di prudenza cauata dagl' aforismi, che si discorrono nell'opre di Lorenzo Gratiano, mandalo in luce d. Vicenzo Giovanni de Lastanosa in Lisbona nell'officina di Enrico Vanlente de'Olliuiera l'anno 1657, Tradotta dalla lingua spagnuola nell'itagliana l'anno 1670* . . . (Parma: Mario Vigna, 1670).

51. These quotes come from the *Criticón* and *El Discreto*, cited by Karl-Ludwig Selig in *The Library of Vincencio Juan de Lastanosa, Patron of Gracián* (Geneva: Droz, 1960), p. 7.

52. E. Correa Calderón, *Baltasar Gracián: Su vida y su obra* (Madrid: Editorial Gredos, 1970), pp. 21–37.

53. On Gracián's humanism, see Egidio, *La rosa del silencio,* pp. 138–44; see also, in general, Egidio, *Las caras de la prudencia,* pp. 11–25.

54. On these authors, see the classic work by José-Antonio Maravall, *La philosophie politique espagnole au XVIIe siècle dans ses rapports avec l'esprit de la Contre-Réforme* (Paris: J. Vrin, 1955). I list the Tacitist works in the order and form in which they are found in the Lastanosa catalog: *Aphorismos sacados de Cornelio tacito* (Barcelona, 1614); *Alma o aforismos de Cornelio Tacito por D. Antonio de fuertes y Biota en Amberes* (1651); *Cornelio tacito illustrado por Don Balthasar Alamos de Barrientos* (Madrid, 1614); *Don Joachin Setanti, los aphorismos de cornelio tacito en vulgar tacito en bulgar [sic]* (Barcelona, 1614).

55. See the following essays in the catalog *Libros libres de Baltasar Gracián* (Zaragoza: Gobierno de Aragón, 2001): Fernando Bouza, " 'Aun en lo material des papel y impression': Sobre la cultura escrita en el siglo de Gracián," pp. 11–50; Aurora Egidio, "Gracián y sus libros," pp. 51–93.

56. Emmanuel Bury, *Littérature et politesse: L'invention de l'honnête homme 1580–1750* (Paris: Presses Universitaires de France, 1996), pp. 131–42.

57. Only the original German version of Elias's *Über den prozess der Zivilization* contains this reference to psychology (2nd ed., vol. 2, pp. 479–82). See Chartier, "Trajectoires," p. 316. Chartier cites Elias, *La société de cour*, p. 108.

58. Chartier, "Trajectoires," pp. 316–23.

59. On questions of authorship in Gracián's works, see Egidio, *Las caras de la prudencia,* p. 149.

60. Amelot de La Houssaye, *L'Homme de cour,* p. 1 of the preface: "Titre que j'ai changé en celui de L'Homme de cour, qui, outre qu'il est moins fastueux et moins hiperbolique, explique mieux la qualité du Livre, qui est une espèce de Rudiment de Cour et de Code-Politique."

61. Ibid., p. 2 of the preface.

62. Baltasar Gracián, *El Discreto,* ed. Aurora Egido (Madrid: Alianza Editorial, 1997), pp. 158–59.

63. Ibid., p. 159.

64. Amelot de La Houssaye, *L'Homme de cour,* pp. 4–5 of the preface: "la sçavante Comtesse d'Arande (Dona Luisa du Padille), dont le nom reste écrit des six plumes imortelles, se formalisait de ce que des matières si hautes, et qui ne sont propres, que pour des Héros, deviennent communes par l'impression; en sorte que le moindre bourgeois peut avoir pour un écu des choses, qui à cause de leur excellence, ne sçauroient être bien

en de telles mains. . . . Ainsi, quoi que les Oeuvres de Gracián soient imprimées, elles n'en sont pas plus communes, car en les achetant l'on n'achéte pas le moyen de les entendre. Tout le monde voit le festin qu'il donne, mais trés peu de gens en font: peut-être aussi a-t-il voulu mettre tout le monde en appetit. Car, à son dire, n'écrire que pour les habiles gens, c'est un hameçon genéral, parce que chacun le croit être, ou ne l'étant pas, se sent piqué du désir de le devenir."

65. Ibid., p. 7 of the preface.

Chapter 6

1. Augustine, *Confessions* (Harmondsworth: Penguin, 1964), 4.16 (pp. 87–90). On Augustine's attitudes toward reading, see Carol Everhart Quillen, *Rereading the Renaissance: Petrarch, Augustine, and the Language of Humanism* (Ann Arbor: University of Michigan Press, 1998), pp. 50–60.

2. Augustine, *De doctrina Christiana*, ed. and trans. R. P. H. Green (Oxford: Clarendon Press, 1995).

3. Jacqueline Hamesse, "The Scholastic Model of Reading," in Cavallo and Chartier, *A History of Reading*, p. 118. On the rich and varied practices of medieval reading, see Mary Carruthers, *The Book of Memory: A Study of Memory in Medieval Culture* (Cambridge: Cambridge University Press, 1990), chaps. 4 and 5.

4. Umberto Eco, *The Name of the Rose* (London: Picador, 1984), p. 400. The passage comes from 22:18–19 (KJV).

5. Grafton, "The Humanist as Reader," pp. 181–83.

6. On Luther's own frustration with establishing a stable version of the New Testament, see Jane O. Newman, "The Word Made Print: Luther's 1522 New Testament in an Age of Mechanical Reproduction," *Representations,* summer 1985, pp. 95–133.

7. Jean-François Gilmont, "Protestant Reformations and Reading," in Cavallo and Chartier, *A History of Reading*, p. 218.

8. Dominique Julia, "Reading in the Counter-Reformation," in Cavallo and Chartier, *A History of Reading*, p. 243.

9. Cited by Julia, ibid., p. 239.

10. Gilmont, "Protestant Reformations and Reading," p. 237.

11. Jean Delumeau, *Le Catholicisme entre Luther et Voltaire* (Paris: Presses Universitaires de France, 1971), p. 43.

12. Nicolas Le Maire, *Le sanctuaire fermé aux profanes ou la Bible défendue au vulgaire* (Paris: S. and G. Cramoisy, 1651), cited by Julia in "Reading in the Counter-Reformation," p. 246.

13. Julia, "Reading in the Counter-Reformation," p. 250.

14. Ibid, p. 249.

15. Jonathan Israel, *Radical Enlightenment: Philosophy and the Making of Modernity, 1650–1750* (Oxford: Oxford University Press, 2001), p. 447.

16. Ibid. See also the excellent study by Klaus Scholder, *The Birth of Modern Critical Theology: Origins and Problems of Biblical Criticism in the Seventeenth Century,* trans. John Bowden (London: SCM Press; Philadelphia: Trinity Press, 1990), pp. 138–41, originally published as *Ursprünge und Probleme der historisch-kritischen Theologie* (Munich: Christian Kaiser Verlag, 1966).

17. Israel, *Radical Enlightenment,* p. 449. Richard Simon, *Histoire critique du Vieux Testament* (Paris: Veuve Billaine, 1678). Jean Le Clerc is another important Bible critic. See Maria Cristina Pitassi, *Entre croire et savoir: Le problème de la méthode critique chez Jean Le Clerc* (Leiden: Brill, 1987).

18. Cited by Israel, *Radical Enlightenment,* p. 449. See Richard Simon, *Réponse au*

livre intitulé Sentimens de quelques théologiens de Hollande sur l'Histoire critique du Vieux Testament (Rotterdam: Reinier Leers, 1686), p. 213.

19. On the dangers of historical criticism and theology, see April G. Shelford, "Thinking Geometrically in Pierre-Daniel Huet's *Demonstratio evangelica* (1679)," *Journal of the History of Ideas* 63 (2002): pp. 599–617.

20. See Grafton, "Teacher, Text, and Pupil"; Hamesse, "The Scholastic Model of Reading," pp. 104–6.

21. On Medieval compilers, see Bernard Guenée, *Histoire et culture historique dans l'Occident médiéval* (Paris: Aubier Montaigne, 1980), pp. 112–15. On the rise of indexing information, see Ann Blair, "Annotating and Indexing Natural Philosophy," in *Books and the Sciences in History,* ed. Marina Frasca-Spada and Nick Jardine (Cambridge: Cambridge University Press, 2000), pp. 69–89.

22. Rouse and Rouse, *Authentic Witnesses,* chaps. 4–7; Hamesse, "The Scholastic Model of Reading," p. 110.

23. Stephen A. Barney, ed., *Annotation and Its Texts* (Oxford: Oxford University Press, 1991).

24. Jacob Soll, introduction to "The Uses of Historical Evidence in Early Modern Europe," Special issue, *Journal of the History of Ideas* 64 (2003): pp. 149–57.

25. On Valla's practices, see Grafton, *Footnote,* pp. 73–75; in n. 21, Grafton provides an extensive bibliography on Valla.

26. Grafton, "The Humanist as Reader," p. 199.

27. On the roles and uses of Renaissance compendia, see Barbara M. Benedict, *Making the Modern Reader: Cultural Mediation in Early Modern Literary Anthologies* (Princeton: Princeton University Press, 1996).

28. On the influence of correctors on the texts they edited, see Anthony Grafton, "Correctores corruptores? Notes on the Social History of Editing," in *Editing Texts/Texte edieren,* ed. Glenn W. Most (Göttingen: Vandenhoeck and Ruprecht, 1998), pp. 54–76. Also see the first two sections of Paul Eggert and Margaret Sankey, eds., *The Editorial Gaze: Mediating Texts in Literature and the Arts* (New York: Garland Publishing, 1998).

29. Stackelberg, *Tacitus in der Romania,* p. 190.

30. On the relationship between editing and textual appropriation, see George Hoffman, "Writing without Leisure: Proofreading as Work in the Renaissance," *Journal of Medieval and Renaissance Studies* 25 (1995): pp. 17–31.

31. Machiavelli, *The Prince,* p. 61.

32. These editions are Nicolo Machiavelli, *Princeps, item aliorum contra Machiavellum scripta de potestate et officio principum contra tyrannos, quibus accessit Ant. Possevini Judicium de Nic. Machiavelli et Jo. Bodini scriptis, Item Bruti vidiciae contra tyrannos, sive de principis in populum populique in principem legitma potestate, Item tractatus de jure magistratuum in subditos, et officio subditorum erga Magistratus* (Ursella: Cornelium Sutorium, 1600); *Le Prince,* trans. Gaspard d'Auvergne (Paris: C. Chappelain, 1613); and Amelot's version, *Le Prince de Nicolas Machiavel* (Amsterdam: Henry Wetstein, 1684).

33. Amelot de La Houssaye, *Le Prince* (1684), p. 1 of the dedication.

34. Sacchini, *Moyens de lire avec fruit,* p. 6.

35. Ibid., p. 45.

36. Ibid., pp. 45–46: "Je crois qu'il est plus commode d'écrire à la marge extérieure de la page un abrégé de ce qu'il y a de plus beau; si vous le faites avec intelligence, vous pourrez, en une petite heure, vous rappeller tout ce qu'il y a de plus faillant dans un livre volumineux. Quelques-uns ont la coutume de tracer certaines marques arbitraires, pour indiquer différentes choses qui s'offrent à eux comme dignes d'être recueillies; cette méthode a son avantage, et approche de celle des anciens. Suidas nous raconte que Suétone

composa un ouvrage sur les marques qui se trouvaient encore dans les livres des anciens; on peut voir dans Laërce quelle était jadis la figure de ces marques, dans les œuvres de Platon, les unes pour désigner ses tours de phrases, les autres pour indiquer ses belles sentences; comme aussi les signes faits pour montrer l'accord des ses dogmes, et d'autres signes pour ce qu'on devait y corriger, ou en rejeter."

37. Ibid., p. 48.

38. Ibid., p. 55: "C'est de là que sont venus les livres des *Variantes,* et des anciennes leçons, les mêlanges, les recueils les plus curieux, les abrégés, les sommaires, les compilations, les journaux et autres livres semblables. Si ces ouvrages faits de la main d'autrui nous sont utiles, combien plus nous le feront-ils, en les faisant nous-mêmes!"

39. For a more detailed study of this book and Amelot's annotations in it, see Soll, "Amelot de La Houssaie Annotates Tacitus."

40. For examples, see Soll, "Amelot de La Houssaie Annotates Tacitus."

41. Ibid., p. 176.

42. For example, on page 94, the word "Æserninum" is underlined in red pencil, and the number "205" is written in the margin. On page 205, the word "Æsernini" is underlined, and the number "94" is written next to it in the margin. Also written in the margin is the note "Esernie, ville du Samnium." In this case, Amelot references the subject of the city of Æsernia with a historical annotation that refers to another example of a similar word, with a clarifying historical note. This annotation aids in translating "Æsernia" and contextualizing it historically. See "Amelot de La Houssaie Annotates Tacitus," pp. 176–78.

43. Examples of this practice are found on page 101, where a symbol resembling a quotation mark is written next to the word "pertinerent" and also in the margin next to the reference number "60." On the same page, a cross is also written next to the word "sententiae" and next to the reference number "98."

44. On the culture of textual correction in the printing shop, see Anthony Grafton, "Printers' Correctors and the Publication of Classical Texts," in *Bring Out Your Dead,* pp. 141–55.

45. "Desqu'on se méle d'écrire, il faut se metre au dessus de l'opp'e et de la crainte, pour avoir la force de dire toujours la vérité." This passage is drawn from René Rapin's *Instructions pour l'histoire* (Paris: Sebastien Marbre-Cramoisy, 1677), p. 34: "Et comme elle est sans cesse corrompuë, et mesme profanée par la lâcheté des flateurs, la pluspart des Historiens estant d'ordinaire pensionnaires des Cours: on doit se mettre au dessus de l'esperance, ou de la crainte, dés qu'on se mesle d'escrire, pour avoir la force de dire toujours la verité." Amelot's quote was probably made from memory, for it is out of order and lacks the first part of the passage. See "Amelot de La Houssaie Annotates Tacitus," p. 182.

46. Amelot de La Houssaye, *Le Prince* (1684), pp. 6–7 of the preface: "Or comme Machiavel les [les maximes politiques] a, pour la pluspart, empruntées de Tacite, le Maître et l'oracle ordinaire des Princes, j'ai cité les passages de cet Auteur, pour faire toucher au doîgt, que Machiavel n'est que son disciple, et son interpréte."

47. Amelot de La Houssaye, *Le Prince* (1684), p. 12 of the preface: "Outre plusieurs Notes, tirées des autres Oeuvres de Machiavel, et des Histoires de Nardi et de Guichardin, j'ai mis au-dessous du texte divers passages de Tacite, qui servent de preuve, de confirmation, ou d'exemple à ce que Machiavel dit. Et cela fait une espéce de concordance da la Politique de ces deux Autheurs, par où l'on verra, que l'on ne sauroit ni approuver, ni condamner l'un sans l'autre: de sorte que si Tacite est bon à lire pour ceux, qui ont besoin d'apprendre l'art-de-gouverner, Machiavel ne l'est guères moins; l'un enseignant, comment les Empereurs Romains gouvernoient, et l'autre, comment il faut gouverner aujourd'hui."

48. Soll, "Amelot de La Houssaie Annotates Tacitus," pp. 183–84.

49. For a detailed analysis of the other examples, see Soll, "Amelot de La Houssaie Annotates Tacitus."

50. Amelot de La Houssaye, *Le Prince* (1684), p. 61, n. 1: "Mais depuis, le Duc craignant, qu'une autorité si excessive ne devint odieuse, I. Nec unquam satis fida potentia, ubi nimia est, dit Tacite, (Hist. 2.)."

51. Ibid., p. 61, n. 2: "Et comme il voiot, que les rigueurs du passé lui avoient atiré de la haine, il s'avisa, un matin, de faire pourfendre Remiro, et de faire exposer sur la Place de Cesene les pièces de son Corps, plantée sur un pieu, avec un couteau ensanglanté à côté, pour montrer au peuple, que les Cruautés commises ne venoient pas de lui, mais du naturel violent de son Ministre. 2. C'est l'ordinaire des Princes de sacrifier, tôt ou tard, les instrumens de leur cruauté. *Scelerum Ministros,* dit Tacite de Tibèrc, *ut perverti ab aliis nolebat: ita plerumque satiatus, veteres et praegraves adflixit.* (Ann. 4.) *Levi post admissum scelus gratia, dein graviore odio.* (Ann. 14.)."

52. The full title of this work is *Mémoires de M. D. L. R., contenant les brigues pour le gouvernement à la mort de Loüys XIII, guerre de Paris, retraitte de M. de Longueville en Normandie, récapitulation, ou abrégé de tout ce que dessus, avec l'emprisonnement des trois princes, ce qui s'est passé depuis la prison des princes jusqu'à la guerre de Guyenne, guerre de Guyenne avec la dernière de Paris, etc., auxquels sont adjoustés les Mémoires de M. de La Chastre* (Cologne: P. Van Dyck, 1662).

53. Amelot de La Houssaye, *Tacite: Les six premiers livres des Annals* (Paris: Martin, Boudot et Martin, 1690), p. xxxiv of the "Discours critique": "D'ABORD on sera surpris de voir nommer ici ce Duc, mais ceux, qui auront lû ses Mémoires et les Oeuvres de Tacite avec quelque atention, devineront sans peine, pouquoi je le mets dans ce Catalogue; car bien que sa rélation des *brigues faites pour le Gouvernement à la mort de Loüis XIII. et de la Guerre de Paris,* ne soit rien moins, en aparence, qu'un Commentaire sur Tacite, néanmoins c'en est véritable, où il a eu l'adresse de faire une aplication juste des plus beaux traits de Tacite aux afaires de la Regence, et aux Ministres, qui les ont maniées."

54. Ibid., p. xxxv: "je dirai sans hésiter qu'il ne s'est jamais rien écrit en nôtre langue, qui approche tant du caractère de Tacite."

55. La Rochefoucauld, *Mémoires de la minorité de Louis XIV,* ed. Amelot de La Houssaye (Villefranche: Jean de Paul, 1688), pp. 171–73.

56. Ibid.

57. Ibid., p. 173: "la concorde et la puissance sont incompatibles en un même lieu: Arduam eodem loci potentiam et concordiam esse. *Ann. 4.*"

58. Ibid., p. 4 of the "Avertissement": "C'est pour en donner quelques preuves qu'on a eu soin de mettre au bas de chaque page des extraits du texte latin de Tacite, et pour faire voir la conformité de ses maximes avec celles de nôtre Autheur."

59. He is referring to the anonymous *Abrégé de la vie de M. de Turenne, ou Réflexions sur quelques affaires du temps* (Villefranche: Charles de la Vérité, 1676).

60. Michel de Certeau, *The Practice of Everyday Life,* trans. Steven Rendall (Berkeley: University of California Press, 1984), pp. xii–xiii, originally published as *L'invention du quotidien,* vol. 1, *Arts de faire* (Paris: Gallimard, 1980), pp. xlix. "Poacher" is a translation from the French *braconnier.*

61. Ginzburg, *The Cheese and the Worms,* especially p. 21.

62. Pierre Bayle, *Dictionnaire critique et historique* (Rotterdam: A. Leers, 1697), p. 2 of the preface.

63. Ibid.: "J'ai divisé ma composition en deux Parties: l'une est purement Historique, un Narré succinct des Faits: l'autre est un grand Commentaire, un mêlange de Preuves et de Discussions, où je fais entrer la Censure de plusieurs Fautes, et quelquefois même une tirade de Réflexions Philosophiques; en un mot, assez de variété pour pouvoir croire, que par un endroit ou par un autre chaque espece de Lecteur trouvera ce qu'il l'accommode."

64. Henri-Jean Martin, *Mise en page et mise en texte du livre manuscrit* (Paris: Editions du Cercle de la Librairie, 1991).

65. E. J. Kenney, *The Classical Text: Aspects of Editing in the Printed Age* (Berkeley: University of California Press, 1974), pp. 63–64; Grafton, *Footnote,* 197. On the close cultural connection between seventeenth-century historians and antiquarians, see Barbara Shapiro, *A Culture of Fact: England, 1550–1720* (Ithaca: Cornell University Press, 2000), p. 51; see Momigliano's work in general; Miller's fundamental study, *Peiresc's Europe;* and Pocock, *Barbarism and Religion,* vol. 2.

66. Bayle, *Dictionnaire,* vol. 1, p. 1046, cited by Grafton, *Footnote,* p. 141.

67. Lawrence Lipking, "The Marginal Gloss," *Critical Inquiry* 3 (1976–77): p. 625, n. 2. Also see Lipking's *The Ordering of the Arts in Eighteenth-Century England* (Princeton: Princeton University Press, 1970), p. 77.

68. Lipking, "The Marginal Gloss," p. 625.

69. Amelot de La Houssaye, *Tibère: Discours politiques sur Tacite* (Paris: Frédéric Léonard, 1684), pp. 5–6 of the preface: "Car je me suis presque toujours assujéti à le commenter par lui même, tenant pour maxime incontestable, que le Commentateur ne doit jamais emprunter d'autres lumières, que de l'esprit même de l'Auteur qu'il commente, quand c'en est un, qui excelle en son genre par dessous tous les autres, comme fait Tacite en fait de Politique. De sorte que mon Commentaire est aussi une espèce de Concordance des meilleurs Axiomes et Aforismes de Tacite, comme il est aisé d'en juger par les passages, qui sont à toutes les marges. Où l'on en trouvera aussi plusieurs du Jeune-Pline, de qui je me suis servi d'autant plus volontiers qu'il étoit le Compagnon d'études de Tacite, et qu'ils se servoient de Maitre l'un à l'autre."

70. Ibid., p. 3 of the preface: "Car comme le dessein, l'ordre, et les paroles sont de ma façon, les préceptes et les enseignemens, qui s'adressent aux Princes, à leurs Ministres, et à leurs Courtisans, sont presque tous de Tacite, comme vous le verrés par la multitude des passages, que j'ai mis à la marge, lesquels d'ailleurs vous serviront de clef, pour entrer dans les plus hauts mistères de sa Politique."

71. The idea of commenting on an author with his own work is a concept as old as scholarship itself. On the case of Aristarchus's criticism of Homer, see L. D. Reynolds and N. G. Wilson, *Scribes and Scholars: A Guide to the Transmission of Greek and Latin Literature* (Oxford: Clarendon Press, 1991), p. 13. For a detailed examination of Aristarchus's practice of criticism and commentary, see R. Pfeiffer, *History of Classical Scholarship: From the Beginnings to the End of the Hellenistic Age* (Oxford: Clarendon Press, 1968), pp. 210–33.

72. Amelot de La Houssaye, *La Morale de Tacite: De la flaterie* (La Haye: Adrien Moetjens, 1686), p. 31 of the "Discours critique": "Je finis en avertissant le lecteur, que tous les passages de Tacite sont marquez par les létres de l'alfabet, et ceux du Jeune-Pline et de Patercule, par des chifres; et les notes Françoises par des étoiles; . . . car comme mon texte sert de version à mes notes, mes notes en servent réciproquement à mon texte."

73. Ibid., pp. 243–48.

74. Ibid., pp. 248–50.

75. Bayle, *Nouvelles de la république des lettres,* January 1686, p. 628.

76. Ibid., June 1686, p. 631.

77. Ibid., June 1684, p. 623.

78. Ibid., p. 627.

79. Ibid., p. 628.

80. Ibid., June 1686, p. 625: "Une des choses sur laquelle les jugemens des hommes s'accordent le plus à l'égard de cet ancien Historien, c'est que ses Histoires sont l'image de la conduite de toutes les Cours, et par là l'on satisfait aisément à ceux qui se plaignent que son Ouvrage est une Ecole de pernicieuse politique, car il est juste de s'imaginer qu'une

chose qui se répand dans tous les lieux et dans tous les siécles est si bien fondée sur l'etat corrompu de L'Homme, qu'elle ne seroit pas moins en vogue si Tacite n'eût jamais écrit. Ses maximes d'Etat sont presque devenuës un mal nécessaire, et ceux qui les blâment quand ils ne font que simples particuliers, en font bien souvent les plus fidéles observateurs quand ils sont appellez au Ministére."

81. Ibid., July 1684, pp. 522–24.

82. Ibid., January 1687, p. 99.

83. Ibid., p. 100: "Il est surprenant qu'il y ait si peu de personnes qui ne croient que Machiavel aprend aux Princes, qui ont apris à Machiavel ce qu'il a écrit. C'est l'etude du monde, et l'observation de ce qui s'y passe et non pas une creuse mediation de Cabinet qui ont été les Maitres de Machiavel. Qu'on brule ses livres, qu'on les refutc, qu'on les traduise, qu'on les commente, il n'en sera ni plus ni moins par raport au gouvernement."

84. Adrien Baillet, *Journal des Savants* (Amsterdam: Wolfgang, Waesberge, Boom and van Someren, 1687), p. 183: "Les sçavans en jugeront par l'opposition qu'il en fait au sens qu'il donne aux endroits de Tacite qu'il a choisis, après en avoir rapporté le Texte latin. Ces endroits sont ou des sentences concernant le caractere, les effets et les usites de la flaterie, ou des préceptes pour les Princes contre ce poison des Cours. M. de la Houssaïe les éclaircit et les commente par mille beaux traits d'histoire et par des passages du jeune Pline, de Patercule et de Tacite même, qui font egalement connoître et sa lecture et son bon goût. Ainsi sans entrer dans un détail qui nous méneroit trop loin. . . ."

85. Amelot de La Houssaye, *Tacite: Les six premiers livres des Annales* (Paris: Veuve de Jean Boudot, 1690), p. 10 of the "Avertissement": "Quelqu'un m'aïant averti, que l'on disoit dans le monde, que les Notes historiques et politiques, qui servent de commentaire à ma traduction, ne pouvoient être qu'une redîte de tout ce qui est dans mon TIBERE, je suis obligé de déclarer ici, qu'elles en sont pour le moins aussi diférentes, que ma version l'est de celle de d'Ablancourt. Et je suis assuré, que ceux qui voudront prendre la peine de conférer ce Commentaire avec l'autre, avoüeront que mon travail est double."

86. Amelot de La Houssaye, *Tacite* (La Haye: Henri Van Bulderen, 1692), vol. 2, p. 532, nn. 4–5: "4. Le Gouvernement Républicain est toujours odieux aux Rois et aux Princes voisins, parce qu'il fait à leurs Sujets une perspective de liberté, qui leur rend la servitude insuportable, et les fait quelquefois succomber à la tentation chatoüilleuse de s'en délivrer. 5. Aujourd'hui, il n'y a plus de flaterie à inventer, l'esprit humain est épuisé de ce côté-là. Les siècles à venir auront céte obligation au nôtre, que l'impossiblité de passer outre les métra à couvert de l'infamie qu'ils auroient pû encourir, si nôtre exemple ne les eût pas prévenus."

87. Robert Darnton, "Readers Respond to Rousseau: The Fabrication of Romantic Sensitivity," in *The Great Cat Massacre*, pp. 215–56.

88. Jean-Jacques Rousseau, *Du contrat social; ou Principes du droit politique* (Amsterdam: Marc Michel Rey, 1762), book 3, chap. 6, p. 105.

89. Ibid., p. 109.

Chapter 7

1. Frederick II, King of Prussia to Voltaire, November 6, 1739, in François Marie Arouet de Voltaire, *Correspondence*, ed. Theodore Besterman et al. (Geneva: Institut et Musée Voltaire, 1970), vol. 91, p. 35: "Je m'étois ouvers à quelqun du Desein que j'avois de réfutér Machiavel, ce quelqu'un m'assura que c'étoit peine perdue puisque l'on trouvoit dans les Notes politiques d'Amelot de la Houssai sur Tacite une réfutation complète du Prince politique. J'ai donc lû Amelot et ces Notes mais je n'y ai point trouvé ce qu'on m'avoit dit, ce sont quelques Maximes de ce politique Dangereux et Détestable qu'on réfute, mais ce n'est pas l'ouvrage en corps." Besterman's notes do not shed any light on the identity of Frederick's "someone."

2. Voltaire to Frederick, February 23, 1740, and Voltaire to Frederick, March 10, 1740, in Voltaire, *Correspondence*, vol. 91, pp. 110, 120. The letter of March 10 mentions Frederick's request to have his refutation published alongside Amelot's version of *The Prince*.

3. Frederick II von Hohenzollern, *Anti-Machiavel, ou Essai de critique sur le Prince de Machiavel, publié par Mr. De Voltaire, Imprimé sur l'Edition Originale de l'Editeur* (Amsterdam: Aux dépens de La Compagnie, 1742), p. xxx of Frederick's introduction: "Le Prince de Machiavel est en fait de Morale ce qu'est l'Ouvrage de Spinosa en matiére de Foi. Spinosa sapait les fondemens de la Foi, et ne tendait pas moins qu'à renverser l'édifice de la Religion; Machiavel corrompit la Politique, et entreprit de détruire les préceptes de la saine Morale." The modern edition published by Theodore Besterman— *L'Anti-Machiavel*, ed. Charles Fleischauer (Geneva: Voltaire Foundation, 1958)—retains Voltaire and Frederick's prefaces but omits Amelot's preface and notes.

4. *Antimachiavel*, p. vi: "J'ose prendre la défense de l'humanité contre ce monstre qui veut le detruire; j'ose opposer la raison et la justice à l'iniquité et au crime. . . ."

5. Amelot's version of *The Prince* was reedited in Paris at least three times during the twentieth century, by Garnier Frères in 1941 and 1960 and by La Tradition in 1948.

6. Voltaire to Frederick, December 28, 1739, and Frederick to Voltaire, February 3, 1740, in Voltaire, *Correspondence*, vol. 91, pp. 54, 99. The letter of February 3 contains Frederick's request to remain anonymous.

7. Voltaire to Van Duren, June 13, 1740, in Voltaire, *Correspondence*, vol. 91, p. 96: "Imprimez à côté *le texte de la traduction du Prince de* Machiavel *par Amelot de La Houssaye, et les mêmes titres courants de chapitres.* Cependant, monsieur, faites moi tenir un exemplaire de cette traduction afin que je me règle sur elle pour composer la Préface, dont on m'a fait l'honneur de me charger." In letter 2118, Voltaire displays his concern about the *mise en livre* of the different texts and how they will complement one another: "Puisque vous avez la traduction d'Amelot, ne manquez pas de l'imprimer à côté de mon auteur. Ma préface précédera celle d'Amelot et celle de Machiavel, qu'Amelot a traduite, et annoncera l'oeconomie de tout le livre." On Voltaire's relationship with Fredrick II, see Christiane Mervaud, *Voltaire et Frédéric II* (Oxford: Voltaire Foundation, 1985), pp. 89–100.

8. Voltaire to Van Duren, June 27, 1740, in Voltaire, *Correspondence*, vol. 91, p. 221.

9. Voltaire to Frederick, October 12, 1740, in Voltaire, *Correspondence*, vol. 91, pp. 314–15.

10. *Antimachiavel*, p. III.

11. Ibid.

12. Ibid.: "Il parle beaucoup de *raison d'État* dans son Épitre Dédicatoire; mais un homme, qui, aiant été Sécretaire d'Ambassade, n'a pas eu le secret de se tirer de la misére, entend mal, à mon gré, la raison d'État."

13. Ibid.

14. Ibid., p. V: "Enfin, la Houssaye prétend que Machiavel haïssoit la tyrannie; sans doute tout homme la déteste, mais il est bien lâche et bien affreux de la détester et de l'enseigner."

15. Ibid.

16. Voltaire, *Correspondence*, vol. 90, letter 18280 (1775), p. 138.

17. Denis Diderot, ed., *Encyclopédie, ou Dictionnaire raisonné des sciences des arts et des métiers, par une société de gens de letters,* 17 vols. (Neufchâtel: Samuel Faulche, 1765), vol. 12, p. 918, s.v. "Politique."

18. Ibid., vol. 13, p. 527, "Prudence": "On le définit plus exactement: *la vertu qui nous fait prendre des moyens pour arriver à une fin,* je suppose que l'on sous-entend une

fin *louable* ou *raisonnable:* la fin donnant le prix à toute notre conduite, comment y auroit-il du mérite à savoir atteindre un but qui ne méritoit pas d'étre atteint?"

19. Ibid.: "Il y a . . . une grande différence entre la prudence et la mauvaise foi; et quoique dans ce siecle corrompu on leur donne le même nom, le sage les distingue très-aisément. La véritable prudence n'a pas besoin de regles qui lui apprennent le moyen de secouer le joug de la vertu et de l'honneur. . . . Un grand coeur, dans quelque état qu'il soit placé, prend toujours la vertu pour guide. Le crime est toujours crime, et rien ne lui fait perdre sa noirceur."

20. Ibid., vol. 13, p. 776, s.v. "Raison d'État."

21. Ibid., vol. 4, pp. 489–97.

22. Ibid., vol. 4, p. 492.

23. Ibid., vol. 4, p. 493.

24. Ibid., vol. 4, p. 494.

25. Ibid.

26. Ibid.: "Par-là l'Histoire, dans sa partie morale, est une espèce de labyrinthe où l'opinion du lecteur ne cesse de s'égarer; c'est un guide qui lui manque: or ce guide seroit un *critique* capable de distinguer la vérité de l'opinion, le droit de l'authorité, le devoir de l'intérêt, la vertu de la gloire elle-même; en un mot de réduire L'Homme quel qu'il fût, à la condition de citoyen; condition qui est la base des lois, la regle des moeurs, et dont aucun homme en société n'eut jamais droit de s'affranchir."

27. Ibid., vol. 4, p. 496.

28. Pierre Richelet, *Dictionnaire de la langue française,* (Geneva: Jean Herman Widerhold, 1685), p. 158 of the Second Part: "POLITIQUE. C'est l'art de gouverner les États. La politique a pour but d'établir un État naissant, de conserver heureusement l'État qui est établi, de soûtenir celui qui est sur son penchant et d'empêcher qu'il ne tombe en décadence. La prudence est l'âme de la politique."

29. *Encylopedie,* vol. 13, pp. 917–19.

30. Ibid., vol. 13, p. 917.

31. Ibid., vol. 9, p. 793: "Lorsque Machiavel écrivit son traité du prince, c'est comme s'il eût dit à ses concitoyens, *lisez bien cet ouvrage. Si vous acceptez jamais un maître, il sera tel que je vous le peins; voilà la bête féroce à laquelle vous vous abandonnerez.*"

32. Momigliano, "Tacitus and the Tacitist Tradition," in *Classical Foundations of Modern Historiography,* p. 127.

33. Louis Desgraves and Catherine Volpilhac-Auger, *Catalogue de la bibliothèque de Montesquieu à La Brède* (Paris: Universitas, 1999), p. 302. Catherine Volpilhac-Auger claims in *Tacite et Montesquieu* (Oxford: Voltaire Foundation, 1985) that Montesquieu was heavily influenced by Tacitus.

34. Dr. Hoefer, ed., *Nouvelle biographie générale depuis les temps les plus reculés jusqu'à nos jours* (Paris: Firmin Didot Frères, 1855), vol. 7, p. 670.

35. Amelot de La Houssaye and François Bruys, trans., *Tacite: Avec des notes politiques et historiques* (The Hague: Henri Scheurleer, 1730), pp. 1–5 of the preface.

36. Ibid., p. 7 of the preface.

37. Ibid., p. 8 of the preface.

38. Ibid., p. 12 of the preface: "Je parois un peu Républicain dans mes Notes Politiques; mais on auroit tort d'en conclure que je désaprouve le Gouvernement Monarchique. J'en connois trop bien les avantages: je ne blâme que les Tyrans et la Tyrannie."

39. Jean-Jacques Rousseau, "Traduction du premier livre de l'Histoire de Tacite," in *Oeuvres complètes* (Paris: Chez Furne, 1837), vol. 3, pp. 302–29.

40. Lionel Gossman, *Medievalism and the Ideologies of the Enlightenment: The World and Work of La Curne de Sainte-Palaye* (Baltimore: Johns Hopkins Press, 1968), p. 115.

41. I refer to the later reprint, Jean Lerond d'Alembert, *Mélanges de littérature, d'histoire et de philosophie* (Amsterdam: Zacharie Chatelain and Fils, 1777), vol. 3, containing three internal volumes.

42. Ibid., the final volume contained in the single book, pp. 5–19.

43. Jean-Philippe-René, abbé de La Blétterie, *Tibère: Les six premiers livres des Annales de Tacite* (Paris: Imprimerie Royale, 1768), p. vj.

44. Ibid., pp. vij–viij: "Dans le cours de vingt-deux années, dont je traduis l'histoire, on suit les progres du despotisme. On le voit marcher d'abord à pas lents, et comme sondant le terrein; avancer ensuite plus rapidement; arriver enfin à son comble, toujours sous le voile des formes républicaines, toujours abusant de la lettre des loix pour en detruire l'esprit."

45. Ibid., p. xxviij: "Dans cette compilation de maximes et de traits empruntés pour la plupart des auteurs Espagnols, parmi beaucoup de choses communes on rencontre quelquefois de l'or."

46. Daniel Roche, *Les républicains des lettres: Gens de culture et Lumières au XVIIIe siècle* (Paris: Fayard, 1988), p. 91.

47. Ibid., p. 177.

48. Amelot de La Houssaye, "Observations historiques et politiques sur le traitez des princes," p. 2 in Léonard, *Recueil.*

49. Gossman, *Medievalism,* p. 92. For the clearest description of Boulainvillier's work and its historical context, see Harold A. Ellis, *Boulainvilliers and the French Monarchy: Aristocratic Politics in Early Eighteenth-Century France* (Ithaca: Cornell University Press, 1988), pp. 64–91.

50. On Peiresc and his international document network, see Peter Miller, *Peiresc's Europe: Learning and Virtue in the Seventeenth Century* (New Haven: Yale University Press, 2000).

51. Roche, *Les républicains des lettres,* pp. 189–92.

52. Daniel Roche, *La France des Lumières* (Paris: Fayard, 1993), pp. 251–53.

53. Ibid., pp. 92–98.

54. Baker, *Inventing the French Revolution,* pp. 34–36.

55. Ibid. See also Franklin L. Ford's classic study, *Robe and Sword: The Regrouping of the French Aristocracy after Louis XIV* (Cambridge: Harvard University Press, 1962), pp. 232–52.

56. On Moreau, see Barret-Kriegel, *Les historiens,* vol. 1, pp. 216–67; Baker, *Inventing the French Revolution,* pp. 37–68.

57. Coincidentally, Silhouette translated a version of *L'Homme de cour* in which he claimed in the preface that he wanted to be a modern Amelot de La Houssaye: Etienne de Silhouette, *Réflexions politiques de Baltasar Gracián sur les plus grands princes et particulièrement sur Ferdinand le Catholique, ouvrage traduit de l'espagnol, avec des notes historiques et critiques, par M. D. S***** (Paris: B. Alix, 1730).

58. Baker, *Inventing the French Revolution,* pp. 40, 63.

59. Ford, *Robe and Sword,* p. 252.

60. Margaret C. Jacob, *The Radical Enlightenment: Pantheists, Freemasons, and Republicans* (London: Allen and Unwin, 1981).

61. Napoleon Bonaparte, *Manuscrits inédits,* pp. 338–49.

62. Gay, *The Enlightenment,* vol. 1, p. 142.

Catalog of Works by Abraham-Nicolas Amelot de La Houssaye

A basic premise of this book is that Amelot de La Houssaye is the author of the books he edited. Thus, this bibliography, though not possibly exhaustive, contains all works he wrote, translated, and edited. Works by other authors—such as Baltasar Gracián, Machiavelli, Paolo Sarpi, La Rochefoucauld, and Tacitus—that were edited by Amelot are found here and not in the principal bibliography; the original author's name is found at the head of the reference.

Manuscript Sources by Amelot de La Houssaye

C. Corn. Tacitus, et in eum M. Z. Boxhornii et H. Grotii observations. Venice: Juntas and Baba, 1645. Réserve of the Bibliothèque Nationale de France, Rés. J. 2353. This copy contains manuscript annotations by Amelot de La Houssaye that were used to write the notes of Amelot's version of *The Prince*.

Histoire du concile de Trente de la Bibliothèque de l'archeveque de Reims mis dans celle du Roy. N.d. Bibliothèque Nationale de France, MS fr. 8375. The first printed version of the *Histoire* (Amsterdam: G. P. and J. Blaeu, 1683) is based on this undated manuscript first edition.

Histoire du gouvernement de Venise. Paris: Frédéric Léonard, 1677. Personal collection of Mr. François Moureau. This copy contains manuscript annotations by Amelot de La Houssaye that were integrated into the 1685 edition of the *Histoire.*

Printed Books by Amelot de La Houssaye

Abrége du procès des Juifs de Metz. Paris: Frédéric Léonard, 1670.

Bruys, Fránçois. *Tacite: Avec des notes politiques et historiques.* The Hague: Henri Scheurleer, 1730.

Gracián, Baltasar. *L'Homme de cour.*
    Paris: la Veuve Martin and Boudot, 1684.
    Paris: la Veuve Martin and Boudot, 1685.
    London: John Taylor, 1687.
    Paris: la Veuve Martin, Boudot and Martin, 1687.
    Paris: la Veuve Martin, Boudot and Martin, 1688.
    Paris: la Veuve Martin, Boudot and Martin, 1690.
    Paris: Edme Couterot, 1693.
    La Haye: Abraham Troyel, 1701.
    Paris: Damien Beugnié, 1702.
    Paris: Pierre Humbert, 1708.
    Augsburg: Paul Kühtze, 1710.

Paris: Paulus du Mesnil, 1716.

Venice: Gabriel Hertz.

Rotterdam: Jean Hofhout, 1748.

Paris: Leopold Colin, 1808.

Paris: Léon Pichon, 1924.

Paris: Grasset, 1924.

Paris: Éditions Champ Libre, 1972.

Paris: Éditions Champ Libre, 1980.

Paris: Éditions Gérard Lebovici, 1990.

Paris, Éditions Ivrea, 1993.

Paris: Éditions Gérard Lebovici, 1995.

Paris: Éditions Mille and Une Nuits, 1997.

Histoire du gouvernement de Venise.

2 vols. Paris: Frédéric Léonard, 1676.

2 vols. Paris: Frédéric Léonard, 1677.

Paris: Frédéric Léonard, 1685. This edition contains the *Examen de la liberté originaire de Venise* (Ratisbonne: Jean Aubry, 1677).

2 vols. Amsterdam: Pierre Mortier, 1695.

Lyon: Jacques Certe, 1740.

La Cueva, Alphonse de. *Examen de la liberté originaire de Venise.*

Ratisbonne: Jean Aubri, 1677.

Ratisbonne: Jean Aubri, 1677.

Ratisbonne: Jean Aubri, 1677. This edition is bound with *Le supplément* à *l'Histoire du gouvernement de Venise* (Paris: Frédéric Léonard, 1685).

Ratisbonne: Jean Aubri, 1678.

Ratisbonne: Jean Aubri, 1684. This edition is bound in the *Histoire du gouvernement de Venise* (Paris: Frédéric Léonard, 1685).

La Rochefoucauld, François. *Mémoires de la minorité de Louis XIV.*

Villefranche: Jean de Paul, 1688.

Villefranche: Jean de Paul, 1689.

Villefranche: Jean de Paul, 1690.

Villefranche: Jean de Paul, 1700.

Amsterdam: Aux dépens de la Compagnie, 1723.

Trevoux: Aux dépens de la Compagnie, 1754.

———. *Réflexions, sentences et maximes morales.*

Paris: Etienne Ganeau, 1711.

Paris: Etienne Ganeau, 1725.

Paris: Veuve Ganeau, 1743.

Paris: Veuve Ganeau, 1746.

Paris: Ganeau, Bauche et d'Havry, 1754.

Amsterdam: n.p., 1765.

Paris: Nyon l'Aîné, 1777.

Paris: Bailly, 1777.

Machiavelli, Niccolò. *Le Prince de Nicolas Machiavel.*

Amsterdam: Henry Wetstein, 1683.

Amsterdam: Henry Wetstein, 1683.

Amsterdam: Henry Wetstein, 1684.

Amsterdam: Henry Wetstein, 1686.

Amsterdam: Henry Wetstein, 1694.

Machiavelli, Niccolò, Frederick II von Hohenzollern, and François Marie Arouet de Voltaire. *The Prince* edited with the *Antimachiavel.*

La Haye: Jean Van Duren, 1740.

London: Guillaume Meyer, 1740.

La Haye: Jean Van Duren, 1740.

La Haye: Aux dépens de l'Éditeur, 1740.

La Haye: Pierre Paupie, 1740.

Brussels: R. François Foppens, 1740.

Copenhagen: Jacques Preuss, 1741.

Amsterdam: Jacques La Caze, 1741.

Gottingen: A. Vandenhoek, 1741.

La Haye: Jean Van Duren, 1741.

London: G. Meyer, 1741.

Amsterdam: Aux dépens de la Compagnie, 1742.

La Haye: Aux dépens de la Compagnie, 1743. This edition is part of the *Oeuvres de Machiavel*, vol. 6.

Amsterdam: Aux dépens de la Compagnie, 1750.

Geneva: Henri-Albert Gosse, 1759.

15 vols. Berlin: Voss and Fils, 1789. This edition is part of the *Oeuvres de Frédéric II*.

Amsterdam: Lemarié, 1790.

8 vols. Paris: Volland, 1793. This edition is part of the reedition of the *Oeuvres de Machiavel*.

Hambourg: F. Perthes, 1834.

15 vols. Berlin: R. Decker, 1848. This edition is part of the *Oeuvres de Frédéric II*, vol. 8.

Paris: Garnier Frères, 1941.

Paris: La Tradition, 1948.

Paris: Garnier Frères, 1960.

Maurier, Aubery du. *Mémoires pour servir à l'histoire de la République des Provinces Unies.* London: Aux dépens de la Compagnie, 1754.

Mémoires historiques, politiques, critiques et littéraires.

Amsterdam: Michel-Charles Le Cene, 1722.

Amsterdam: Michel-Charles Le Cene, 1722.

Amsterdam: Michel-Charles Le Cene, 1731.

Amsterdam: Michel-Charles Le Cene, 1737.

Amsterdam: Zacharie Chatelain, 1737.

Amsterdam: Zacharie Chatelain, 1742.

Minucci, Minuccio, and Paolo Sarpi. *Histoire des Uscoques.*

Paris: Veuve Louis Billaine, 1682.

Paris: Robert Pepie, 1684.

Ossat, Cardinal d'. *Lettres du Cardinal d'Ossat.*

Paris: Jean Boudot, 1698.

Amsterdam: Pierre Humbert, 1708.

Amsterdam: Pierre Humbert, 1714.

Paris: André Cailleau, 1724.

Amsterdam: Pierre Humbert, 1732.

Palafox, Juan de. *Homélies théologiques et morales sur la passion de Jesus-Christ.* Paris: Jean Boudot, 1691.

———. *Modèle d'une sainte et parfaite communion.* Paris, 1693.

Préliminaires des traitez faits entre les rois de France et tous les princes de l'Europe.

Paris: Frédéric Léonard, 1692.

Paris: Frédéric Léonard, 1692.

Paris: Frédéric Léonard, 1693.

Rélation du conclave de MDCLXX. Paris: Frédéric Léonard, 1676.

Sarpi, Paolo. *Histoire du concile de Trente.*
  Amsterdam: G. P. and J. Blaeu, aux dépens de la Compagnie, 1683.
  Amsterdam: G. P. and J. Blaeu, aux dépens de la Compagnie, 1686.
  Amsterdam: G. P. and J. Blaeu, aux dépens de la Compagnie, 1686.
  Amsterdam: P. and J. Blaeu, Waesbergen, Boom, à Someren and Goethals, 1699.
  ———. *Traité des bénéfices.*
  Amsterdam: Henry Wetstein, 1685.
  Amsterdam: Henry Wetstein, 1687.
  Amsterdam: Henry Wetstein, 1690.
  Amsterdam: Henry Wetstein, 1699.
  Amsterdam: Henry Wetstein, 1706.
  N.p., 1765.

Supplément à l'Histoire du gouvernement de Venise. Paris: Frédéric Léonard, 1677. This compilation of Venetian and papal texts concerning the excommunication of 1606, translated and commented on by Amelot, was published attached to the *Examen de la liberté originaire de Venise.* It is found in all editions of the *Histoire du gouvernement de Venise.*

Tacitus. *Tibère: Discours politiques sur Tacite.*
  Amsterdam: Héritiers de Daniel Elzevier, 1683.
  Paris: Frédéric Léonard, 1684.
  Paris: Frédéric Léonard, 1684.
  Paris: Frédéric Léonard, 1685.
  Amsterdam: Abraham Wolfgang, 1686.
  Amsterdam: Les Héritiers de Daniel Elzevier, 1688.
  ———. *La Morale de Tacite: De la flaterie.*
  Paris: Veuve Martin and Boudot, 1686.
  Paris: Veuve Martin and Boudot, 1686.
  La Haye: Adrian Moetjens, 1686.
  Paris: Veuve Martin and Boudot, 1686.
  ———. *Tacite: Les six premiers livres des Annales.*
  Paris: Martin, Boudot and Martin, 1690.
  Paris: Veuve Martin, Boudot and Martin, 1690.
  La Haye: Henri Van Bulderen, 1692.
  Rotterdam: Fritsch and Böhm, 1709.
  Paris: André Cailleau, 1724.
  Amsterdam: Michel-Charles Le Cene, 1731.

Foreign Language Editions of Amelot's Works

Caratere dei Veneziani, articolo tratto dalle Storia del governo di Venezia. Venice: Francesco Andreola, 1797.

Gracián, Baltasar. *The Modern Courtier; or, The Morals of Tacitus upon Flattery; Paraphras'd and illustrated with Observations by Amelot de La Houssaye, Newly done out of French.* London: John Taylor, 1687.
  ———. *The Art of Prudence, Illustrated with Amelot de La Houssaie's Notes.* London: n.p., 1702.
  ———. *The Art of Prudence; or, A Companion for the Man of Sense; Written originally in Spanish by that Celebrated Author, Baltasar Gracián; now made English from the best edition of the original and Illustrated with the Notes of the Sieur Amelot de La Houssaye,* trans. by Mr. Savage. London: J. Bowyer, 1705; London: n.p., 1714.

———. *Baltasar Gracián's Homme de cour oder Kluger Hof, une Welt-Mann nach Monsieur Amelot de La Houssaye seiner frantzösischen Version.* N.p., 1711.

———. *L'uomo di Corte, o sia l'Arte di Prudenza di Baldassar Graziano; Tradotto dal Spagnuolo nel Francese Idioma et comentato dal Signor Amelot de La Houssaye.* Venice: Gabriel Hertz, 1718.

The History of the Government of Venice. London: John Starkey, 1677; London: W. Hawes, 1702.

La storia del governo di Venezia, d'Amelotto della Houssaia. Colonia: Pietro Martello, 1681.

Machiavel und Anti-Machiavel: Regierungstuhft eines sörfen mit herr Amelots de La Houssaye historischen und politischen ummerlungen. Frankfurt and Leipzig: n.p., 1745.

Machiavelli. *Il Principe: Con la prefazione e le note istoriche e politiche di Mr. Amelot de La Houssaye.* Cosmopoli: n.p., 1745; Cosmopoli: n.p., 1768, 1769.

Sarpi, Paolo. *Father Paul of Beneficiary Matters, with the Notes of Amelot de La Houssaye.* London: n.p., 1730.

———. *A Treatise of Ecclesiastical Benefices and Revenus, with Notes by A. de La H.* London: n.p., 1736.

Tacitus. *The Annals and History of Cornelius Tacitus: His Account of the Antient Germans, and the Life of Agricola, Made English by Several Hands, With the Political Reflections and Historical Notes of Monsieur Amelot de La Houssaye, and the Learned Sir Henry Savile.* London: Matthew Gillyflower, 1698.

———. *Tacyt Polski albo neczy moralia Tacyta nad pod chlebstewenn.* N.p., 1744.

Bibliography

Archival Sources

Archives Nationales de France, KK 601.
Bibliothèque de l'Institut, Fonds Godefroy, no. 287.
Bibliothèque Nationale de France, MS fr. 2454.
Bibliothèque Nationale de France, MS fr. 8122.
Bibliothèque Nationale de France, MS Thoisy 94.
Cambridge University Library, no. Q.8.2.

Primary Sources

Alembert, Jean Lerond d'. *Mélanges de littérature, d'histoire et de philosophie.* 5 vols. Amsterdam: Zacharie Chatelain and Fils, 1777.

Ammirato, Scipione. *Discorsi sopra Cornelio Tacito.* Florence: F. Giunti, 1594.

Aristotle. *La Morale d'Aristote.* Trans. M. Catel. Toulouse: Pierre Bosc, 1644.

———. *Nicomachean Ethics.* Trans. H. Rackham. London: Heinemann, 1968.

Augustine. *Confessions.* Harmondsworth: Penguin, 1964.

———. *De doctrina Christiana.* Ed. and trans. R. P. H. Green. Oxford: Clarendon Press, 1995.

Baillet, Adrien. *Journal des Savants.* Amsterdam: Wolfgang, Waesberge, Boom and van Someren, 1687.

Baudoin, Jean. *Les oeuvres de Tacite et de Velleius Paterculus.* 2 vols. Paris: J. Gesselin, 1610.

———. *Les oeuvres de Tacite et de Velleius Paterculus.* 2nd ed. Paris: J. Richer, 1619.

———. *Les oeuvres de Tacite et de Velleius Paterculus.* 3rd ed. Paris: E. Richer, 1628.

———. *Le Prince parfait et ses qualitez les plus éminentes, avec des conseils et des exemples moraux et politiques tirez des oeuvres de Juste-Lipse et des plus célèbres autheurs anciens et modernes. . . .* Paris: Cardin Besongne, 1650.

Bayle, Pierre. *Nouvelles de la république des lettres.* 6 vols. Amsterdam: Henri Desbordes, 1684–88.

———. *Dictionnaire historique et critique.* 4 vols. Rotterdam: Abraham Leers, 1697.

———. *Lettres de Mr. Bayle, publiées sur les Originaux, avec les Remarques par Mr. Des Maizeaux.* 3 vols. Amsterdam: Aux dépens de la Compagnie, 1729.

———. *Choix de la correspondance inédit de Pierre Bayle, 1670–1706.* Ed. Emile Gigas. Copenhagen: G. E. C. Gad, 1890.

Boccalini, Trajano. *De' ragguagli di Parnaso.* Milan: G. B. Bidelli, 1614.

———. *Advices from Parnassus, in two centuries, with the Political touchstone, and an appendix to it, Written by Trajano Boccalini, To which is added, a continuation of the*

Advices, by Girolamo Briani . . . All tr. from the Italian by several hands, Rev. and cor. by Mr. Hughes. London: Printed by J. D. for D. Brown, 1706.

Bodin, Jean. *Juris universi distributio.* Cologne: J. Gymnicum, 1580.

———. *Oeuvres philosophiques de Jean Bodin.* Ed. and trans. Pierre Mesnard. Paris: Presses Universitaires de France, 1951.

———. *Method for the Easy Comprehension of History.* Ed. and trans. Beatrice Reynolds. New York: Columbia University Press, 1945; New York: W. W. Norton, 1969.

———. *Les six livres la republique.* Paris: Jacques Dupuy, 1976.

———. *Les six livres de la république.* Paris: Livre de Poche, 1993.

Bonaparte, Napoleon. *Manuscrits inédits.* Ed. Frédéric Masson and Guido Biagi. Paris: Société d'Éditions Littéraires et Artistiques, 1907.

Botero, Giovanni. *Della ragion di stato.* Rome: V. Pellagallo, 1590.

*Catalogue des Livres de M. ***** (Henri de Fourcy), dont la vente se fera en détail le Lundy 13. May 1737. et jours suivans, depuis deux heures de relevée jusqu'au soir, ruë de Joüy dans le Cul-de-sac de Fourcy.* Paris: Gabriel Martin, 1737.

Caussin, Nicolas. *De regno Dei.* Paris: D. Bechet, 1650.

Cauvigny, François de. *Observations politiques, topographiques et historiques sur Tacite.* Paris: Imprimerie de A. Estiene, 1613.

Chapelain, Jean. *Lettres.* Ed. Philippe Tamizey de Larroque. 2 vols. Paris: Imprimerie Nationale, 1880–83.

Charron, Pierre. *De la sagesse.* Bordeaux: S. Millanges, 1601.

———. *De la sagesse.* Ed. Amaury Duval. 3 vols. Geneva: Slatkine, 1964. Reedition of the edition of 1824.

Cicero. *De officiis.* Trans. Walter Miller. Cambridge: Harvard University Press, 1913.

Colbert, Jean-Baptiste. *Lettres, instructions et mémoires.* 7 vols. Paris: Imprimerie Impériale, 1861–73.

Contarini, Gasparo. *De magistratibus et republica Venetorum.* Paris: M. Vascosani, 1543.

———. *The Commonwealth and Government of Venice.* Trans. Lewes Lewkenor. London: John Windet, 1599.

Daniel, Gabriel. *Histoire de France.* 10 vols. Paris: Jean-Baptiste Delespine, 1713.

Diderot, Denis, ed. *Encyclopédie, ou Dictionnaire raisonné des sciences des arts et des métiers, par une société de gens de letters.* 17 vols. Neufchâtel: Samuel Faulche, 1765.

Du Tillet, Jean, sieur de la Bussière. *Pour la majorité du roi treschrestien contre les escrits des rebelles.* Paris: G. Morel, 1560.

———. *Recueil des roys de France, levrs couronne et maison.* 2 vols. Paris: Jean Houzé, 1607.

Erasmus, Desidirius. *The Education of a Christian Prince.* Ed. Lisa Jardine. Trans. Neil M. Cheshire and Michael J. Heath. Cambridge: Cambridge University Press, 1997.

Frederick II von Hohenzollern, king of Prussia. *L'AntiMachiavel.* Ed. Charles Fleischauer. Geneva: Voltaire Foundation, 1958.

Furetière, Antoine. *Dictionnaire universel.* Rotterdam: A. & R. Leers, 1690.

Giry, Louis, trans. *Des causes de la corruption de l'éloquence, dialogue attribué par quelques-uns à Tacite et par autres à Quintilien.* Paris: C. Chappelain, 1630.

Godefroy, Denis II. *Recueil des traités de confédération et d'alliance entre la couronne de France et les princes et états étrangers, depuis l'an MDCXXI jusques à présent; avec quelques autres pièces appartenantes à l'histoire.* Amsterdam: P. Van Dyke, 1664.

Gournay, Marie de Jars. *Harangue de Galba . . . Versions de quelques pièces de Virgile, Tacite et Saluste. . . .* Paris, 1619.

Gracián, Baltasar. *El Discreto.* Ed. Don Juan de Lastanosa. Huesca: Juan Nogués, 1646.

———. *El Héroe.* Lisbon: Manuel da Sylva, 1646.

———. *El Político Fernando.* Huesca: Juan Nogués, 1646.

————. *Oráculo manual y arte de prudencia.* Huesca: Juan Nogués, 1647.

————. *Agudeza y arte de ingenio.* Ed. Don Juan de Lastanosa, with a preface by Eduardo Overjero y Maur. Huesca: Juan Nogués, 1648.

————. *El Criticón.* Madrid: P. de Val, 1653.

————. *Oracolo manvale e arte di prvdenza cauata dagl' aforismi, che si discorrono nell'opre di Lorenzo Gratiano, mandalo in luce d. Vicenzo Giovanni de Lastanosa in Lisbona nell'officina di Enrico Vanlente de'Olliviera l'anno 1657, Tradotta dalla lingua spagnuola nell'itagliana l'anno 1670.* . . . Parma: Mario Vigna, 1670.

————. *The Oracle: A Manual of the Art of Discretion.* Ed. and trans. L. B. Walton. London: J. M. Dent and Sons, 1953.

————. *Oráculo manual y arte de prudencia.* Ed. M. Romera-Navarro. Madrid: Revista de Filologia Española, 1954.

————. *Manuel de poche d'hier pour hommes politiques d'aujourd'hui.* Ed. and trans. Benito Pelegrín. Paris: Hallier, 1978.

————. *El Discreto.* Ed. Aurora Egido. Madrid: Alianza Editorial, 1997.

Guicciardini, Francesco. *Ricordi.* Ed. Nicolai Rubenstein. Trans. Mario Domandi. Phildelphia: University of Pennsylvania, 1965.

Guichenon, Samuel. *Histoire généalogique de la royale maison de Savoie.* Lyon: Guillaume Barbier, 1660.

Harlay de Champvallon, Achilles de, trans. *Les oeuvres de Corneille Tacite.* Paris: Jean Camusat, 1644.

————. *Les oeuvres de Corneille Tacite.* 2nd ed. Paris: Veuve de Jean Camusat, 1644.

————. *Les oeuvres de Corneille Tacite.* 3rd ed. Paris: Veuve de Jean Camusat, 1645.

Hobier, Ithier, trans. *La Vie de Julius Agricola.* Paris: Jean Camusat, 1639.

Kant, Immanuel. *Foundations of the Metaphysics of Morals and What Is Enlightenment?* Ed. and trans. Lewis White Beck. New York: Liberal Arts Press, 1959.

La Blétterie, Jean-Philippe-René, abbé de. *Tibère: Les six premiers livres des Annales de Tacite.* Paris: Imprimerie Royale, 1768.

La Planche, Étienne de, trans. *Les oeuvres de C. Cornelius Tacitus.* Paris: Abel L'Anglier, 1582.

————. *Les oeuvres de C. Cornelius Tacitus.* 2nd ed. Paris: Abel L'Anglier, 1584.

————. *Les oeuvres de C. Cornelius Tacitus.* 3rd ed. Paris: Abel L'Anglier, 1585.

————. *Les oeuvres de C. Cornelius Tacitus.* 4th ed. Geneva: Les Héritiers de C. Vignon, 1594.

————. *Les oeuvres de C. Cornelius Tacitus.* 5th ed. Douai: B. Bellère, 1609.

La Planche, Étienne de, and Claude Fauchet, trans. *C. Cornelii Tacitus opera latina, cum versione gallica.* Frankfurt: Excudebat v. Hoffmanus, Sumptious, I Rhodij, 1612.

La Rochefoucauld, François, duc de. *Mémoires de M. D. L. R., contenant les brigues pour le gouvernement à la mort de Loüys XIII, guerre de Paris, retraitte de M. de Longueville en Normandie, récapitulation, ou abrégé de tout ce que dessus, avec l'emprisonnement des trois princes, ce qui s'est passé depuis la prison des princes jusqu'à la guerre de Guyenne, guerre de Guyenne avec la dernière de Paris, etc., auxquels sont adjoustés les Mémoires de M. de La Chastre.* Cologne: P. Van Dyck, 1662.

Latassa, Don Felix de. *Biblioteca nueva de los escritores Aragoneses.* 6 vols. Pamplona: Joaquin de Domingo, 1799.

Le Maire, Nicolas. *Le sanctuaire fermé aux profanes ou la Bible défendue au vulgaire.* Paris: S. and G. Cramoisy, 1651.

Le Maistre, Rodolphe. *L'Institution du Prince: Ensemble la sagesse des anciens.* Paris: Michel Sonnius, 1613.

————. *Le Tibère Français, ou les six premiers livres des Annales de Cornelius Tacitus.* 2nd ed. Paris: Robert Estienne, 1616.

————. *Les oeuvres de Tacite.* Paris: C. Cramoisy, 1627.

————. *Les oeuvres de Tacite.* 2nd ed. Paris: J. Dugast, 1636.

————. *Les oeuvres de Tacite.* 3rd ed. Rouen: J. Berthelin, 1650.

Le Moyne, Pierre. *De l'histoire.* Paris: A. Billaine, 1670.

Léonard, Frédéric. *Recueil des traitez de paix faits entre les rois de France et tous les princes de l'Europe depuis le règne de Charles VII.* Paris: Léonard, 1693.

Lipsius, Justus. *C. Cornelii Taciti Historiarum et Annalium libri qui exstant, Justi Lipsii studio emendati . . . Ejusdem Taciti Liber de moribus Germanorum, Julii Agricolae vita. Incerti scriptoris Dialogus de oratoribus sui temporis. . . .* Antwerp: Plantin, 1574.

————. *C. Cornelii Taciti opera omnia quae exstant. . . .* Antwerp: Plantin, 1581.

————. *Politicorum sive ciuilis doctrinae libri sex.* Leiden: Plantin, 1589.

————. *Les six livres des politiques, ou Doctrine civile de Justus Lipsius, où il est principalement discouru de ce qui appartient à la principauté.* Trans. Charles Le Ber. La Rochelle: H. Haultin, 1590.

————. *Les politiques ou doctrine civile . . . avec Le traité de la constance . . . reveus et augm. d'annotations en marge.* Trans. Simon Goulart. Tours: G. Montreul and J. Richer, 1594.

Louis XIV. *Mémoires pour l'instruction du Dauphin.* Ed. Pierre Goubert. Paris: Imprimérie Nationale, 1992.

Machiavelli, Niccolò. *The Prince.* Ed. Quentin Skinner and Russel Price. Trans. Russell Price. Cambridge: Cambridge University Press, 1988.

————. *The Discourses.* Ed. Bernard Crick. Trans. Leslie J. Walker. London: Penguin Books, 1970.

————. *Discours de l'estat de paix et de guerre de messire Nicolas Macchiavelli . . . sur la première décade de Tite-Live, traduict d'italien en Françoys, plus un livre du mesme auteur intitulé: Le Prince.* Trans. Gaspard d'Auvergne. Paris: H. de Marnef and G. Cavellat, 1571.

————. *Il Principe.* Rome: A. Blado, 1532.

————. *Le Prince.* Trans. Gaspard d'Auvergne. Poitiers: E. de Marnef, 1553.

————. *Le Prince.* Trans. Gaspard d'Auvergne. Paris: C. Chappelain, 1613.

————. *Le Prince.* Trans. Guillaume Cappel. Paris: Charles Estienne, 1553.

————. *Le Prince.* Trans. Jacques Gohory. Paris: R. Le Mangnier, 1571.

————. *Princeps, item aliorum contra Machiavellum scripta de potestate et officio principum contra tyrannos, quibus accessit Ant. Possevini Judicium de Nic. Machiavelli et Jo. Bodini scriptis, Item Bruti vidiciae contra tyrannos, sive de principis in populum populique in principem legitma potestate, Item tractatus de jure magistratuum in subditos, et officio subditorum erga Magistratus.* Ursella: Cornelium Sutorium, 1600.

Maistre, Joseph de. *Les Soirées de Saint-Petersbourg, ou entretiens sur le gouvernement temporel de la Providence.* Lyon: J. B. Pélagaud, 1850.

Montaigne, Michel de. *Essais.* 3 vols. Paris: Garnier Frères, 1962.

Montesquieu, Charles-Louis de Secondat de La Brède de. *Considerations sur les causes de la grandeur des Romains et de leur decadence.* Amsterdam: Chez J. Desbordes, 1734.

————. *De l'esprit des loix.* Geneva: Barrollot and Fils, 1748.

Montfaucon, Bernard de. *L'antiquité expliquée et représentée en figures.* 5 vols. Paris: F. Delaulne, 1719.

Morosini, Andreus. *Historia Veneta ab anno M.D.XXI. vsque ad annum M.DC.XV.* Venice: Antonium Pinellum, 1623.

Nani, Giovan Battista. *Historia della Republica Veneta.* 2 vols. Venice: Combi and La Noue, 1662–79.

————. *Histoire de Venise.* Trans. L'abbé Tallement. 4 vols. Paris: Louis Billaine, 1679–80.

————. *Relazione de Francia fatta al senato veneto dapo l'ambasciata straodinaria a* quella corte e letta in senato il 3 febrajo 1661, dal. cav. Gio. Battista Nan, ora la prima volta interamente publicata dal Marchese Giuseppe Melchiorri. Rome: Tipografica della Minerva, 1844.

Naudé, Gabriel. Considérations politiques sur les coups d'état. Rome, 1639.

———. Considérations politiques sur les coups d'état. Ed. Louis Marin. Paris: Les Editions de Paris, 1988.

Niceron, Jean-Pierre. Mémoires pour servir à l'histoire des homes illustres de la république des lettres. 44 vols. Paris: Briasson, 1727–45.

Paschalius, Carlus. C. Cornelii Tacitii equities romani ab excessu divi Augusti Annalium libri quatuor priores, et in hos observations C. Paschalii cuneatis. Paris: Aldus, 1581.

P. D. B. Les oeuvres de C. Cornelius Tacitus. Paris: M. Orry, 1599.

Perrot d'Ablancourt, Nicolas, trans. Les Annales de Tacite. 2 vols. Paris: La Veuve de Jean Camusat, 1640.

———. Oeuvres de Tacite. Paris, A. Courbé, 1658.

Plato. Philebus. Trans. H. N. Fowler. London: Heinemann, 1962.

Pliny. Panegyricus. Trans. Betty Radice. Cambridge: Harvard University Press, 1969.

Polybius. The Histories. Trans. W. R. Paton. 6 vols. London: W. Heinemann; New York: G. P. Putnam's Sons, 1922–27.

Puget de La Serre, Jean. Maximes politiques de Tacite, ou la Conduite des gens de cour. Paris: J. Ribou, 1664.

———. Maximes politiques de Tacite, ou la Conduite des gens de cour. 2nd ed. Paris: Chez J. Baptiste Loyson, 1667.

Rapin, René. Instructions pour l'histoire. Paris: Sebastien Marbre-Cramoisy, 1677.

Renaudot, Théphraste. Pièces Historiques contenant les Couriers, Mercures, Relations, et autres semblables Observations curieuses sur l'Estat et gouvernement de France, comme il est en la présente année, 1649, C'est comme une notice générale pour servir de fondement à toute l'Histoire du temps. Paris: Sebastien Martin, 1649.

Richelet, Pierre. Dictionnaire de la langue françoise (Geneva: Jean Herman Widerhold, 1685).

Richelieu, Armand du Plessis, Cardinal de. Testament politique. Ed. Françoise Hildesheimer. Paris: Société de l'Histoire de France, 1995.

Rousseau, Jean-Jacques. Du contrat social; ou Principes du droit politique. Amsterdam: Marc Michel Rey, 1762.

———. "Traduction du premier livre de l'Histoire de Tacite." In Oeuvres complètes, vol. 3, pp. 302–29. Paris: Chez Furne, 1837.

Sacchini, Francesco. De ratione libros cum profectu legendi libellus, deque vitanda moribus noxia lectione, oratio Francisci Sacchini. Sammieli: F. Du Bois, 1615.

———. Moyens de lire avec fruit. Tran. Durey de Morsan. La Haye: Guillot, 1786.

Sarpi, Paolo. Histoire du concile de Trente. Trans. Giovanni Diodati. Geneva: E. Gamonet, 1621.

———. Discorso dell'origine, forma, leggi ed uso dell'ufficio dell'Inquisitione nella Città, e Dominio di Venetia. Venice: n.p., 1639.

Seignelay, Jean-Baptiste Colbert, Marquis de. L'Italie en 1671: Relation d'un voyage du marquis de Seignelay, suivie de lettres inédites à Vivonne, Du Quesne, Tourville, Fénelon, et précédée d'une étude historique. Paris: Didier, 1867.

Silhouette, Etienne de. Réflexions politiques de Baltasar Gracián sur les plus grands princes et particulièrement sur Ferdinand le Catholique, ouvrage traduit de l'espagnol, avec des notes historiques et critiques, par M. D. S****. Paris: B. Alix, 1730.

Simon, Richard. Histoire critique du Vieux Testament. Paris: Veuve Billaine, 1678.

———. Réponse au livre intitulé Sentimens de quelques théologiens de Hollande sur l'Histoire critique du Vieux Testament. Rotterdam: Reinier Leers, 1686.

Swift, Jonathan. *Travels into Several Remote Nations of the World by Lemuel Gulliver.* 3 vols. London, Benjamin Motte, 1726.

Theveneau, Adam. *Les Morales.* Paris: Toussaincts du Bray, 1607.

Thou, Jacques-Auguste de. *Advis et notions.* Paris: Toussaincts du Bray, 1608.

———. *Iac. Augusti Thuani Historiarum sui temporis libri CXXV.* 11 vols. Paris: H. Drouart, 1609–14.

———. *Histoire universelle.* 10 vols. La Haye: Henri Scheurleer, 1740.

Varillas, Antoine. *Histoire de l'hérésie de Viclef, Jean Hus et Jérôme de Prague, avec celle des guerres de Bohême qui en ont esté les suites.* Lyon: J. Certe, 1682.

Voltaire, François Marie Arouet de. *Correspondence.* Ed. Theodore Besterman et al. 107 vols. Geneva: Institut et Musée Voltaire, 1970.

Zuccolo, Ludovico. *Della ragione di stato.* In *Politici e moralisti del seicento: Strada, Zuccolo, Settala, Accetto, Brignole Sale, Malvezzi,* ed. Benedetto Croce and Santino Caramelle, pp. 25–40. Bari: Laterza and Figli, 1930.

Secondary Sources

Aldridge, John W. *The Hermeneutic of Erasmus.* Richmond, Va.: John Knox Press, 1966.

Allott, Terence. "Undermining Absolutism: The Disguised Critique of Amelot de La Houssaie." *Seventeenth Century* 7 (1992): pp. 71–81.

Aubenque, Pierre. *La prudence chez Aristote.* Paris: Presses Universitaires de France, 1963.

Baker, Keith. *Inventing the French Revolution: Essays on French Political Culture in the Eighteenth Century.* Cambridge: Cambridge University Press, 1990.

Baldini, Enzo. "Le guerre di religione francesi nella trattatistica italiana della ragion di stato: Botero e Frachetta." Special issue, *Dal machiavellismo al libertinismo: Studi in memoria di Anna Maria Battista, Il pensiero politico* 2 (1989): pp. 301–24.

———, ed. *Botero e la "Ragion di stato."* Florence: Olschki, 1992.

———. *Aristotelismo politico e ragion di stato.* Florence: Olschki, 1995.

"Baltasar Gracián: Selección de estudios, investigación actual y documentación." Special issue, *Suplementos: Materiales de Trabajo Intelectual* 37 (1993).

Barney, Stephen A., ed. *Annotation and Its Texts.* Oxford: Oxford University Press, 1991.

Baron, Hans. "The Secularization of Wisdom and Political Humanism in the Renaissance." *Journal of the History of Ideas* 21 (1960): pp. 131–50.

Barret-Kriegel, Blandine. *Les historiens et la monarchie.* 4 vols. Paris: Presses Universitaires de France, 1988.

Battista, Anna Maria. *Alle origini del pensiero politico libertino: Montaigne e Charron.* Milan: Giuffrè, 1966.

———. "Morale 'privée' et utilitarisme politique en France au XVIIe siècle." In Lazzari Christian and Dominique Reynié, eds. *La pouvoir de la raison d'état,* pp. 191–230.

———. *Politica e morale nella Francia dell'età moderna.* Geneva: Name, 1998.

Bély, Lucien. *Espions et ambassadeurs au temps de Louis XIV.* Paris: Fayard, 1990.

Benedict, Barbara M. *Making the Modern Reader: Cultural Mediation in Early Modern Literary Anthologies.* Princeton: Princeton University Press, 1996.

Benzoni, Gino, and Tiziano Zanato, eds. *Storici e politici veneti del cinquecento e del seicento.* Milan: Riccardo Ricciardi, 1982.

Birely, Robert. *The Counter-Reformation Prince: Anti-Machiavellianism or Catholic Statecraft in Early Modern Europe.* Chapel Hill: University of North Carolina Press, 1980.

Blair, Ann. "Humanist Methods in Natural Philosophy: The Commonplace Book." *Journal of the History of Ideas* 53 (1992): pp. 541–51.

————. *The Theater of Nature: Jean Bodin and Renaissance Science.* Princeton: Princeton University Press, 1997.

————. "Reading Strategies for Coping with Information Overload ca. 1550–1700." *Journal of the History of Ideas* 64 (2003): pp. 11–28.

Bleznick, Donald. "Spanish Reaction to Machiavelli in the Sixteenth and Seventeenth Centuries." *Journal of the History of Ideas* 19 (1958): pp. 542–50.

Borghero, Carlo. *La certezza et la storia.* Milan: Franco Angel, 1983.

Borrelli, G. *Ragion di stato e leviantano: Conservazione e scambio alle origini della modernità politica.* Bologna: Il Mulino, 1993.

Bourdieu, Pierre. *Les règles de l'art: Genèse et structure du champ littéraire.* Paris: Seuil, 1992.

Bouwsma, William J. *Venice and the Defense of Republican Liberty: Renaissance Values in the Age of the Counter Reformation.* Berkeley: University of California Press, 1968. Paperback, 1984.

Bowers, Fredson. *Textual and Literary Criticism.* Oxford: Clarendon Press, 1972.

Bradford, A. T. "Stuart Absolutism and the Utility of Tacitus." *Huntington Library Quarterly* 46 (1983): pp. 127–55.

Brown, Elizabeth A. R. "Jean Du Tillet et les archives de France." *Histoire et Archives* 2 (1997): pp. 29–63.

Brown, John L. *The Methodus ad Facilem Historiarum Cognitionem of Jean Bodin: A Critical Study.* Washington, D.C.: Catholic University of America Press, 1939.

Brucker, Gene. *The Civic World of Early Renaissance Florence.* Princeton: Princeton University Press, 1977.

Burger, Pierre-François. "Deux documents sur Amelot de La Houssaie." *Dix-Septième Siècle* 131 (1981): pp. 199–202.

Burke, Peter. Introduction to *The History of Benefices and Selections from the History of the Council of Trent,* by Paolo Sarpi, ed. and trans. Peter Burke, pp. xix–xx. New York: Washington Square Press, 1967.

————. *The Renaissance Sense of the Past.* New York: St. Martin's Press, 1969.

————. "Tacitism." In *Tacitus,* ed. T. A. Dorey, pp. 149–71. London: Routledge and Keegan Paul, 1969.

————. "Ranke the Reactionary." In *Leopold von Ranke and the Shaping of the Historical Discipline,* ed. Georg G. Iggers and James M. Powell, pp. 36–44. Syracuse: Syracuse University Press, 1990.

————. "Tacitism, Scepticism, and Reason of State." In *The Cambridge History of Political Thought,* ed. J. H. Burns and Mark Goldie, pp. 479–98. Cambridge: Cambridge University Press, 1991.

————. *The Social History of Knowledge from Gutenburg to Diderot.* Cambridge: Polity Press, 2000.

Burns, J. H., and Mark Goldie, eds. *The Cambridge History of Political Thought, 1450–1700.* Cambridge: Cambridge University Press, 1991.

Bury, Emmaneul. *Littérature et politesse: L'invention de l'honnête homme 1580–1750.* Paris: Presses Universitaires de France, 1996.

Busson, Henri. *La pensée religieuse française de Charron à Pascal.* Paris: J. Vrin, 1933.

Butterfield, Herbert. *The Statecraft of Machiavelli.* London: G. Bell, 1940.

Calderón, E. Correa. *Baltasar Gracián: Su vida y su obra.* Madrid: Editorial Gredos, 1970.

Cardascia, G. "Machiavel et Jean Bodin." *Bibliothèque d'Humanisme et Renaissance* 3 (1943): pp. 129–67.

Carruthers, Mary. *The Book of Memory: A Study of Memory in Medieval Culture.* Cambridge: Cambridge University Press, 1990.

Cassirer, Ernst. *The Myth of the State*. New Haven: Yale University Press, 1946.

Cavaillé, Jean-Pierre. *Dis/simulations: Jules-César Vanini, François La Mothe Le Vayer, Gabriel Naudé, Louis Machon et Torquato Accetto; Religion, morale et politique au XVIIe siècle.* Paris: Honoré Champion, 2002.

Cavallo, Gugliemo, and Roger Chartier, eds. *A History of Reading in the West.* Trans. Lydia G. Cochrane. Amherst: University of Massachusetts Press, 1999.

Cave, Terence. *The Cornucopian Text: Problems of Writing in the French Renaissance.* Oxford: Clarendon Press, 1979.

Céard, Jean. "Les mots et les choses: Le commentaire à la Renaissance." In *L'Europe de la Renaissance: Cultures et civilizations,* ed. Jean-Claude Margolin and Marie-Madelaine Martinet, pp. 25–36. Paris: J. Touzot, 1988.

Certeau, Michel de. *L'invention du quotidien.* Vol. 1, *Arts de faire.* Paris: Gallimard, 1980.

———. *The Practice of Everyday Life.* Trans. Steven Rendall. Berkeley: University of California Press, 1984.

Chartier, Roger. *Lectures et lecteurs dans la France de l'Ancien Régime.* Paris: Seuil, 1987.

———. *The Cultural Origins of the French Revolution.* Durham: Duke University Press, 1991.

———. *L'ordre des livres.* Aix-en-Provence: Alinea, 1992.

———. "Trajectoires et tensions culturelles de l'Ancien Régime." In *Les formes de la culture: Histoire de la France,* ed. André Burguière and Jacques Revel, vol. 3, pp. 25–142. Paris: Seuil, 1993. 2nd ed., 2000.

Cherel, Albert. *La pensée de Machiavel en France.* Paris: L'Artisan du Livre, 1935.

Chrétien-Goni, Jean-Pierre. "*Institutio arcanae:* Théorie de l'institution du secret et fondement de la politique." In *Le pouvoir de la raison d'état,* ed. Christian Lazzari and Dominique Reynié, pp. 135–89. Paris: Presses Universitaires de France, 1992.

Church, William F. *Richelieu and Reason of State.* Princeton: Princeton University Press, 1973.

Clair, Pierre. "L'information au quotidien: Discours politique et vision du monde dans le Mercure François et quelques autres gazettes." In *L'état Baroque: Regards sur la pensée politique de la France du premier XVIIe siècle,* ed. Henri Méchoulan, pp. 301–33. Paris: J. Vrin, 1985.

Collas, George. *Un poète protecteur des lettres au XVIIe siècle, Jean Chapelain, 1595–1674.* Paris: Perrin, 1912.

Coron, Antoine. " 'Ut prosint aliis': Jacques-Auguste de Thou et sa bibliothèque." In *Histoire des bibliothèques françaises,* vol. 2, pp. 101–25. Paris: Promodis, 1988.

Coster, Alphonse. *Baltasar Gracián, 1601–1658.* Paris: Revue Hispanique, 1913.

Couzinet, Marie-Dominique. "Jean Bodin: État des lieux et perspectives de recherches." *Bulletin de l'Association d'Étude sur l'Humanisme, la Réforme et la Rénaissance* 21 (1995): pp. 11–36.

———. *Histoire et Méthode à la Renaissance: Une lecture de la Methodus de Jean Bodin.* Paris: J. Vrin, 1996.

Coyle, J. K. *Augustine's De Moribus Ecclesiae Catholicae: A Study of His Work, Its Composition, and Its Sources.* Fribourg: University Press, 1978.

Dalcourt, G. J. "The Primary Cardinal Virtue: Wisdom or Prudence." *International Philosophical Quarterly* 3 (1963): pp. 55–79.

Darnton, Robert. "In Search of the Enlightenment: Recent Attempts to Create a Social History of Ideas." *Journal of Modern History* 43 (1971): pp. 113–33.

———. *The Literary Underground of the Old Regime.* Cambridge: Harvard University Press, 1982.

———. *The Great Cat Massacre, and Other Episodes in French Cultural History.* New York: Vintage Books, 1985.

————. *Édition et sédition: L'Univers de la littérature clandestine au XVIIIe siècle.* Paris: Odile Jacob, 1991.

————. *Forbidden Best-Sellers of Pre-Revolutionary France, 1769–1789.* New York: W. W. Norton, 1996.

————. "Two Paths through the Social History of Ideas." In *The Darnton Debate: Books and Revolution in the Eighteenth Century,* ed. Haydn T. Mason, pp. 251–94. Oxford: Voltaire Foundation, 1998.

Davies, Martin. *Aldus Manutius: Printer and Publisher of Renaissance Venice.* London: British Library, 1995.

Davila, Arrigo Catarina. *Historia delle guerre civile di Francia.* Venice: T. Baglioli, 1630.

Dean, Leonard F. "Bodin's *Methodus* in England before 1625." *Studies in Philology* 39 (1942): pp. 160–66.

Delisle, Léopold. *Histoire générale de Paris: Le Cabinet des Manuscrits de la Bibliothèque Impériale.* 3 vols. Paris: Imprimerie Impériale, 1868.

Delumeau, Jean. *Le Catholicisme entre Luther et Voltaire.* Paris: Presses Universitaires de France, 1971.

Desan, Philippe. "Jean Bodin et l'idée de méthode au XVIe siècle." *Corpus* 4 (1987): pp. 3–18.

Desgraves, Louis. *Catalogue de la bibliothèque de Montesquieu.* Geneva: Droz, 1954.

Desgraves, Louis, and Catherine Volpilhac-Auger. *Catalogue de la bibliothèque de Montesquieu à La Brède.* Paris: Universitas, 1999.

Dewerpe, Alain. *Espion: Une anthropologie historique du secret d'état contemporain.* Paris: Gallimard, 1994.

Dini, Vittorio. *Il governo della prudenza: Virtù dei privati e disciplina dei custodi.* Milan: Franco Angeli, 2000.

Dini, Vittorio, and Giorgio Stabile, eds. *Sagezza e prudenza: Studi per la ricostruzione di un'antropologia in prima età moderna.* Naples: n.p., 1983.

Dionisotti, Carlotta. "Polybius and the Royal Professor." In *Tria corda: Scritti in onore di Arnaldo Momigliano,* ed. E. Gabba, pp. 179–99. Como: Edizioni New Press, 1983.

Dodds, Muriel. *Les récits de voyages: Sources de l'Esprit des lois de Montesquieu.* Paris: Honoré Champion, 1929.

Dooley, Brendan. *A Social History of Skepticism: Experience and Doubt in Early Modern Culture.* Baltimore: Johns Hopkins University Press, 1999.

————. "*Veritas Filia Temporis:* Experience and Belief in Early Modern Culture." *Journal of the History of Ideas* 60 (1999): pp. 487–504.

Duhem, Pierre. *Medieval Cosmology: Theories of Infinity, Place, Time, Void, and the Plurality of Worlds.* Ed. and trans. Roger Ariew. Chicago: University of Chicago Press, 1985.

Eco, Umberto. *The Name of the Rose.* London: Picador, 1984.

Eden, Kathy. *Hermeneutics and the Rhetorical Tradition: Chapters in the Ancient Legacy and Its Humanist Reception.* New Haven: Yale University Press, 1997.

Eggert, Paul, and Margaret Sankey, eds. *The Editorial Gaze: Mediating Texts in Literature and the Arts.* New York: Garland Publishing, 1998.

Egidio, Aurora. *La rosa del silencio: Estudios sobre Gracián.* Madrid: Alianza Editorial, 1996.

————. *Las caras de la prudencia y Baltasar Gracián.* Madrid: Editorial Castalia, 2000.

————. *Humanidades y dignidad del hombre en Baltasar Gracián.* Salamanca: Ediciones Universidad de Salamanca, 2001.

Eisenstein, Elizabeth. "Le livre et la culture savante." In *Histoire de l'édition française,* ed. Roger Chartier and Henri-Jean Martin, vol. 1, pp. 563–83. Paris: Promodis, 1982.

————. *Grub Street Abroad: Aspects of the French Cosmopolitan Press from the Age of Louis XIV to the French Revolution.* Oxford: Clarendon Press, 1992.

Elias, Norbert. *The Civilizing Process: The History of Manners.* Trans. Edmund Jephcott. New York: Urizen Books, 1978.

———. *Über den prozess der Zivilization: Soziogenetische une psychogenetische Untersuchungen.* Basel: Haus zum Falken, 1939. 2nd ed., 2 vols., Frankfurt: Suhrkamp, 1981.

———. *La société de cour.* Trans. Pierre Kamnitzer and Jeanne Etoré, with a preface by Roger Chartier. Paris: Flammarion, 1985.

Ellis, Harold A. *Boulainvilliers and the French Monarchy: Aristocratic Politics in Early Eighteenth-Century France.* Ithaca: Cornell University Press, 1988.

Erasmus. *Adages.* Paris, 1500.

Fabre, L'abbé A. *Chapelain et nos deux premières académies.* Paris: Perrin, 1890.

Fell, London A. *Origins of Legislative Sovereignty and the Legislative State.* Vol. 3, *Bodin's Humanistic Legal System and Rejection of "Medieval Political Theology."* Boston: Oelgeschleger, Gunn and Hain, 1987.

Ferrari, Giuseppe. *Histoire de la raison d'état.* Paris: Michel Lévy Frères, 1860.

Findlen, Paula. "Possessing the Past: The Material World of the Italian Renaissance." *American Historical Review* 103 (1998): pp. 83–114.

Firpo, Luigi, ed. *Relazioni Ambasciatori Veneti.* 13 vols. Turin: Fondazione L. Firpo, 1975.

Flandrois, Isabelle. *L'Institution du Prince au début du XVIIe siècle.* Paris: Presses Universitaires de France, 1992.

Ford, Franklin L. *Robe and Sword: The Regrouping of the French Aristocracy after Louis XIV.* Cambridge: Harvard University Press, 1962.

Foucault, Michel. "What Is Enlightenment?" In *The Foucault Reader,* ed. Paul Rabinow, pp. 32–50. New York: Pantheon Books, 1984.

Franklin, Julian. *Jean Bodin and the Rise of Absolutist Theory.* Cambridge: Cambridge University Press, 1973.

———. *Jean Bodin and the Sixteenth-Century Revolution in Law and History.* Westport, Conn.: Greenwood Press, 1977.

———. "Sovereignty in Bodin's Account of Law." In *Historians and Ideologues: Essays in Honor of Donald R. Kelley,* ed. Anthony T. Grafton and J. H. M. Salmon, pp. 40–47. Rochester: University of Rochester Press, 2001.

Frasca-Spada, Marina, and Nicolas Jardine, eds. *Books and the Sciences in History.* Cambridge: Cambridge University Press, 2000.

Fumaroli, Marc. *L'âge de l'éloquence.* Paris: Albin Michel, 1984.

———. "Histoire et mémoires." In *Chateaubriand mémorialiste: Colloque du cent ciquantenaire 1848–1998,* ed. Jean-Claude Berchet and Philippe Berthier, pp. 11–34. Geneva: Droz, 2000.

Funck-Brentano, F. *Les lettres de cachet à Paris.* Paris: Imprimerie Nationale, 1903.

Garver, Eugene. *Machiavelli and the History of Prudence.* Madison: University of Wisconsin Press, 1987.

Gauchet, Marcel. *Le désenchantement du monde: Une histoire politique de la religion.* Paris: Gallimard, 1985.

———. "L'état au miroir de la raison d'état: La France et la chrétienité." In *Raison et déraison d'état: Théoriciens et théories de la raison d'état aux XVIe et XVIIe siècles,* ed. Yves-Charles Zarka, pp. 193–244. Paris: Presses Universitaires de France, 1994.

———. "État, monarchie, public." Special issue, *Cahiers du Centre de Recherche Historique* 20 (1998).

Gay, Peter. *The Enlightenment: An Interpretation.* 2 vols. New York: Vintage Books, 1968.

Gelderen, Martin van. *The Political Thought of the Dutch Revolt, 1555–1590.* Cambridge: Cambridge University Press, 1992.

————. "Holland und das Preußentum: Justus Lipsius zwischen niederländischen Aufstand und Brandenburg-preußischem Absolutismus." *Zeitschrift für Historische Forschung* 23 (1996): pp. 29–56.

Genette, Gérard. *Seuils*. Paris: Seuil, 1987.

Gigas, Emile. *Choix de la correspondance inédit de Pierre Bayle, 1670–1706*. Copenhagen: G. E. C. Gad, 1890.

Gilbert, Felix. *Machiavelli and Guicciardini: Politics and History in Sixteenth-Century Florence*. Princeton: Princeton University Press, 1965.

————. *History, Choice, and Commitment*. Cambridge: Belknap Press, 1977.

Gilissen, J., ed. *La preuve: Recueils de la Société Jean Bodin pour l'histoire comparative des institutions* 17 (1965).

Gilmont, Jean-François. "Protestant Reformations and Reading." In *A History of Reading in the West*, ed. Gugliemo Cavallo and Roger Chartier, trans. Lydia G. Cochrane, pp. 213–37. Amherst: University of Massachusetts Press, 1999.

Gilmore, Myron. "Myth and Reality in Venetian Political Theory." In *Renaissance Venice*, ed. John R. Hale, pp. 431–33. London: Faber, 1974.

Ginzburg, Carlo. *Il formaggio e i vermi: Il cosmo di un mugnaio del'500*. Turin: Einaudi Editore, 1976.

————. *The Cheese and the Worms: The Cosmos of a Sixteenth Century Miller*. Trans. John and Anne Tedeschi. Baltimore: Johns Hopkins University Press, 1980.

————. "Montrer et citer." *Le Débat* 56 (1989): pp. 43–54.

Gleason, Elizabeth. "Reading between the Lines of Gasparo Contarini's Treatise on the Venetian State." *Historical Reflections/Reflexions Historiques* 1 (1988): pp. 252–70.

————. *Gasparo Contarini: Venice, Rome, and Reform*. Berkeley: University of California Press, 1993.

Godefroy-Menilglaise, D. C. *Les savants Godefroy: Mémoires d'une famille*. Paris: Didier, 1873.

Goldgar, Ann. *Impolite Learning: Conduct and Community in the Republic of Letters, 1680–1750*. New Haven: Yale University Press, 1995.

Gossman, Lionel. *Medievalism and the Ideologies of the Enlightenment: The World and Work of La Curne de Sainte-Palaye*. Baltimore: Johns Hopkins Press, 1968.

Goyet, Francis. *Le sublime du "Lieu Commun": L'invention rhétorique dans l'antiquité et à la Renaissance*. Paris: Honoré Champion, 1996.

Grafton, Anthony. "Teacher, Text, and Pupil in the Renaissance Classroom: A Case Study from a Parisian College." *History of Universities* 1 (1981): pp. 37–70.

————. *Defenders of the Text: The Traditions of Scholarship in an Age of Science, 1450–1800*. Cambridge: Harvard University Press, 1991.

————. *The Footnote: A Curious History*. Cambridge: Harvard University Press, 1997.

————. "Correctores corruptores? Notes on the Social History of Editing." In *Editing Texts/Texte edieren*, ed. Glenn W. Most, pp. 54–76. Göttingen: Vandenhoeck and Ruprecht, 1998.

————. "The Humanist as Reader." In *A History of Reading in the West*, ed. Gugliemo Cavallo and Roger Chartier, trans. Lydia G. Cochrane, pp. 179–212. Amherst: University of Massachusetts Press, 1999.

————. *Bring Out Your Dead: The Past as Revelation*. Cambridge: Harvard University Press, 2001.

Grafton, Anthony, and Lisa Jardine. *From Humanism to the Humanities: Education and the Liberal Arts in Fifteenth- and Sixteenth-Century Europe*. London: Duckworth, 1986.

————. "Studied for Action: How Gabriel Harvey Read His Livy." *Past and Present* 129 (1991): pp. 30–78.

Grafton, Anthony, and Nancy Siraisi, eds. *Natural Particulars: Nature and the Disciplines in Renaissance Europe.* Cambridge: MIT Press, 1999.

Greenleaf, W. H. *Order and Empiricism in Politics: Two Traditions of English Political Thought, 1550–1700.* Oxford: Oxford University Press, 1964.

Grell, Chantall. *L'histoire entre érudition et philosophie: Étude sur la connaissance historique à l'âge des Lumières.* Paris: Presses Universitaires de France, 1983.

Grendler, Paul. *Schooling in Renaissance Italy: Literacy and Learning, 1300–1600.* Baltimore: Johns Hopkins University Press, 1989.

Guellouz, Suzanne. "Du bon usage des textes liminaires: Le cas d'Amelot de La Houssaie." *Littéraires Classiques* 13 (1990): pp. 261–75.

Guenée, Bernard. *Histoire et culture historique dans l'Occident médiéval.* Paris: Aubier Montaigne, 1980.

Guillermou, Alain. *St. Ignace de Loyola et la Compagnie de Jésus.* Paris: Seuil, 1960.

Guthrie, W. K. C. *A History of Greek Philosophy.* 6 vols. Cambridge: Cambridge University Press, 1981.

Habermas, Jürgen. *The Structural Transformation of the Public Sphere: An Inquiry into a Category of Bourgeois Society.* Trans. Thomas Burger and Frederick Lawrence. Cambridge: MIT Press, 1989.

Hafter, M. C. *Gracián and Perfection: Spanish Moralists of the Seventeenth Century.* Cambridge: Harvard University Press, 1966.

Hamesse, Jacqueline. "The Scholastic Model of Reading." In *A History of Reading in the West,* ed. Gugliemo Cavallo and Roger Chartier, trans. Lydia G. Cochrane, pp. 103–19. Amherst: University of Massachusetts Press, 1999.

Hampton, Timothy. *Writing from History: The Rhetoric of Exemplarity in Renaissance Literature.* Ithaca: Cornell University Press, 1990.

Hazard, Paul. *La crise de la conscience européenne.* Paris: Arthème Fayard, 1961.

Heger, K. *Baltasar Gracián: Estilo lingüístico y doctrina de valores.* Zaragoza: Catedra Gracián-Institución Fernando El Católico, 1960.

Heninger, S. K. *Touches of Sweet Harmony: Pythagorian Cosmology and Renaissance Poetics.* San Marino, CA: Huntington Library Press, 1974.

Hirstein, James S. *Tacitus' Germania and Beatus Rhenanus (1485–1547): A Study of the Editorial and Exegetical Contribution of a Sixteenth-Century Scholar.* Frankfurt am Main: Peter Lang, 1995.

Hoefer, Dr., ed. *Nouvelle biographie générale depuis les temps les plus reculés jusqu'à nos jours.* 46 vols. Paris: Firmin Didot Frères, 1855.

Hoffman, George. "Writing without Leisure: Proofreading as Work in the Renaissance." *Journal of Medieval and Renaissance Studies* 25 (1995): pp. 17–31.

Homenaje à Gracián. Zaragoza: Institución Fernando el Católico, 1958.

Horkheimer, Max, and Theodor W. Adorno. *Dialectic of Enlightenment.* Trans. John Cumming. New York: Herder and Herder, 1972.

Index librum prohibitorum. Rome: Typis Vaticanis, 1901.

Israel, Jonathan I. *Radical Enlightenment: Philosophy and the Making of Modernity, 1650–1750.* Oxford: Oxford University Press, 2001.

Jacob, Margaret C. *The Radical Enlightenment: Pantheists, Freemasons, and Republicans.* London: Allen and Unwin, 1981.

Jaeger, Werner. *Aristotle: Fundamentals of the History of His Development.* Trans. R. Robinson. Oxford: Clarendon Press, 1934.

Jardine, Lisa. *Worldly Goods: A New History of the Renaissance.* London: MacMillan 1996.

Jehasse, Jean. *La Renaissance de la critique: L'essor de l'humanisme érudit de 1560 à 1614.* Saint-Etienne: Publications de l'Université de Saint-Etienne, 1976.

Johns, Adrian. *The Nature of the Book: Print and Knowledge in the Making.* Chicago: University of Chicago Press, 1998.

Jonsen, A. R., and S. Toulmin. *The Abuse of Casuistry: A History of Moral Reasoning.* Berkeley: University of California Press, 1988.

Jouhaud, Christian. "Histoire et histoire littéraire: Naissance de l'écrivain." *Les Annales* 4 (1988): pp. 849–66.

———. *La main de Richelieu ou le pouvoir cardinal.* Paris: Gallimard, 1991.

———, ed. Special issue, *Cahiers du Centre de Recherche Historique* 20 (1998).

———. *Les pouvoirs de la littérature histoire d'un paradoxe.* Paris: Gallimard, 2000.

Julia, Dominique. "Reading in the Counter-Reformation." In *A History of Reading in the West,* ed. Gugliemo Cavallo and Roger Chartier, trans. Lydia G. Cochrane, pp. 238–68. Amherst: University of Massachusetts Press, 1999.

Kahn, Victoria. *Rhetoric, Prudence, and Skepticism in the Renaissance.* Ithaca: Cornell University Press, 1985.

———. *Machiavellian Rhetoric from the Counter-Reformation to Milton.* Princeton: Princeton University Press, 1994.

Kantorowicz, Ernst H. *The King's Two Bodies: A Study in Medieval Political Theology.* Princeton: Princeton University Press, 1957.

Kassier, T. L. *The Truth Disguised: Allegorical Structure and Technique in Gracián's Criticon.* London: Tamesis Books, 1976.

Kelley, Donald. "Jean Du Tillet, Archivist and Antiquary." *Journal of Modern History* 38 (1966): pp. 337–54.

———. *The Foundations of Modern Historical Scholarship: Language, Law, and History in the French Renaissance.* New York: Columbia University Press, 1970.

———. "Murd'rous Machiavel en France: A Post-mortem." *Political Science Quarterly* 85 (1970): pp. 545–59.

———. "The Rise of Legal History in the Renaissance." *History and Theory* 9 (1970): pp. 174–94.

———. "The Development and Context of Bodin's Method." In *Jean Bodin: Verhandlungen der Internationalen Bodin Tagung,* ed. Horst Denzer, pp. 123–50. Munich: C. H. Beck, 1973.

Kenney, E. J. *The Classical Text: Aspects of Editing in the Printed Age.* Berkeley: University of California Press, 1974.

Keynes, Geoffrey. *The Library of Edward Gibbon.* London: St. Paul's Bibliographies, 1980.

King, James E. *Science and Rationalism in the Government of Louis XIV, 1661–1683.* Baltimore: Johns Hopkins University Press, 1949.

Kinser, Samuel. *The Works of Jacques-Auguste de Thou.* The Hague: Martinus Nijhoff, 1966.

Kolb, R. "Teaching the Text: The Commonplace Method in Sixteenth-Century Biblical Commentary." *Bibliothèque d'Humanisme et Renaissance* 49 (1987): 571–85.

Koselleck, Reinhart. *Kritik und Krise: Ein Beitrag zur Phatigenese der Bürgerlichen Welt.* Freiburg: Verlag Karl Alber, 1959.

———. *Le règne de la critique.* Paris: Éditions de Minuit, 1979.

———. *Critique and Crisis.* Oxford: Berg, 1988.

Krieger, Leonard. *Ranke: The Meaning of History.* Chicago: University of Chicago Press, 1977.

Kühlmann, Wilhelm. *Gelehrtenrepublik und Fürstenstaat: Entwicklung und Kritik des deutschen Späthumanismus in der Literatur des Barockzeitalters.* Tübingen: Max Niemeyer, 1982.

Lagrée, Jacqueline. *Juste Lipse et la restauration du stoïcisme: Étude et traduction des traités stoïciens de La Constance, Manuel de philosophie stoïcienne, Physique des stoïciens.* Paris: J. Vrin, 1994.

———. *Le Politiques: Livre IV de Juste Lipse.* Caen: Presses Universitaires de Caen, 1994.

Lazzari, Christian, and Dominique Reynié, eds. *Le pouvoir de la raison d'état.* Paris: Presses Universitaires de France, 1992.

Lepreux, Georges. *Gallia typographica: Série parisienne; Livre d'Or des Imprimeurs du Roi.* 4 vols. Paris: Honoré Champion, 1911.

Lethen, Helmut. *Cool Conduct: The Culture of Distance in Weimar Germany.* Berkeley: University of California Press, 2002.

Levi, A. *The French Moralists.* Oxford: Clarendon Press, 1964.

Levine, Joseph. *Humanism and History: The Origins of Modern English Historiography.* Ithaca: Cornell University Press, 1987.

Lewis, C. S. *The Discarded Image: An Introduction to Medieval and Renaissance Literature.* Cambridge: Cambridge University Press, 1964.

Libros libres de Baltasar Gracián. Zaragoza: Gobierno de Aragón, 2001.

Lipking, Lawrence. *The Ordering of the Arts in Eighteenth-Century England.* Princeton: Princeton University Press, 1970.

———. "The Marginal Gloss." *Critical Inquiry* 3 (1976–77): pp. 609–55.

Lossky, A. "The Absolutism of Louis XIV." *Canadian Journal of History* 19 (1984): pp. 1–15.

Lovejoy, Arthur O. *The Great Chain of Being: A Study of the History on an Idea.* Cambridge: Harvard University Press, 1936.

Luce, T. J., and A. J. Woodman, eds. *Tacitust and the Tacitean Tradition.* Princeton: Princeton University Press, 1993.

MacCormack, Sabine. *Art and Ceremony in Late Antiquity.* Berkeley: Univeristy of California Press, 1981.

Macek, Johann. "La *Fortuna* chez Machiaveli." *Le Moyen Age* 77 (1971): pp. 305–28.

Maclean, Ian. *Interpretation and Meaning in the Renaissace: The Case of Law.* Cambridge: Cambridge University Press, 1992.

———. "From Prudence to Policy: Some Notes on the Prehistory of Policy Sciences." In *Guest Lectures,* pp. 5–27. Nijmegen: Katholieke Universiteit, 1993.

Magendie, Maurice. *La politesse mondaine et les théories de l'honnêteté en France au XVIIe siècle, de 1600 à 1660.* Paris: Alcan, 1925.

Maldonado, Francisco. *Baltasar Gracián como pesimista y político.* Salamanca: Imprenta et Libreria de Francisco Nuñez Izquierdo, 1916.

Maravall, José-Antonio. *La philosophie politique espagnole au XVIIe siècle dans ses rapports avec l'esprit de la Contre-Réforme.* Paris: J. Vrin, 1955.

Marin, Louis. *Le portrait du roi.* Paris: Éditions de Minuit, 1981.

———. "La logique du secret." *Traverses* 30–31 (1984): pp. 60–69.

Martin, Henri-Jean. *Livre, pouvoirs et société à Paris au XVIIe siècle 1598–1701.* 2 vols. Geneva: Droz, 1984.

———. *Mise en page et mise en texte du livre manuscrit.* Paris: Editions du Cercle de la Librairie, 1991.

Mason, H. T. *Pierre Bayle and Voltaire.* Oxford: Oxford University Press, 1963.

Mattei, Rodolfo de. *Il problema della "Ragion di stato" nell'età della controriforma.* Milan: Riccardo Ricciardi, 1979.

McIlwain, C. H. *Constitutionalism Ancient and Modern.* Ithaca: Cornell University Press, 1958.

McKenzie, Donald F. *The Bibliography and Sociology of Texts.* London: British Library, 1985.

———. *La bibliographie et la sociologie des livres.* Trans. Marc Amfreville. Paris: Editions du Cercle de la Librairie, 1991.

Meinecke, Friedrich. *Machiavellism: The Doctrine of Raison d'État and Its Place in Modern History.* Trans. D. Scott. London: Routledge and Kegan Paul, 1957.

Mellot, Jean-Dominique. *L'édition rouennaise et ses marchés, vers 1600–vers 1730.* Paris: École des Chartes, 1998.

Merighi, U. Rossi, ed. *Segreto di stato tra politica e amminitrazione.* Naples: ESI, 1994.

Merlin, Hélène. *Public et littérature en France au XVIIe siècle.* Paris: Belles Lettres, 1994.

———. *L'absolutisme dans les lettres et la théorie des deux corps: Passions et politique.* Paris: Honoré Champion, 2000.

Mervaud, Christiane. *Voltaire et Frédéric II.* Oxford: Voltaire Foundation, 1985.

Mesnard, Pierre. *L'essor de la philosophie politique au XVIe siècle.* Paris: J. Vrin, 1951.

Miller, Peter. *Peiresc's Europe: Learning and Virtue in the Seventeenth Century.* New Haven: Yale University Press, 2000.

———. "The 'Antiquarianism' of Biblical Scholarship and the London Polyglot Bible (1653–57)." *Journal of the History of Ideas* 62 (2001): pp. 463–576.

———. "Nazis and Neo-Stoics: Otto Bruner and Gerhard Oestreich before and after the Second World War." *Past and Present* 176 (2002): pp. 144–86.

Momigliano, Arnaldo. "The First Political Commentary on Tacitus." *Journal of Roman Studies* 37 (1947): pp. 91–101.

———. *Contributo alla storia degli studi classici.* Rome: Edizioni di Storia e Letteratura, 1955.

———. "Les études classiques aux XIXe et XXe siècles: Leur place dans l'histoire des idées." *Entretiens sur l'Antiquité Classique* 26 (1979): pp. 127–57.

———. *Settimo contributo alla storia degli studi classici e del mondo antico.* Rome: Edizioni di Storia e Letteratura, 1984.

———. *Essays in Ancient and Modern Historiography.* Middletown, Conn.: Wesleyan University Press, 1987.

———. *The Classical Foundations of Modern Historiography.* Berkeley: University of California Press, 1990.

Moreau, Pierre-François, ed. *Le stoïcisme au XVIe et au XVIIe siècle.* Paris: Albin Michel, 1999.

Morford, Mark. *Stoics and Neostoics: Rubens and the Circle of Lipsius.* Princeton: Princeton University Press, 1991.

———. "Tacitean *Prudentia* and the Doctrines of Justus Lipsius." In *Tacitust and the Tacitean Tradition,* ed. T. J. Luce and A. J. Woodman, pp. 129–51. Princeton: Princeton University Press, 1993.

Mornet, Daniel. "Les enseignements des bibliothèques privées (1750–1780)." *Revue d'Histoire Littéraire de la France* 17 (1910): 449–96.

———. *Les origines intellectuelles de la Révolution française 1715–1787.* Paris: Armand Colin, 1933.

Moss, Ann. *Printed Commonplace-Books and the Structuring of Renaissance Thought.* Oxford: Clarendon Press, 1996.

Newman, Jane O. "The Word Made Print: Luther's 1522 New Testament in an Age of Mechanical Reproduction." *Representations,* summer 1985, pp. 95–133.

Oestreich, Gerhard. *Neostoicism and the Early Modern State.* Ed. Brigitta Oestreich and H. G. Koenigsberger. Trans. David Mclintock. Cambridge: Cambridge University Press, 1982.

Omont, Henri. "Jean Du Tillet et le trésor des chartes (1562)." *Bulletin de la Société de l'Histoire de Paris* 31 (1904): pp. 79–81.

Palacios, Leopoldo Eulogio. *La prudencia política*. Madrid: Instituto de Estudios Políticos, 1945.

Pelegrín, Benito. Preface to *Manuel de poche d'hier pour hommes politiques d'aujourd'hui*, by Baltasar Gracián. Ed. and trans. Benito Pelegrín. Paris: Hallier, 1978.

———. *Éthique et esthétique du Baroque: L'espace jésuitique de Baltasar Gracián*. Arles: Actes Sud, 1985.

Pemble, John. *Venice Rediscovered*. Oxford: Clarendon Press, 1995.

Pfeiffer, R. *History of Classical Scholarship: From the Beginnings to the End of the Hellenistic Age*. Oxford: Clarendon Press, 1968.

Pintard, René. *Le libertinage érudit dans la première moitié du XVIIe siècle*. Paris: Boivin, 1943.

Pitassi, Maria Cristina. *Entre croire et savoir: Le problème de la méthode critique chez Jean Le Clerc*. Leiden: Brill, 1987.

Pocock, J. G. A. *The Machiavellian Moment: Florentine Political Thought and the Atlantic Republican Tradition*. Princeton: Princeton University Press, 1975.

———. *Barbarism and Religion: The Enlightenments of Edward Gibbon, 1737–1764*. 3 vols. Cambridge: Cambridge University Press, 2001–3.

Popkin, Richard. *The History of Skepticism from Erasmus to Spinoza*. Berkeley: University of California Press, 1979.

Post, Gaines. *Studies in Medieval Legal Thought: Public Law and the State, 1100–1322*. Princeton: Princeton University Press, 1964.

Preto, Paulo. *I servizi segreti di Venezia*. Milan: Il Saggiatore, 1994.

Queller, Donald E. "The Development of Ambassadorial Relazioni." In *Renaissance Venice*, ed. John R. Hale, pp. 174–96. London: Faber, 1974.

Quillen, Carol Everhart. *Rereading the Renaissance: Petrarch, Augustine, and the Language of Humanism*. Ann Arbor: University of Michigan Press, 1998.

Ranum, Orest. *Artisans of Glory: Writers and Historical Thought in Seventeenth-Century France*. Chapel Hill: University of North Carolina Press, 1980.

Ravaisson, François. *Archives de la Bastille: Documents inédits; Règne de Louis XIV 1675–1686*. Paris: A. Durand and Pédone-Lauriel Libraires, 1876.

Reynolds, L. D., and N. G. Wilson. *Scribes and Scholars: A Guide to the Transmission of Greek and Latin Literature*. Oxford: Clarendon Press, 1991.

Ricciardi, M. "Appunti su segreto di stato e principio di transparenza." *Politico del Diritto* 24 (1993): pp. 35–50.

Rice, Eugene. *The Renaissance Idea of Wisdom*. Cambridge: Harvard University Press, 1958.

Richelet, Pierre. *Dictionnaire de la langue française*. Geneva: Jean Herman Widerhold, 1685.

Ricuperati, Giuseppe, ed. *La reinvenzione dei lumi: Percorsi storiografici del novecento*. Florence: Olschki, 2000.

Roche, Daniel. *Les républicains des lettres: Gens de culture et Lumières au XVIIIe siècle*. Paris: Fayard, 1988.

———. *La France des Lumières*. Paris: Fayard, 1993.

Rothkrug, Lionel. *Opposition to Louis XIV: The Political and Social Origins of the French Enlightenment*. Princeton: Princeton University Press, 1965.

Rouse, Mary A., and Richard H. Rouse. *Authentic Witnesses: Approaches to Medieval Texts and Manuscripts*. Notre Dame: University of Notre Dame Press, 1991.

Rubenstein, Nicolai. "The Beginning of Niccolò Machiavelli's Career in the Florentine Chancery." *Italian Studies* 9 (1956): pp. 72–91.

Rummel, Erika. "God and Solecism: Erasmus as a Literary Critic of the Bible." *Erasmus of Rotterdam Society Yearbook* 7 (1987): pp. 54–72.

Ruysschaert, José. *Juste Lipse et les Annales de Tacite: Une méthode de critique textuelle au XVIe siècle.* Turnhout: Brepols Press, 1949.

Salmon, J. H. M. "Francois Hotman and Jean Bodin: The Dilemma of Sixteenth-Century French Constitutionalism." *History Today* 23 (1973): pp. 1–7.

———. "Clovis and Constantine: The Uses of History in Sixteenth-Century Gallicanism." *Journal of Ecclesiastical History* 41 (1990): pp. 584–605.

———. "The Legacy of Jean Bodin: Absolutism, Populism, or Constitutionalism?" *History of Political Thought* 17 (1996): pp. 500–522.

Santoro, Mario. *Fortuna, ragione e prudenza nella civiltà letteraria del cinquecento.* Naples: Ligouri Editore, 1977.

Saunders, J. L. *The Philosophy of Renaissance Stoicism.* New York: Liberal Arts Press, 1955.

Sauvy, Anne. *Livres saisis à Paris entre 1678 et 1701.* La Haye: Martinus Nijhoff, 1972.

Schmitt, Carl. *Politische theologie: Vier Kapitel zur Lehre von der Souvränität.* Berlin: Dunker and Humblot, 1922.

———. *Political Theology: Four Chapters on the Concept of Sovereignty.* Trans. George Schwab. Cambridge: MIT Press, 1985.

Schneider, Robert. "Political Power and the Emergence of Literature: Christian Jouhaud's Age of Richelieu." *French Historical Studies* 25 (2002): pp. 357–80.

Schnur, Roman, ed. *Staatsräson: Studien zur Geschichte eines politischen Begriffs.* Berlin: Dunker and Humblot, 1975.

Scholder, Klaus. *Ursprünge und Probleme der historisch-kritischen Theologie.* Munich: Christian Kaiser Verlag, 1966.

———. *The Birth of Modern Critical Theology: Origins and Problems of Biblical Criticism in the Seventeenth Century.* Trans. John Bowden. London: SCM Press; Philadelphia: Trinity Press, 1990.

Selig, Karl-Ludwig. *The Library of Vincencio Juan de Lastanosa, Patron of Gracián.* Geneva: Droz, 1960.

Senellart, Michel. *Machiavellisme et raison d'état.* Paris: Presses Universitaires de France, 1989.

———. *Les arts de gouverner: Du regimen médiéval au concept de gouvernement.* Paris: Seuil, 1995.

———. "Le stoïcisme dans la constitution de la pensée politique: *Les Politiques* de Juste Lipse (1589)." In *Le stoïcisme au XVIe et au XVIIe siècle,* ed. Pierre-François Moreau, pp. 117–39. Paris: Albin Michel, 1999.

Sgard, Jean, ed. *Dictionnaire des journalists 1600–1789.* Grenoble: Presses Universitaires de Grenoble, 1976.

Shapiro, Barbara. *A Culture of Fact: England, 1550–1720.* Ithaca: Cornell University Press, 2000.

Shelford, April G. "Thinking Geometrically in Pierre-Daniel Huet's *Demonstratio evangelica* (1679)." *Journal of the History of Ideas* 63 (2002): pp. 599–617.

Sherman, William H. *John Dee: The Politics of Reading and Writing in the English Renaissance.* Amherst: University of Massachusetts Press, 1995.

Siraisi, Nancy. "Anatomizing the Past: Physicians and History in Renaissance Culture." *Renaissance Quarterly* 53 (2000): 1–30.

———. "History, Antiquarianism, and Medicine: The Case of Girolamo Mercuriale." *Journal of the History of Ideas* 64 (2003): pp. 231–51.

Skinner, Q. R. D. *The Foundations of Modern Political Thought.* 2 vols. Cambridge: Cambridge University Press, 1978.

———. *Machiavelli.* Oxford: Oxford University Press, 1981.

———. " 'Social Meaning' and the Explanation of Social Action." In *Meaning and Con-*

text: Quentin Skinner and His Critics, ed. James Tully, pp. 79–96. Princeton: Princeton University Press, 1988.

Soll, Jacob. "Une bibliographie matérielle d'Amelot de La Houssaie: Les traces d'une stratégie d'auteur." Diplôme d'Études Approfondies diss., École des Hautes Études en Sciences Sociales, Paris, 1993.

———. "The Hand-Annotated Copy of the *Histoire du gouvernement de Venise;* or, How Amelot de La Houssaie Wrote His History." *Bulletin du Bibliophile* 2 (1995): pp. 279–93.

———. "Amelot de La Houssaie and the Tacitean Tradition in France." *Translation and Literature* 6 (1997): pp. 186–202.

———. "Amelot de La Houssaie (1634–1706) Annotates Tacitus." *Journal of the History of Ideas* 2 (2000): pp. 167–87.

———. "Healing the Body Politic: French Doctors, History, and the Birth of a Nation, 1570–1634." *Renaissance Quarterly* 55 (2002): pp. 1259–86.

———. "Empirical History and the Transformation of Political Criticism in France from Bodin to Bayle." *Journal of the History of Ideas* 64 (2003): pp. 297–316.

Solomon, Howard M. *Public Welfare, Science, and Propaganda in Seventeenth-Century France: The Innovations of Théophraste Renaudot.* Princeton: Princeton University Press, 1972.

Soman, Alfred. "Press, Pulpit, and Censorship in France before Richelieu." *Proceedings of the American Philosophical Society* 120 (1976): pp. 439–63.

Somerville, J. P. "Absolutism and Royalism." In *The Cambridge History of Political Thought, 1450–1700,* ed. J. H. Burns and Mark Goldie, pp. 347–73. Cambridge: Cambridge University Press, 1991.

Spini, Giorgio. "The Art of History in the Italian Counter Reformation." In *The Late Italian Renaissance,* ed. Eric Cochrane, pp. 91–133. London: MacMillan, 1970.

Spink, J. S. *French Free-Thought from Gassendi to Voltaire.* London: Athlone Press, 1960.

Stackelburg, Jürgen von. *Tacitus in der Romania: Studien zur literarichen Rezeption des Tacitus in Italien un Frankreich.* Tübingen: Max Niemeyer, 1960.

Stagl, Justin. *A History of Curiosity: The Theory of Travel, 1550–1800.* Chur, Switzerland: Harwood Academic Publishers, 1995.

Stegmann, André. "Le Tacitisme: Programme pour un nouvel essai de définition." In *Machiavellismo e Antimachiavellismo nel cinquecento.* Special issue, *Il Pensiero politico* 2 (1969).

Stolleis, Michael. *Staatsraison, Recht und Moral in philosophischen Texten des späten 18. Jahrhunderts.* Monographien zur Philosophischen Forschung 86. Meisenheim am Glan: Verlag Anton Hain, 1972.

———. "Arcana imperii und Ratio status: Bemerkungen zur politischen Theorie des frühen 17. Jahrhunderts." *Studie an d. Herzog-August-Bibliothek* 39 (1980): pp. 5–34.

———. "Machiavellismus und Staatsräson: Ein Beitrag zu Conrings Politischem Denken." In *Hermann Conring (1606–1681): Beiträge zu Leben und Werk,* ed. Michael Stolleis, pp. 173–214. Berlin: Dunker and Humblot, 1983.

———. *Staat und Staatsräson in der frühen Neuzeit: Studien zur Geschichte des öffentlichen Rechts.* Frankfurt am Main: Suhrkamp, 1990.

———. "L'idée de la raison d'état de Friedrich Meinecke, et la recherche actuelle." In *Raison et déraison d'état: Théoriciens et theories de la raison d'état aux XVIe et XVIIe siècles,* ed. Yves-Charles Zarka, pp. 11–39. Paris: Presses Universitaires de France, 1994.

Strauss, Leo. *Persecution and the Art of Writing.* New York: Free Press, 1952. 3rd ed., Chicago: University of Chicago Press, 1988.

Streuver, Nancy. *The Language of History in the Renaissance: Rhetoric and Historical Consciousness in Florentine Humanism.* Princeton: Princeton University Press, 1970.

Syme, Sir Ronald. *Tacitus.* Oxford: Clarendon Press, 1958.

Thuau, Etienne. *Raison d'état et pensée politique à l'époque de Richelieu.* Paris: Armand Colin, 1966.

Todeschi, Fabio. " 'Lector Scepticus': La recezione della tradizione scettica e formazione del publico in area tedesca 1680–1750." Ph.D. diss., European University Institute, Florence, 1998.

Toffanin, Giuseppe. *Machiavelli e il Tacitismo: La politica storica al tempo della Controriforma.* Naples: Guida, 1972.

Tribble, E. *Margins and Marginality: The Printed Page in Early Modern England.* Charlottesville: University Press of Virginia, 1993.

Trinkaus, Charles. *In Our Image and Likeness: Humanity and Divinity in Italian Humanist Thought.* London: Constable, 1970.

Tuck, Richard. *Philosophy and Government, 1572–1652.* Cambridge: Cambridge University Press, 1993.

Vattimo, Gianni, ed. *La filosofia tra pubblicità e segreto.* Rome-Bari: Laterza, 1994.

Viala, Alain. *La naissance de l'écrivain.* Paris: Éditions de Minuit, 1985.

Villari, Pasquale. *The Life and Times of Niccolò Machiavelli.* Trans. Linda Villari. 2 vols. London: T. Fisher, 1892.

Villari, Rosario. *Elogio della dissimulazione: La lotta politica nel siecento.* Rome: Editori Laterza, 1987.

Viroli, Maurizio. *From Politics to Reason of State: The Acquisition and Transformation of the Language of Politics, 1250–1600.* Cambridge: Cambridge University Press, 1992.

Vivo, Filippo de. "Le armi dell'ambasciatore: Voci e manoscritti a Parigi durante l'interdetto di Venezia." In *I luoghi dell'imaginario barocco,* ed. Lucia Strappini, pp. 189–201. Naples: Liguori Editore, 1999.

———. "Dall'imposizione del silenzio alla 'Guerra delle Scriture': Le pubblicazione ufficiali durante l'interdetto del 1606–1607." *Studi Veneziani* 41 (2001): pp. 179–213.

———. "Quand le passé résiste à ses historiographes: Venise et le XVII siècle." *Cahiers du Centre de Recherches Historiques* 28–29 (2002): pp. 223–34.

Voegelin, Eric. *Anamnesis.* Ed. and trans. Gerhart Niemeyer. Notre Dame: University of Notre Dame Press, 1978.

Volpilhac-Auger, Catherine. *Tacite et Montesquieu.* Oxford: Voltaire Foundation, 1985.

Wade, Ira. *The Intellectual Origins of the French Enlightenment.* Princeton: Princeton University Press, 1971.

Wasznik, Jan. "*Inventio* in the *Politica:* Commonplace-Books and the Shape of Political Theory." In *Lipsius in Leiden: Studies in the Life and Works of a Great Humanist,* ed. K. Enenkel and C. Heesakkers, pp. 141–62. Voorthuizen, Holland: Florivallis, 1997.

Wintroub, Michael. "The Looking Glass of Facts: Collecting, Rhetoric, and Citing the Self in the Experimental Natural Philosophy of Robert Boyle." *History of Science* 35 (1997): pp. 189–217.

Wood, N. "Machiavelli's Concept of *Virtù* Reconsidered." *Political Studies* 15 (1967): pp. 159–72.

Wootton, David. *Paolo Sarpi: Between Renaissance and Enlightenment.* Cambridge: Cambridge University Press, 1983.

Zagorin, Perez. *Ways of Lying: Dissimulation, Persecution, and Conformity in Early Modern Europe.* Cambridge: Harvard University Press, 1990.

Zarka, Yves-Charles. *Raison et déraison d'état: Théoriciens et théories de la raison d'état aux XVIe et XVIIe siècles.* Paris: Presses Universitaires de France, 1994.

Index

Ablancourt, Nicolas Perrot d', 15, 39, 74, 110

absolutism, 24; and reason of state, 47, 58

Académie Française, 60, 123; and Tacitism, 39, 47

Acton, Emerich Edward Dalberg, Lord, 62

Alembert, Jean Le Rond d', 122

Alexander the Great, 50

Anne of Austria (queen of France), 39, 67, 91

annotation, 97–99; and Amelot, 113, 116; and Bayle, 104–5, 111. *See also* marginalia

Antistius Labeo, Marcus, 81

Aquinas. *See* Thomas Aquinas, Saint

Aranda, Dona Luisa de Padilla, countess of, 87, 121

arcana imperii, 26, 40

archives, 29–30, 123; and Gallicanism, 52; and politics in the eighteenth century, 123–25; and Théodore Godefroy, 53; and Venice, 62

Aristotle, 50; on ethics, 84; on prudence, 23

Augustine, Saint, 89

authorship, 68; Amelot's strategies of, 10–13, 19, 111, 117; and humanism, 95; surreptitious style of, 74–82, 86

Auvergne, Gaspard d', 100

Bagni, Giovanni Francesco, Cardinal, 73

Baillet, Adrien, 111

Baker, Keith, 124

Balzac, Honoré de, 125

Bastille, 12, 68, 69, 94

Battista, Anna Maria, 82

Bayle, Pierre, 1, 3–5, 8–10, 18, 19, 74, 88, 110, 113–14, 118, 121, 126; on erudition and political criticism, 7, 65; reads Amelot, 15, 103–6

Bellay, Joachim du, 42

Benedictine Order, 52, 123–24

Bentham, Jeremy, 126

Beza, Théodore de, 53

Bentivoglio, Guido, Cardinal, 48–49

Bible reading, 3–4, 91–92, 94, 97, 100; textual criticism of, 4, 33, 89–90

Bibliothèque Mazarine, 3

Bibliothèque Nationale de France, 34, 38, 73

Boccaccio, Giovanni, 100

Boccalini, Trajano, 3, 45; Diderot on, 120

Bodin, Jean, 2, 43, 65, 73; and absolutism, 24; and comparative political science, 64; Diderot on, 120; and prudence, 27; and reading, 28, 93

Bonaparte, Napoléon (emperor of France), 10, 126

Bonaventura, Federico, 46

Borgia, Cesare, duke de Valentino, 102

Bossuet, Jacques-Bénigne de, 4, 24

Botero, Giovanni, 44–45, 77

Boulainvilliers, Henri, count de, 123

Bourbon, French royal family, 76; relations with scholars, 13

Bowers, Fredson, 13

Brandolini, Marcantonio, 70

Brethren of the Common Life, 90

Briencour, sieur de, 73

Bruni, Leonardo, 62

Bruys, François, 121–22

197

Budé, Guillaume, 31
Burke, Peter, 20
Butterfield, Herbert, 23

Cabinet des Chartes, 125
Calvin, Jean, 52, 91
Calvinism, 4, 95
Cambridge University: Library, 34; Press,
    5
Candia (Crete), war of, 70
Cappel, Guillaume, 73
Cassirer, Ernst, 22–23
casuistry, 83
Cauvigny, François de, 39
Certeau, Michel de, 103–4
Chapelain, Jean, 48–50
Charles IX (king of France), 29–30
Charron, Pierre, 36, 46
Chartier, Roger, 86
Choisy, François Timoléon, abbé de, 47
Christina (queen of Sweden), 10
church, the, 1, 4, 89; and Bible criticism,
    91–92; and Counter-Reformation in
    Spain, 83; and historical scholarship,
    27, 42–43, 92; and religious wars, 31, 41
Cicero, Marcus Tullius, 38, 97, 100, 119;
    Ciceronian historiography, 50, 52, 55,
    118; on ethics, 84; on prudence, 24, 27
Cistercian Order, 92
Clement IX (pope), 67
Colbert, Jean-Baptiste, 39, 74–75, 123–25;
    and critical history, 48–49, 51; and the
    Godefroy family, 53–56; sponsors pane-
    gyric history, 50–51
commentary, 2, 4, 61, 92–95; Amelot's
    commentary on Tacitus, 104–7; readers
    and, 113, 116
Commines, Philippe de, 42, 100
commonplaces (*loci communes*), 33; and
    Tacitism, 34; in Spain, 85, 97–99, 107.
    See also reading, for fruit
compilation, 4, 60–61, 65, 104–5
Congress of Münster, 53
Congreve, William, 13
Contarini, Gasparo, 44, 63, 125
Contarini, Nicolas, 69
copyists, 12
correctors, 12, 60, 75, 93
Council of Trent, 18, 44, 90, 91
critical culture, 3–4, 87, 93, 119, 121
critical history, 8, 18, 42, 118, 124; as an

antidote to flattery, 81; decline of,
    48–50, 57; and emendation, 93; and
    Gallicanism, 44; and politics, 4; and
    prudence, 22, 29–30; and the Scrip-
    tures, 90; transformation of, 76; and
    Venetian archives, 62, 71; and the
    Venetian interdict, 43
Cujas, Jacques, 93

Daniel, Gabriel, 51–52
Darnton, Robert, 5
Davila, Arrigo Catarina, 51, 52
Desbordes, Henri, 15
Diderot, Denis, 1, 119–21
Diodati, Giovanni, 74
Diogenes Laertes, 100
diplomacy: and ambassadorial culture, 11,
    62–63; and ambassadorial relations, 66
disenchantment, 8, 19, 25, 82
dissimulation, 62, 74, 84, 86
document analysis, 12, 26, 28–29, 65,
    68–70
dominationis arcana, 65, 77
Don Quixote, 84
Dupuy, Jacques, 42, 53–54
Dupuy, Pierre, 53–54
Duren, Jean van, 116–17
Durey de Meinières, Octavie, 124
Dutch Wars, 53
Du Tillet, Jean, the Elder, 28, 30, 32, 52,
    54, 73, 123–24; and document analysis,
    29; and prudence, 29

Eco, Umberto, 89
Edict of Nantes, 41
editing, 2, 5, 11, 12, 14, 32, 60–61, 94–97;
    editors as authors, 77
Elias, Norbert, 38, 86
Elizabeth I (queen of England), 48
eloquence, 51, 56
Elzevier, Daniel, 76
Emile, Paul, 42
Enlightenment, 72; Amelot and, 126; ideas
    about, 2–5, 10; relationship to the
    Renaissance, 20
Erasmus, Desiderius, 3, 33, 83, 90, 93,
    98
erudition, 2, 4, 60; and political criticism,
    65
ethics, 84
exegesis. *See under* reading

Fénélon, François, 91
Ferrault, Jean, 44
flattery, 15, 79, 107, 110; and prudence, 81
Florence, 23
Florus, Publius Annius, 103
Fontenelle, Bernard Le Bovier de, 74
footnotes. *See* textual references
Foucault, Michel, 20
Fourcy, Henri de, Abbé, 11, 125
François I (king of France), 73
François II (king of France), 29
Frederick II (king of Prussia), 115–17
French monarchy, 25, 29; and the church, 44
Fronde, the, 73

Galileo, 49
Gallicanism, 29, 30, 44, 58, 62, 66, 69, 91, 120, 123–25; and archivists, 52, 54; and Venice, 23
Gauchet, Marcel, 8, 25, 46, 82
Gay, Peter, 5
Gibbon, Edward, 1, 10, 126; and the idea of decline, 64
Ginzburg, Carlo, 9, 126
Giovo, Paulo, 42, 51
Godefroy, Denis II, 52–56
Godefroy, Denis III, 55–56
Godefroy, Jean, 55–56
Godefroy, Théodore, 52–53
Gohory, Jacques, 73
Goulart, Simon, 34
Gournay, Marie Jars de, 79
Gracián, Balthasar, 8–10, 14, 95, 100, 102, 110, 113, 125; and authorship, 13; Diderot on, 120; and the *Oráculo,* 85–87; and Tacitus, 87; his theory of prudence, 84
Grafton, Anthony, 93
Grasaille, Charles de, 44
Graves, Robert, 65
Grotius, Hugo, 98
Grub Street, 2
Guicciardini, Francesco, 42, 46, 47, 49, 52, 100
Guichenon, Samuel, 74
Gutenberg, Johannes, 38

Habermas, Jürgen, 20, 26
Harlay de Champvallon, Achilles de, 30, 39, 53, 91

Hazard, Paul, 2–3
Henri IV (king of France), 31, 37, 41, 42
Herbin, Charles, 60–61
Herrera, Antonio de, 85
history. *See* critical history
Hobbes, Thomas, 2, 82, 126
Hobier, Ithier, 79
Hotman, François, 65
humanism: Aragonese, 84; decline of, 120; Dutch, 3; and Dutch scholarship, 15; and editing, 60–61; and history, 26; and pedagogy, 33; and political culture, 72–73, 117–18, 127; reading practices, 32, 104; and the Renaissance sense of the past, 20; textual practices, 19. *See also* Jesuits

individualism, 82, 122; and Jesuit culture, 85

Jansenism, 91
Jars de Gournay, Marie de, 39
Jerome, Saint, 89
Jesuits, 11, 12, 62, 94; and casuistry, 83; and Ciceronian historiography, 51; and pedagogy, 82, 84; and prudence in Spain, 83–85; and reason of state, 45, 84; and Tacitism, 84, 93; textual practices of, 10; and writing manuals, 94
Jouhaud, Christian, 48

Kant, Immanuel, 20, 123
Kelley, Donald, 44
Koselleck, Reinhard, 3–4, 19

La Blétterie, Jean-Philippe-René, abbé de, 122
La Planche, Etienne de, 38
La Reynie, Gabriel Nicolas, 18–19
La Rochefoucauld, François, duc de, 8, 100, 102–3
Lastanosa, Don Juan de, 84–87, 111, 116
Latin scholarship, 32, 84, 90
Laval, Antoine de, 46
Le Ber, Charles, 34
Le Maire, Nicolas, 91
Le Maistre, Rodolphe, 37, 39
Le Moyne, Pierre, Abbé, 51–52
Léonard, Frédéric, 9, 12, 56–58, 63, 98, 106; print shop, "L'Écu de Venise," 59–60; strategy for publishing the

Port Royal, 91

print shops. *See* publishing

Protestants, 88; and reading, 92, 94; the Reformation, 90, 91

prudence, 23, 27, 36; Amelot's theory of, 81; examples of in ancient Rome, 80–81; Enlightenment critique of, 118–21; and flattery, 81; and history, 30; and royal pedagogy, 37; and *phronesis,* 23; *prudentia,* 24; *prudenza,* 24; publication of theory, 8, 121; and reason of state, 25–26

public sphere, 8, 26, 124

publishing, 2, 12; historical information, 9; illicit, 79; *The Prince,* 102, 116; printing Tacitus's works, 38–39; use of pseudonyms, 78; works on reason of state, 8

Puget de La Serre, Jean, 74

Quintilian, 50

Racine, Jean, 50

Ranke, Leopold von, 12; and historical accuracy, 61–62

Rapin, René, 51, 52, 66, 99

ratio studiorum, 84

reading: for action, 94; and Amelot, 93, 110; critical style of, or textual criticism, 8, 15, 26–28, 65, 90, 93, 100, 118; Diderot on, 119–20; and exegesis, 93, 96; for fruit, 33, 93, 97–99; and humanism, 3–4, 22; *lectura,* 92; Machiavelli on, 22–24; and the Middle Ages, 89–90; sacred form of, 91–92; Tacitean style of, 32. *See also* Bible reading

reason of state, 2, 25, 69, 72; Amelot's critique of, 78; decline of, 73; Enlightenment critique of, 119; and Gallicanism, 44; Italian works on, 45–46; literature of, 8; and Richelieu, 47; of the self, 83, 87, 111, 121

Reformation, 4, 31, 97; Counter-Reformation polemics, 41. *See also* Bible reading

relations (*relazioni*), 12, 65–68, 70, 102

remonstrances, 124

Renaissance. *See* humanism

Renaudot, Théophraste, 66–67

republicanism, 1, 3, 31, 80, 119, 127; Amelot on, 114; Venetian, 67–69

republic of letters, 18, 42–43, 48–49, 85, 117

Revocation of the Edict of Nantes, 76

Richelet, Pierre, 120

Richelieu, Armand du Plessis de, Cardinal, 39, 48, 50, 74, 82, 95; and information culture, 67; and Tacitism and reason of state, 47

Robespierre, Maximillien, 1, 8, 20

Roche, Daniel, 123–24

Rome, ancient political institutions of, 68

Rousseau, Jean-Jacques, 5, 95, 114; translates Tacitus, 122

Saavedra Fajardo, Diego de, 85

Sacchini, Francesco, 33, 85, 97–98

Saint-André, Nicolas Prunier de, 11, 62

Salic Law, 29

Sallust, 38, 42, 100, 103

Sarceno, Scipione, 70

Sarpi, Paolo, 3, 8, 9, 18, 42, 49, 52, 54, 65, 67, 70, 72–74, 100, 102, 124, 126; and critical history and the interdict, 43–44, 70; critical technique of, 66

Savile, Henry, 113

scholasticism, 83; and reading, 89–90, 93

Scientific Revolution, 24

secrecy, 26, 126; Amelot exposes Venetian secrets, 64; and Colbert, 56; and reason of state, 77; secrets of princes, 107

secular culture, 2, 19, 24–25, 93, 126; de-Christianization, 26; political theory of, 4; *saeculum,* 9; and the state, 82

Seneca, 100

Senellart, Michel, 34

Silhouette, Etienne de, 125

Simon, Richard, 3–4; and Bible criticism, 92

skepticism, 1, 3, 43, 82

Skinner, Q. R. D., 23

Spain, empire of, and political culture, 83–85

Sparta, 68

Spinoza, Baruch, 4, 92, 115

Stackelberg, Jürgen von, 94

St. Bartholomew's Day massacre, 31, 41

St. Mark's Library (Bibliotéca Marciana), Venice, 11, 69, 70

Strauss, Leo, 74–75

Suarez, Juan, 85